ACCLAIM FOR *David Remnick*'s

RESURRECTION

"Remnick's skilled technique as a reporter produces the utmost liveliness . . . his eye for the amusing detail rarely fails."
—*The New York Times*

"Inquisitive and humorous, [Remnick] captures the Russsian scene in all its dramatic contrariness."
—*Wall Street Journal*

"Insightful . . . vivid . . . Mr. Remnick writes passionately."
—*Washington Times*

"*Resurrection* is the best of the current books on the rapidly evolving country."
—*Milwaukee Journal-Sentinel*

"David Remnick is a marvel."
—David Halberstam

"A writer who has the ace reporter's nose for a good story, and the cultural range and fluency of a classical belles-lettrist. . . . A pleasure to read."
—E. L. Doctorow

"[Remnick's] reporting is reliable, his knowledge is deep, and his judgment is sound."
—*Christian Science Monitor*

"By turns blackly comic and deadly serious, [*Resurrection*] reads like a fast-paced novel, filled with sharp and unforgettable characters."
—Henry Louis Gates, Jr.

"*Resurrection* is a work of enormous power and distinction. David Remnick is an acute political analyst and an equally acute observer of the small movements of life. As I read his brilliant, horrific report from Chechnya, I thought of Orwell."
—Janet Malcolm

"An extraordinarily good writer with a vivid sense of the comic and a wonderful dramatic sense . . . reads like an entertaining novel."
—*New York Review of Books*

David Remnick

RESURRECTION

David Remnick is a staff writer for *The New Yorker*. He received a Pulitzer Prize in 1994 for his first book, *Lenin's Tomb: The Last Days of the Soviet Empire,* which was selected by *The New York Times Book Review* as one of the nine Best Books of the Year. Mr. Remnick is also the author of *The Devil Problem and Other True Stories.* He lives in New York City with his wife and two sons.

RESURRECTION

DAVID REMNICK

RESURRECTION

THE STRUGGLE FOR
A NEW RUSSIA

Vintage Books

A DIVISION OF RANDOM HOUSE, INC.

NEW YORK

FIRST VINTAGE BOOKS EDITION, JUNE 1998

Copyright © 1997, 1998 by David Remnick

All rights reserved under International and Pan-American
Copyright Conventions. Published in the United States by Vintage Books,
a division of Random House, Inc., New York, and simultaneously in Canada by
Random House of Canada Limited, Toronto. Originally published in slightly different
form in hardcover in the United States by Random House, Inc., New York, in 1997.

The Library of Congress has cataloged the Random House edition as follows:
Remnick, David.
Resurrection—the struggle for a new Russia/David Remnick.
p.   cm.
Includes bibliographical references and index.
ISBN 0-679-42377-X
1. Russia (Federation)—Politics and government—1991–   . I. Title.
DK510.763.R46   1997
947.086—dc21   96-47360

Vintage ISBN: 0-375-75023-1

Author photograph © Gasper Tringale
Book design by J. K. Lambert

Random House Web address: www.randomhouse.com

Printed in the United States of America
10   9   8   7   6   5   4   3   2   1

To Esther

CONTENTS

PREFACE

To live in Moscow at century's end is to exist in a strange and contradictory landscape, one filled with both ruin and possibility. The signs of a fallen totalitarian state persist: Lenin gazing out over October Square; the apartment buildings on Leninsky Prospekt built by prisoners of the gulag; the old and the poor marching on May Day, sometimes even carrying portraits of Stalin. At the same time, the newspapers (when they are not shilling for the government at election time) are alive with real news and varied commentary; stores with high-quality goods are opening all over; the airports are mobbed with people traveling abroad as often as their incomes will allow. On Lubyanka Square, the statue of the founder of the secret police, Feliks Dzerzhinsky, is gone (it was torn down after the collapse of the August coup); and, nearby, a stone from Solovki, the first of Lenin's concentration camps, honors the millions killed under the old regime. And yet the old KGB structures (using new names and old methods) are still at work. All around, the bright lights of commerce flare while the mayor orders police to arrest the homeless and put them on trains.

In the provinces, the contrasts are more subtle, but they are there all the same: Japanese businessmen eating in the sushi bars of Khabarovsk while laborers in town wait six months or more for their wages; in Ivanovo, where three quarters of the workforce has been laid off from the textile mills, television carries up-to-the-minute reports from the film festival at Cannes; the scholars and scientists of Novosibirsk arrive home after yet another conference at Harvard and walk past refugees living in the airport; the shoppers in Murmansk try to read the labels on bottles of Norwegian shampoo and try not to worry too much about the nuclear waste threatening their city, their harbor; on the Leningrad Highway, a new Mercedes with dark-tinted windows streaks past a beggar. The symbols of transformation are stark and banal and true.

But the transformation of Russia is not merely a matter of its outward signs—its relics and innovations. The process roils in the mind and heart of every Russian. Although the epochal news stories are now a matter of history—the end of the Cold War, the end of communism, the end of empire—every Russian (even the young) lives in multiple worlds: in a past that still shapes his thinking and language and habits; in the sometimes unbearable present, with its economic and psychological shocks; and in the future, which is even more unknowable, more unpredictable, than it is elsewhere.

After having endured an inhuman, unthinkable epoch, every Russian is, in some way, engaged in building a new reality, a new state, a new identity, a place in the greater world. An American might look for a parallel in the late eighteenth century, but there are important differences: the colonists could draw on English law and custom to create American political and legal culture; they were also a relatively healthy people, not one recovering from a history of annihilation, propaganda, and neglect. In one way or another, Russians struggle almost daily with essential questions about themselves: What is our country? Who are our heroes? What is our past? What do we believe in? Who are our friends and who are our enemies? Are we Europeans, or are we Asians, or are we wholly other? What experience can we borrow and what is alien and unusable?

Ever since the Soviet Union collapsed and the threat of nuclear confrontation subsided, American interest in Russia has eased. Enrollment in Russian language and history courses has plunged. Having been denied the front page or a chance at prime time, some news bureaus grow bored, frustrated with the indifference back home. This is a serious mistake, for the process of creating a new country—a country that will undoubtedly reassert itself in every sense in the twenty-first century—is at least as interesting, as essential, as the process of erosion and collapse. It is not, however, an easy subject to grasp. The events of 1991 provided a dramatic ending to the Soviet era; the story of the new state is only just beginning, evolving, often in ways that are hard to see. The texture of Russian life after 1991 is so fluid, so changeable and supercharged, that it is nearly impossible to capture in words and images. One of the best writers of the dissident generation, Vladimir Voinovich, explained to me one afternoon that while his existence as a man and as a citizen is now easier—he happily splits his time between Moscow and his place of exile, Munich—his job as a writer is no less difficult than it was in the days of Leonid Brezhnev.

"The absurd in Russia is permanent, it just takes different forms," Voinovich told me. "Under Soviet rule, life had congealed; it was organized and static. Writers could regard Soviet reality like Cézanne regarding a bowl of fruit. It was easier. Now the well-established life is collapsing and a new one is being built all in a fast and chaotic way, and it's hard to write about it. It's like writing about a sinking ship while sitting on deck. When I wrote *The Ivankiad*"—a mock epic about his struggle for a larger apartment—"it was as if I were painting a portrait of something as solid as a tree. Now I can't do this. One would have to be constantly rewriting, catching up. The trick now is to try to write about eternal matters—friendship, love, envy, hatred—in conditions that are constantly changing."

I sympathize with Voinovich, but as a journalist I don't have the luxury of avoiding the fluidity, the quickness of Russian life. Unlike my first book, *Lenin's Tomb,* which was an account of the decline and fall of the Soviet Union, *Resurrection* is more limited in geography and scope. The story of postimperial, postcommunist transformation is so enormous that I have limited myself to one state—Russia—and, in the main, to one rather broad theme—the struggle for a definition of the new Russian state. In describing what is newest in Russia (real politics, oligarchs and businessmen, postcensorship culture, nationalist wars), other subjects are left for other writers and other books. Yevgenia Albats and Amy Knight have written well about the post-Soviet secret services; Stephen Handelman has explored the Russian mafia; and a range of scholars is now at work on post-Soviet economics, foreign policy, poverty, and many other subjects.

This book covers the period from December 1991, when the leaders of the republics decided to squeeze out Mikhail Gorbachev and create fifteen independent states, to the beginning of Boris Yeltsin's second term as Russian president in the fall of 1996. As the book went to press, Yeltsin underwent quintuple bypass surgery. Since a twilight atmosphere dominated the Kremlin even before Yeltsin's victory over Gennady Zyuganov and the communists, the book ends with a consideration of the Russian future, post-Yeltsin.

Two highly contradictory stories run through these years and through this book. The first is Yeltsin's own story, one whose tragic ending is best symbolized by the bombed-out buildings of Grozny and his own exhausted condition. There has never been a Russian leader more triumphant than Yeltsin was in 1991 and rarely one associated with such promise. Having vanquished the August coup, he seemed on the brink of leading this new state, quickly and smoothly, into the world. At least that is what so many, in their hope and in their naiveté, thought might happen. But Russians and Westerners alike have learned that transformation, especially on this scale, is at least as painful as the collapse that precedes it. Because of an intransigent opposition, because of his own errors and failures of character, morality, and imagination, because of his inability— and unwillingness—to create a consensus for change in society, Yeltsin began to suffer a series of tainted victories and terrible defeats. In Chechnya, eighty thousand people paid with their lives for Yeltsin's vanity, his insistence on using the most violent and authoritarian means to solve a highly complex problem of nation-building. At least in the short term, those defeats went a long way toward eclipsing his victories.

The second story, which runs parallel to Yeltsin's own, is the development of Russia itself: the rise of a market economy, the development of political liberties (and their limits), the struggle for a national identity, and a recovery from postimperial funk. And here the story is deeply complicated. Russia is now a state with features of democracy (mainly elections), but also elements of oligarchy and authoritarianism. In writing a history of this jumbled period, I have tried to provide a small gallery of characters who represent this sense of transition: Zyuganov, Yeltsin, his bodyguard Aleksandr Korzhakov, the business magnate Vladimir Gusinsky, Aleksandr Solzhenitsyn, and others. Without ever regretting for an instant that the days of communist rule are over, I also see that this second strand of my story is filled with error and pain, with uncertainty, and this is likely to be the pattern for quite a long time. How could it be otherwise? Russia is emerging from seventy years of barbaric rule and hundreds of years of authoritarianism. It must still climb out *iz pod glib*—

from under the rubble, in Solzhenitsyn's phrase. That Russia has survived at all is remarkable; that the situation today is not worse—far worse—than it is seems to me a miracle. For all its trials, for all its mistakes, the story of Russia at the end of the century must be counted as a kind of revival, a resurrection.

David Remnick
New York City
November 1996

RESURRECTION

CHAPTER 1

THE LOST EMPIRE

In the years after his fall, Mikhail Gorbachev would leave his dacha outside Moscow, fold himself into the backseat of a Volga sedan, and, on the way downtown to his office, survey the contours of the new Russian world. Billboards and beggars. Strip joints and traffic jams. A small fascist parade. Neon brightness and construction everywhere: a quarter-billion-dollar cathedral rising on the Moscow River embankment, an underground shopping mall burrowing in outside the gates of the Kremlin.

It had been more than four years since the leaders of the union republics dissolved the Soviet Union and declared Gorbachev's job moot. On December 21, 1991, leaders of eleven republics put together a retirement package for him that included a small house in the countryside, office space for a foundation in town, and a pension worth (as it turned out) $140 a month. The nominal head of the republican leaders, Russian president Boris Yeltsin, drank heavily throughout the session, and, with time, his head slumped to the desk. Once in a while, he would raise his head, mutter, "What you say is right," and then fall off again into a stupor. At the end of the meeting, he had to be helped from the room.

"This is terrible! Who's ruling Russia?" the Armenian president, Levon Ter-Petrossian, asked one of Yeltsin's aides. "How are you Russians going to live? We don't envy you."

Gorbachev was the last general secretary of the Communist Party, the first—and last—president of the Soviet Union. He resigned Christmas night 1991, an event that marked the end of Soviet history and, in many ways, the twentieth century. His fate, unique in a thousand years, was to be a retired czar, free to accept plaudits and lecture fees abroad, free to suffer the disdain of a people he did so much to liberate. For their part, the republican leaders divvied up the perquisites of traditional Kremlin power: the private jets and limousines, the communications systems and palaces, thousands of nuclear warheads. The dissolution of the Soviet Union had become inevitable after the collapse of the August coup, but the haste and vanity of those who dissolved it were extraordinary. Although they portrayed themselves to their people as national heroes, many had supported or, at least, were ready to knuckle under to the leaders of the August 1991 coup attempt. In time, the leaders of Uzbekistan, Belarus, and Turkmenistan would establish authoritarian regimes more severe than anything seen in the Soviet Union since the days of Andropov and Chernenko. Yeltsin, for his part, would bloody a record of liberal reform and political bravery with corruption, war, and retreat.

Change came so quickly in modern Russia that a few years marks an epoch, so what Gorbachev saw from the car window on his rides to the office on Leningradsky Prospekt no longer stunned him: not the marble-and-glass banks, not the bulletproof limousines, not the Museum of the Revolution where old men now came to pawn their busts of Lenin and Western tourists came to buy them for a laugh.

"Shocked?" Gorbachev said. "What on earth could ever shock me now?"

At first, Gorbachev was humiliated by his abrupt eclipse. Whenever Yeltsin, his successor and antagonist, slighted him, or whenever the media failed to show him the respect that was once his due, Gorbachev suffered. Invariably, he took his suffering public. Talking to a clutch of reporters, his face would redden, his syntax would falter until his speech was a stream of pure rage. His aides learned to soothe him or, barring that, to avoid him. But that, too, changed with time. Anatoly Chernyaev, who remained after fifteen years Gorbachev's most trusted aide, told me, "When Mikhail

Sergeyevich first came to the foundation after leaving power, he would be mortified when things were published about the supposed grandeur of his house, about how he supposedly squirreled away for himself the Party's gold reserves. All that nonsense. But he has adapted. He realized that under the conditions of free expression he has to expect that kind of thing. He holds it all in contempt but he tries to ignore it."

It was not easy. In 1993, Andrei Razin, the lead singer for a pop band called Sweet May, duped Gorbachev's ailing mother into selling her house in Privolnoye, a village in southern Russia. Razin then gave an interview to *Komsomolskaya Pravda* accusing Gorbachev of abandoning his mother—and this, Razin declared, is "even more immoral when it's being done by a person who used to claim the role of leader of the entire Russian nation." Gorbachev, who was born in Privolnoye, where his father was the chairman of the local collective farm, was enraged by Razin and the bad publicity. But anger did him no good. He was reduced to imploring Razin to sell him back the house.

For the young, Gorbachev soon became a figure of fun. One of the biggest hits of 1995, the music that seemed to blare from every taxi radio, was a techno-pop song by the group Gospodin Daduda (Mr. Daduda). As a synthesizer throbs in the background, there is a hilarious Dada interplay between a woman in a state of sexual ecstasy and a "Gorbachev"—complete with southern accent, bureaucratic clichés, and grammatical tics:

> "In the village, cattle mortality rates are up."
> *(Orgasmic cries)*
> "I understand your reaction."
> *(Orgasmic cries)*
> "And this is the main thing."
> *(Orgasmic cries)*
> "Da-doo-da."
> *(Orgasmic cries)*
> "We need to get more control."
> *(Orgasmic cries)*
> "And Raisa Maximovna is also aware of it."
> *(Especially loud orgasmic cries)*
> "Da-doo-da."

Had there ever been a figure of such historical stature who left the throne so easily and then lived on with so little fuss? Certainly not in Russia, where monarchs either died in office or were shot. Even Khrushchev, after he was overthrown by Brezhnev, in 1964, was banished to a KGB-monitored dacha in the woods outside Moscow and was not allowed to publish or pronounce on the politics of his successors. Gorbachev, by contrast, published constantly in his retirement. He ran his foundation, which raised money for various academic, environmental, and first-aid projects. He wrote accounts of the August coup and the collapse of the Soviet Union and, with the help of a team of advisers, a two-volume memoir called *Zhizn i Reformi* ("Life and Reforms"). In Moscow, no one seemed terribly interested in Gorbachev's memoirs; the books were expensive, the sales paltry.

Gorbachev left office saying he was not "going off to the taiga," though no one imagined that he would ever return to politics. It was not just a matter of age and the futility of a second act; politics in Russia had changed, and while Gorbachev was the master of the one-party system, its true Nijinsky, he had always avoided the elective system he had done so much to create. Among his greatest failures as the leader of the Soviet Union was his reluctance to test himself in the marketplace of politics; instead he looked on as Yeltsin, playing the populist card, won elections and therefore a measure of legitimacy that he could never claim.

And yet, at the age of sixty-five, Gorbachev still dreamed of a return to power and a redemption. When the presidential race of June 1996 began, it seemed wide open. None of the contenders, not the communist Gennady Zyuganov, not the nationalists Vladimir Zhirinovsky and Aleksandr Lebed, not the liberal Grigory Yavlinsky, not even Yeltsin himself, could be considered prohibitive favorites. The communists swept the parliamentary elections in December 1995; the communists proved themselves to be the one party in Russia with a sizable membership base, grassroots organization, and a viable set of myths. Zyuganov artfully abandoned orthodox Leninist rhetoric and replaced it with a more appealing language of wounded national pride; however, he had been a former midlevel Central Committee apparatchik and looked it. Zhirinovsky continued to attract support, but it was doubtful that a majority of the electorate would vote for a man who promoted a neofascist ideology and, in his time in parliament, had slugged a woman deputy and posed naked in the shower for photographers. Lebed was a general, well regarded in military circles, but could he make it in politics? No one knew. Yavlinsky, a young economist, could count on support from intellectuals in the biggest cities, but his liabilities included a self-defeating ego, a narrow political base, and a Jewish mother. Yeltsin remained a formidable politician, especially so since he could exploit the tools of Kremlin power during the race, but it was hard to imagine that he had not ruined himself by now. The crime rate, the rampant corruption, the war in Chechnya, and his own failing health were not a prescription for victory. A number of Yeltsin's hard-line advisers, men who feared for their own political lives, told him to use whatever pretense necessary to call off the election.

Not that any of this would help Gorbachev. He was despised by the communists, who regarded him as no better than the CIA; despised by the "great power" nationalists, who believed he was responsible for the humiliation of a great power and its army; and despised as well by liberal democrats, who felt he had never fully shed his allegiance to the nomenklatura that raised him. Running was a risk that only he seemed willing to consider. Late in 1995, when I spoke with a number of his old inner circle, none of them was eager to see their man run.

"Gorbachev is a great historical figure and this is known all over the world, but he has achieved enough," the loyal aide Anatoly Chernyaev told me one afternoon at the Gorbachev foundation. "He should live up to the level of his historical greatness and not stoop to the level of campaign bickering. Maybe he could run and win in a normal country. But that will take maybe twenty years. I don't know. Maybe he should wait and run then."

Gorbachev was not through desiring. Aleksandr Gelman, a playwright and a friend of the former president, told me, "Gorbachev is a cunning man, but he is also totally demoralized without power. He can't imagine himself without power. It's almost as if he's gone mad. He won't run for the Duma, but he is serious about running for the presidency. Which is too bad. The role of an ex-president is an important enough one. If only Yeltsin would join Gorbachev in the ranks of the ex-presidents, this would be a great gain for a fledgling democracy.

"I saw Gorbachev a few months ago and he told me that he gets a lot of letters telling him he should run for president. I said, 'Why should you run? Why do you need this? You've done enough.' But he is a difficult man. He wants to move back into power. As a writer, I am very interested in this quality, the way that the yearning for power can blind a man."

After meeting with Chernyaev at the foundation, I walked up a set of marble steps to Gorbachev's office. The building once housed a Party institute; there are still some of the old-style columns and draperies, the same red runner carpets that the Party favored in the days of Stalin. After several battles with Yeltsin's staff, Gorbachev had lost some of his office space. The business school kids from down the hall strolled by outside Gorbachev's door and thought nothing of it.

Unlike Yeltsin, who had grown as fragile at times as the old general secretaries, Gorbachev seemed, if anything, revived. When I saw him, he looked fit, tanned, and trim. He wore a dark-blue Italian-made double-breasted jacket. The long rest suited him, and it did not take him long to explain what he planned to do with his new reserve of energy.

"I haven't really decided yet to run, but I am getting more positive about it all the time," Gorbachev said. "When I travel around Russia I find that the cliché that Gorbachev has been forgotten is overturned. Everyone who travels with me sees what goes on, despite the opposition to these trips from Moscow. Recently I went to Cheboksary and Yeltsin's people called the local leadership and asked them to limit my contacts there. But I met with all the press there—communists, noncommunists, reformist, nonreformist—and they all wrote about me. I answered questions on the air for an hour. Some of the university officials tried to deny me an auditorium. Under student pressure the administration gave me the philharmonic hall, and instead of fifteen hundred people, *twenty-five* hundred people came. Not just students, but communists and Zhirinovsky people, too! Everyone! I answered questions for three hours. I met with workers there, too. They came up to touch me and test whether Gorbachev is still alive. They said, 'How is your health, Mikhail Sergeyevich?' And I replied, 'My health is just as you see it.' Then they'd say, 'Well, do you have the guts to run? One more time?' And they would look me right in the eye."

———

This was not the first time I had met with Gorbachev in his retirement, and sitting there in his bare and nearly bookless office, listening to him once more, I had the sense that his vanity, charm, and self-delusion were wisdom itself. He has the gift. You sit across from Gorbachev and react with an idiot's awe, a fixed smile, intermittent nods of agreement. He takes you in before you've had a chance to sort through what he's actually said.

It could only have been the power of personality—a form of magic—that allowed Gorbachev to guide the Communist Party to its own transformation, purge, and eventual crack-up. Despite various forces suggesting the need for economic and technological reform, the Party did not have to take Gorbachev's radical course. Vitaly Vorotnikov, a conservative Politburo member, in his diaries—published under the title *This Is How It Was* . . . —recounts how he would sit in at the meetings of the top Party leadership and listen to Gorbachev propose changes that everyone knew would mean the weakening, if not the end, of one-party rule. Why do we all sit still for it? Vorotnikov wondered. Why do we all vote our assent? Vorotnikov and the rest still ask themselves the same questions. When I asked one of Gorbachev's key conservative rivals in the Politburo, Yegor Ligachev, how it could have happened, he sneered. "Mikhail Sergeyevich played us for dupes," Ligachev said. "When we caught on, it was too late."

To his allies, Gorbachev's deceptiveness, his instrumental amorality, was his political talent. "Gorbachev is a figure who refutes the law that by evil means no good can be done," said Gelman, who besides writing plays also served briefly on the Party Central Committee. "He lied to his circle of Communist Party people. He had a double personality. He was two-faced to nearly everyone. Next to Gorbachev, Ligachev was a moral genius. Ligachev, after all, said what he thought and was clear about his principles. Gorbachev had to operate among people who would have killed him had they known what he was really up to. And sometimes Gorbachev deluded himself, too. So on the basis of classic moral principles, Gorbachev was a bad man, a dishonest man. But what he achieved was enormous. Thanks largely to Gorbachev, the world was redivided in a sensible way without war."

Gorbachev himself is entirely aware of the power he exerted over other people. "I think a lot of it is about human nature," he told me. "As early as boyhood, among the other kids, I was always the leader. This is just a natural quality, like the curiosity I have that pushes me to get to the bottom of things. It never occurred to me to get into politics. But then when I got involved in Komsomol politics someone said, 'Okay, who here is Gorbachev?' I stood and climbed up on my chair. Then, suddenly, someone pulled the chair out from under me and everyone laughed. That's how my career began! But my conclusion was always to get up off the floor and keep going. Keep going. That's what my experience tells me."

Gorbachev's memoirs chronicle a small-town boy's climb up through the only political hierarchy his country offered: the hierarchy of tyranny. Without apology, Gorbachev writes of his uncanny ability to win over the old Party leaders and make them his mentors, and his willingness to stifle disagreement and even laughter in the presence of his age-fogged superiors. In scene after scene, Gorbachev plays the courtier to Brezhnev, who, in his dotage, was unable to frame a clear thought, much less utter one. In one episode he describes how, in 1982, one Politburo ancient, Andrei Kirilenko, was eased into retirement only after receiving assurances that he could keep his dacha and other perks; when the time came for Kirilenko to write his resignation papers, tears filled his eyes and he asked the general secretary, Yuri Andropov, to draft the letter for him. Kirilenko could not hold the pen.

"Oh my God! I couldn't write about everything—but Kirilenko!" Gorbachev told me, collapsing in laughter. "The man could not put two words together. This was, simply put, a problem. I think now, when we look back at such things years from now, we simply won't be able to imagine them."

———

Language was a foundation of the old regime. The old Communist Party controlled language absolutely (banning writers, creating the Newspeak of official doctrine and media) and, like God almighty, gave everything its name. Brezhnev's inability to speak coherently was a fair representation of the regime's decline—imitations of the old man's garbles were common comic currency in the late seventies. When he took power in 1985, Gorbachev displayed a fluency that held out the illusion that the regime, now in command of its faculties again, could express itself, revive itself, and endure.

The most important speech Gorbachev ever gave while he was in power (and still popular) came in November 1987 on the seventieth anniversary of the Bolshevik Revolution. Hidden among phrases that now seem painful in their obeisance to Leninist theology, Gorbachev returned to the theme of Soviet history and anti-Stalinism that Khrushchev had first raised in 1956 in the "secret speech." Gorbachev described Stalin's regime as "criminal" and went on from there. Even though he took time to redeify Lenin and skimmed over numerous episodes of his brutality, Gorbachev had, in a public, televised forum, opened the political history—and system—of the Soviet Union to criticism, doubt, and question. In spite of Gorbachev's own intentions for the system's renewal, the suicide had begun.

One of the rallying cries of the revived Russian Communist Party as it began its campaign for the presidency in 1996 was that the "democrats," beginning with Gorbachev, had "blackened" the Soviet past, crossed out all its triumphs and glories. Russian school texts, at least in the big cities, have now been sufficiently revised to include a version of the Revolution that is closer to that of an American historian like Richard Pipes than to Lenin's. Schoolchildren now read of the weakness of Nicholas II, the vacuum of power that followed his fall, and then the ruthlessness of the Bolshevik seizure of power; the new texts are a litany of cruelties as well as of achievements. The Communist Party standard-bearer, Gennady Zyuganov, did not vow a return to censorship and the Stalinist version of history, but he was intent on battling what he insisted were "criminal distortions."

"At first there was criticism of Brezhnev, then of Stalin, then of the period going all the way to Lenin," Zyuganov said in one of his speeches. "Today all that was glorious is eliminated. In our schools today textbooks practically do not mention Pushkin and Tolstoy, Dostoevsky and Nekrasov . . . instead we have literary and political pornography. And these textbooks are written with the sponsorship of the Soros Fund. . . . This is done to kill our memory. . . . Today one hears terrible lies, that the October Revolution was a plot, a coup. We hear it said that the revolution was the product of several people, a limited number of people. No. The revolution was a social earthquake which decided the most burning contradictions."

The resentment against Gorbachev never abated. For the men who led the communist opposition, he was the man who had betrayed everything: the Party, history, the empire. One afternoon, I went to see Anatoly Lukyanov, a leading communist, a key figure in the Duma, and one of Zyuganov's gray cardinals. Under Gorbachev, Lukyanov had been a Politburo member and chairman of the Supreme Soviet; he was also a key supporter of the August 1991 coup. Lukyanov and Gorbachev first met at Moscow State University in the early fifties. Lukyanov was Gorbachev's protégé in the Party. After Lukyanov and the other coup plotters were released from prison under a general amnesty, he no longer spoke of his friendship with Gorbachev, only his hatred. When Gorbachev's name came up, Lukyanov's face darkened, his fists clenched and whitened.

When I visited Lukyanov at his office, he greeted me the way a fighter greets his opponent in the center of the ring. He thrust out his chest and stared hard. I began by asking about various publications in the communist press that blamed the collapse of the Soviet Union on Western intelligence agencies and their "agents of influence"——men like the former adviser to Gorbachev Aleksandr Yakovlev. Did Lukyanov really believe that?

"Are you a naive person?" Lukyanov said. (He now made sure his nose was about six inches from mine.) "I know this to be a fact. It is enough to read the Americans from John Foster Dulles through Zbigniew Brzezinski and Henry Kissinger. Their role in this was enormous. The West simply didn't want the competition of the Soviet Union. Geopolitically, the United States wanted to break up the Soviet Union and turn it into a raw-materials annex. This was the eternal policy of the West. They wanted to create a vast new market. They wanted to 'liberate' the market, give jobs to their unemployed and use our people for cheap labor. And still the Americans are producing ten times more weapons than ever. All the rest is superficial. The West even managed to lead on young, inexperienced Soviet politicians who could be bought with nice words. It was enough in 1984 for Margaret Thatcher to praise Gorbachev and he became theirs. And sitting next to Gorbachev was Yakovlev, who had spent twelve years in Canada as ambassador, where he became a rabid anticommunist. I have known Gorbachev for forty years and Yakovlev for thirty. I know these men."

While Lukyanov was in power, he was always next to Gorbachev, forever reminding reporters of their great partnership in perestroika. After the coup collapsed, he begged for Gorbachev's indulgence. But now he portrayed their relationship quite differently: as a wise counselor failing to sway a foolish king.

"All that happened with Gorbachev could have been predicted at the end of 1990," Lukyanov went on. "He was a confused politician. He was like a child who refuses to see that some stories have scary endings. I knew by April 1991 that all of this would end in arrests and catastrophe. But what happened in August 1991 was not a coup, not a plot. It was an attempt to save the country, and that is all. In Gorbachev, we were dealing with a politician who was out of his depth, a man who had never known anything except Komsomol politics and Party politics. In me, you are talking to a man who worked as a lathe operator at a factory in 1943. The metallic dust has come out of my pores only in these last ten years. Gorbachev was just a functionary given to great outbursts of suggestions and then irresponsible implementation. He was a brilliant actor."

But surely Gorbachev wanted to preserve the union? Was he to blame for its collapse?

Lukyanov smiled, indulging once more the naiveté of his visitor.

"Gorbachev could have stopped it all," he said. "Belovezhskaya Pushcha"—the hunting lodge near Minsk where the leaders of Belarus, Russia, and Ukraine first declared an end to the union—"is just a few kilometers from the Polish border. It would have been enough just to give them a little shove and they would have all fled to shelter under Lech Walesa. Gorbachev was never a master at seeing three steps ahead. But he knew the collapse was coming. He had at his disposal forces that could have prevented it. He could have acted decisively. But he was so naive he thought these people would have mercy on him."

Before leaving, I asked Lukyanov about the possibility of Gorbachev's return to politics.

Lukyanov grinned almost maniacally. "Before he thinks about his future and running for president, Gorbachev ought to try walking the streets of Moscow and let's see if he comes back in one piece," he said. "He needs to get out among workers and farmers and see if he returns in one piece. Let him visit a military base and see if he can come back in one piece. Then we'll talk about running for president.

"You see, sooner or later there will be a trial. A Duma deputy named Viktor Ilyukhin held a trial and sentenced Gorbachev to the people's eternal shame, and this was a conviction and punishment worse than capital punishment. Do you know how Gorbachev will persist in people's memories? As the destroyer of the Soviet Union. Nothing more. Just that. Yeltsin will be the man who fired on the parliament. Nothing more."

"And you, Anatoly Ivanovich? How will you be remembered?" I asked.

"Me?" he said. "I will be the man who realized his power too late, who, together with some others, was responsible for letting happen what happened. I should have been more resolute."

On a dismal winter afternoon, I took the subway out to the northern fringe of Moscow to watch Zyuganov work a crowd of faithful constituents. At the Polyarni movie theater, several hundred people, most of them past retirement age, filled the seats and the aisles to hear their man. The theater was warm enough, but in customary Russian style, everyone wore his coat and hat. The place had a steamy wet-wool smell. After Zyuganov arrived, we all stood. The "Internationale" played on the loudspeakers, and in this crowd nearly everyone still knew the words—and sang.

Older voters were Zyuganov's most visible supporters, but they were far from alone. The Party was able to revive itself not because of any individual, but rather because it is the one political organization with a resonant mythology. In its electoral programs and in its newspapers, the Party combined elements of the old ideology (collectivism, social equality) and elements of the nationalist agenda (the reestablishment of Russia as a rival to the United States, the restoration of the Soviet Union, an allergy to foreign influences). At the Polyarni theater, Zyuganov unleashed his standard speech, his travelogue across "this long-suffering country," his description of how the United States destroyed the Soviet Union with "lies, provocations, and money." Yeltsin, of course, came in for a beating, but Gorbachev did no better. "Gorbachev is responsible for the banditry in this country," Zyuganov said. "He is responsible for police having to wear bulletproof vests. Gorbachev got the Nobel Peace Prize, and for that Alfred Nobel must have spun ten times in his coffin."

What was unforgivable for Zyuganov and his constituents was the humiliation they felt at the collapse of the Soviet Union. While in the West many scholars and journalists came to see the political battles between

Gorbachev and Yeltsin as the great struggle of the late eighties and early nineties, the story line of an era, the Russian opposition forces saw one man as the extension of the other. The men were equally despised for their complementary roles in destroying the empire. No matter what the angle of vision, there is no doubt that the relationship between the two men, and the effect it had on Soviet history, loomed over all Russian politics. Countless empirical factors contributed to the collapse of the Soviet Union—a rotting economy, a bankrupt ideology, percolating intellectual and moral dissidence, foreign military and political pressure, and then, under Gorbachev, the catalytic effect of a little freedom and the rise of nationalism in the republics.

"The Soviet Union was doomed to collapse as a multinational empire. But it was an entirely different matter *when* this historical moment would happen," said Galina Starovoitova, a member of the Duma who had been close to Andrei Sakharov and then worked in the early nineties as an adviser to Yeltsin on ethnic issues. "My feeling is that the disintegration was inevitable but the historical moment, the timing, was accidental. If it hadn't been for a number of subjective factors—and not just the personal feud between Yeltsin and Gorbachev—it all could have happened thirty or fifty years later than it did."

Starovoitova had traveled extensively throughout the Soviet Union, both as a scholar and as a dissident, and her sense of the empire was as keen as anyone's in the Kremlin. "The Soviet Union brought together one hundred and twenty-six different nations and tried to homogenize them, managing it only superficially," she told me. "They were different in terms of language, which ranged from the Ural-Altaic linguistic families to Indo-European, and in religion, which ranged from Christianity to Islam. Religion and language usually determine the mentality of a nation, and so there were great differences. The layer of *Homo sovieticus* was extremely superficial. The thickness, so to speak, of this layer was probably greater in Russia or Ukraine than in Tadjikistan, Estonia, Turkmenia, or Azerbaijan."

For decades the Soviet empire was held together by ideology and coercion and even the perversity of the imperial economy. Under Stalin, especially, whole nations were directed to assume responsibility for economic monocultures: cotton in Uzbekistan, for instance, or rocket parts in

Ukraine, cigarette filters in Armenia. To challenge that imperial arrangement was to invite not only brutal punishment but economic disaster.

"When Gorbachev began perestroika, he certainly did not understand
all these factors," Starovoitova said. "He was simply a younger and more
energetic leader who wanted to look civilized in the eyes of the West,
where he had traveled a little. He wanted to be regarded as a decent man,
not another senile character of the Brezhnev, Chernenko type. Thatcher
played a role in this—encouraging him—and he tried to live up to her
expectations. Of course, Gorbachev wanted to renovate the facade, not
modify the foundation or the construction itself. He did not understand
that he was cutting the very branch that he was sitting on. In criticizing
the Communist Party and disclosing information about the crimes of the
Party and Stalin, he inevitably—even though he didn't understand it—
arrived at a conclusion that one-party power was illegitimate. His two
liberal advisers, Aleksandr Yakovlev and Eduard Shevardnadze, claim they
were the only ones who understood everything, but I doubt that even
they did at first. Gorbachev certainly did not understand. I know this
from personal talks with him."

Gorbachev announced many times that while the Soviet Union suffered
from serious failings, even crises, "the nationalities problem has been
solved." Such had been the propaganda, and the genuine belief, of the
Party for many years. "No Catholic priest, and certainly no pope, can be a
nonbeliever," Starovoitova said, "and so it is with general secretaries and
high Party functionaries: they believe what they proclaim. So the subject
of the nationalities went banned and unexplored." In 1988 and 1989,
when the various people's fronts began to show enormous political
strength in the Baltic states and in Armenia, Georgia, and Azerbaijan, Gorbachev reacted as if he were being challenged by extremists, marginals,
even madmen—and it is clear now that he was encouraged to think so by
the reports he was getting from the KGB. In every case, Moscow made arrests of local leaders and sent troops and tanks into the republican capitals;
and while casualties were relatively few, the military reaction only built
support for nationalism on the periphery of the empire. "Gorbachev's belief," Starovoitova said, "that it was all a provocation by some extremists—
his belief that we had, in fact, a Soviet people—was a more important
subjective factor in all this than even his relations with Yeltsin."

In May 1992, Gorbachev was in Washington as a guest of the librarian of Congress, James Billington, and during a breakfast with a small group of scholars and other guests, he was asked what had been his most difficult problem as Soviet president and general secretary. "The nationalities issue," Gorbachev said. And when did you really grow aware of it? he was asked.

"In the fall or winter of 1990," came the answer. At least two years too late.

———

So there were many factors, political and economic, undermining the union. But as Sergei Parkhomenko, one of the best-known journalists in Moscow, put it to me, "The hatred between Gorbachev and Yeltsin was the engine." Gennady Yanayev, one of the leaders of the August coup, agreed: "The animal hatred between Gorbachev and Yeltsin, this was the subjective factor that played an evil trick on the nation, this is what eventually led to the disintegration of the country."

Boris Yeltsin was not a part of Gorbachev's original inner circle. When Gorbachev came to power in March 1985, Yeltsin was a regional party secretary, in the Urals; it was a provincial career distinguished, above all, by his accepting the order to destroy the Ipatiev house, where the Romanov family had been executed. But as Gorbachev was trying to build a core of support for himself in the Central Committee, his two closest political allies in the Party at the time, Nikolai Ryzhkov and Yegor Ligachev, debated the wisdom of bringing Yeltsin, a construction foreman and Party apparatchik, to Moscow from the city of Yekaterinburg (which was then called Sverdlovsk). Yeltsin had a mixed reputation in Party circles: he was energetic and intelligent, but also erratic and quick to take offense.

"I remember when I was first told about Yeltsin, I had my doubts," Gorbachev told me. "I talked about it with Ryzhkov, and he said, 'Don't take him, you'll be in trouble with him.' You see, he really knew Yeltsin from the Urals. But then the process sort of started. Ligachev was in charge of personnel and he said, 'Let me go down and check it out.' Ryzhkov said no, but I thought maybe Ryzhkov and Yeltsin had a conflict, so I said to Ligachev, 'Yegor Kuzmich, go ahead and check it out.' He went and called me a few days later and said, 'Yeltsin is okay. He's what we need. He's our man.' " Even this early incident is fraught with irony, for it was Ligachev, the Party traditionalist, who would become Yeltsin's fiercest enemy.

As the first party secretary of the Moscow Party organization, Yeltsin made his mark not with sophisticated political arguments or ideological speeches, but rather through a technique utterly alien to Soviet political culture: raw populism. He began firing dozens of officials and bragged about it to the press. He visited stores and rode the Moscow metro, and was always careful to see that the press covered the event. At least in the capital, Yeltsin competed with the general secretary for attention.

"When Yeltsin worked as first secretary I didn't criticize him, or if I did it wasn't on a Politburo level, only on a personal level," Gorbachev said. "It was never public. But more and more I had the suspicion that he was too much about breaking things over his knee. I spoke to him about this and said that if it ever seems that we are conducting reforms like this, the question will arise, 'Can you really call these democratic reforms?' That's when the crisis arose.

"Also, Ligachev demanded a lot from everyone, and that included Yeltsin, and Yeltsin didn't like that. Yeltsin began to complain, saying, 'Why am I being castigated for every little thing? Ligachev is always try-ing to push me around.' Such was Yeltsin. He began to sense that he could use his populism. He would take a little tram or he'd go 'shopping' for food or meet the press. And by the way, I supported his meetings, his openness. I did not try to change him. I wanted him to be absorbed in this process, like all of us. But he was so full of hurt feelings that he began to hold things against us sometimes. Then he'd go off and say, 'The Politburo is so old, filled with mastodons who should be fired.' But I had changed the entire Politburo, I made a clean sweep, like there had never been be-fore, even in Stalin's time. We had to go about these things in a proper way, not like Yeltsin thought. I think he only brought these things up to exploit them, so that he could put himself forward under this banner. They were really careerist claims. He also took it hard that he was not a full member of the Politburo. Maybe if he had had full Politburo status he would have behaved differently. There was something about Yeltsin, something inside him, maybe hard feelings, even vengefulness, and he still carries around these qualities. He doesn't forgive anything."

Gorbachev, of course, tells the story in a language and version totally in his favor. He was tolerant of Yeltsin, it is true, but he also turned on him when he thought the occasion demanded. In October 1987, Yeltsin made the mistake at a closed Central Committee session of trying to challenge Ligachev's authority in the Party and what he saw as a tendency in the leadership to create a "cult" around Gorbachev. Within minutes, one speaker after another rushed to the podium to denounce Yeltsin, setting off the pattern of confrontation that would define Soviet politics thereafter.

As we talked about this old sequence of events—Yeltsin's exile, then his reemergence as the leader of the opposition and then as the first democratically elected president of Russia—Gorbachev assumed an expression of pained disgust. When the subject is Yeltsin, he cannot be stopped.

"I don't believe Yeltsin was ever really a democrat," he said angrily. "Yes, he got incorporated into democratic and intelligentsia circles. But I think he joined with these forces deliberately and took advantage of them to break through to the top.

"When he was on the Politburo he would write letters to me while I was on vacation telling me how disappointed he was. In Moscow he realized he just couldn't manage. He would reshuffle personnel, disband various Party committees. He acted as if he were still a Party chief in Yekaterinburg. But it's not the same level. Moscow is a state within a state, with all its bureaucrats and politicians watching our every move. Then he realized he was losing his grip and tried to turn a failure into a victory, to make himself seem more democratic, more pro-reform, as if he had ever been prevented from having this opportunity."

There has never been a politician, Russian or otherwise, who has believed more in the power of personality than Gorbachev. And the personality he believed in was his own. He was convinced of his ability to reconcile and balance forces of all kinds, and so long as he was dealing with the Communist Party in its old and obedient form, while it still observed the rules of Party discipline, he was right in admiring his own mastery. He had the gift of Stalin's manipulations without resorting to Stalinist means.

But when the rules of politics changed in the Soviet Union, Gorbachev could not change his personality. He tried to lecture and cajole men like Yeltsin and the other republican presidents as if they had no power or will or ambition of their own. In the spring of 1991, Gorbachev brought together nine republican leaders, including Yeltsin, to begin a process of negotiations on a new, less centralized Soviet Union. The negotiations, which took place in the dacha village of Novo-Ogarevo outside Moscow, were seen as a sign of great promise. Gorbachev, after so many battles with Yeltsin and the others, had finally decided to compromise, to cede power to the republics without giving up entirely the importance of Moscow as an imperial center.

But during the Novo-Ogarevo process, Gorbachev spoke mainly in monologues, the way he would at Politburo sessions in years past. The various republican presidents grumbled among themselves about how Gorbachev was behaving like a *glukhar*, a bird that goes deaf while making its mating calls. Even Stanislav Shushkevich of Belarus, not an especially powerful personality from not an especially powerful republic, told his colleagues he was getting fed up. He had things to do, meetings to attend. Gorbachev was taking them all for a ride. The others nodded in agreement.

One day, Ruslan Khasbulatov, who was sitting in for Yeltsin as the Russian representative, interrupted Gorbachev, mid-monologue, and said, "Okay, Mikhail Sergeyevich, if you want us to continue with these talks, you'll have to apologize to all of us here. Here lined up in front of you are the representatives of the sovereign states as the Soviet constitution defines them."

Gorbachev went pale, then red, and then apologized. The meetings went on. By July 1991, the group reached agreement on a union treaty that would result in a far more decentralized, federative union than any known before in Soviet history. The republics would tend to their own economies and pay far less into the central government. Gorbachev and Yeltsin, as well as the other republican presidents, argued over taxation, security, and dozens of other issues, but it was clear, as the August vacation began, that the treaty, scheduled for signing on August 20, would undermine the power of the central authorities.

The leaders of the KGB, the army, and the Interior Ministry police had listened to wiretaps of the union treaty negotiations. For them, the treaty would mean the end of their singular power—the KGB chief, Vladimir Kryuchkov, for one, heard from the tapes that he would soon be fired—and to put an end to it, they attempted the coup.

The failure of the coup was the spark that lit a bonfire beneath the old union structures. Lithuania had already declared independence in 1990, but with the failure of the coup and the weakness it revealed, one republic after another declared its sovereignty. Even in republics where the presidents welcomed or at least showed no resistance (even rhetorical) to the coup, independence became the politics of the day. Gorbachev struggled in every way he could to return the situation to what had existed before August 19—he convened sessions of the old Soviet Congress of People's Deputies, he called on a core of liberal advisers he had abandoned only a year before—but he had lost power and could no longer control the political game.

"The August putsch and its failure was the Chernobyl of the old system—that is the most precise image," Yeltsin's chief aide at the time, Gennady Burbulis, told me. "The putschists revealed the depths of the system's deterioration and collapse. All the long-term decay of the military, the political system, the economy was all expressed by the August coup. After that, our goal was simply to give some *shape* to the collapse."

"After the coup, Gorbachev was in a state of shock," said Galina Starovoitova, who was in the middle of all these negotiations. "He didn't know what to do or what to say, and so he tried to go on singing the old song. He tried to keep up the Novo-Ogarevo process, but it was a balloon with no more air left in it. It was too late. Before the coup, everything was possible, but not now, not afterward. Now he had to face all these new partners and talk to them on an entirely different level. . . . Who was he? A king without a kingdom."

Sensing Gorbachev's weakness and tired of his old song, the republican presidents became more active in their disdain. "And it wasn't Yeltsin alone who disliked him," Starovoitova went on. "Everyone was sick of him and his garrulity. I heard this from Shushkevich [of Belarus] and Nazarbayev [of Kazakhstan]. Kravchuk, the Ukrainian president, simply despised him. Yes, they wanted to push him out. Not just Yeltsin wanted to do it. And they couldn't find another way of pulling out his chair without abolishing his post. There was no other way. For Gorbachev, everything was collapsing. The ground was slipping from under him."

Yeltsin, especially, began to intensify a double game he had been flirting with for nearly a year. Even while he continued negotiating with Gorbachev about a new union—the terms had shifted from federation to confederation—his advisers explored the possibility of what would happen if there were no union at all. Yeltsin's top aide, Gennady Burbulis, his legal adviser Sergei Shakhrai, his economic guru, Yegor Gaidar, and his foreign minister, Aleksandr Kozyrev, began working with their staffs on alternatives to the union. "We began looking into various examples around the world: the United Arab Emirates, the European Community, the British Commonwealth, all the possibilities," Kozyrev told me. Burbulis added that as early as the beginning of 1991, he and his staff were seriously considering the organization of a four-sided union of Russia, Ukraine, Belarus, and Kazakhstan. Gorbachev was aware of this double game, but he never even tried to take action. Even to the distraction of his last remaining loyal aides, he acted as if he were still capable of steering events through sheer force of personality and will.

"This was utterly characteristic of Gorbachev," his aide Anatoly Chernyaev said. "I remember when those ministers—Dmitri Yazov, Vladimir Kryuchkov, and Boris Pugo, the eventual coup plotters—I remember when they went into the Supreme Soviet in June 1991 and railed against Gorbachev, tried to seize power, quietly. I called Gorbachev on the phone and I said, 'Do you know what they are saying about you in the Supreme Soviet? Your own people?' And Gorbachev said, 'Why should I care?' So this was his habit, a kind of confidence or innocence, so that he would not pay heed. Gorbachev could never believe that someone close to him, not even Yeltsin, would raise a hand against him. Here he was, surrounded by hatred, and he remained completely alone. Even while the so-called democrats were criticizing him and insulting him, he couldn't believe that such a deal would be done, that people would abandon all common sense and try to disband the union."

Yeltsin, in fact, did not make an overt move to disband the union until December. In meetings in November, Gorbachev was still able to convince Yeltsin that without a confederative structure and a union center in

Moscow, economic and political disaster was inevitable. (Or, at least, Yeltsin *pretended* to be convinced of this.) More and more power was being ceded to the republics with each passing week, but Gorbachev had still managed to retain a few prerogatives for Moscow, not least his own office, the union presidency. But on November 25, with Ukraine scheduled to vote on an independence referendum one week later, Yeltsin balked at initialing a draft treaty, telling Gorbachev that he did not want to alienate the Ukrainians. Gorbachev once more went back to treating the men assembled as if they were his Politburo.

"I don't understand how you plan to get along," he said in a long and often obscene rant. "You know, when you set up your shantytown instead of a united state you will put your people through torture. We are strangling in the shit as it is! . . . If you reject the confederated state version, then just go on without me!" Gorbachev stormed out of the meeting.

A little while later, Yeltsin went to calm Gorbachev down and tell him that he and the others had agreed to submit the draft treaty to their national legislatures. Gorbachev kept referring to Yeltsin as "Czar Boris"— a reference to the tragic Boris Godunov.

The truth was, Yeltsin did not really know how Ukraine would vote. He had said all along that without Ukraine, there could be no union of any kind. Around the time of the ill-fated meeting with Gorbachev, Yeltsin asked Starovoitova how she thought the vote would go in Ukraine. Starovoitova had sent a team of pollsters and ethnologists to the republic to canvass public opinion there. She told Yeltsin that she thought that as much as 75 percent would vote for Ukrainian independence.

"How is that possible?" Yeltsin said. "It can't be!"

Yeltsin refused to believe the news.

"They are brother Slavs," he said. "There are so many Russians there. If you had said fifty-one percent, I would believe you, maybe. But seventy-five percent?"

But then Yeltsin collected himself and said, "Okay, well, if this is so, then we'll be forced to accept it. So this is what we'll do. One week later, when the euphoria subsides, I'll bring together the leaders of the Slavic republics. Not in Kiev, where they have just seceded, not in Moscow, which is like an imperial center, but in Minsk. And we'll begin to build something new, a new union, a commonwealth."

On December 1, a few votes shy of 90 percent voted for Ukrainian independence. Eighty-four percent of the eligible voters went to the polls, and even ethnic Russians in the eastern part of the republic voted overwhelmingly for independence. Almost no one had confidence in Moscow or the old union structures any longer. For Yeltsin, the vote clarified everything. There could be no more double game.

One day after the vote, Yeltsin's ethnic relations adviser, Starovoitova, went to see the plenipotentiary representative of Ukraine in Russia, Pyotr Kryzhanovsky.

"On the way over I bought a big bunch of roses," Starovoitova recalled. "I came to him and he was frightened and confused. He didn't know how to react. He was an old communist apparatchik and suddenly his republic has seceded from the union and here he was sitting in Moscow with no instructions and no idea what to do. He was thinking, Maybe tanks will be moved into Kiev as they were sent into other republics. And suddenly I show up as an official adviser to Yeltsin with a bunch of roses and say, 'I've come to congratulate you on the first day of Ukrainian independence!' He was completely confused. In my presence he called Kravchuk in Kiev and said, 'Galina Vasilievna is here.' And they switched to Ukrainian and he said, 'It's the first time in my life that a *zhinka* [a woman] has given me flowers.' They were thinking tanks and they got roses. This was an official signal. I told him, 'Boris Nikolayevich recognizes the new reality and Russia will recognize you.' "

In their opposition to Yeltsin, Gorbachev and Zyuganov would agree: the new regime began its habit of flouting the legal order when on December 7, 1991, Yeltsin, Kravchuk, and Shushkevich met at a government compound in Belarus near the Polish border and declared the Soviet Union defunct. A couple of weeks later, eleven of the fifteen republics confirmed the decision (the Baltic states and Georgia thought the meeting superfluous) in the Kazakh capital, Alma-Ata. It is common knowledge in Russia that the meeting in Belarus was lubricated, at least part of the time, in traditional fashion. On the door of one of Gorbachev's aides at the foundation is a picture of Yeltsin, Kravchuk, and Shushkevich looking indecently happy. Underneath is the caption "Three split a bottle and millions get a headache."

"Remember this," Gorbachev's aide Anatoly Chernyaev said of the decision to end the union. "All these men wanted their own state. I remember Karimov, of Uzbekistan, always complained about how when an African head of state would come to Moscow he would be greeted with a red carpet and a real Kremlin reception and so on, but for him—the leader of a place with ten times the population and a great industrial base—the reception was a yawn. So, yes, ego played a role. The union only lasted as long as it did mainly due to Communist Party discipline. In every republic, Moscow put ethnic Russians in charge of the military and the KGB and the Party. And it stayed together through force or the threat of force. But when the republics saw what had happened in Eastern Europe, when they saw that Gorbachev would not venture to use force on any scale, the disintegration process grew quicker."

The three-way meeting in Belarus was not exactly a secret. Yeltsin told Gorbachev that he was going to Minsk to go over some "bilateral business," nothing of great importance. "What we did," Kozyrev told me, "was to use the opportunity of a long-standing date we had with Shushkevich for a bilateral meeting. We wanted to explore what Belarus wanted. Since they were, by nature, closest to Russia, we wanted to see what was maximally feasible. We knew if Belarus didn't want to maintain a union, then we had to go on to something else. The idea was also to avoid meeting in Moscow. If we met in Moscow, Gorbachev would be drawn in and the game would go around in circles."

In the last two days before going to Minsk, Kozyrev put together a four-page memo for Yeltsin suggesting various options ranging from a "renewed union"—more or less what Gorbachev was hoping for—to a loose confederation. To get a sense of how improvised this period of history was, to understand the lack of sophistication involved, one need only know that on the night before he left Moscow for Minsk, Kozyrev went to the Savoy Hotel not far from the KGB headquarters and met with an old friend, Allan Weinstein, head of the Washington-based Democracy Project and the author of a book on the Alger Hiss case.

"Allan," Kozyrev said, "what is the difference between a commonwealth, a federation, and an association?" The discussion proceeded from there. But while Yeltsin would certainly bring up the subject of a union,

Kozyrev, Shakhrai, Burbulis, and Gaidar—his key advisers on this issue—
knew that would not stay on the table for long.

"The idea behind the whole meeting in Belarus was that while you
couldn't take Gorbachev out of the country, you could take the country
away from Gorbachev," the journalist Sergei Parkhomenko said.

At the start of the meeting, Yeltsin asked Shushkevich if Belarus was
prepared to join in a union. Shushkevich said that it was not. They then
called Kravchuk in Kiev and invited him to meet them in an informal setting, a hunting lodge near the Polish border. Once Kravchuk arrived in
Belarus, Yeltsin asked him if there was any chance that Ukraine would
join a confederate union. Yeltsin said he felt he had to ask, if only to satisfy Gorbachev.

"All our efforts at this point were directed at Kravchuk to participate
in the Novo-Ogarevo process," Burbulis recalled. Later, Kravchuk would
say, "When we went to Belovezhskaya Pushcha, I did not know what the
outcome of the meeting would be. We had to talk together. If we had invited more delegates, it would have been pointless. Russia, Ukraine, Belarus—these were the founding states, the foundation, of the old union
[in 1922]. Our logic was that we should meet and then talk with the
others."

When Kravchuk said that Ukraine would refuse to join a new union of
the sort that Gorbachev was insisting on, the negotiations moved to a far
different, a revolutionary, plane. "The mood was tense, reflective, inspired, somewhat worried," Burbulis said. "The person who was most
worried was Yeltsin himself. We really had to convince him, to prod him,
because he, more than anyone else, felt the scale of the consequences."

The three parties agreed that they would try another possibility, a commonwealth of sorts. They had only the vaguest notion of where they were
moving. The team of Russian and Belarussian experts and ministers began
working at a smaller dacha while the heads of state began what can only be
called a celebratory dinner. As it became ever clearer that the three presidents would now move on without Gorbachev, that they would be the
leaders of their own independent states, the atmosphere lost its tension.
The working group finished at about two in the morning, and what it conceived was a declaration that would effectively end the Soviet Union and
propose a new voluntary commonwealth. Kozyrev and others worried

that various generals might stage a coup in the name of defending the union state, but Shakhrai insisted that since these three republics organized the union in 1922, they had the legal right to dissolve it.

Meanwhile, "Yeltsin got very drunk," according to someone close to the negotiations. "Yeltsin was so drunk he fell out of his chair just at the moment that Shushkevich opened the door and let in Burbulis, Kozyrev, and the others. Everyone began to come into the room and found this spectacular scene of Shushkevich and Kravchuk dragging this enormous body to the couch. The Russian delegation took it all very calmly. They took him to the next room to let him sleep. Yeltsin's chair stayed empty. Finally, Kravchuk took his chair and assumed the responsibility of chairman. When Kravchuk finished his short speech to everyone about what had been decided, he said, 'There is one problem that we have to decide right away because the very existence of the commonwealth depends on it: don't pour him too much.' Everyone nodded. They understood Kravchuk perfectly."

Yeltsin's version of events is less spectacular and more sober-minded. "I well remember how a sensation of freedom and lightness suddenly came over me," he wrote of his experience that day in the memoir *The Struggle for Russia*. "Russia was choosing a different path, a path of internal development rather than an imperial one. . . . Russia had chosen a new global strategy. She was throwing off the traditional image of 'potentate of half the world,' of armed conflict with Western civilization, and the role of policeman in the resolution of ethnic conflicts. . . . The Belovezhsky agreement was not a 'silent coup,' but a lawful alteration of the existing order of things."

None of the leading players will confirm this account of Yeltsin's rather buoyant and impulsive behavior in that historic session. ("I believe I was in the sauna," Kozyrev told me with an impish and knowing smile. Burbulis said the scene was "not so Chaplinesque.") But it is clear that Yeltsin had enough presence of mind to make sure that word of the dissolution of the union would reach Gorbachev in a way that would be maximally insulting.

The next morning, the presidents discussed the draft declaration for about an hour. Then they agreed that Shushkevich, by far the least significant of the three, would make the call to Gorbachev. (Yeltsin, quick to assume the role of the international player, called the American president, George Bush.) According to former American ambassador Jack Matlock, who spoke later with Shushkevich, the first thing Gorbachev said after getting the news about the end of the Soviet Union was "What happens to me?"

———

In late 1995, just before the parliamentary elections, I traveled to the northern port city of Murmansk with Kozyrev. This was just a few weeks before he was forced out as foreign minister—part of Yeltsin's purge of liberal advisers. Kozyrev is a smooth and cautious man. He rarely falters, rarely shows emotion to an outsider. But as we sat together on his Foreign Ministry jet, he betrayed a degree of contempt for what had happened in Belarus four years before. He said he would have preferred a "tight" rather than a "loose" confederation.

"Yes, it was improvised in some sense, especially by some," Kozyrev said. "For me, it was more or less a choice between trying to establish a kind of European union or of trying to keep together a former state in a confederative way. As you know, history-making is full of improvisation at the level of the heads of state. One of the issues is that they have a different level of experience. Their international experience was very limited. It boiled down to a few foreign visits and receiving two or three foreign visitors—a kind of superfluous protocol function. They had a very, very limited knowledge of foreign affairs. It did not end as well as it might have, but not as badly as it could have, either."

Back in Moscow, I met with Giorgi Satarov, one of Yeltsin's top political aides and a key strategist for the 1996 election. He knew that the collapse of the union remained, nearly five years later, a burning issue for millions of Russians, but he would not say a word against the decisions taken in Belarus or Alma-Ata. Satarov said the collapse was "the natural outcome of the events. We had a choice between a controlled and an uncontrolled collapse. An uncontrolled collapse would have reached every neighborhood. I don't think that those who did this were literally thinking in these terms, necessarily, but they probably had an intuitive sense of it. To have continued the old Novo-Ogarevo process would be like putting makeup on a boil—a cover-up. The participants no longer controlled anything, nor did Gorbachev."

A few days later, I met with Sergei Stankevich, a Duma deputy who had worked as a political adviser to Yeltsin in the Kremlin until 1994. Now Stankevich was literally on the run; he had been accused in the Russian press of accepting a $10,000 bribe. As we sat and talked about the last days of the union and the first steps taken toward a new order, Stankevich kept stealing glances at a rather oafish fellow at the next table. He was convinced he was being followed by agents from the KGB.

"After August 1991, Yeltsin sensed triumph but could not resist the temptation to humiliate Gorbachev," Stankevich said. "It was such a horrible scene. The first thing he did was to manipulate Gorbachev so that he was completely humbled and stripped of all power. But Gorbachev would not accept his new role, and Yeltsin decided to remove him entirely. Gorbachev had no intention of ruining the Soviet Union and he had no clear picture of what he wanted Russia to be. The tension with Ukraine was seen as temporary. They went to Belarus with the intention of finding a legitimate way to remove Gorbachev from power. The real plan was to remove Gorbachev and the union state and then reconcile with Ukraine and join with Belarus and Kazakhstan in a union of states, like a new federation but with more serious power to the republics.

"Everyone was very mysterious about the meeting in Belarus. I was not involved in its preparation. It's my understanding that a lot was improvised, but the main purpose was not the destiny of the USSR but the destiny of Gorbachev. That was the reason they met in such secrecy. The idea of a declaration came about right there, and it was written on site. It was a triumph for them, and in Russia, after a triumph it is the custom to drink."

The poet Anna Akhmatova once said, "If you only knew the trash that poems come from." The lesson of the Gorbachev-Yeltsin drama was "If you only knew the trash that history comes from."

When I asked Gorbachev himself to reflect on his relationship with Yeltsin, he used a favorite provincial Russian expression that means to put something over on someone: "Yeltsin always wanted to hang noodles on my ears."

"Although there were many other factors at work, do you think Yeltsin's main goal was to get rid of you?" I asked.

"I think that was the main thing, yes," Gorbachev said. "They really couldn't find another solution, so they went in for this adventurous solution. And it's because of this scheme that we're where we are now. The main thing was the destruction of the country. It just fed all fears of disintegration: social, political, cultural, and defense. It wasn't really about a drunken revel. Yeltsin actually hesitated. He was afraid of taking the step. In November he did say there had to be a union. But there were other influences. It was in October that Burbulis went to Sochi with a memo in which he tried to prove to Yeltsin that Russia and the Russian leadership were losing the momentum they had gained after the August revolution. He said that sly old Gorbachev was spinning his web and was taking away the fruits of their victory. Russia, he said, can do without the Soviet Union because Russia is the source of all finance and resources: let everyone come and beg Russia for help, let them come to Czar Boris. Yeltsin finally believed that once he had freed himself of the other republics, having the money and the resources and the oil, he would be able to move faster and show the world what a great reformer he was. This was such shoddy thinking on his part. So superficial."

When he was in power, Gorbachev surrounded himself with aides and factions of varying ideologies. It was his conceit that he could never afford to veer in one direction for long, he had to balance warring forces. Until the end of his time in power, he was a lonely figure. And now more than ever. When I suggested to Gorbachev that this might have been the case, that he was a solitary figure who trusted only his wife and few others, he nodded gravely.

"During a time of reform, such is the fate of the leader," he said. "As one great man once said, there is no such thing as a happy reformer. Most reformers begin as a reformer and then shift toward reaction. In Russian history, Alexander I was originally associated with Speransky, a liberal, and then ended up with Arakcheyev, a reactionary. Napoleon had this, too. Any reformer, in making his decision, unleashes new forces and new ideas and new movements. He inevitably enters into conflict with the people of his time. He is in conflict with those in power who wouldn't relinquish their power, and this is always complicated. Remember the French Revolution. Many people anathematize the October Revolution, but the French Revolution was even more complicated. Robespierre, the

THE LOST EMPIRE | 31

day before his execution, marched before the crowd as an idol and then his head was cut off. So this is the fate of the politician who assumes the burden of reforms and then tries to fit in the revolutionary flow and tries to influence those new streams and tendencies. The fact is that such people make their guesses intuitively."

Gorbachev said he was sure that Yeltsin could never win reelection, and while he himself favored a range of "centrist" parties—not least the Gorbachev party, whatever that might be—he was not fearful of a restoration of communist government.

"I think it's more about a reaction of Western politicians and press to this. It smells of panic," he said. "What it's all about is a reaction to the way the democrats carried out reforms and the price people had to pay for them. The price they paid pushed them toward these neocommunists. . . . The cost is tremendous. I think if Americans had to pay such a cost they would have had themselves another civil war. Our people have swallowed so many wars that they have become a cautious people.

"Some people say that Russians are now apolitical and interested only in their own property and vegetable gardens. It's not so. I travel around Russia, and even with the opposition shown by the local bosses, people rush to see me. The Russian situation is heated. Fifty-five million people do not have enough to eat every day. Except for those few who found a place in business, the rest are insecure about tomorrow. They have lost their anchor. There are no social guarantees. Under Soviet power, social guarantees existed, even if they were at a modest level. All this makes it possible for the pro-communists to make a return. It all came from the shock therapy and the collapse of the union. The army has suffered. People cannot afford to go visit their relatives. This is what people hold this new team accountable for. And so the communists and the communist radicals collect the dividends."

It was curious to me that Gorbachev could be so calm about the potential return of the communists. These, after all, were not the liberal communists of his time, but rather those who were left behind, those who supported the August coup of 1991. They were not merely calling for Yeltsin's head, they were calling for Gorbachev's, as well.

"It's true," Gorbachev allowed rather sadly. "They treat me as a traitor." And yet he was so calm about it that I had the sense he did not know how true it was.

The morning after I saw Gorbachev, I flew south to Stavropol, the small city in southern Russia where he had reigned as regional leader before coming to Moscow in the late Brezhnev era. At the Stavropol airport I found a driver willing to make the two-hour drive through a nasty windstorm to Gorbachev's old village, Privolnoye.

On a similar trip in 1989, local KGB authorities made sure I never got close to the village. First, I was told at my hotel in Stavropol that Privolnoye was afflicted with an undetermined cattle-related virus and that the village was under strict quarantine. When I tried to go anyway, I managed only a glimpse of Privolnoye before it was clear that the KGB presence there was roughly what it was on the Chinese border.

Now, no one much cared.

"Why do you want to go to Privolnoye?" the driver asked as we journeyed farther into a kind of snow-fog. I said I wanted to see Gorbachev's old neighbors, see how their lives had changed since I had been there last.

"Oh," he said. "Well, don't expect perestroika."

He wasn't kidding. The villages in the region, it would seem, should have prospered. The soil is rich, the weather far milder than that of the Russian north. In the Russian Far East, in Siberia, in the north, I had been in villages of stunning poverty: the wooden huts seemed almost to sink into the muck; the diet was strictly kasha and bread; the men drank themselves to death; the old went without all but the most rudimentary medical care. Privolnoye looks better than the average village: the houses are made of brick and concrete, the prospects are good. And yet, Privolnoye turned out to suffer from nearly every symptom of "post-communist stress."

Not long after I arrived I met a seventy-year-old woman named Maria Kraiko, whose family had lived in Privolnoye for generations—"more generations than I know." She remembered Gorbachev well. She had worked as an accountant in the peasants' brigade under his father. She invited me inside her hut, and as we sat around her tiny table, she remembered the central memory of all Russians of her—and Gorbachev's—generation.

"The Germans were here, they came August 2, 1942, and they left February 23, 1943, when they were kicked out," she said. "I worked in the village office. In those days one thousand seven hundred men were drafted, and only half of them, maybe less, came back. There is a monument to them at the local cemetery. We had an eternal flame to their memory—but now it's been turned off. That happened about a year ago. Everything is so expensive now. To maintain it became impossible."

The region was not far from the war in Chechnya, and Privolnoye and the surrounding villages were now filled with refugees. The economy had collapsed. The local movie theater had closed down because no one could afford a ticket. The local hospital could no longer afford to feed the patients. Under the new regime, the local collective farm—the kolkhoz—had been free to turn itself into a "joint stock company," but that had done nothing but sour everyone on capitalism. Without subsidies from Moscow, the farm had fallen into a dismal state. Besides, no one wanted to buy its products: wheat, sunflowers, corn, cattle, sheep. The farmers could hardly afford to repair their equipment or buy the supplies they needed. There was not enough fertilizer, so it was impossible to sow in time. Crops rotted in the fields. There was not enough fodder for the cattle. Pensioners were still living decently on around $100 a month for a couple, but the young and middle-aged, who were dependent on the new world, the new rules of economic life, were suffering. People got by, they admitted, by stealing food from the farm. In the last days of Gorbachev, a new man, full of energy, named Ivan Mikhailenko, had come from Stavropol to reform the collective farm. Soon he was accused of building houses for himself, piling up a fortune. There were rumors he had a private plane, a helicopter. After a while, the local people threw him out and brought in another man, Nikolai Brizhalkin, a former Party official from the area. The farm only got worse, and now the people wanted the first man back.

Even someone as old and relatively secure as Maria Kraiko could no longer find it in her heart to remember Mikhail Gorbachev with much fondness. She was happy to be able to read a decent newspaper (though they were rarely available) and to watch soap operas on television. And yet she yearned for the past, not because she was a bedrock reactionary, a nostalgic Stalinist, but because she feared for the future of her children and her grandchildren.

"It's a pity there is no more Soviet Union. We had more rights then, I think," she said. "We don't need capitalists. We need the same decent life for everyone. Millionaires have two-story houses and two cars. They don't keep their money in a stocking. And how they make this money, God knows. This is what the majority of people here think. Only those who are close to money or really have a lot of it think otherwise."

Did she think Gorbachev was at fault?

"I wouldn't say that Gorbachev is to blame," she said. "He just got lost and fell under some sort of power. But I was really ashamed of him when the union collapsed. He walked away from the struggle, like a mother who just leaves her husband and children behind."

Maria's husband, Dmitri, walked in and said, "Mikhail Sergeyevich did not do the right thing. We have hard feelings about him now. We won the Great Patriotic War and then along came these people and now who are we? We are nothing. Gorbachev was one of us and then he went and did this."

———

One of the first signs of capitalism in the big cities like Moscow, St. Petersburg, and Nizhni Novgorod was the appearance of kiosks, street-side booths, some of them no bigger than a freezer, where people sold whatever goods they could get: liquor, candy, stockings, children's clothing. In Privolnoye there were just three kiosks. The one private store, a television and refrigerator repair shop, closed down a few months after it opened because the owner couldn't pay his taxes. A young man named Aleksandr Gordubel, who helped to run one of the kiosks, sold me a German chocolate bar and told me that while he thought "Mikhail Sergeyevich did more for the world than he did for the country," he was glad for the chance to make a living on his own.

Galina Tarasovich ran the one enterprise in town resembling a good time. After the local grocery store closed down for the day, she opened up shop as a bar. She was twenty-nine years old and her husband was one of those young farmers in town who made almost nothing in salary—$4 a month. The bar was their one chance to make a little cash. She was barely breaking even, mainly because hardly anyone in town had the money for a night out.

When I asked Tarasovich why she didn't move to Stavropol or some other city nearby, she stared at me with a look of infinite pity.

"Where else is he supposed to work? Where else is he supposed to go? I might think about leaving for Stavropol, but then where would we live?" she said. "At least here we have a few ducks, some chickens."

It was all very depressing. I thought if there was one man in this mournful village willing and eager to say a nice word for Gorbachev it would be Aleksandr Yakovenko, a pensioner who had known Gorbachev for more than fifty years. Yakovenko worked with Gorbachev in the fields and knew his entire family. When the KGB did allow a few journalists to visit Privolnoye in the late eighties, it invariably set them up to see Yakovenko. The surveillance was long gone, but no journalists had been by in years. As he led me into the living room, Yakovenko laughed and said, "Before they sent Hedrick Smith to see me, the KGB called and said that the foreigners don't like to take off their shoes in the house and that we had to serve them something to eat!"

Yakovenko was retired, but he still tended a small private plot and stayed abreast of the gossip in town. He did nothing to hide his disappointment.

"Before the collapse of the union, everything was more or less all right. But after that there was dramatic change. They freed prices and suddenly the twenty thousand rubles my wife and I had saved—we thought we could retire on it, even help our children with it—all of it was worth no more than a taxi ride. The government says it might compensate us for that, but will it really? I doubt it.

"You see, we were raised on communist ideology. We were used to it," Yakovenko said. "For us it provided discipline, it meant education, it meant free medical care and a guaranteed retirement. It meant that even we provincial people could travel a little or go on vacation to rest houses. Now no one can afford to travel. So of course we have nostalgia for the old days.

"Of course, we're not stupid. We know better than you that there were repressions. In 1937 and 1938, people were beaten and tortured. They were enemies of the people, Stalin said, but I don't think there were real enemies of the people—at least not here in Privolnoye. We don't miss that sort of thing. The fifties and the sixties were hard, but the period of Brezhnev until the collapse of the union—I would say that was the peak of the good old days. Under Brezhnev we could buy a car. Houses were built. This lasted through Andropov and Chernenko, even Gorbachev. Then it all became impossible."

Yakovenko was reluctant to criticize Gorbachev or Yeltsin. In fact, at one point he said, "Are you sure it's okay for you to be here? The, uh, people in Moscow. They don't mind?" But it was clear that while his own house was a fine one and his pension enough to live on, Yakovenko was no different from everyone else in Privolnoye. He feared for the future, and he was more than a little ashamed that the greatest son of the village had done so much to unleash this new and uncertain wave of history.

"Lots of people in town are hurt by Gorbachev because they feel he is responsible for us living so badly now," he said. "People are desperate and sometimes they resort to stealing. We never had that before. The big-time mafia hasn't come to this village yet, but that will come, too."

As I was leaving, Yakovenko pointed out his door and toward a cemetery not far off. Gorbachev's parents were buried there. It is quite possible that Gorbachev will meet a similarly modest end. In another time, a place would have been held for him against the walls of the Kremlin. That is not a sure thing any longer. And Yakovenko, his great friend from childhood, his great supporter for so long, said he had decided which way Russia needed to go now. "I'm voting for the communists," he said. "We need the Party again." What Yakovenko wanted most of all was a return of the Soviet Union.

CHAPTER 2

THE OCTOBER REVOLUTION

It may be hard to imagine now, but there was a time not long ago when a belief in the politics of Boris Yeltsin was a requirement for membership in the post-Soviet society of right-thinking Russians. (That time may be defined roughly as the period between Yeltsin's successful defense of the Russian White House in August 1991 and his successful attack on the same building twenty-five months later.) For some, that belief was even a prerequisite for carnal engagement, as in this personal ad, which ran in late 1991 in the newspaper *Vechernyaya Moskva:* "Attractive Moscow woman, height 165 centimeters, higher musical education, never married, constantly improving herself in every way, seeking man up to 33 years old with goal of starting family. Those not sharing the political views of Yeltsin need not apply." With Gorbachev and the Soviet Union out of the picture, Yeltsin pretended to the role of a Russian George Washington; he would lead the creation of a new state after the triumphal elimination of the old.

Russian liberals did not entirely trust Yeltsin. They well understood that Yeltsin's career was that of the Communist Party apparatchik; he was not especially cerebral or kind; he specialized in the politics of confrontation, rather than compromise; his ability over time to slide too easily from communist to populist, democrat to nationalist, when the political moment suited him, was always apparent. Andrei Sakharov, in his time, had joined forces with Yeltsin, but warily. Like many in the democratic camp, Sakharov sensed in Yeltsin a desire to do good, but also intellectual limitations and a powerful ambition. On the night before voting for Yeltsin in the 1989 elections for the Soviet parliament, Sakharov wept, telling his friends he could not entirely trust in the candidate's self-proclaimed commitment to democracy. And yet, when the Party and the union collapsed in 1991, Yeltsin was what remained—he was the country's singular politician—and the vast majority of the public supported the man and sympathized with the unthinkable scale of the tasks he faced.

As a public figure, on television and on the speaking platform, Yeltsin radiated a sureness, even an arrogance, in power. He spoke in a deep, bluff voice, more like the construction foreman he started out as than as a statesman. Privately, however, he was utterly overwhelmed by the job before him. In 1991, when Yeltsin was elected president of the Russian Republic, he and his longtime assistant Lev Sukhanov took a tour of their new offices in the Russian White House. The rooms were vast, far more sumptuous in fact than the old Communist Party headquarters across town on Old Square. The chandeliers were out of a ballroom scene; the desks had the grandeur of battleships. Yeltsin and Sukhanov could not contain their sense of awe.

"Look, Boris Nikolayevich, what an office we've seized!" Sukhanov said.

"I have seen many an office in my life," Yeltsin recalled later, "but I got a pleasant tingle from the soft modern sheen, all the shininess and comfort."

"Well, what next?" Yeltsin remembered thinking. "After all, we haven't just seized an office. We've seized an entire Russia."

In those first moments of power, Yeltsin's popularity was enormous, his authority in parliament strong, if only because so many deputies were still in shock after the events of 1991. (Years later, communist and nationalist deputies would complain about Yeltsin's dissolution of the Soviet Union, but they conveniently forgot that the vast majority voted to endorse the new arrangement.) When Yeltsin had a chance to look back and survey his mistakes, he would castigate himself for having failed to start with an even cleaner slate: he should have dissolved parliament and called for new post-Soviet elections; he should have initiated a political party. But at the time, Yeltsin was reluctant to eliminate what little visible structure he had behind him.

All at once, Yeltsin was faced with the job of creating a market economy, a political democracy, and social peace; he had to shape the meaning and identity of Russian statehood in a time of weakness and, in the eyes of many, humiliating defeat; and he had to do all of this in a country in which nearly all the men and women of experience and managerial competence had been loyal to the system he had wrecked. "I can't say that we had to start from scratch, but almost," Yeltsin would write later. "Meanwhile, we had to figure out everything from the start. What was a vice president? How should a Russian constitutional court look? There was nothing but blank space because no such institutions had previously existed in Russia. . . . As a result, there emerged beautiful structures and pretty names with nothing behind them." Not only did Yeltsin have to shoulder the burden of state-building, he had to do it at a moment of unprecedented public expectations: "They expected paradise on earth, but instead got inflation, unemployment, economic shock, and political crisis."

Just months after the August coup it also became clear to Yeltsin that his team, which had fought the coup together, was far from unified. Yeltsin faced political opposition even from his own vice president. In the spring of 1991, Yeltsin had cast about for a running mate who could bring him votes outside "the democratic camp." The mass movement Democratic Russia could never bring in enough votes to assure him majority support; in fact, Democratic Russia was already starting to splinter. In American terms, Yeltsin needed some regional and ideological balance for his ticket.

Yeltsin chose Aleksandr Rutskoi, a prominent officer in the war in Afghanistan, who had been the leader of Communists for Democracy, a faction in the Russian parliament that had split from the more hard-line Communists of Russia. Rutskoi's faction had helped give control of the parliament to Yeltsin. Rutskoi seemed to Yeltsin a tolerable—and tolerant—conservative. As a pilot during the war in Afghanistan, Rutskoi had been shot down twice; the second time he was held prisoner in a Pakistani prison and had to be exchanged for prisoners on the other side. He was acquainted during the war with other military men who would come into Yeltsin's orbit, including Pavel Grachev and Aleksandr Lebed, and, like those commanders, he came to have contempt for the old Soviet guard and its disregard for the honor of the army in Afghanistan. But like Grachev and Lebed, Rutskoi was no Westernizer; he had, after all, faced Stinger missiles, launched by the mujahideen and paid for by the Central Intelligence Agency. There was, in fact, a quality of strangeness to Rutskoi; he told friends that while he was at war, he had gone through a sort of visionary experience that led him to believe he would one day play a crucial role in Russian history. In liberal circles, Rutskoi was not well known, but those who did know him did not approve. When Rutskoi ran for deputy in 1989 for the Soviet-era Congress of People's Deputies, his campaign manager, Colonel Valery Burkov, answered a question about the human rights movement by saying, "I'd like to hang Sakharov."

Yeltsin may have acted the supplicant before Sakharov in 1989, but that was then, this was now. Sakharov was dead. Yeltsin decided he needed Rutskoi; he would bring him votes in the military, in the provinces, in regions where precious few people thought much about civil liberties or free markets. Yeltsin even had a suspicion that Rutskoi, with his thick brush mustache and blue eyes, his military bearing, would look good on television and on campaign posters. "He had the look of an accomplished actor," Yeltsin recalled. "He was a combat pilot, a recipient of the Hero of the Soviet Union award, and he spoke firmly and eloquently. A real tiger! Middle-aged matrons would swoon with delight at the sight of such a vice president!"

Yeltsin would later say he learned a lesson: never to be drawn to "a beautiful form" or "a logic of externals." But he learned that lesson far too late. Even before Rutskoi started objecting to various policies, even before he went to war with various ministers in the cabinet, Rutskoi began to grate on the president. Before he knew it, Rutskoi was coming into his office saying, "Boris Nikolayevich, where did you get those shoes?" The next day, Yeltsin recalled, Rutskoi would come to the office with a half-dozen pairs of Italian shoes. Then it was on to jackets.

What was more irritating to Yeltsin was that Rutskoi would not accept that the Russian vice presidency (at least in Yeltsin's mind) was designed to be even less important than the American version. Theirs was a doomed marriage.

———

In the first years of Yeltsin's Kremlin, Gennady Burbulis was the organizational and strategic master. Before coming to Moscow as a deputy in the Soviet congress, Burbulis had been a professor of Marxist-Leninist doctrine at Sverdlovsk's Advanced Training Institute of the Ministry of Nonferrous Metals. He wrote a dissertation on "Marxist-Leninist guidance of the worldview of young scientists and technicians." Strange credentials for the putative leader of the Kremlin's "Westernizers," but like so many others he had shed one skin for another. He had grown close to Yeltsin when they were both members of the Interregional Group, the democratic opposition in the Soviet parliament.

Burbulis had the narrow, penetrating eyes and clenched expression of a dangerous man; in fact, danger was an image he cultivated. It was Burbulis, as Yeltsin's chief strategist, who masterminded the meeting at Belovezhskaya Pushcha that put an end to the Soviet Union. For his role in that episode, Burbulis became known among Russian reporters as "the Political Killer." He was a man inclined toward overarching theories of the world, and when he made his conversion from socialism to capitalism, he did it with the passion of the convert. After a couple of years, Yeltsin would grow weary of Burbulis, his arrogance, his penchant for walking into any meeting and sitting next to the president. "I got tired of seeing the same face in my office, in meetings, at receptions, in my home, at my dacha, on the tennis court, in the sauna. . . . He overstepped some boundary in our personal relations." But for the time being, Yeltsin relied absolutely on the Political Killer.

Burbulis promoted the careers of the two most influential Westernizers in the early days of Yeltsin's reign: Andrei Kozyrev and Yegor Gaidar. Kozyrev had been a promising diplomat in the Soviet Foreign Ministry when Eduard Shevardnadze was still in office and then became Yeltsin's foreign minister in 1990. Kozyrev was intelligent and polished, and, unlike the rest of the Yeltsin circle and Yeltsin himself, he had been in many foreign capitals. Kozyrev formed relationships with American and European leaders that seemed so friendly, even accommodating, that he would soon be considered Enemy No. 2 in nationalist circles.

Enemy No. 1 was, undoubtedly, the young, pudgy economist Yegor Gaidar. It is hard to imagine an American parallel to the career of Gaidar. Burbulis began suggesting him to Yeltsin in 1991. Gaidar was the scion of a famous Bolshevik family. His grandfather, Arkady, was a Red Army hero in the Civil War and the author of children's books for brave young communists. General Pershing meets Dr. Seuss. Gaidar's father, Timur, was known throughout the Soviet Union as the subject of one of Arkady's tales; as an adult he carved out his own notoriety and privileged existence as a rear admiral in the Soviet navy and as a foreign correspondent for the Communist Party daily newspaper, *Pravda*. Yegor Timurovich was a member of that happy breed of Soviet times called the *zolotaya molodyozh,* the "golden youth." As a child, he lived in Cuba and Yugoslavia with his father. At Moscow State University, he studied under two economists who would play crucial advisory roles in the perestroika years, Stanislav Shatalin and Gavriil Popov. In 1983, Gaidar was one of a team of young economists involved in trying to work out an economic reform plan under Yuri Andropov—a project that ended with Andropov's death in 1984. Although the project did not go far, Gaidar came into contact with other economists like Anatoly Chubais and Pyotr Aven, both of Leningrad, who also were interested in going well beyond the old Soviet dogmas of a planned, centralized economy. As young men, they had read the classics of Western economic and political thought, especially Adam Smith, F. A. Hayek, John Maynard Keynes, and Milton Friedman.

In the Gorbachev years, Gaidar occupied two editorial posts that allowed him to explore (gingerly at first, then with few restrictions) the possibility of adopting market mechanisms in the Soviet Union. First as the economics editor of the political journal *Kommunist* and then as a columnist for *Pravda,* Gaidar wrote articles on economic reform and began attracting attention in government and intellectual circles in Moscow. By 1991, Gaidar was also studying the Polish experiment with "shock therapy" and meeting some of the Western economists who influenced the Warsaw government, scholar-activists like Jeffrey Sachs of Harvard and Richard Layard of the London School of Economics.

Yeltsin was intent on finding an economic guru who would be willing to commit an act of political daring: a kamikaze minister. If Yeltsin had one goal, it was to smash the old system of central planning and false economies. He knew that the pattern of Russian history had always been one of one step forward, two steps back. Change had always been followed by reaction. "Not a single reform in Russia has ever been completed," Yeltsin would write. "The purpose of Peter the Great's reforms, for example, was to create 'Russian Europeans.' Obviously, that was an extremely ambitious goal that could not be achieved within one generation. In a certain sense, Peter the Great's reforms have not been achieved to this day." The freeing of the serfs, land reform, the New Economic Policy under Lenin, the Kosygin reforms—all of them were followed by periods of reaction. Yeltsin, under the influence of Burbulis and Gaidar, became convinced that he must move quickly and decisively—even brutally—to avoid the old pattern. In his memoir, Yeltsin remembers hearing Aleksandr Solzhenitsyn's comment "Would you treat your own mother with shock therapy?" Yeltsin turns the question around, saying that Russia is us, and "I would use shock therapy on myself, and not just one time. By choosing the path of shock therapy, I did not choose it for some immature Russia or some abstract people. I chose this path for myself as well." A rather disingenuous statement for a man who lived as a czar, but it was his conviction all the same.

Certainly, the Russian government could not afford to delude itself about the depths of the economic crisis. The evidence was inescapable. It is a kind of journalistic and psychological custom in Russia to fear the worst for the winter ahead, but in 1991 there really was fear of starvation, even famine. The government had no cushion: gold reserves, long thought to be enormous, had been cashed in by the communist regime. Foreign exchange reserves were down to $100 million and foreign debt was climbing, mainly because Gorbachev had borrowed $20 billion in 1991. Because of fluctuations in world markets and horrific management in the energy bureaucracies, oil revenues fell from $22 billion in 1986 to $7 billion in 1991.

On October 28, 1991, with the Soviet Union still alive, if barely, Yeltsin went before the Russian parliament and made his case for radical reform. He told the legislators that they were facing "one of the most critical moments in Russian history. It will be decided right now what sort of country Russia will be in the coming years and decades." He made no secret that he was calling for an abrupt turn: "The time for small steps is over." Gaidar, the author of the speech, would be made deputy prime minister. Yeltsin asked for and received from the parliament what amounted to a yearlong vote of absolute confidence: he could reform the economy by decree. The vote was 876 to 16 in favor. Yeltsin was now free to implement Gaidar's radical vision of freed prices, financial stabilization, and privatization. As of January 2, 1992, all prices would be liberated. The exchange rate would float until it found its level on world financial markets. In those days, Yeltsin and Gaidar also figured they would get a great deal of help from the West, and they appealed in the speech to the World Bank, the International Monetary Fund, the European Bank for Reconstruction and Development, and, above all, the developed countries themselves.

Gaidar created his team from among the young technocratic intellectual elite of Moscow and St. Petersburg. The top officials were between thirty and forty, and their aides and number-crunchers were often far younger. Nearly all of them had been Communist Party members for career reasons, but, as one foreign adviser, Anders Aslund, points out, they were neither "real communists" nor activists in the democratic movement in the perestroika years. They were possessed of an academic brilliance and a certain arrogance and energy of youth. No one at the University of Chicago, no one in the cabinets of Margaret Thatcher or Ronald Reagan, could have had a more idealized picture of the West or free markets than Gaidar. The former staff pundit at *Pravda* and *Kommunist* now wrote in the tones of Hayek:

Despite all the wars and disasters in Europe, modern civilization became possible there because most European nations had lived a settled life for over ten centuries—there were no great migrations, no conquests made by nomadic tribes, just a long tradition of handing down estates, land lots, and rights to land property to descendants. Hereditary title to land emerged and was reinforced by many centuries of tradition. Europe, inhabited by settled peoples, became the fountain-

head of the myriad innovations which formed the basis of its civilization and gave rise to a gigantic upsurge in material and spiritual wealth
in the second half of the present millennium. One physically feels the
effect of this culture as one takes a stroll through some German or
British campus, where soil has never been bulldozed away, as over
here, but cultivated assiduously by countless generations.

It is rather surprising that Lenin, who spent years and years in Europe and worked long hours in the British Museum, absorbed nothing
of this atmosphere, becoming, on the contrary, an implacable enemy
of this civilization and its culture, although he felt like a European
when in Russia. I guess he just did not believe in the Russian people.
His radicalism came from lack of faith in the natural course of
events—especially since the latter promised him a rather modest role
in society. Russian communism was a consistent and aggressive reaction to the growth of the world market civilization. In a sense, it was
Europe's response to Europe's challenge, a desperate attempt to get
through the industrial stage by creating immense tensions within society and establishing a superstate.

Gaidar saw himself as a reformer out to dismantle an essentially feudal
society whose sole incentive had been fear. He wanted to end the state's
control over society and allow Russia to move toward "a normal path of
development." Normalcy, in his eyes, meant a state based on private
property and the protection of property rights. From his reading of
Adam Smith and other Western economists, Gaidar recognized that the
only way to build a strong legal order and a prosperous economy was to
make what had once been anathema to the Bolsheviks—that is, private
property—a treasured value of the Russian people. He was setting out,
of course, with myriad disadvantages—the legacy of history. As he
started out in 1991, Gaidar realized "we had to start building a country
which had no borders, no army, no customs, no banking system with
links to foreign economies, no clear-cut concept of citizenship, and no
foreign trade management." But unlike Poland, Russia did not have any
broad-scale private sector in industry or agriculture. The Central Bank
also still controlled the money supply, making market reform even more
complicated.

With a sense of messianic zeal, and without ever really educating the public or winning its approval, the Gaidar reforms moved ahead. The period of Russian "shock therapy" was indeed a shock to Russians, who had grown used to artificially low prices—a few kopecks for bread, a few rubles for vodka, virtually free rent and utilities. Prices accelerated with the new year, a frightening experience for nearly everyone. Gaidar also instituted vast cuts in defense spending and tried hard to cut way back on subsidies to industries and enterprises that could not otherwise exist.

Even though Gaidar could not go nearly as far as he wanted, it was not long before his reforms showed some astonishing results. Shortages were vastly reduced; stores filled up with goods. Although state-run stores were often empty, ambitious (and mainly young) traders ran kiosks on the streets of some of the leading cities: Moscow, St. Petersburg, Nizhni Novgorod, Yekaterinburg. Imports of all kinds—toilet paper, liquor, candy, videocassettes—became available. Goods, mainly from abroad, began moving around the country in a manner that began to resemble a functioning, if crude, market economy. At the same time, the kiosks and bazaars also revealed the terrible pain of transition. Living standards plunged, as they did in all the Eastern European countries after 1989. Older people, who were at a loss to keep pace with inflation and lived on their meager pensions, could be seen selling anything they could grab on to: their pets, their shoes, homemade sweaters and tablecloths. The poverty level soared. Older people, the disabled, and the unemployed could no longer depend on the state and had to depend instead on "invisible income," that is, help from their more successful children and grandchildren. Far from everyone got such help. State institutions—clinics, hospitals, and schools—continued to deteriorate. Industries that had relied for decades on the state delayed, or even stopped, paying salaries to their workers. The most frightening statistic of all—an index of misery—was the drop in life expectancy, especially among men. Life expectancy peaked for Russian men in 1987 at sixty-five years; by 1993 the average age of death was just fifty-nine.

On a macroeconomic scale, after a year, Russia's foreign exchange market was established with a monthly turnover of $1 billion, compared with $18 million previously. Foreign exchange reserves went from $100 million to $1.5 billion. A privatization plan—the biggest in human history—was in the works.

Rutskoi objected gravely to Gaidar's reforms. In another country, a vice president would have been discreet about his opinions; it did not work that way in Russia. Burbulis and Yeltsin had tried to neutralize Rutskoi by giving him busywork. In the tradition of the Soviet Communist Party, they asked him to take on the thankless task of writing reports on the country's agricultural prospects. Rutskoi, who was not the brightest man in government, dutifully submerged himself in agricultural minutiae. But even he eventually saw through that ploy. More and more he made his opposition to the radical reforms clear. He toured the country, especially military bases and defense plants, and made caustic remarks about the government—"boys in pink shorts," he called Gaidar's team. On December 19, 1991, he wrote an article for *Nezavisimaya Gazeta* describing the Kremlin as a palace of intrigue and promising to resign if the reforms continued. Rutskoi, acting as the chairman of a government commission on defense conversion, met with a group of state enterprise directors and, by way of sympathizing with them, said that Yeltsin's reforms were nothing less than "another experiment performed on the Russian people" and that loans from the International Monetary Fund were "free cheese in a mousetrap." So brazen were Rutskoi's forays against the president and so powerful were his connections to many of the higher-ups in the Russian army that rumors were constantly afloat in Moscow that Rutskoi might be preparing Yeltsin's overthrow with backing from the military.

Gaidar, for his part, was starting to grow wary of Rutskoi and the leader of the parliament, Ruslan Khasbulatov. Rutskoi, on his own, may not have possessed enough power or guile to be much trouble, but Khasbulatov did. Khasbulatov ran the parliament as his instrument, his vassal. Without any real political parties in evidence and with the entire body fragmented into small factions, Khasbulatov could manipulate the parliament with ease. As the months went by, he became more and more resistant to Yeltsin's economic reforms, not least because he saw that Yeltsin was losing support among regional leaders.

The radical reform of the economy almost instantly divided the parliament, and not in Yeltsin's favor. Of the 1,033 members of the Russian

Congress of People's Deputies, four hundred were members of the "irreconcilable opposition," two hundred were for Yeltsin, and the rest were members in good standing of the *boloto*, the swamp. The factions were divided not only by ideology—democrats, nationalists, communists, etc.—but also by economic interests. Deputies from regions that depended hungrily on industrial subsidies or where collective farm leaders were resisting privatization abandoned Yeltsin. Arkady Volsky, the head of a powerful industrial lobbying organization, the Russian Union of Industrialists and Entrepreneurs, and a former adviser to Andropov, led a large faction called Civic Union which argued for a more "gentle" reform; that is, it argued for continued subsidies to military and industrial plants that were otherwise dying.

The economic reforms were so painful to so many Russians that Khasbulatov and Rutskoi no longer concealed their opposition to Yeltsin. There was political advantage to be gained. By 1992, it was clear that in Russian politics a system—or better, a situation—of *dvoevlastie,* double power, had evolved. Yeltsin, for his part, was intent on a system of presidential dominance, which he, in fact, enjoyed for the one year he could rule the economy by diktat. He had every intention of pushing through a constitution modeled roughly on the de Gaulle–era constitution of the Fifth Republic in 1958, which allowed the president to dissolve parliament and rule by decree. Meanwhile, the parliament, led and manipulated by Khasbulatov, exploited the Soviet-era slogan "All power to the soviets." Remarkably, the new Russian state was still operating under the Soviet constitution written under Brezhnev in 1978; the rules of the game allowed the parliament (which had been a rubber stamp in Soviet times) to amend the constitution easily and without limit. In his battle against Yeltsin, Khasbulatov pushed through no less than 320 changes to the constitution. Khasbulatov also cynically exploited people's economic fears, promising subsidies and social welfare spending where no funds existed. He regularly pushed budgets that would, if implemented, have sent the country into a spiral of hyperinflation and, most likely, social unrest.

In sum, for Khasbulatov the weakening and embarrassment of the president seemed to be the highest of all goals. Khasbulatov campaigned so fiercely against Yeltsin that even his own deputy, Nikolai Ryabov, admitted that the speaker of the parliament had ordered local councils to neutralize Yeltsin's representatives in the regions. Khasbulatov, who himself had to take an unexpected leave because of "tobacco poisoning," regularly told reporters that the president was nothing more than an erratic drunk who could not be trusted with the nuclear button. As more than one opposition member admitted, Khasbulatov was aiming for power and the reduction of Yeltsin to the status of a modern English sovereign.

The rise of a powerful and angry opposition also heightened the growing sense of confrontation in Moscow. Right-wing nationalist sentiment had been a staple of Soviet political thinking for decades, even centuries, but it was not until 1992, when Yeltsin came under attack, that the right-wing forces began to organize themselves seriously and publicly into various fronts and alliances. In September 1992, *Sovetskaya Rossiya* published a critical manifesto titled "A Political Declaration of the Left and Right Opposition" and then, one month later, an "appeal to the citizens" by the new National Salvation Front. Both documents put forward an increasingly familiar critique of the Yeltsin government—that is, it was too Western in orientation, too draconian in its reforms, too amenable to foreign influence. What was more impressive was the array of politicians and intellectuals who had agreed to line up under the same banner: there were leaders from the industrial lobby; communists like Gennady Zyuganov and Richard Kosolapov; military men like Viktor Alksnis, Valentin Varennikov, and Albert Makashov; a KGB general, Aleksandr Sterligov; Russian nationalists like Vasily Belov, Ilya Konstantinov, and Valentin Rasputin; and journalist-ideologues like Valentin Chikin of *Sovetskaya Rossiya* and Aleksandr Prokhanov, the publisher and editor of *Dyen* ("the Day"). When the National Salvation Front held its opening meeting, the stage was decked out with both czarist and communist banners. Guarding the stage was a group of young neo-Nazis led by Aleksandr Barkashov. Barkashov first became known in Moscow as a bodyguard and "physical education instructor" for the head of the anti-Semitic group Pamyat and the partner of a neofascist who dreamed of creating a Nazi-Russian superstate.

By the end of 1992, the impasse between the president and the parliament had reached a crisis point, with both sides showing no sign of cooperation with the other. From December 1992 to September 1993, Russia was witness to a series of parliamentary sessions and scandals that had everyone in Moscow (always a conspiracy-minded city) worried about the possibility of civil war. In the event of a heightened conflict, what role would the army play? Yeltsin, after all, represented imperial dissolution, massive budget cuts, capitulation to old enemies, wounded pride.

In June 1992, a demonstration organized by militant communists gave a sense, a foreshadowing, of the year to come. Viktor Anpilov, a firebrand who had once worked as a KGB operative for Radio Moscow, led his group of disgruntled pensioners and lumpen crazies to march on the television center known as Ostankino, carrying portraits of Lenin and Stalin as well as banners demanding punishment (if not execution) for Yeltsin, Gaidar, Jews, and (the latest of enemies) the Caucasian minorities, known on the street as *cherno zhopiye,* "black asses." Anpilov did everything he could to goad the police who were on the scene, and, predictably, before the day was through, there were scuffles and even a little blood.

"That's what I do," Anpilov told me with a wide and prideful grin. "I stir things up."

Yeltsin's vulnerability was immediately evident at the Seventh Congress, a two-week-long political battle in the first half of December 1992. For days, deputies attacked Yeltsin for "shock therapy," for letting the former Soviet republics go their own way, for "kowtowing" to the West in foreign policy. One angry speech followed another, and each was more disconnected from the ostensible topic under debate than the last. On the very first day, a deputy from Irkutsk, Ivan Fedoseev, managed to put forward an impeachment vote, one that Yeltsin survived by a vote of 352 for and 429 against. Another vote that would have stripped Yeltsin of the ability to select and retain his own ministers lost, but this time by only four votes. Yeltsin proposed a referendum on both elections and reform for April, but it was clear the congress would resist.

Yeltsin was utterly demoralized with the way the congress was moving. He had not felt this way since 1987, when Gorbachev demanded he leave a hospital bed and come before the Moscow Communist Party Committee to endure a session denouncing him. Yeltsin arrived at his house outside the city, walked quickly past his wife, Naina, and their children, and shut himself up in the *banya*—the steam bath. He stayed there for such a long time that the family began to worry. He would not come out until his bodyguard and trusted friend Aleksandr Korzhakov wedged open the door and persuaded him that enough was enough. Later, Yeltsin would say there were times when the pressure nearly defeated him:

"The debilitating bouts of depression, the grave second thoughts, the insomnia and headaches in the middle of the night, the tears of despair, the sadness at the appearance of Moscow and other Russian cities, the flood of criticism from the newspapers and television every day, the harassment campaign at the Congress sessions, the entire burden of the decisions made, the hurt from people close to me who did not support me at the last minute, who didn't hold up, who deceived me—I have had to bear all of this."

In the end, the most serious defeat of all was that Yeltsin had to sacrifice his most important minister; reluctantly, but with no real choice, he dumped Gaidar and replaced him with Viktor Chernomyrdin, a former oil and gas minister in the Soviet era and then the head of the privatized natural gas corporation Gazprom. Chernomyrdin promptly declared an end to "market romanticism," setting off a round of fretful articles in the Russian and Western press and apocalyptic comments in foreign capitals. In the end, however, Chernomyrdin would turn out to be loyal to Yeltsin and far less conservative than many expected. During his tenure at Gazprom, it was rumored that he had become the wealthiest man in Russia, and one of the richest in the world. Once in office, Chernomyrdin preached the need for low inflation, tight monetary control, and other basics of the market.

The shift from the intellectual Gaidar to the more technocratic Chernomyrdin marked an overall shift in the government. "It was inevitable," Gennady Burbulis told me. "The early democratic movement of 1989, 1990, 1991, was led by Russian intellectuals, bookish, romantic. We had read books, we knew what was happening elsewhere in the world. In our time, we managed to attract the political will of the people and the political authority of Yeltsin to our side. But there was little firsthand experience of politics, so when reforms started to falter, when there were inconsistent moves and patience ran out, Yeltsin replaced the bookish men with the practitioners."

As a personality, Chenomyrdin was Gaidar's opposite: an industrialist where Gaidar was a theoretician. But, for the moment, the point was that

Yeltsin had been forced to yield when he did not want to do it. He had no recourse. In the battle of the two powers, the parliament had won the upper hand.

Three months later, Khasbulatov called two more congressional sessions, the Eighth and the Ninth Congresses, and the conflict was even sharper. During the Eighth Congress, Khasbulatov's forces, under the guise of representing the interests of the Russian people, voted to cancel the referendum (they called it "inexpedient"). The vote ignored the fact that over two million people had signed petitions calling for the vote and that tens of thousands of people had gathered to support a referendum on Red Square. Many of Yeltsin's critics criticized him for failing to win popular support for radical reform; the referendum, as he envisioned it, would have asked the population their opinion of perhaps the most essential component of radical economic change, private property; the congress preferred not to hear the answer.

Two weeks later, Yeltsin planned to issue a decree declaring "special rule" in Russia. Before the announcement, he thought he had even won the support of two crucial figures: Rutskoi and Yuri Skokov, the conservative chairman of the Security Council. Instead, Rutskoi and Skokov came out against the decree.

Yeltsin was now vulnerable. He also seemed to be behaving more and more strangely. He went before the congress and gave a rambling speech defying the calls for his resignation or impeachment. His face was puffy and clenched, his white hair flopped over his eyes. His baritone dipped toward the basso, and he slurred the grace notes. Yeltsin's enemies, the communists and the hard-line nationalists, who dominated the floor, were convinced that the Russian president had been drinking and said so—loudly—from the floor of the legislature.

After Yeltsin left the chamber, a diminutive journalist from the Moscow daily *Kuranty* looked up at his president and said, "Uh . . . er . . . Boris Nikolayevich, have you, uh, been drinking?"

Yeltsin stopped in his tracks and peered down at the little man.

"Smell my breath!" he said.

And with that the leader of the largest landmass on the globe exhaled into the face of the Fourth Estate.

"Well?" Yeltsin said.

The *Kuranty* reporter allowed that the air expelled did not noticeably reek of vodka or any of the president's other preferred spirits.

In his public appearances, Yeltsin tried to maintain the bluff and vivid image of his days in opposition, but his health, the pressure of the presidency, and his drinking wore away at him to such a degree that there were days when he resembled some of the dinosaurs of the Soviet Politburo. His speech was garbled and aimless, his gait that of an infirm retiree; at more than one public occasion, Yeltsin's guards had to grasp him firmly at the elbow and guide him (practically carry him) to his seat. The diplomats and reporters in Moscow became obsessed with Yeltsin's health. Political conversations began to resemble the deathwatch days when Andropov's kidneys were collapsing. There were rumors that Yeltsin was dying of a brain tumor or wasting away with cirrhosis of the liver. The rumors were false. The truth was that Yeltsin suffered from depression and he was plagued with high blood pressure. The arteries near his heart were clogged and in need of bypass surgery. His speech problems probably had less to do with vodka than with the drugs he took to take the edge off the pain in his back and legs stemming from a plane accident in Spain in 1990. Unlike Gorbachev, who seemed to appear endlessly on television almost every night of the perestroika era, Yeltsin fanned rumors of his ill health by avoiding the press, especially television. His absences created mystery, even foreboding. He could even be elusive to foreign leaders. More than once, Bill Clinton's aides had him in place for a conversation with Yeltsin over a secure telephone line only to be told by the Russian handlers that their man was unable to come to the phone. During one winter vacation, Yeltsin's aides made sure to have him photographed swimming in the Crimea, the better to promote an image of vigor. The Kremlin began a pattern of lying about Yeltsin's health—a habit that would worsen with the years and with Yeltsin's health. One leading adviser, Giorgi Satarov, told the weekly paper *Argumenti i Fakti* that Yeltsin was a bundle of energy, playing tennis, swimming in freezing waters, and even picking up his not insubstantial wife, Naina, for the hell of it. "And, as for lack of health," Satarov said, "who in our country is in perfect health? Psychological study confirms that to be a politician—well, that is itself a diagnosis." Yeltsin himself even told journalists he would allow them to test his blood and urine. "Let them see what I have inside me!"

———

Yeltsin's escape from impeachment was, relatively speaking, a victory—one he celebrated with tens of thousands of supporters behind the spiraling cupolas of St. Basil's Cathedral. On April 25, 1993, he scored an even more important victory, one which he hoped would end the standoff with the parliament. Yeltsin managed to get the legislature to pass on a nationwide referendum, though it would not question the population on private property. The ballot was limited to four questions:

1. Do you support the president of the Russian Federation?
2. Do you support the social and political policies of the government?
3. Do you advocate early elections for the president?
4. Do you advocate early elections for the parliament?

The campaign to pass the referendum would be the last time in his first term of office when Yeltsin would have the unambiguous support of the intelligentsia. On referendum day, he scored a victory that even his most ardent supporters did not dare predict. (Some critics, of course, charged vote fraud, media manipulation, and other malfeasance.) On questions one and two, Yeltsin won with "yes" votes of 58 percent and 53 percent. On the question of early elections, 67.2 percent favored electing a new parliament, but only 49.5 percent wanted early elections for the president.

The margins, while not overwhelming, could certainly not have encouraged Khasbulatov and Rutskoi to rely on popular support. And so, in the late spring and into the summer of 1993, the opposition forces, led by Rutskoi, tried to paint themselves as the champions of the insulted and the injured, the millions of people either impoverished or humiliated by the new order.

From the very start, the Russian people saw that the rise of a market economy would not be fair, in the sense that incomes and wealth would no longer be more or less equal; and far worse and less explainable was that the new system would bring with it a wave of corruption far worse than anything seen under the communist regime. No one doubted that the old Communist Party, with its absolute control of the economy, behaved like a mafia clan; Party secretaries and functionaries, everyone understood, were the only ones who lived under "true communism." But even the Politburo members lived with at least an overture to Leninist modesty; the Central Committee members I knew tended to wear dismal Soviet-made suits and shoes; they vacationed at Party rest homes in the Crimea, not in Monaco. Under the new rules, the wealthy often did very little to hide their gains. I went to numerous interviews and meetings with aides in the Kremlin and found them wearing fine Italian and English suits; they showed off snapshots of their golf vacations in Spain, their ski trips to Zermatt; there were rumors of Swiss bank accounts. The new breed of bankers and entrepreneurs was even more blatant: like Miami drug lords, they built gated mansion communities on the edge of Moscow and sent their children to finishing schools abroad; their wives went on European shopping binges.

By 1992–93, desperate to win back the public after the loss in the referendum, Rutskoi reiterated, and amplified, the charge that he had "eleven suitcases" filled with evidence of Kremlin corruption. Rutskoi hoped that the resonant phrase "eleven suitcases" would toll ominously in the Russian imagination. There was no doubt that there was corruption everywhere in government: in the Kremlin and the parliament, quite obviously; ministers were brazenly selling licenses and permissions; officers and former officers of the KGB were using their connections to become some of the biggest property owners in Russia; army generals with control over Russian arsenals and warehouses sold everything from rifles to tanks to helicopters to arms dealers from Germany to Chechnya to Vladivostok; even street cops had no shame—a friend of mine who was stopped on the highway for no reason at all suddenly discovered that the patrolman wanted nothing more than to sell him tins of black-market caviar, a comically petty crime in the new Moscow. The recipe for corruption—low government salaries and tremendous amounts of loose money floating around—was simple and almost irresistible. In 1993, policemen earned a salary of about $30 a month—a pittance. The chief of the Moscow police force admitted that 95 percent of his men were on the take. Judges were also badly paid. The legal order was, in all, almost nonexistent. In the United States there are about 800,000 lawyers—seventeen times the number of lawyers in Russia.

In May, Yeltsin was attending a reception at the opening of the new Palace Hotel when he was called away by his KGB minister, Viktor Barannikov. According to Yeltsin, Barannikov wanted him to come to a state dacha not for urgent business but rather to meet an émigré businessman named Boris Birshtein, who ran a company called Seabeaco in Switzerland. Barannikov went on about how the businessman had become the top economic adviser to Kyrghizia and how he had brokered a peace agreement between Russia and Moldova.

The fullest account of and investigation into government and business corruption in Russia is Stephen Handelman's *Comrade Criminal* (1995). It is pointless to truncate Handelman's complicated and bizarre narrative. For my purposes, that is, to sketch out the atmosphere and maneuverings that led to the confrontation between Yeltsin and the parliament in October 1993, it is enough to know that the summer of corruption accusations ended with all sides losing. Barannikov was fired after it was discovered that his wife and another wife of a high-ranking official had been Birshtein's guests in Switzerland, where they were allegedly treated to a three-day-long shopping spree worth $350,000; according to Yeltsin, they returned to Moscow with twenty suitcases crammed with fur coats, jewelry, clothes, and whatever else could be flung across a counter. Barannikov, for his part, had turned on Yeltsin and was helping Rutskoi build a criminal case against politicians close to the president. In the end, no government officials went to jail. But there were millions of Russians who wished they would all go to hell.

There are a few axioms about Soviet (and now Russian) politics that are not necessarily true, yet everyone seems to believe them: winter, with its threat of hunger and calamity, breeds conservatism; summer works in favor of reformers; the czar runs into trouble when he goes on vacation; everything ends badly. The last is a particularly Russian formulation, and it was, in fact, becoming clearer by the day that the conflict between Yeltsin and parliament would end badly. As he proved from nearly the first moment he arrived in Moscow to join the Gorbachev leadership, Yeltsin thrived on conflict, the bold gesture. Sometime in late summer, he made a fateful decision that would change completely the political, intellectual, and moral tenor of the post-Soviet landscape.

Yeltsin decided to cut the Gordian knot. Flouting existing law, he would use his mandate in the nonbinding April referendum and dissolve parliament and call new elections for December, a decision that could bring only conflict. For a long time, Yeltsin had been relying on an ever-constricting circle of aides, but this decision he kept to himself. "No one knew this, not even my closest aides," he admitted later. Yeltsin gave only hints of what was to come, warning darkly of a difficult autumn, of "artillery preparations."

Early in September, Yeltsin started preparing the move against the parliament. He called in his loyal aide Viktor Ilyushin and asked him to draft a presidential decree dissolving the congress. Ilyushin nodded and went off to do his job, calmly, Yeltsin recalled, "as if he were being assigned to draft a decree about cattle fodder for the upcoming winter."

Yeltsin knew the move could lead to conflict, even armed conflict, but he was not naive: he could not assume that the military and the KGB would flock to his side. After all, their loyalties had been in question in August 1991; what was more, Rutskoi, especially, had close ties to leading generals in the army, and the defense minister, Pavel Grachev, had already declared publicly that the army should be "above" politics. The military was worn out, sick of coups, weary of being sent into murky border conflicts in Moldova, Tajikistan, and other regions. They were weary, too, of the deep cuts in military budgets that resulted in unpaid salaries, pathetic living conditions, and a deep sense of humiliation. Yeltsin visited two key bases with Grachev, the Taman and Kantemir divisions not far from Moscow. "After work on this decree began," he wrote, "this visit took on new meaning for me." All the while Yeltsin kept thinking, How would these military people behave? How would they react?

Slowly, Yeltsin brought more of his aides into the picture: first, Yuri Baturin, his legal counselor, and then the leading ministers, Grachev, Kozyrev, Viktor Yerin of the Interior Ministry police, Acting Security Minister Nikolai Golushko. On September 11, they all met at a government dacha outside Moscow and Yeltsin informed them of his plan.

"I have a serious comment," Kozyrev said gravely. "I am not in agreement with one fundamental point, Boris Nikolayevich. Such a decree should have been passed long, long ago."

At first, Yeltsin and his advisers chose September 19, a Sunday, as the day to issue the decree. Rutskoi and Khasbulatov would not be in the White House. They would have no access to the hundreds of weapons available to the parliamentary guard. The plan seemed perfect to Yeltsin: "Without the White House, the rebel deputies would turn into a handful of loudmouths. What were six hundred people compared to the whole population of Moscow? No one would listen to them."

But by September 15, it was clear that the news of an impending decree had leaked. Rutskoi and Khasbulatov knew the plan and were getting ready to call a special session of the legislature for Sunday the 19th, the better to establish a bunkered position. Yeltsin called off the decree for a few days, thinking that his opponents would find themselves with nothing to fight against and then go home. But it soon became apparent that this tactic would not work either. The Kremlin was leaking every plan the instant it was decided on.

As the tension grew in the White House, some of Yeltsin's advisers began to sense disaster. Sergei Filatov, Yeltsin's chief of administration, had until recently worked under Khasbulatov. He was wary of his old boss's gift for political infighting. He told Yeltsin that the West and millions of Russians would not support the decree, that it would be better to work out a deal. But Yeltsin said that it was too late. Filatov, he believed, "was living in the past, in the world of compromises and concessions that I had been dwelling in until recently." At a meeting later with Mikhail Barsukov, chief of the Kremlin guard, Yeltsin heard more objections. At dinner with the security ministers, Barsukov said that he was afraid that the entire episode would end in disaster, bloodshed, and even political failure. Once more, Yeltsin dismissed the advice.

"Mikhail Ivanovich," Yeltsin told Barsukov, "perhaps you really should take a vacation now, and when it's all over, then you can come back and get to work." Chastened, Barsukov changed his mind. He would fight alongside the president.

By the weekend, Khasbulatov and Rutskoi were plotting strategy. Khasbulatov blithely told reporters that "after he's had a few" drinks,

Yeltsin would sign anything. The opposition now had its own plan. At the instant that Yeltsin's decree became public, they would declare Yeltsin banned from office; Rutskoi would assume the presidency and an entirely new set of ministers would assume office, including the renegades Achalov and Barannikov as defense and interior ministers. Achalov had supported the first coup, the coup of August 1991. The "constitutionalists," as Khasbulatov and Rutskoi called themselves, clearly thought they could win the battle and assume power. They were well aware that there would be hesitation in the military hierarchy; the generals would not necessarily obey the orders of their commander in chief.

September 21

At around 5:00 p.m., Yeltsin taped a speech to be broadcast three hours later on the evening news. He announced that he was signing Order Number 1400: "On Step-by-Step Constitutional Reform in the Russian Federation." To keep the secret from leaking out even more than it already had, Yeltsin ordered the television crew to stay at the Kremlin until the broadcast. Yeltsin seemed serenely confident that he would be able to carry out his plan—the dissolution of parliament and new elections—with relative ease. He skipped rather lightly over the fact that he was acting with no legal basis; he was hoping that the mandate of the April referendum, the support of the West, and the public's impatience with the status quo would carry him through. "Russia was entering a new epoch," he wrote later. "Just a few more shakes and we would all start to breathe more easily and purely."

In the evening, Russian television played the tape of Yeltsin's announcement. Veronika Kutsillo, a twenty-six-year parliamentary reporter for the newspaper *Kommersant,* rode over to the White House to see what was happening. Like so many in Moscow who had grown weary of the permanent state of crisis in politics, she wondered if this was not just another gambit of minimal consequence. Would it be like Yeltsin's abortive attempt in March to institute "special rule"?

Outside the White House, about two thousand people had assembled. Many of them were carrying red banners and the red flag of the old Soviet Union.

September 22

Khasbulatov, as expected, called an emergency session of the full Congress of People's Deputies. While the Yeltsin supporters and dozens of "undecideds" did not come, he had more than enough for a quorum of the smaller body, the Supreme Soviet—a symbolic victory at least. Working at breakneck speed, the Constitutional Court declared Yeltsin's decree unconstitutional; the legislature, meanwhile, then approved Rutskoi's elevation to the presidency and a slate of new hard-line ministers, including Vladislav Achalov as minister of defense, and Iona Andronov, a former KGB man who worked undercover in the Soviet era as a foreign correspondent, as minister of foreign affairs.

Rutskoi, acting as president, immediately began the campaign to win over the military. In one of many such acts, he sent out an appeal by telegram to a key unit, the Dzerzhinsky Motorized Division:

> I come to you with hope and faith. Today, you, the strength and soldiers of Russia, must decide to live by conscience and law; if not you will have taken the road of lawlessness against the people. In my executive capacity as president of the Russian Federation, as a general in the Russian army, I request with great alarm for you to deviate not one step from your constitutional duty and military code. I am sure that you will not take up arms against your fellow countrymen, against the law of the Russian Federation. I call on you to endure, to fulfill calmly and firmly my orders regarding the defense of constitutional order in Russia and to support the security of the state.
>
> A. Rutskoi. Moscow.

On the floor of the Congress, the speeches, following Khasbulatov's lead, were confident and full of rage. There were even calls for the death penalty for "the former president" and his aides. Veronika Kutsillo, who decided that she should camp out in the White House until the crisis was over, noticed that not all the "defenders of constitutional order" were members of parliament. She wondered why young men wearing "red swastika-like" armbands and berets were marching around the hallways.

September 23

In the first days of the crisis, reporters could get in and out of the White House fairly easily, and, once inside, they could meet with Khasbulatov and Rutskoi. At first, both men were sure not only of victory but of support. Their first defeat was the overwhelming evidence that the leaders of the United States, France, Germany, and Britain, using phrases like "support of the democratically elected president" and "support for the cause of reform," had cast their lot with Yeltsin. Khasbulatov promptly told reporters that the West was betraying not only the White House, a democratically elected parliament, but also the cause of democracy. The West was hypocritical. In fact, Khasbulatov said, Yeltsin had briefed the Western countries ahead of time to be sure of their support; the West, in turn, supplied Yeltsin with intelligence. The Western intelligence capability was enormous, he said. In 1991, the CIA had known ahead of time that the KGB and the army were plotting a coup and had tried to inform Gorbachev. (This, of course, was true.)

Khasbulatov found (or imagined) signs of hope in Russia itself. "The regions are not supporting this anticonstitutional coup," he said. "You should understand that it's all over for Yeltsin. He is hanging by a thread. My God, if I hadn't been by his side before, history would have long ago forgotten about him! The regional leaders say that if legality is not restored, they will stop paying taxes, shut down transportation, call strikes, and destroy the economy."

As a cold rain came down outside his window, Khasbulatov said that he knew that if the White House was lost, he would go to prison. But he would not lose, he said. Yeltsin would fail, and he would be judged at last for destroying the Soviet Union and for conducting a foreign policy "in the interest of the West."

Rutskoi, as usual, was more blunt. When he was asked about the Clinton administration's support for Yeltsin, he said, "It's not surprising that the countries which supported the destruction of the country support Yeltsin."

September 24

On Yeltsin's orders, Moscow city officials shut off the electricity, heat, and phone lines in the White House. Yeltsin even tried to bribe the fence-sitters inside the White House, saying he would pay deputies' salaries and benefits through 1995 if they would only leave the building. To Rutskoi and Khasbulatov's surprise and fury, many deputies accepted the offer.

At first there was only a light police presence near the building. But when one of the parliament's extremist military leaders, Stanislav Terekhov of the Union of Officers, tried to attack the military communications office of the Commonwealth of Independent States, there was first blood: a woman was killed in the incident. Now Yeltsin ordered the Interior Ministry to cordon off the White House. The police parked a yellow armored car outside the building to play booming music and progovernment propaganda at top volume day and night; the car soon became known as the Yellow Goebbels.

But while Yeltsin and his aides worked the phones trying to shore up support in the regions and among military leaders, there was a sense of chaos in the Kremlin. "We had no battle plan," Yeltsin admitted afterward. "Internally, I simply could not accept the possibility that a constitutional dispute could lead to shooting people."

If the Kremlin was disorganized, the White House leaders were growing more and more desperate. While the soldiers and paramilitaries walked around with rifles and grenade launchers, the more ordinary folk piled up stones, the better to hurl them out the windows when the final attack came. Every day there were new rumors: the storming of the White House would come that night without doubt; help was on the way from this or that army division. Each night the guns would come out; nerve-shot old men and women and young soldiers and guards shivered in the darkened hallways; the night would pass. Then the next day there would be the same rumors, the same sense of alarm and apocalypse. Day after day, the deputies and their supporters grew more and more tired, more frazzled, more convinced of a bloody end.

Rutskoi's telegrams were bringing no rewards. His call for strikes went nowhere. Khasbulatov's request that the Trans-Siberian Railroad shut down went unheeded. By now, there were hundreds of arms inside the White House, but the men who would bear them did not look like a force able to defeat anyone, much less the Russian army. Albert Makashov, a Stalinist general who had run for the Russian presidency promising a return of the gulag, swaggered around the White House like Colonel Blimp telling everyone, "We have adequate force to defend the deputies, the building, and Soviet power in general!" Makashov announced the arrival of a detachment of Cossacks, strange men with spectacular mustaches, high boots, and furry headgear. Makashov and the others also recruited troops returning from Moldova and Latvia, peach-cheeked recruits AWOL from local bases, students at military academies. Aleksandr Barkashov's young fascists did not seem to offend anyone, including the men and women old enough to remember the Great Patriotic War.

September 25

Rutskoi decided impulsively to scout the area around the White House. Trailed by a pack of reporters, he walked outside and met a police officer—one of the dozens assigned to cordon off the building.

"Comrade Officer!" Rutskoi shouted, his face reddening with anger. "A criminal regime wants you to spill the blood of innocent people! Don't do it! Don't take criminal orders! I'm telling you with all my authority: soldiers and police who cross over to the side of the law will be freed of all responsibility." There was in Rutskoi's voice, Kutsillo wrote, a "kind of helplessness, a hopelessness."

Asked by a reporter about the possibility of a compromise with Yeltsin, Rutskoi said, "I will not make any sort of compromise!"

September 26

On Red Square, Mstislav Rostropovich and the National Symphony Orchestra performed in front of a huge crowd, including Yeltsin. The climax of the concert came with the firing of cannons and the ringing of the Kremlin bells. The wind was sharp and chill—the musicians were so cold that they had a difficult time getting from bar to bar—but there was a sense of triumph on the square. The night before, Rostropovich had performed with the son of an old friend. With Ignat Solzhenitsyn at the piano, he conducted Shostakovich's Piano Concerto No. 1. At the end of the performance Rostropovich and Solzhenitsyn embraced. Politically, they had also embraced Yeltsin.

At the White House there was music of another kind. Some of the older people sat around the candlelit chamber singing old Soviet songs of war and patriotism. The rumors were worse than ever. The army was coming. That night! Absolutely! There was some rejoicing when one deputy announced, with great confidence, that the United States Senate was preparing to arrest Bill Clinton for his support of Yeltsin. He was sure. His information was absolute.

Someone asked Rutskoi if he thought Yeltsin would dare to storm the White House.

"That depends on how much the president drinks," he said.

September 27–28

As time went by, the atmosphere in the White House became more and more charged with a sense of impending martyrdom. By now, Khasbulatov looked haunted: he often wore a black shirt; the bags under his eyes and his dark ramblings about Yeltsin and the attack to come made him seem to the reporters he met with like a man over the line. Khasbulatov announced that the White House would be stormed on the night of the 28th. Without doubt. The KGB's Alpha troops, who had refused to storm the White House in 1991, were preparing their assault, he said. Wearing a bulletproof vest, he herded the remaining deputies into the Hall of the Soviet of Nationalities. (Many deputies had already gone home.) Rutskoi wore his army camouflage. If Yeltsin's tactics, through intelligence agents and sheer persistence, were meant to put his opponents on edge, they were succeeding beyond all expectation. General Achalov commanded everyone to stay up, not to sleep. No one went to sleep until four in the morning. The military commanders, including Rutskoi, started sketching out grandiose plans about capturing the Ostankino television buildings, the wire service ITAR-TASS, and other key points around the city. To pass the time, the deputies sang their Soviet songs and read Soviet poetry; the troops, an increasingly bizarre and menacing sight, paced the halls and traded rumors—one rumor more terrifying and confident than the last. Khasbulatov told reporters that Yeltsin had turned the White House into "a closed concentration camp."

"This is just ordinary fascism," he said, but added, "the regime will fall."

———

With so many factions roaming the White House—communists, nationalists, neo-Nazis, Cossacks, etc.—there could be no one absolute leader. It was unclear, really, who spoke for the White House forces: even Rutskoi and Khasbulatov went back and forth on the crucial issue of negotiations. But now it was becoming clear that Aleksei II, the patriarch of the Russian Orthodox Church, was preparing to insert himself between the two warring sides. Certainly both sides had done what they could to co-opt the church and its symbolic importance as the spiritual center of a "new Russia." Yeltsin and Rutskoi both had gone many times to Russian Orthodox ceremonies and were photographed in church holding candles and standing next to Aleksei. Yeltsin's government had already spent billions of rubles for the restoration of churches and monasteries abandoned or destroyed under communism. In the first week of the White House crisis, Rutskoi wrote a letter to the patriarch, saying, "As a religious believer and as a citizen of Russia invested with high authority, I assure you that I will do everything possible to overcome the crisis by peaceful means."

Outside it was snowing. An armored personnel carrier took up position near the Mir Hotel, a few hundred yards away from the White House.

September 29

Yeltsin convened his Security Council once more. It was clear to all that the tactics they had used until now—cutting off the lights and heat, the barrage of disinformation—was not going to drive anyone out of the building. There were reports from inside the White House that the troops there were getting more and more arms; they were mining the building's system of underground tunnels, setting up barricades around the building and at key points inside. Police said that the White House guard had accumulated an arms cache of sixteen hundred automatic weapons, two thousand pistols, twenty machine guns, and several grenade launchers. That was the guard's legal arsenal. In the preceding two weeks, White House supporters and troops had brought in hundreds more automatic weapons and machine guns. Rutskoi had at his command a significant force, including three battalions of Moscow reservists, one hundred crack troops who had been serving in Moldova, police troops back from Riga, a detachment of Cossacks, various paramilitaries from Workers of Russia and other communist groups, and more than a hundred troops trained by the neo-Nazi commander Aleksandr Barkashov. This motley army was nearly as menacing to some of the deputies inside the White House as it was to the government. Yeltsin's Security Council decided to issue an ultimatum: the defenders of the White House had four days to get out. Kozyrev, the foreign minister, went on CNN and said that the situation was growing more unstable, that Rutskoi was mentally "unbalanced."

Meanwhile, Aleksei II, Patriarch of Moscow and All Russia, issued a proclamation warning of impending violence, even civil war. "Don't give in to provocations," he wrote. "Today's troubled situation could be exploited by extremists, criminal elements, and simply unhealthy people."

Both sides agreed to begin negotiations the next morning under church auspices at the Danilovsky Monastery, one of the holiest sites in the capital.

October 1

At the monastery, Sergei Filatov, Oleg Soskovets, and Moscow mayor Yuri Luzhkov represented Yeltsin; Ramazan Abdulatipov and Venyamin Sokolov spoke for the parliament. In the presence of the patriarch, the talk at the table was reasonably polite, and, to the amazement of everyone, the two sides agreed to "Protocol No. 1"—the government would turn on the lights and hot water in the White House when the parliament forces gave up their weapons. The agreement, however, fell apart in just a few hours. Rutskoi and Khasbulatov quickly backed out of the deal, and when negotiations resumed, the White House added to its team Yuri Voronin, an orthodox communist firebrand whose stalling tactics made it clear that the talks at the monastery were doomed.

At the White House itself, the scene was becoming more bizarre: "a theme park of oddities, a Disneyland of paranoia, a Jurassic Park of menace," Lee Hockstader of *The Washington Post* wrote. The grounds of the parliament were now dominated by mercenary soldiers, Cossacks, neo-Nazis, priests, exhausted-looking legislators, old women, army deserters, children. There were signs supporting a monarchy, signs supporting Lenin and Stalin, signs calling for the blood of Yeltsin, the blood of Gaidar, the blood of the Jews. There were posters of the Virgin Mary, graffiti denouncing the West. As at past meetings of the National Salvation Front, the red Soviet flag flew side by side with the black-white-and-gold flag of the Romanovs—a vision that would surely have stunned Lenin and the Romanovs alike.

"We are at a turning point," Rutskoi announced within earshot of a reporter from Reuters. "I firmly believe we shall win. Give us two or three more days."

October 2

For several days there had been a series of increasingly menacing demonstrations near the White House. Now the level of tension was about to increase. On the afternoon of October 2, the Workers of Russia, the most militant of the communist groups, staged a demonstration on Smolensk Square near the Foreign Ministry building and the start of the Arbat pedestrian mall. The site was just a fifteen-minute walk from the White House. Led by Viktor Anpilov, the former Radio Moscow operative, the crowd reached several thousand and seemed prepared, even hungry, for violence. They got it. Marching under the red flag, the demonstrators tore apart a stage and used the steel parts as truncheons to attack the police. They built barricades on the Ring Road and set buses on fire. The police seemed pitifully undermanned and ill-prepared. They fired off some tear-gas canisters and rubber bullets, but to little effect. The crowd was overrunning them. The only mercy was that Anpilov and a member of the Moscow City Council, Nikolai Gonchar—men from opposing camps—finally called off the mob; the demonstrators even handed over a couple of Molotov cocktails. But before they left for home Anpilov told them to rest up: there would be a greater battle the next day, he said.

Yeltsin was informed of the clashes and wondered what to do, whether to move in more arms and police or go the other way, loosen the security, let time do its work.

"I later exhausted myself trying to understand whether I'd done the right thing, believing that we shouldn't let ourselves be provoked and that our restraint would force the outlaws to stop their armed resistance," he would write later. "Now that the bloody events are over, it can probably be said that we were tragically mistaken. If the police had been armed, if the Interior Ministry officers had the chance from the start to react properly to the armed attack, the ferocious barbarism of the night of October 3–4 in Moscow would have been avoided. The rebels were drunk with their own impunity. Yet if the police had been armed, an even greater tragedy might have occurred. All told, I don't know and to this day I cannot be sure."

October 3

Sunday morning and the sky was bright and the air was warm. A perfect Indian-summer morning. The patriarch, who had seen the negotiations at the Danilovsky Monastery going nowhere, shifted to more elevated means of peace-making. Trailed by priests dressed in black robes, he went to the Yelokhovsky Cathedral and paraded the icon of the Mother of God, which had been used to ward off Tamerlane's invasion in 1395. The icon was the holiest in Moscow and had been kept until now at the Tretyakov Gallery. Aleksei II prayed that Russia be saved from catastrophe yet again.

Veronika Kutsillo, the reporter for *Kommersant,* was utterly worn out from her days and nights in the White House. She wandered down to one of the main halls of the parliament and saw Khasbulatov, a Muslim from Chechnya, attending a makeshift service led by Orthodox priests. When the service was finished, he walked over to a few reporters (by now they were nearly as familiar with one another as friends or family) and said the time had come for Yeltsin to be punished for his "evil." The CIA and the other Western secret services were infiltrating the building and feeding information to the Kremlin. "A terrible war is coming," he said and eerily drifted off down the hall, a ghost.

———————

A little while later, the crowds in the White House heard a gathering noise out on the street: cheering, slogans, commotion. People rushed to the windows, looked down at the street. There were thousands of people, and they were carrying red banners. The crowd had started out at October Square and worked its way through one police line after another, breaking through with stunning, even mysterious, ease. Met at the Krymsky Bridge by several rows of crack Interior Ministry troops (the OMON), the demonstrators started shouting and surging forward and hurling paving stones. Armed only with riot shields and truncheons, the police gave way, and the crowd crossed the bridge and headed along the

Ring Road toward the White House. So frightened were the police that some of them threw their shields into the Moscow River and ran for the nearest metro station. Some officers even left behind trucks and squad cars, which the demonstrators promptly took as their own. All along the road to the parliament, militiamen would hastily try to form lines of defense blocking the crowd's way, but each time they fell out and scattered. When the demonstrators reached the White House, they were jubilant. Police fired a few shots over the demonstrators' heads—whether live rounds or blanks is unclear—but when it became evident that the militia were preposterously outnumbered, they, too, abandoned the scene and retreated to the nearby headquarters of the Moscow mayor. By 3:30 P.M., the White House blockade had been shattered.

This was the moment that Rutskoi had been picturing for days. With his bodyguards flanking him, he walked to the balcony of the White House and barked a call to arms through a megaphone at the crowd.

"We've won!" Rutskoi declared feverishly. "Thank you, dear Muscovites! Now we must form detachments and take the mayor's office—and then Ostankino!" The mayor's office (the former COMECON building) was just a few hundred yards away. The police had been using the building as a temporary headquarters during the crisis. The Ostankino television complex was six miles to the north.

Under the balcony, Generals Achalov and Makashov started to form detachments out of the deserters and Cossacks and neo-Nazis available to them. Then Khasbulatov took the bullhorn: "I call on our troops to come and our tanks to come to take the Kremlin and its usurper, its criminal leader, Yeltsin. . . . Yeltsin should be jailed in Sailor's Rest!" The reference was to the prison where the coup plotters of 1991 had been jailed.

From the moment he used his bullhorn, Rutskoi changed the crisis utterly. Now there could be no doubt that the violence would escalate. Rutskoi and Khasbulatov never reconsidered their calls to arms; they issued an appeal, saying:

Dear Friends! The victory is not yet final; armed units under the commanders who have sold out may still be flung at you. They are supported by Yeltsin's stooges and underlings. Be vigilant and stand firm. We appeal to all collectives, to all citizens of our motherland: do not obey the criminal decrees and orders of the Yeltsinites. Unite around the lawfully elected government bodies—the soviets of people's deputies. . . . We call on soldiers of the Russian army and navy: display civic courage, preserve your military honor in loyalty to the constitution, support the concrete deeds of popular power and the law. Russia will be grateful to you and will give genuine patriots their deserved appreciation. . . . The Yeltsin group, having usurped power, is falling apart. In the next few days the congress will pass laws and decisions which will guarantee a dignified life to our people and return to our homeland the glory of its past.

Kutsillo went downstairs and watched in horror at what happened next: with the generals leading the charge, the White House forces took two military trucks in their possession and drove them through the glass front of the mayor's offices. The few soldiers and police who were still there threw down their weapons and ran. There was shooting—who was shooting and at whom was unclear, confused—but there was no doubt that the White House forces were on the offensive. "Now I knew what real fear was," Kutsillo wrote in her diary. "I stood and watched as they beat a man. I did nothing so that I wouldn't be beaten, too. I just did not want to be beaten."

———

The trip from the mayor's office north to Ostankino is all the way across town—long and traffic-ridden. The attackers from the White House had no idea of what they were heading toward. Although they had little information about what was going on in the rest of the city, those who stayed behind in the White House, Khasbulatov included, were elated. They were positive that victory was only hours away: once television was seized, they could take to the airwaves and dominate communications from Moscow to Sakhalin; they imagined the army and the police joining them; they imagined Yeltsin and his aides under arrest and in jail. The atmosphere inside the White House was delusional, insane. "Events have shown that people instinctively reject tyranny," Khasbulatov said. "I am convinced that the troops will not open fire on the defenders of democracy. We must take the Kremlin. Ostankino is captured, and so is the mayor's office."

The only way that the reporters left in the White House knew that the Yeltsin government was still in office was that the news reports were still referring to "former legislators" and "former deputies." Anatoly Shabad, one of the leading liberals in the parliament, had heard the demonstrators calling for executions and now feared that he was in real personal danger. Shabad called his wife and told her to leave their apartment. There was, in fact, panic everywhere: Yevgeny Savostyanov, the head of the municipal secret services, was told by his field officers that the crowds had overrun the mayor's office and were heading for Ostankino. He announced that there was no force in the city to stop Rutskoi.

———

Amazingly, Yeltsin himself was not yet in command. He was at his country retreat enjoying a leisurely meal with his family when he heard the news that the demonstrators had run through the police lines and were heading for Ostankino. Many of his deputies were blithely doing work that had nothing to do with the immediate crisis. A team of aides was working at Old Square, drafting legislation for a new civil code that was not scheduled for discussion for months to come. Yeltsin's chief of administration, Sergei Filatov, was still engaged in the same ridiculous negotiations at the Danilovsky Monastery! When his aides finally told Yeltsin what was happening in the city, he declared a state of emergency in Moscow and ordered a helicopter to come pick him up and take him to the Kremlin. As his security aide briefed him further, Yeltsin recalled "my heart heaving in my chest, thinking to myself, Oh Lord, is it really starting? They had done what we had kept believing to the end they would not do. They had crossed the line that the Russian people should never cross. They had started a war, the most terrible kind of war—a civil war."

Sergei Kovalyov, Andrei Sakharov's greatest disciple in the human rights movement and a deputy in parliament, recounted his experience among the demonstrators: "I was in the crowd today and they moved under red flags and black-and-yellow flags to the White House, and they were hitting and screaming at the policemen. They cried, 'All power to the Soviets!' 'Down with Yeltsin!' But they were also yelling, 'Beat!' Beat

the democrats, beat the Jews, beat the police, beat the Caucasians. . . .
We were naive. We tried to work out a crisis through negotiations with
people who are today showing their true face—the face of homegrown
fascism. We cannot allow this. Everyone who wants to defend our democracy, our future, should fulfill his civil duty. Soldiers must be true to
the law of the president and the government; the citizen must calmly fulfill his duty. . . . We, the prisoners under Stalin, Khrushchev, and Brezhnev, do not want our children and grandchildren to live under Soviet
power. The shadows of the dead and murdered are with us."

Sometime after four, special detachments of the special operations
forces of the Interior Ministry raced from their posts outside the American embassy to Ostankino. Yeltsin's aide Sergei Stankevich told *The Washington Post* that he drove up alongside the armored personnel carriers and
asked which side they were on.

"We don't know," came the answer. "We'll see when we get there."

With Yeltsin still outside the city, the scene at the Kremlin's presidential offices was one of absolute disorganization. Sergei Parkhomenko, a
columnist at the time for the newspaper *Sevodnya* ("Today"), wandered
from office to office and saw high-level aides at an utter loss. They bick-
ered with one another. They were ill informed. Nothing was happening.
They did not know what to do. Parkhomenko reported that the few aides
who were there argued about who had been more naive and had believed
that a compromise with the "bandits" was possible.

"So what are you going to do now, peacemaker?" one aide shouted at
another.

"I'm a peacemaker?" came the answer. "You're the peacemaker!"

At one point, Parkhomenko asked an aide who was going to guard the
Kremlin should it come to that. After a while, the aide, sick of Par-
khomenko's questions, told him to call General Mikhail Barsukov of the
KGB.

So he did. Parkhomenko picked up a special Kremlin phone and called
Barsukov. The general picked up his own phone. Sergei asked his question.

"Where are you calling from?" Barsukov said.

"Filatov's office," Sergei said (without exactly identifying himself).

"Well, two battalions," Barsukov said. "Why? Don't you think that's
enough?"

Parkhomenko mumbled something incoherent.

"I can give orders for reinforcements," Barsukov added. "Do you think I should?"

"Go ahead," Parkhomenko said.

For the rest of his career, Parkhomenko would call the incident "How I organized the defense of the Kremlin."

———

As Muscovites learned what was happening near the White House, those who feared the forces under Rutskoi and Khasbulatov had nowhere to go, no sense of what to do. It was not until Yegor Gaidar went on the radio station Echo of Moscow and called on people to rally in support of the government outside City Hall on Tver' Street that there was any sign of popular resistance to what was being called "the counterrevolution." At first, only small numbers of people came to City Hall, but by eight or nine o'clock, there were thousands, maybe fifteen or twenty thousand people on the streets. The crowd listened to speeches and traded rumors of fighting elsewhere in the city, but mostly people came to show at least themselves that all was not lost. "We wanted most of all to prove that we exist," one friend told me. "It was cold and frightening, but we stayed all night. All night until the shelling began."

———

While Yeltsin was making his way back to the Kremlin by helicopter, Rutskoi was at the White House issuing orders that had all the detail and precision of a standard coup d'état: his troops, in fact, did attack ITAR-TASS, the main official wire service, and then issued orders to blockade airports and train stations and make assaults on radio stations and telephone exchanges. There were assaults on sixteen different electricity-switching stations.

Finally, aides started pouring into the Kremlin. Yeltsin's helicopter executed a U-turn maneuver before settling on the Kremlin lawn in case one of the White House forces decided, as Yeltsin put it, to give him a "whack with a Stinger or something."

The key question now was the behavior of the military. Defense Minister Grachev told Yeltsin that he had given orders for army units to come into Moscow. Assured initially that he would have no problems from Grachev, Yeltsin and two other military leaders, Dmitri Volkogonov and Yevgeny Shaposhnikov, started calling military bases around the country, wanting to make sure of their support. Meanwhile, at the Defense Ministry building, not far from the Kremlin, deputy ministers and three-star generals were reduced to guarding the building's myriad entrances. They had good reason to fear; the country's nuclear codes and command centers were inside.

The main concern, however, was Ostankino, the television complex. Seizing the means of communications is the cardinal rule of any struggle for power—especially in a banana republic like Russia, many Muscovites were quick to add—and the race for the tower was on. From the moment of Rutskoi's call to seize Ostankino, Vyacheslav Bragin, the chairman of Russian state television, was on the phone with Yeltsin's ministers asking for instructions. The most important maneuver, however, came not from the Kremlin's initiative. Another television executive, Oleg Poptsov, made plans for alternate means of broadcast that would end-run the demonstrators.

"Ostankino has been seized!" Khasbulatov told his deputies back at the White House. "Today we must seize the Kremlin!" But the battle had hardly begun. At around 6:40 P.M., General Makashov was at Ostankino brandishing a bullhorn; he was surrounded by thousands of supporters and even more onlookers who were simply curious to see what was going on. The Interior Ministry had already installed troops inside the building. Makashov shouted his demands: the troops must leave the building and give up their arms. There was a sense of imminence, of euphoria, among the White House forces now. Someone with a guitar was singing old victory songs from the Soviet past. Others shouted battle cries from wars past. And then, without warning, someone near Makashov fired a grenade into the Ostankino building. With that, a firefight that would last into the early morning began.

At exactly 8:00 P.M., Ostankino officials shut down Channels 1, 3, and 4. (Channel 1 is the most powerful station of all, covering nearly all the states of the former union.) But using a backup broadcasting studio all the way across town, newspeople loyal to the government went on the air on Channel 2—the "Russian channel." This would probably be the most decisive and best-planned maneuver for the Yeltsin forces (though Yeltsin had nothing to do with it). A stream of broadcasters came on the air: Svetlana Sorokina, Nikolai Svanidze—all of them familiar to viewers, all of them urgent and informative. Frantic and disheveled, the broadcasters sat in shabby chairs in the makeshift studio reading one wire report after another. Another well-known broadcaster, Sergei Torchinski, stayed on the air all night interviewing some of the best-known politicians and intellectuals in the country. Perhaps the most memorable appearance was that of Liya Akhedzhakova, a popular comic actress. Her hair in disarray, her eyes furious, even desperate, she appealed to whoever was watching.

"This all shows that we have not learned anything in seventy years!" she said. "People look at the past and they think the past was all fine because 'we had sausage.' They say, 'It's not important that millions were imprisoned in the camps.' " She said that those acting in the name of the constitution were actually lunatics and the law-abiding citizens of the capital were unprotected. "Where is our army? Why aren't they protecting against these so-called defenders of the constitution? My friends! Wake up! Don't sleep! Tonight the fate of our unhappy country will be decided, our unhappy motherland. Our unhappy motherland in peril! Don't go to sleep! They are threatening us with terrible things! The communists are coming again!"

Yelena Bonner, Sakharov's widow, made a rather cooler appeal to the people. She said that what was happening at Ostankino and the White House was a "fascist act" planned in advance. "I always thought that negotiations with the White House and the former Supreme Soviet were futile," she said. "When terrorists hijack a plane, is it really possible to talk them out of it? Of course, the answering action of the president and the government has come late, but it seems that the president sincerely tried to end the conflict peacefully and until the last he believed in the common sense of the other side."

———

Late into the night, the crisis was still unresolved. There was still no sign of the army troops that Grachev had promised earlier in the evening. Every time Yeltsin barked at him, Grachev kept saying the tanks were on their way, they were coming soon. Outside City Hall, the thousands of demonstrators loyal to the government became more worried by the minute that the troops would never come, that all would be lost. Then Yeltsin heard from the head of the Moscow traffic police that there were still no tanks on the road. Yeltsin was furious. "Many of those on television asked why I was remaining silent, and they demanded that I address the country," Yeltsin would say later. "At that moment, however, I had a far more important job to do, and speeches were the last thing on my mind. I was trying to bring my combat generals out of their state of stress and paralysis."

Grachev told Yeltsin that the Military Collegium would soon meet at the Defense Ministry. That meeting would decide the course of battle.

October 4

No one slept. Not the broadcasters on Channel 2, not the deputies inside the White House, no one. At first, Yeltsin sent the prime minister, Viktor Chernomyrdin, to the meeting at the Defense Ministry, but it was clear, long after midnight, that there had been no definitive decision. The generals, hesitant after August 1991, hesitant after Baku and Tbilisi and Vilnius, wanted no part of this latest political war.

Sometime after 2:00 A.M., Yeltsin climbed into his bulletproof limousine and made the short ride from the Kremlin gates to the Defense Ministry. A pair of armored personnel carriers blocked the driveway at the ministry, but when they were told that Yeltsin was in the car, the two vehicles glided apart like sliding doors. Yeltsin's driver steered down into an underground garage. Yeltsin took the elevator to the fifth floor, where the leading generals in the Russian army were seated around an enormous table.

When Yeltsin walked through the door, the generals averted their gaze. They stared at their hands, at the table, at their shoes, anywhere but at Yeltsin. After an inconclusive round of comments, Yeltsin's bodyguard and security aide, Korzhakov, took the floor. He asked that a man named Zakharov of the Chief Security Directorate come into the room and give a briefing about contingency plans to attack the White House. Somehow this focus on details rather than on political and moral questions captured the attention of the generals.

Before the discussion shifted entirely to tactics, however, Grachev raised his hand and asked Yeltsin, "Boris Nikolayevich, are you giving me sanction to use tanks in Moscow?"

"Pavel Sergeyevich, what are you saying?" Chernomyrdin broke in. "You've been assigned to command an operation! Why should the president decide what precise means you require for it?"

Grachev grumbled that he needed to verify matters.

Yeltsin rose from his seat and said that the generals should work out the details themselves, and, turning to Grachev, he said, "I'll send you a written order."

Yeltsin returned to the Kremlin. There his aide Viktor Ilyushin drafted the order. Yeltsin signed it, and it was rushed back to the Defense Ministry and handed to Grachev.

With that out of the way, Yeltsin summoned a team of television technicians and taped a message to the nation which would go on the air in the morning just before the tanks began firing at the White House, a building that had so recently been a symbol of liberation. Yeltsin turned to the camera. "The armed mutiny," he declared, "is doomed."

At around 7:00 A.M. armored personnel carriers and T-80 tanks took positions around the White House and on the Novo Arbatsky Bridge. The tanks had come rumbling down Kutuzovsky Prospekt, the same approach to the center of the city that Napoleon had taken in 1812, the same approach that the coup plotters had used in 1991. Shortly before nine, a T-80 from the Kantemirovsky Division fired a 150-millimeter cannon at one of the higher floors in the White House. Windows shattered; water mains snapped, flooding the hallways. Fires started in the upper floors and the black smoke stained the building, which soon would be known as the Black House. "When the tanks fired it was something terrible," said Veronika Kutsillo, the *Kommersant* reporter who stayed inside the building. "It felt as if the building would collapse like a house of cards." The tanks were aiming to shatter the morale of the White House defenders, who had, from the start, been congregated mainly on the lower floors. As the shots came, they tried to keep calm, some still singing old Soviet songs—"My dear capital, the enemy will never make you bow your head, my dear capital . . ."

The White House leaders, who only hours before had sensed victory and the imminent possession of the Kremlin, now knew that the army was not with them, that they were doomed. By midmorning, a wire reporter came across Khasbulatov, who was slumped on a couch. He was pale, ghostly, talking nonsense. "Get out now," Khasbulatov told the reporter. "You don't know what it will be like in here." Then he lit his pipe and said, as if to himself, "I have known Yeltsin for a long time but I never would have expected anything like this from him."

Meanwhile Rutskoi was on the phone shouting nonstop obscenities and pleas at the chief justice of the Constitutional Court, Valery Zorkin, who had supported him in September: "I'm asking you, have someone call the embassies! Have the foreign ambassadors come! I beg you, Valera, you are a believer—fuck your mother!—you will have this sin on your soul! They are murderers. Do you understand that or not?" In a similar vein, Rutskoi shouted at yet another phone companion: "Fuck . . . come here! . . . Fuck! Tell me . . . damn it . . . fuck your mother. I am a hero, don't you realize that? What's on TV is all bullshit! Bullshit! Damn it!"

———

The White House forces fired rifles out the window, and the troops below, with their superior firepower and organization, fired back. The strangest part of the spectacle was the sight of hundreds of people watching the action along the streets and bridges as if they were at a sporting event.

Rutskoi knew now that he had no chance to win his war, but he said he would kill himself rather than surrender. Then he changed his mind, telling one of the politicians who was trying to negotiate a truce that there were already five hundred dead. He was ready to leave his bunker, just make sure to send the foreign ambassadors—he would not leave the building without them. No matter how inflated Rutskoi's casualty count may have been, the grounds of the White House were strewn with dead bodies—bodies of old people, soldiers, and children alike with limbs blown off, holes in their chests. One doctor on the scene said that nearly half the bodies coming to the morgue were kids, probably gawkers. There is no telling how many of the 150 killed and hundreds more wounded were spectators, but there were a lot of them. It was insane: teenagers dashing across the battlefield, desperate perhaps to appear on the one news channel that was showing every minute of this war—CNN.

Leonid Roshal, head of one of the main pediatric clinics in Moscow, treated dozens of people and was amazed that the White House forces waited until late afternoon to walk out of the building. "I don't always agree with Yeltsin, but it's worth imagining what things would have been like under Rutskoi and Khasbulatov," the doctor said. "If those two are normal people and not fascists, why is it they didn't put up a white flag and come out much sooner? They would have saved many lives, including the lives of their own people. . . . I thought that Rutskoi would have taken his own life. Instead he called for help from the ambassadors of those same Western countries which he had insulted and libeled from the speaker's tribune."

In the end, Rutskoi and Khasbulatov walked out the main entrance of the White House and were herded onto a caravan of police buses and driven off to prison. Like the coup plotters of 1991, they needn't have worried much. They would not stay in jail very long.

———

The day did not end with the arrests of Rutskoi, Khasbulatov, and the other White House leaders. The area around the building was the scene not only of carnage from the hours before but of sniping from the rooftops and beatings down below. Oleg Rumyantsev, a scholar-politician in his thirties who had gone from supporting Yeltsin to standing side by side with the nationalists in the parliament, had tried to help negotiate a settlement to the crisis. Now he found himself with his life in danger. Rumyantsev was a peculiar figure: as a legal expert for Yeltsin, he had drafted a version of a new constitution. In a piece I wrote about him for *The Washington Post* in 1990 I said that he was being referred to as a Russian James Madison. As an ally of Khasbulatov, he wrote a constitutional draft calling for a parliamentary system. Now Alpha troops were taking him to the courtyard of a building not far from the burning White House.

According to Rumyantsev, he was told to lie down on the ground. Then a drunken soldier grabbed him by his beard and said, "Come here, you Jewish shit." The soldier hit Rumyantsev in the face and then searched him for money. When the soldier discovered no riches on Rumyantsev, he beat him some more. Beatings were going on all over. A few weeks later, I went to see Rumyantsev. He looked drawn, haunted, depressed. He railed at the treachery of the West, at Yeltsin's betrayal of parliament. He was now saying that the West, with its talk of liberty and individualism, was "not right" for Russia. Russia was a "special case," its people were a "special people." He had changed. "The Oleg Rumyantsev you met in 1990—the one you wrote about for the *Post* in 1990—came all from my studies, from what I had learned from books," he said. "Until 1990, I had two universities: Moscow State University and the Moscow Institute for Legal Studies. Then came the universities of the Congress of People's Deputies, the university of life. I will never be the same."

———

Russians have been building Potemkin villages since the time of Catherine the Great. Now, as they slopped paint over the charred facade of the White House, they had nearly finished one on the banks of the Moscow River. In 1991, the building, in all its sprawling vulgarity, had been the scene of Russia's greatest historical triumph since the end of World War II—the defeat of a Bolshevik coup and the fall of the old regime. Overnight, the Russian White House became a symbol of liberty more vivid than the Bastille: the storming of the Bastille had not been on CNN; Boris Yeltsin standing on a tank was.

In October 1993, Yeltsin won another victory at the White House, not by defending it but by blasting it. Because Yeltsin came so close to losing power to a leadership that would have been infinitely worse than his, many Russians expressed relief. In fact, most people were disgusted with both sides. There was no sense anywhere of celebration. There were funerals this time, not fireworks.

The hangover in Moscow was deadening. Everywhere I went—from the Central Market to the villages outside town, from newspaper offices to Kremlin anterooms, where aides sat around dully watching music videos—there was a sense of hopelessness about political life. No more heroes, no great expectations. "The October events" obliterated any shred of triumphalism left from August 1991. The relatively easy verities of the old political struggle—good versus bad, reformers versus tionaries, democrats versus communists—dissolved into a bitter soup of uncertainty.

Even as the papers filled with news of Yeltsin's plans for a new, two-chambered parliament, or Duma, and elections on December 12 to fill it, Russia was no longer deluded (if it ever was) about being a democratic country. Intellectuals and government officials who were once prepared to enjoy the moral clarity of First Amendment absolutists now claimed that a country as unstable as Russia could not afford the luxury of having newspapers that supported armed insurrection. Yeltsin's government ordered fifteen newspapers to suspend publication in punishment for their support of the rebellion; Yeltsin allowed *Pravda* to resume publication only after it agreed to replace its editor in chief. Aleksandr Yakovlev, who was the leading advocate for a free press within the Gorbachev inner circle, told me, "You just cannot compare our situation with that in America, where there is stability. *Pravda* cannot be considered merely an opposition paper when it calls for workers' detachments to come to the White House—that is an open call to arms. There is as much blood on the hands of the editor of *Pravda* as there is on General Makashov's." Eventually, nearly all the papers began publishing again.

Yeltsin's reputation would never fully recover after the October events. The novelist Andrei Sinyavsky, who had been sent to prison under Brezhnev before emigrating to Paris, wrote a scathing article in *Nezavisimaya Gazeta* comparing Yeltsin unfavorably to Gorbachev, saying that Gorbachev had given hope, he had worked through peaceful means, while Yeltsin thrived on confrontation and now blood. "Why am I against Yeltsin?" Sinyavsky wrote. "Because in the clash of two forces there must not be any winners. Both sides should leave the political scene, because the art of government consists in the mastery of compromise and cooperation. Victory for one side is a defeat for democracy, and victory at the cost of so much bloodshed is a crime. . . . The worst thing is that some of my old enemies are beginning to speak the truth, while my own tribe of Russian intellectuals, instead of opposing Yeltsin to help correct his mistakes and his team's mistakes, are welcoming what the great leader does and calling for tough measures. It has all happened before. This is how Soviet power began."

...eksandr Gelman acknowledged the brutality of the ...their ambiguity, but he also invited the readers of ...onsider the alternative outcome: "Imagine if it had gone ...—they took the Kremlin, arrested Yeltsin, Chernomyrdin, ...government. They took over the cabinet, closed democratic ne...ers. Could this really have happened? It could have. This is the main lesson to take away from this. In Germany, the U.S., France, England, Canada, Spain, and Japan, fascists cannot take power today. Here they could have. This we should always preserve in our souls and keep in our minds."

Even at the Kremlin there was no sense of triumph. Narrow escape was more like it. "We were on the verge," Andrei Makarov, a presidential adviser, told me. "We won by accident."

One afternoon I went to visit Leonid Batkin, a historian, whose involvement in the movement toward democracy in Russia was evidently so compelling to the authorities that, beginning in the mid-eighties, the KGB had assembled a five-volume collection of his phone conversations. Batkin had won this peculiar honor for being one of those political-academic heroes of the Gorbachev era, but now, he said, all that was in the past. "That wasn't politics," he said. "That was history."

Like most of the other democracy activists I talked to in Moscow, Batkin was relieved that Yeltsin had prevailed in the October events, but he was convinced that Yeltsin in 1993 was beginning to look like Gorbachev in 1990—erratic, confused, reaching the end of the line as an effective leader.

"For the problems we face, we need a politician with the range of someone like Franklin Roosevelt," Batkin said. "We need someone shrewd, intelligent, imaginative, someone who can change direction. We have no such figure ready on the horizon, because until very recently serious people in this country just did not do politics." Now, Batkin said, it was finally time for Russia to develop a professional class of politicians: the era of revolutionary giants and moral saints was over. "If Andrei Sakharov had lived to the present day, he would not have the same effect he did when he was able to impress the whole country with a speech. The time has come for institutions—real politicians and parties. Politics now is not a matter of saying the unsayable. It is a professional activity, far most of the professionals are still from the old regime."

———

Years later, after he had left the Kremlin, Gennady Burbulis felt himself free enough from the constraints of power to talk about what he called the "phenomenon of Yeltsin and Russian power"—a paradox that had revealed itself most acutely in the October events.

"You cannot comprehend the Yeltsin personality without understanding the constitutional limits he operates in," Burbulis told me one day in 1996. "The paradox of Russia in the 1990s is that the constitution of 1993 was written essentially without any alternatives; it was written in the personal interests of Yeltsin and, like him, it contains both democratic and authoritarian tendencies. This is the reality we deal with.

"Let me put it this way," Burbulis went on. "The tree of power in Russia has two roots: the roots of authoritarianism and of democracy, and this is very much in tune with Yeltsin himself. Yeltsin's entire life, his entire human experience, was that of being an outstanding representative of the administrative side of a totalitarian system. That was his schooling, and he was trained in mobilizing himself for extreme decision making, for an authoritarian style of exercising political power. But at the same time, he is a creative, untamed personality, and in the late eighties he came in contact with the democratic moods of society and he came to be in tune with this. So he began to combine these two traditions, so at once he is forceful, with a powerful urge to simplify complicated things, and yet he is also capable of rebelling against the Communist Party. These roots are present in Russian society and they are at war within Yeltsin; he personifies this strange political garden. It's as if he has two hearts, two motors, two ideas inside him. And so if he is a democrat, it is situational. With Yeltsin there is always the possibility of ruling with an authoritarian hand, of skipping the difficult processes of analysis, of bargaining for consensus. It's that war of urges, of roots, that describes us in transition, and Yeltsin personifies it all."

CHAPTER 3

THE GREAT DICTATOR

The price of October was a sustained period of reaction, a political struggle in which the Yeltsin government could not hope to claim an easy moral superiority. The politics of Russia had now become ambiguous, confused, and while a few lonely democrats longed for the moral authority of the dissidents, a far greater number yearned for an opposite clarity—the absolutes of the Soviet system itself. It may be that any revolution carries with it the risk of reaction, of a longing for the old regime. The events of October had not erased that nostalgia at all; it was only now beginning to form, to take hold as a social impulse, a hardening, radicalized opposition.

Nostalgia was everywhere and took varied shapes. In early 1994, I went to a show at the Manezh exhibition hall, near the Kremlin, of the paintings of Dmitri Nalbandyan, one of the last living specimens of Kremlin artist. (He died in 1995.) A winner of the Lenin Prize and a Hero of Socialist Labor for his portraits of the Soviet leaders, Nalbandyan was one of many lackeys whose great misfortune it was to have lived long enough to witness the indignity of the collapse of the regime and its official aesthetic. The exhibition catalog was without irony, but it seemed to me that at least some of the people who had come to see the paintings were making derisive remarks. But far from all: many people, especially older people, were eager to gaze on the relics of the old regime, the pitifully rendered artifacts that had once decorated the halls of Soviet power. A Russian friend and I walked, half stupefied, past these creations: *The Dance of the Collective Farmers in Armenia; Portrait of Stalin; Lenin, Gorky in 1920; The Sea of Youth.*

A few days later, I went to see Nalbandyan, who had an enormous studio on what was once Gorky Street and was now, in the rush of post-Soviet renaming, Tver' Street. I was greeted at the door by an irascible man of eighty-six, and soon found that his conversation consisted of moments of lucidity often interrupted by angry or sentimental meanderings. I asked him about his sessions with Stalin.

"Stalin didn't like to sit for his portrait painters, but he sat for me," he said. "For forty, forty-five minutes! When Stalin saw what I had done, I was immediately named master of the first rank. In those days, this was a tremendous achievement. They printed millions of copies of my portrait of Stalin. When people came to see Stalin, he would point out the portrait and say, 'It was young Nalbandyan who did this.'

"God knows what's written about Stalin now, but he appealed to me as a man and in his appearance. He had a beautiful face and the eyes of a wise man. You could see how smart he was just by looking at those eyes. Churchill once wrote—I think it was Churchill—that even Roosevelt, a cripple, would stand when Stalin came into the room. Stalin was an iron man. They blame Stalin for everything now, and it's all wrong! People ask me why I painted Stalin so grandly when he had pox and a withered arm. Well, what of it! Was Reagan so beautiful?

"People love me as an artist. I am a realist. Even Picasso was a realist, you know. I visited Picasso in Spain, and he told me that he wasn't really interested in Cubism at all, that it was all a bunch of nonsense for the critics. Picasso told me he was a realist. And he was a Jew, you know. Picasso was a Jew. . . ."

I had not said much, and when Nalbandyan began dispensing his opinions of Jews (negative) and flying saucers (positive) I decided that it was probably time to go.

Still, Nalbandyan was no freak. Once more, extreme nationalist and communist parties were forming, fueled by the failures (real and imagined) of the Yeltsin regime and a firm belief in the verities of the past. The new communist parties, led by former apparatchiks at all levels, formulated a conspiratorial version of recent history that had wide currency among the opposition generally. According to leaders of the failed coup in 1991, the real coup, the undermining of Soviet power, was an intricate plot devised by Gorbachev and Yeltsin with help from "foreign agents" in the West.

"Many people started out believing that the 'democrats' were those people who would be able to improve the standard of living and the existing Soviet power," the former defense minister Dmitri Yazov, who helped lead the coup, told the newspaper *Sovetskaya Rossiya*. "Then it became clear that their secret goal was the restoration of capitalism. From the other side, it is well known that already by 1963, under the leadership of Kennedy, there was a plan worked out to weaken Soviet power from the inside."

Vladimir Kryuchkov, the former KGB chief, hatched a conspiracy theory worthy, in its ingenious specificity, of a cheap Cold War thriller. In an article headlined THE AMBASSADOR OF TROUBLE and published in *Sovetskaya Rossiya,* Kryuchkov wrote that while he was head of the secret police he compiled documentary evidence that Gorbachev's closest, and most liberal, adviser, Aleksandr Yakovlev, had been an "agent of influence" recruited by the Central Intelligence Agency and had been working for Washington ever since he had been an exchange student at Columbia University, in 1958–59. Kryuchkov also claimed that he gave Gorbachev a file on the matter but that Gorbachev repeatedly failed on his promise to look into the issue. "They should put up monuments to Yakovlev at the Pentagon and Langley," Yazov said.

The signs of opposition were clear enough to the Yeltsin regime, but the president, a self-proclaimed populist, was still prone to overconfidence and a dismally inaccurate reading of public opinion. For election night— December 13, 1993—the Kremlin scheduled a nationwide televised joyfest called "Celebrating the Political New Year." The idea was as presumptuous as it was simple: the pro-Yeltsin party, Russia's Choice, led by Yegor Gaidar, would waltz to victory in the parliamentary elections and the main state television station would broadcast an all-night vote-counting celebration live from the Kremlin. The horror of October would fade and, as the Bolsheviks would say, "the shining future" would begin.

Yeltsin himself had stayed aloof from the election campaign for the new parliament, the Duma, but it was clear that he supported not only his new draft constitution, which was on the ballot, but also Russia's Choice. The party hoped to call on the support of the old Democratic Russia movement and also link up with the middle class that had presumably begun to grow at a fantastic rate since 1991. Gaidar wanted to flood the Duma with like-minded deputies and thus provide Yeltsin with the political room to move back onto a reform track. Anyway, that was the scenario.

But Russia's Choice ran, all too smugly, as the party of a class that barely existed. If there was a middle class, it was too small to base an election campaign on. There truly was an emerging middle class in Moscow and St. Petersburg, but, as always, those two cities were exceptions. Nearly all other Russian cities and towns had a few preposterously wealthy people (usually crooked) and a majority population whose most distinct attitude toward the new economics was one of immoderate resentment. And yet, somehow, the Russia's Choice leadership and the nouveau riche bankers and industrialists who supported them thought they could count on the middle class for victory. Their calculations seemed to be based more on the electorate of Germany than of Russia. One particularly memorable television ad for Russia's Choice featured a prosperous family with one child and a dog living in a beautiful new house complete with a bright Western kitchen and furniture. As the parents walked out the door to vote for Gaidar, the little boy turned to his dog and said, "Isn't it too bad that we can't vote, too?"

"Yeah, too bad," one could practically hear Russia muttering to its collective self. The ad was, for most Russians, surreal, insulting.

Gaidar himself had no gift for personal connection. He campaigned as if he were running for the head of the math department. He came across on television as the overfed academic, the cool technocrat. His language was complicated, remote, maddeningly serene. He would arrive at factories and lecture the workers on the intricacies of tax rates, financial stabilization, interest rates. He did not often take questions, and when he did, he answered in language fit for the classroom.

With only a couple of weeks to go in the campaign, the leaders of the Russia's Choice campaign team, who were camped out at a political club at 44 Herzen Street, began to realize the seriousness of their predicament. To their amazement, the radical nationalist Vladimir Zhirinovsky, the loony-like-a-fox political performance artist who had come as if from nowhere in 1991 to finish third in the Russian presidential race, promising free vodka and nuclear blackmail, was moving up in the polls.

Yeltsin's advisers, especially Gennady Burbulis, thought they had a solution to ensure the victory they were expecting all along. Rather than stage a debate with Zhirinovsky and risk a walloping from Russia's slickest populist performer since the revolution, they would show a documentary film. Burbulis, especially, calculated that if only the Russian people would see Zhirinovsky for who he was—a hater, a crank, a nut—well, then, victory would follow. Burbulis arranged to have shown Pavel Chukhrai's antifascist propaganda documentary called *The Hawk*. On the weekend before the balloting, Zhirinovsky was seen on the air in all his glory, drinking and carousing, meeting with people like the Iraqi ambassador and European ultrarightists. The film made sure to point out that Zhirinovsky, a rabid anti-Zionist and anti-Semite, had a Jewish father named Volf Edelshtein. For more than an hour, Zhirinovsky ranted about foreign invaders and called for a "last dash to the south," a Russian *Anschluss* that would push so far south that soldiers from Tambov and Podolsk could finally unwind on the shores of the Mediterranean Sea and the Indian Ocean.

In the last days of the campaign, Zhirinovsky was happy to be as outrageous as possible. The lesson he had learned from 1991 was that the more bizarre his behavior, the more attention he got—and Zhirinovsky was a performer who learned well from constant rehearsal. With just days to go before the vote, Zhirinovsky met with former Swedish ambassador to Moscow Rolf Gauffin, who had come to Moscow to interview him for the geopolitical review *Limes*. Zhirinovsky guided Gauffin to a map of the Russian empire on the wall behind his desk; the empire included Alaska and Finland. Zhirinovsky sketched out his imperial designs on the map: Poland would be divided between Germany and Russia;

Germany would take Austria, the Czech Republic, and Slovenia; Russia would get the Baltic republics; Russia would take back Ukraine and Moldova. All the while, Zhirinovsky was carving up the map using a black marker. This mad tableau had a particular resonance for any Russian with even the slightest historical knowledge: Stalin, pen in hand, dividing up the map of Europe with Hitler.

On the 13th, the Russia's Choice leaders gathered at the Kremlin for an election-night banquet and the television broadcast. Before the first results came in they were confident of victory, confident they had staved off the Zhirinovsky challenge simply by "exposing" him on television. But what had been intended as a festival, an event that would put the disaster of October behind, turned into a horror film. As the votes started to come in—first from the Far East, nine and ten hours ahead on the clock, then from Siberia, then the Urals—the tote boards showed that Zhirinovsky's Liberal Democratic Party (neither liberal nor democratic) was winning by a wide margin. The constitution would win narrowly, but Russia's Choice would, most assuredly, not. Zhirinovsky, a neofascist, had won 23 percent of the vote, leaving the rest of the party leaders (the communists, Russia's Choice, the Agrarians, and several others) to split up the rest. No one else was close.

A sense of despair, of terrible fear, surged through the Russia's Choice delegation at the Kremlin. As the returns came in, Yuri Karyakin, a famous Dostoevsky scholar and a liberal deputy in the old Soviet Congress of People's Deputies, cried out, "Russia, come to your senses! Have you gone mad?"

Not long after his victory became apparent, Zhirinovsky himself came strutting into the Kremlin halls. He wore a tuxedo and carried a bottle of champagne. At one point, Zhirinovsky walked over to Telman Gdlyan, a well-known prosecutor, and said to him, in a mocking voice, "So when will you be appointed head of the Armenian army?" Gdlyan replied bitterly, "When you are appointed head of the Jewish army." With that Zhirinovsky bashed Gdlyan in the ear.

Past midnight and into the morning, some of the leaders of Russia's Choice hung around the Kremlin hoping somehow that the very late returns would tell a different story, that somehow a liberal wave from the western, European cities of Russia would overtake the first results. There was no such wave. The men and women who had counted August 1991 as a fin de siècle triumph and October 1993 as a narrow escape now greeted first light knowing that the age of romance and reform was, for the foreseeable future, dead as dust. The pro-Yeltsin forces had planned to stay on the air all night. When it became clear how the vote was turning out, someone close to Yeltsin ordered an end to the program. Farewell from the Kremlin. Say good night, Boris Nikolayevich.

Few people were under any illusions that by holding nationwide elections Russia had established a mature democracy. And yet the fact of elections had enormous meaning—and bore fantastic risk for a society as unstable as Russia's. Adam Michnik, one of the leaders of the Polish Solidarity movement and a keen observer of Moscow politics, wrote, "Russia stands before a dramatic dilemma, to which no one has yet given a reasonable answer. What is better: to disrupt the rules of democracy and chase out the totalitarian parties while they are still sufficiently weak? Or respect the democratic order and open to these parties the road to power?"

Yeltsin chose elections, but it must also be said that he chose that path with every expectation of winning. There was no great mystery why Russia's Choice, as the party of Yeltsin, had failed so miserably. For the great majority of people, economic reform had so far brought only more pain; Zhirinovsky was able to make the demagogic, but highly effective, point that Yeltsin's reforms had meant that one million people had gotten rich and 150 million people had gotten poorer. Pride in the country was at an all-time low: America, still gloating over its victory in the Cold War, was preeminent, unchallenged in world affairs. The Russian army was weak, yet embroiled in various border conflicts. What was more, Russia's Choice had run a pitiful and arrogant campaign. The democratic camp was badly split, still suffering from its "victory" in October.

But while Gaidar proved he had no popular skills, his analysis of his opponent was acute. "During the election campaign, I said that Zhirinovsky reminded me of Hitler in 1929," he wrote in *Izvestia* in early 1994. "Unfortunately, I was mistaken. Zhirinovsky with his 23 percent of the votes has already surpassed Hitler in 1929 and has achieved the result that the Nazis got in the Reichstag elections of 1930. . . . The person whom I write about today is the most popular fascist leader in Russia. This means that he is the biggest threat to my motherland and my people." If there was a difference between Zhirinovsky and Hitler, he said, it was mainly stylistic: "Hitler was serious in the German manner. Zhirinovsky is the opposite. He tries to make people laugh, knowing it is easier to get at the Russian popular consciousness with laughter."

Zhirinovsky would sue Gaidar for calling him a fascist and win a small monetary judgment. But what was Zhirinovsky if not a fascist? The real question was, why had a quarter of the electorate voted for him?

Foreign travelers, even sympathetic ones, have always treated Russia with a measure of condescension and presumed that Russians, more than anyone else, have always had the dismal leadership they deserved. Bertrand Russell once tried to explain to Lady Ottoline Morrell why he thought the despotism of the Bolsheviks was, sadly, a fitting turn of history. "If you ask yourself how Dostoevsky's characters should be governed, you will understand," Lord Russell said. Russia after the fall of communism was not much more fortunate. Consider, by contrast, the fortunes of America during its era of emergence. The colonies were blessed with the inheritance of English history, law, and political culture, as well as an abundance of Enlightenment thinkers and politicians: Washington, Jefferson, Madison, Adams. The Russians had inherited a legacy of terror, xenophobia, and lawlessness; even the presence of artists as great as Pushkin, Turgenev, or Tolstoy could not erase that historical residue.

Even before Zhirinovsky's victory, it was clear that the opposition to Yeltsin was rooted in one form or another of mythic nostalgia: communist nostalgia for the order of Stalin and the supposedly dependable standard of living under Brezhnev; military nostalgia for the fear that the Soviet arsenal once aroused in the Western enemy; nationalist nostalgia for empire and higher spiritual purpose. It was entirely natural that nostalgia should be such a powerful force of politics in Russia, just as it had been for the Ottoman Turks and the British when they had lost their empires. Empires have never been happily lost, and the mourning that follows is a natural response, a form of aesthetics, and a form of politics. Enoch Powell was driven to fits of poetry over the loss of India, and even today "neo-Ottomanism" is a powerful force in Turkish politics.

For tens of millions of Russians, the story of their country since Gorbachev's advent, in 1985, had been one of unremitting loss and injured pride. What took decades for the citizens of Constantinople and London to absorb struck the Russians in an instant: the empire—Russian greatness—had vanished. That the economy had been dying was obvious to any serious analyst. (Certainly it was obvious to Gorbachev when he launched perestroika in the name of economic modernization.) Less obvious, especially to foreigners, was the Russians' anxiety about their place in the world. The jewels of the empire were lost: the beaches of the Crimea, the vineyards of Moldova, the oil fields of Kazakhstan, the port of Odessa—to say nothing of Prague, Budapest, and Warsaw—had become parts of foreign lands. Russians had to absorb the fact that travel to such places would require a visa and foreign exchange.

Zhirinovsky ran especially well among the groups who suffered most from wounded pride and gained the least from civic and economic reforms. He ran strong among army officers and recruits, policemen, disaffected workers, the unemployed, less educated young people. He succeeded among groups that could not abide Gaidar's intellectualism, among groups that yearned for a sense of identity and pride. He succeeded in the Far East, too, where Yeltsin had done so well in 1991 with a populist campaign. Most of all he ran well among groups that adored his talent for direct talk, something no Russian or Soviet politicians had ever dared provide.

Eduard Limonov, a scandalous novelist who fancied himself a militarist and (for a while) a Zhirinovsky supporter, said the key to the Liberal Democratic victory in the December 1993 elections was language. "It was Zhirinovsky who introduced the language of the street into politics," he said. "After the wooden speech of the party, he spoke with the common man in his own language, and the man in the street liked that." When plain language failed to get the message across, Zhirinovsky yielded the stage to one of his "shadow ministers," Sergei Zharikov, the lead singer and lyricist for the punk band DK.

While Yeltsin barely appeared in public or on television during the campaign, thereby denying Russia's Choice the benefit of its one natural populist, Zhirinovsky went on the air as often as he could. He spoke directly to the anxieties of the Russian majority, the workers and peasants, the elderly and the lumpen young. To American ears, he committed career-ending gaffes in nearly every sentence, threatening Japan with "more Hiroshimas" and the Baltic states with radiation; he vowed to become a dictator and immediately jail a hundred thousand "offenders"; he promised cheap vodka to all and vowed that "under my regime, no Russian woman will be lonely." But his voice was well tuned to Russian ears, or at least millions of them. He appealed to people's wounded pride, their resentment of the new rich and the hectoring, superior West.

"The present reforms are being conducted at your expense," he told the voters on one television broadcast. "The leadership wants you to die as quickly as possible, and you are already doing this. . . . Today I wish mainly to address the older generation and, in particular, the pensioners and veterans, because they are the ones who are suffering the most. Chiefly they have been dealt a great psychological blow—they have the impression that they have lived their lives in vain, that everything has been bad, the Revolution, the war, and everything they have done. Our party takes a different position. We do not blame the older generation for anything. On the contrary, we bow down to you and say to all of you that you have done well. You are leaving us a normal country, a good economy in principle, great cities, fine transport, fine science and culture. You did everything you could and now you have the right to a dignified old age."

Zhirinovsky promised to change the world so profoundly that even the images of wealth and Western ways would disappear. No longer would television tantalize and taunt. "Television will be different," he promised. "We shall ban all commercials. They will be allowed only in newspapers. There will be no sneakers, no chewing gum, no beaches. We have eight months of winter. We need fur coats, not beaches and cool drinks. You will be able to watch good Russian films. Ninety percent of all news on our television channels will be about Russia in the good Russian language. You will be spoken to by Russian broadcasters with good, kind, blue eyes and fair hair."

Instead of "bowing down to the West" in the manner of Yeltsin and his foreign minister, Andrei Kozyrev, Zhirinovsky promised new alliances, new conquests. At his forty-seventh birthday party, for example, he raised his glass to the ultraright German ideologue Gerhard Frey and proposed a toast: "To a German Prussia and a Russian Alaska!" He met, and professed his admiration for, right-wing extremists like Jean-Marie Le Pen of France, Gianfranco Fini of Italy, Jorg Haider of Austria, Radovan Karadzic of the Bosnian Serbs. In 1992 he went to Baghdad and embraced Saddam Hussein, saying, "We have the same enemies as Iraq: America, Israel, and Turkey."

By December 1993, many Russians had grown disgusted with what they saw as the pattern of Western—particularly American—behavior. They saw the West celebrate its victory in the Cold War but withdraw from promises of massive aid or a "Russian Marshall Plan." They saw their own government make agreement after agreement, concession after concession to the West, to disarm, to withdraw, to become, in the end, a weaker state, threatening to no one, respected by no one.

Writing in his magazine, *The Liberal,* Zhirinovsky addressed the problem of America in his customary modest terms:

"I will terrorize them! . . . We are hungry, angry, humiliated, and offended. . . . The American won't fight—he can't. . . . If their two submarines come near Crimea and Murmansk, we'll sic our whole fleet on them. If they destroy our fleet, in the Hudson Bay near New York, then New York will fry."

———

There were some in the Kremlin who, in an attempt to reassure themselves and spin the press, pronounced December's elections a "victory for democracy." After all, elections had taken place, and while Russia's Choice had lost the popularity contest it still had the largest single voting bloc in the two houses of the parliament. What was more, the constitution passed with 58 percent of the vote, and the constitution, based largely on the de Gaulle–era French constitution, left Russia with a political system balanced heavily toward the presidency. Compared to the American system, the parliament had almost no power at all.

But for the more clear-eyed in the democratic camp, Zhirinovsky's strong showing, as well as the formidable presence of the renascent Communist Party and pro-communist factions like the Agrarians, was no reason for celebration. If nothing else, the vote described a level of political fury and strange judgment that would never again allow for any euphoria about rapid democratic development.

Galina Starovoitova, who now found herself thrust out of Yeltsin's circle, saw the rise of Zhirinovsky as the sign of a Russian Weimar scenario. The combination of economic distress and wounded self-esteem was combustible, an invitation to a charismatic authoritarian movement. "One cannot exclude the possibility of a fascist period in Russia," Starovoitova said on the radio station Echo of Moscow. "We can see too many parallels between Russia's current situation and that of Germany after the Versailles Treaty. A great nation is humiliated, and many of its nationals live outside the country's borders. The disintegration of an empire has taken place at a time when many people still have an imperialist outlook. . . . All this is happening at a time of economic crisis."

When the new parliament convened, anyone waiting for a new, more refined and statesmanlike Zhirinovsky was about to be disappointed. He immediately played the rube. At first he campaigned hard to win the speaker's chair. At one point, Anatoly Chubais, a Yeltsin loyalist and the architect of the privatization program, pointed to his watch as if to say the debate had dragged on too long. Zhirinovsky, who had already offered to throw various deputies into psychiatric hospitals, was furious. "You will be doing that in a prison cell to call for your lunch," he barked at Chubais.

The next day, in the Duma cafeteria, Zhirinovsky and his aides tried to cut into the chow line. When one deputy, the businessman Mark Goryachev, protested, Zhirinovsky said that when he won the presidency—an event he now counted as inevitable—he would throw him in jail. At which point, Goryachev punched the president-presumptive in the face.

When the foreign minister, Kozyrev, was asked about Zhirinovsky, he would invariably say that this was not so much a political problem as a medical one. And yet, in the months to come, it would be Zhirinovsky and, moreover, the hard-line nationalism he represented that helped to push Kozyrev into positions that he would once have thought beyond his imagining. The problem was not medical at all.

———

I first encountered Zhirinovsky and his taste for performance at a session of the old Soviet parliament in early 1991. Although he was neither a deputy nor a member of the press and had no particular reason to be in the hall, he somehow managed to gain entry. With his chin jutting Mussolini-style, with his arms tightly folded across his chest (as if held by a straitjacket, I could not help thinking), this odd and angry man stood in the lobby, surrounded by journalists and deputies, unreeling fantastic political scenarios and racist jokes. I could be wrong, but that day was when he first unleashed his "plan" for threatening the Baltic states (by burying radioactive waste along the border and blowing the poisons west with gigantic fans, etc.).

More than two years later, Zhirinovsky's performances were no less emphatic or outrageous. One morning I went to see him at one of his regular appearances at the Sokolniki metro station in Moscow. Zhirinovsky lived in the neighborhood in a typical and dowdy two-room apartment. Surrounded by thuggish guards known as Zhirinovsky's Falcons, he trotted out his old jokes and threats. He ranted about the need for Russia to expand south to the Mediterranean and west into Europe "to form a common border with Germany"; he talked of capturing Iran, Turkey, and Afghanistan; he talked about the American-Zionist conspiracy and the creation of a special weapon to "zap" people's brains. These were the final weeks of the campaign, and it should have been clear to Yeltsin's aides comfortably ensconced at the club at 44 Herzen Street that their candidates were not enjoying the sort of applause and laughter and support that Zhirinovsky was.

At about the same time, Zhirinovsky published his autobiography, *The Last Thrust to the South*. The title was a reference to Zhirinovsky's intention to expand Russia and re-create an empire. ("How I dream of our Russian soldiers washing their boots in the warm waters of the Indian Ocean. The pealing of bells from a Russian Orthodox church on the shores of the Indian Ocean or Mediterranean would proclaim to the peoples of this region peace, prosperity, and calm.") The book was filled with Zhirinovsky's ideology in all its outlandish fervor, but just as important, it provided a description of his life, a Dickensian self-portrait of loneliness, poverty, failure, and self-pity. Zhirinovsky hid nothing (except his Jewishness, of course); in fact, he went out of his way to describe every wound, every slight and humiliation.

"There had been other memoirs in Russia," Zhirinovsky told me, "but mine was the first to talk about a real life. After me, they all wrote memoirs, but mine was the first to relate to the people."

It certainly did not take long for Zhirinovsky to be wounded by life. Zhirinovsky was born in the Kazakh capital of Alma-Ata, and on the day of his birth, the ambulance came too late to pick up his mother. She delivered young Volodya at home. His uncle cut the umbilical cord with a kitchen knife. Zhirinovsky clearly understood himself as an "other," as a Russian among Kazakhs. In fact, he was even more alien than he wanted to admit. His father was Volf Edelshtein, and according to Kazakh records, Zhirinovsky did not change his name from Edelshtein to Zhirinovsky until 1964, when he was eighteen. Later in life, as a public figure, he would answer questions about his parents this way: "My mother was Russian, my father was a lawyer." When asked about his patronymic, Volfovich, Zhirinovsky said it no doubt sounded "strange to Russian ears." But not *that* strange.

"There are many lies about me," Zhirinovsky once told me. "And the first lie is that my father was Jewish."

Zhirinovsky's obsession with his father went beyond ethnicity. Volf Edelshtein died in a car crash before Zhirinovsky was a year old. Zhirinovsky's mother, a high school dropout, was left with Vladimir and five children from a previous marriage. They all lived together in one room of a communal apartment. For the first few years of his life, Zhirinovsky slept on a trunk. "It was a joyless childhood," he wrote.

When he was four, his thirty-eight-year-old mother started sleeping with a twenty-three-year-old student. No one bothered to celebrate Vladimir's birthday until he was twelve. "My clothes were bought at the market, the clothes of dead people," he told *La Stampa*. And then to *Die Zeit* he said, "I was always hungry. I was fed from the cafeteria where my mother worked. The food was awful, of course, it caused gastritis. In the flat there were no children's books, no toys, no papers, no telephone." For a couple of years, when he was growing up, Zhirinovsky was sent to live at a local child-care center. "I was in everyone's way, I was the youngest," he wrote in *The Last Thrust to the South*. He was lonely and deprived. "I remember in school that one girl had a ballpoint pen and I did not. Or I would visit a home where they had hot water but we didn't. If I had lived in good conditions, warm and well fed, maybe I wouldn't have become involved in politics."

At his mother's knee, Zhirinovsky learned to resent the Kazakhs around them; according to her, the Russians did all the work and the

Kazakhs got all the breaks: the best apartments, the best jobs. He deeply resented what he saw as imperial affirmative action. "I grew up in Central Asia," Zhirinovsky wrote. "We considered it Russia, not Central Asia. At first, only Russians lived there. Russians brought in civilization while the Kazakhs were living in mud huts without electricity, without anything, just raising animals, sheep, just like the primitive communities of tribes, where there were no states."

For the potential nationalist voters, passages like that one had an attractive resonance, even if they seemed like bigotry to non-Russians. In the most vulgar way, Zhirinovsky played to the Russian sense of betrayal, the sense that the Russians brought everything from nuclear weapons to decent roads to the lowly Asians and now, in the wake of the 1991 crack-up, the ungrateful Asians had merely expropriated these resources. In his autobiography, he also signaled an emotional affinity for one of the most important of all nationalist issues: the diaspora of over twenty-five million ethnic Russians who suddenly found themselves living outside of Russia in places like Estonia, Latvia, Kazakhstan, Ukraine, and Uzbekistan. The fact that Zhirinovsky, like so many other Russians, is of mixed blood goes unmentioned.

After high school, Zhirinovsky made it out of Alma-Ata by winning admission to the Institute of Oriental Languages in Moscow, where he studied Turkish, French, German, and English. At the university he was perennially angry at the "golden youth," the privileged sons and daughters of Communist Party big shots. While he stayed alone in his dormitory room, surviving on a poverty-level stipend, he imagined his classmates were out every night on an endless bacchanalia. Meanwhile, he was a social and sexual misfit. In a series of passages that combine elements of *David Copperfield, Portnoy's Complaint,* and the Kinsey Report, Zhirinovsky regales the reader with tales of his dismal sexual failures:

"At the time when we were supposed to be falling head over heels in love and going out with girls," he wrote, "I was sitting at home studying. And, later, from the age of twenty to twenty-four, it wasn't the same, something had burned out, I had somehow missed that special early surge of romantic lyricism; there was no one to get me in the right mood, and that, of course, impoverished my soul in some way, and, as a result, I never really fell in love with anyone."

He told of his first potential sexual encounter while lying on the beach of Sochi at the age of seventeen. His request to a girl next to him to remove the lower half of her bikini has gone nowhere:

"But what kind of girl is going to be the first one to take off her panties? I didn't know that I was supposed to do that myself, to help. I was embarrassed as well. So we just lay there, until someone broke in on us. That embarrassment and shyness prevented me from beginning a sexual life at the time that I was ready.

"During those student years I didn't have a single girlfriend. . . . I was to blame for it myself. I was too concerned with social issues, was spending too much time and effort on my studies. . . . Apparently that was my destiny, that I would never really experience any love or friendship. . . . Apparently, it's fate." Zhirinovsky, like Freud in *Civilization and Its Discontents,* seemed to believe that sexual energy could be sublimated into productive work—in his case an ability to "better and more deeply understand the political process in society."

The truth is, no one much liked Vladimir Zhirinovsky. As a young man he showed the same arrogance that would make him world-famous in his forties. In his second year at the institute, for example, he went to the dean with a proposal to reorder the plan of study for the entire country. In 1967, he sent a letter to the Kremlin leadership with plans for reordering the Soviet agricultural system. According to Zhirinovsky's astute biographers, Vladimir Solovyov and Elena Klepikova, "Zhirinovsky was the type of boy described by Dostoevsky: if you gave him a map of the stars overnight, he would return it the next morning with corrections."

It was undoubtedly sometime in college that Zhirinovsky's saga shifted from early Dickens to John le Carré. The institute was known as a place to identify espionage talent. After graduation (celebrated alone in his dorm room, of course, "with no one to share my joy" or champagne), Zhirinovsky traveled to Turkey, where he worked as an interpreter at a joint Turkish-Soviet steelworks (a classic intelligence cover). He was arrested there under suspicion of espionage after he was caught trying to get a peek at a nearby American military base. The arrest was a local scandal, and Zhirinovsky was released from jail and sent home only after some tense negotiations between Ankara and Moscow. Then Zhirinovsky got a job at the Soviet Peace Committee, a notorious KGB cover organization. A pattern was beginning to take shape.

"There it is! Lie Number Two!" Zhirinovsky told me. "No matter what they say, I've never been tied to the KGB! But I wish I had been. It's a glorious organization."

Despite his protests of innocence, former spies like Major General Oleg Kalugin and journalists who specialize in the secret service, like Yevgenia Albats of *Izvestia,* say that Zhirinovsky's career has all the earmarks of Lubyanka sponsorship. "There is no evidence, but he was obviously infiltrated into the system early on," Kalugin has said. "Look, for instance, at when he was a student and was allowed to travel outside the country freely, even though he was single, with no family. His was the first party to emerge after communism. He was received by the former KGB chairman, and his party manifestos were printed in the *Pravda* printing house. It is very difficult to get access to it unless you have support from the Party and its henchmen, the KGB. I believe he has immense support from the old structures."

After taking law courses at night at Moscow State University, Zhirinovsky got a job in 1975 working as a lawyer at Inyurkollegiya, a state-run firm. His job was to track down Soviet citizens who had been left money or property by relatives abroad. Although he was considered reasonably competent at his job, he was also a notorious loudmouth, famous for railing against the local communist organizations and the office bosses. He was forced out after he was accused of improperly accepting a gift—a free vacation—from a client. In 1983, he found a new job working at the Mir publishing house. Once more he attracted notice by pronouncing on politics. He wanted to be the labor representative but failed. A few years later, with Gorbachev now in power, Zhirinovsky also began appearing at political meetings for various organizations: Shalom, a Jewish group, and Pamyat, the most notorious of the early nationalist anti-Semitic groups, to name two. Zhirinovsky claimed that he went wherever the rally was, for the sheer pleasure of meeting and making speeches. And yet it is also known that Shalom and Pamyat both were heavily infiltrated by the KGB.

"All that stuff about me having Jewish blood, about associations with the KGB, all of it is lies," Zhirinovsky told me. "But the one thing that is true is that I spent my early life preparing for open political life. Finally, I got my chance."

In 1988, a time when political activity was expanding beyond the Communist Party and Gorbachev's own imagination, Zhirinovsky met an eccentric composer named Vladimir Bogachev and began attending meetings with a new radical party called Democratic Union. Bogachev recognized in Zhirinovsky a talent for performance and decided they should begin something called the Liberal Democratic Party. This came at a time when the infamous Article 6, which preserved one-party rule for the communists, was under attack. Just a few weeks later—a coincidence Zhirinovsky says now—the Democratic Union held its founding congress. Zhirinovsky was elected chairman. Seven months later, under suspicion of being a KGB operative, he was expelled. Zhirinovsky simply regrouped and formed another party: the Liberal Democratic Party of Russia.

The real story of the LDPR, its founding and funding, is still only vaguely known—though all who believe they know, know for sure. Anatoly Sobchak, then the liberal mayor of St. Petersburg, told reporters that the father of perestroika was to blame. "At a Politburo meeting," said Sobchak, who was never a member of the Politburo, "Gorbachev said something to the effect that 'a multiparty system is looming on the horizon; we have to overtake events. We have to create the first alternative party ourselves, but a party that can be managed.' The then KGB was assigned to find a candidate for the leadership. As usual, it fulfilled the assignment nicely—it found in its active service (there is such a notion!) a man with the rank of captain and a name now widely known. The party's name was conceived at the time—'liberal democratic.' It seemed a real find. Obviously, the word 'liberal' has long been compromised in our country. Two weeks later, the new party was officially registered. It was the first political party in the country to obtain such a status." (To this day, Gorbachev denies he gave any such instructions but allows that the KGB might have worked with Zhirinovsky "on its own.") According to Solovyov and Klepikova's biography, Zhirinovsky also got financial help from various criminal groups, East German communists, and various directors of military industries.

No matter who might have supported Zhirinovsky's party in its initial stages, it was his ability as a performer that made him an instant contender from the margins in the 1991 race for the Russian presidency. His special talent was to describe his own misery and the national misery in a way that was vivid, funny, and sympathetic. On one show, for example, he leaned into the radio microphone and spoke as if into the ear of every Russian:

"I am myself an ordinary citizen, I represent the middle stratum which earns two hundred rubles a month and lives in a two-room apartment. I am just like you, and I understand that these awful prices in commercial and cooperative stores are beyond our means. . . . A few days before my mother died, she said, 'Volodya, there is nothing to remember.' In all her seventy-three years she had not known a single day of joy. . . . I share all of your anxieties: the eternal lines, the shortages . . . constant worry about how to feed your family."

In 1991, Zhirinovsky came in third behind Yeltsin and former Soviet prime minister and Communist Party candidate Nikolai Ryzhkov; he won over six million votes—"as many people as live in Switzerland!" Now, as a leader of parliament and the most visible figure in the nationalist opposition, he was a contender to lead a country of 150 million people and thousands of nuclear weapons.

After the "October events" and the December elections, all the early confidence had been completely sapped from the Yeltsin forces. In conversations I had with four of Yeltsin's aides, all of them admitted that their hopes for a smooth, swift transfer from a communist dictatorship to a free-market democracy were now shattered.

The choice, as they saw it, was stark: behave with the manners of a Western democrat and risk allowing the current anarchy to overwhelm Russia, or else take "decisive measures" and risk smothering Russia's newborn civil society in the cradle. Now the talk was of a transitional regime of "enlightened authoritarianism" or "administrative democracy" or some such hybrid that made no secret of the need for a prolonged concentration of power in the presidency. Yeltsin was known to be drinking more and becoming a creature of a tight circle of antireform aides, but he could still be politician enough to read election results and the national mood they described. In the months to come he would put an end to his easy accommodations with the West; he reinstalled Gaidar, but that would not last long. As time went by, one liberal after another would be fired or would resign; the most trusted aides were hard-line careerists from the old military-industrial complex and the security services like the presidential security chief, Aleksandr Korzhakov.

The signs that the period of Western romanticism was over were obvious to all. Yeltsin backed off from returning at least two of four Kurile Islands to Japan for fear of arousing the hatred of the statists. His unwillingness to get more than minimally involved in Bosnia on the Western side was an outright concession to the nationalists, who favored their Orthodox brethren the Serbs. The general line on foreign policy began to grow more confrontational, less out of genuine conviction than a sense of political need. "More and more I found myself getting overruled on foreign policy questions," Kozyrev told me. "I had gotten this reputation as 'Mr. Da' and they decided it was time to start saying *nyet*."

Even some of the last-remaining young "democrats" in the Kremlin were sounding the national theme. One afternoon, I went to see Sergei Stankevich, a political adviser to Yeltsin whom I had first met when he was running for a seat in the Soviet Congress of People's Deputies, in 1989. In those days, Stankevich established himself as one of the brightest young allies of the democratic opposition. Now he was writing articles in the press in which he quoted Ivan Ilyin and other Russian nationalists from the 1920s and argued that Russia would, after all, carve out a "third way" of development, neither capitalist nor socialist.

Stankevich's office, in the Kremlin, was vast and shadowy. He had grown a paunch, and there were bags under his eyes. I asked him how he looked at the current state of affairs and the deadlock that was the plague of Moscow politics.

"The process of change went through three phases," Stankevich said. "The first began with the rise of Gorbachev, in 1985—a time of liberal communists of the sixties generation, who sought to preserve the old system and modernize it. They wanted to introduce only some elements of democracy—a limited free press called glasnost, and limited free elections, which resulted in the Congress of People's Deputies. They wanted to prolong the life of the system and prevent alienation between the people and the state. Gorbachev accomplished this to a great extent and made his major contribution, but he failed to keep pace with the second wave.

"The second wave began, I'd say, with the elections in 1989, which helped sweep away communist ideology and established a desire for real, not limited, democratic institutions. A real constitution, a real legislature, real elections—these were the new values. The coalition supporting them was built around Yeltsin and Andrei Sakharov, who was in his last year of life, and around the Interregional Group of radical deputies, the Baltic leaders, and so on. The high point of that phase came with the unexpected August coup and its complete collapse—a collapse that led to the eradication of the Communist Party and of the state's total control of the economy. But that victory turned out to be a mixed blessing. We had reached a distant shore long before we thought we ever would.

"The third phase began and we were not really ready. We democrats who had been in opposition were suddenly in power, and in many ways we were not prepared. The main weakness was that the idea of what a 'new Russia' should be had not been considered at all. We had to create at least a minimal consensus on the general future of Russia, and so far we've been unable to do that."

Stankevich made no excuses for the nationalism in his recent articles and speeches. "As politicians, we can't afford to think as we once did—as radicals, as opponents," he said. "We are now in power, and we have to reorganize a gigantic country, of more than a hundred and fifty million people, all with their own views and interests. We must democratically represent the interests of these people—some of whom think as nationalists—and not only the interests of our friends in Washington.

"Of course, there is a nostalgia now for the old Russia or the old Soviet empire. But the attempt to invent a specific model should not be interpreted as a reactionary dream. To the contrary, the idea that we can Westernize Russia in three or four years, that we'll be able to travel from Chicago to St. Petersburg and see no difference, is absolutely absurd. I have nothing against the West or Western goods. I have nothing against good hotels or American breakfasts. And from time to time I'll even visit McDonald's here, because, basically, McDonald's was a first window on Western commercialism for many of our people. But we must differentiate between Russia and the West. The United States and France are different culturally, but they are greatly similar as well. Russia is something else. From the early Middle Ages, Western societies have experienced a steady accretion of rationalism in their psychology and their institutions. There was the Reformation, the Renaissance, the Enlightenment. We had none of this. Look at Holland, the Dutch. This is a highly rational society in which everything is for the most part predictable, orderly, and each person and organization has its own place and behavior. Maybe it is even overrational. But Russia has none of this. Without my getting stereotypical, Russia's psychology is more spontaneous, unpredictable, artistic, more inclined to extremes of endless patience and explosions of license. This doesn't mean there is a Great Wall of China between Russia and the rest of the world. We are closer to Europe than to Asia. But these differences exist. They are not the invention of some romantic journalist. We can still have democracy, elections, a constitution, markets, and the rest, but if we intend to get anywhere we have to recognize our qualities—we have to recognize who we are and where we are starting from."

————

The Kremlin's political sales force worked furiously to emphasize the need for order. "The hand of power cannot be totally weak," Yeltsin's legal adviser Yuri Baturin told me one afternoon at his Kremlin office. "When the use of power was necessary during the October events, it was impossible to use it right away, because the so-called power ministries—defense, security, police—were hesitating. If they had used their force more quickly, the victory would have been accomplished sooner, with less blood." I noticed that on Baturin's desk there was a mountain of reports and one book: Lewis Carroll's *Through the Looking Glass.* When I mentioned the book to him, Baturin smiled and said, "I keep it here as a guide to Russian politics. I find it is very helpful, don't you?" In his spare time, Baturin translated Carroll into Russian, an activity that seemed to me an emblem of post-Soviet Russia as a whole.

Yeltsin's advisers also admitted that in trying to restore some degree of order in Russia there was always a danger of drifting into iron rule. All in the name of establishing democracy, of course. "Like Gorbachev's perestroika, everything now, in the development of democracy, is being guided only from above," said Giorgi Satarov, a key adviser to Yeltsin. "It is very easy to slip into dictatorship. There are no checks. Monopolistic rule is responsible for checking itself, and this self-restriction has to hold somehow before there can be real checks and balances. There can be little steps toward dictatorship, each one seeming small in itself, but the trend can drag us into dictatorship. This can happen. But, insofar as I know the president and his motives, I do not think he has any intention of becoming a dictator."

There were more than enough people who called on Yeltsin to become an unabashed autocrat. A poll published in *Izvestia* showed that three-quarters of all Muscovites welcomed the brief state of emergency that followed the October events and wanted to see it prolonged indefinitely. One of Yeltsin's aides stunned Moscow's media corps with an announcement that the government's job was to define "state ideology" and the reporters' job was to spread it. The late Aleksandr Ivanov, a popular satirist, told the president at a meeting of writers that he really ought to become a strongman, a Russian version of Chile's Augusto Pinochet. "Many people in Russia think they admire Pinochet, but they have no idea why," Leonid Radzikhovsky, a well-known journalist and politician, told me. "All they know is that Pinochet shot a lot of communists, and they would like to shoot communists. But that's all they know."

As Yeltsin tacked toward a more nationalist stance, Zhirinovsky could not conceal his pleasure. "I have shoved him forty-five degrees to the right and I will keep on shoving," he told me.

One night, I took Radzikhovsky to dinner at the plush Italian restaurant in the Kempinski, a new, German-owned hotel across from the Kremlin. Hotel restaurants used to be a unique variety of torture for the foreign visitor—places where you might be told that every dish but one, on a ten-page menu, was unavailable—but the new hotels, like the Kempinski, had become islands of foreign luxury. Radzikhovsky, for his part, looked around suspiciously, as if waiting to be thrown out. Then he settled down a bit and, as he plowed through a plate of roast beef and then one of tiramisù, he described the shift in post-1993 politics.

"I was at one of the congresses for a new bloc, Russia's Choice, and I was one of those writing the platform," he said. "It was all about order and combating crime. Two years ago, we would have been writing only about the necessity of freedom and democracy. But who is a democrat and who is not is unclear. It was the rebels inside the White House in October who were describing themselves as 'defenders of the constitution' and 'defenders of democracy.' Yeltsin is no democrat, but he's not going to establish authoritarian rule, either. And I'm not a democrat, because I have no clear idea of what it means. I don't like fascism, that's true, but how would I, a Russian, have a clear idea of what democracy means?"

Before paying the check (enough for a good used car, I thought to myself), I asked Radzikhovsky if his circle of political friends had given themselves a name. Yes, he said. The circle was called Demskitz—Democratic Schizophrenics.

Even if Yeltsin had been inclined to become the leader of a full-scale authoritarian regime he would probably not be able to manage it. Although some of his advisers pointed to South Korea and parts of Latin America as places that built potential democracies under authoritarian rule, the analogy fell flat before Russian realities. Despite the military's decisive role in October, the army showed no signs of a Latin American–style ambition for juntadom; the generals preferred winning higher wages and other social guarantees to taking the upper hand in politics. Nor could Russia rely on an Asian work ethic or on Asian efficiency, to say nothing of a tradition of democratic political culture—a feature of life in Chile before Pinochet. Russia had to build a state with Russians.

The truth was that Yeltsin, or any potential successor, had the nearly impossible task of trying to build a modern state in conditions of almost complete social and economic anarchy. Aleksandr Rutskoi and Ruslan Khasbulatov, the leaders of the anti-Yeltsin uprising in October, were released thanks to an amnesty granted by the Zhirinovsky-led Duma in February; theirs was not likely to be the last episode of rebellion or violence. Even those who accepted—or, at least, were resigned to— Yeltsin's notion of transition understood that the anger and disillusion throughout Russian society was growing ever worse. The dulling realities of Soviet society—equality in poverty, stability born of repression—had come unwound, and now Russia was an unfamiliar, bewildering scene of radical polarization. The fondest wish of the Russian reformers in 1991 had been that out of economic change would emerge a large middle class and a business elite, which would become the main constituencies for further change. As the December elections proved, that had not yet happened.

Instead, Russians watched with fury and envy as a small percentage of people grew rich in an environment of almost general chaos and criminality. Capitalism in Russia had produced far more Al Capones than Henry Fords, more Luca Brasis than Ward Cleavers. In fact, the economy hardly merited the name of capitalism at all, since it operated largely outside the framework of law.

Russia had bred a world-class mafia. Next to the collapse of communism, American prohibition was nothing. This new world was a boon for the mafia. According to Luciano Violante, the chairman of Italy's parliamentary committee of inquiry into the Mafia, Russia was now "a kind of strategic capital of organized crime from where all the major operations are launched." He said that Russian mob leaders had held summit meetings with the three main Italian crime organizations, from Sicily, Calabria, and Naples, to discuss drug-money laundering, the narcotics trade, and even the sale of nuclear material. Russia, he added, "has become a warehouse and clearinghouse for the drug market."

The new Russian mobsters became involved in everything from arms sales to banking and learned to work with former officials in the highest ranks of the Communist Party and the KGB as well as with mob bosses abroad. There was little doubt that the ministries of Yeltsin's government—especially in areas like foreign trade, customs, tax collection, and law enforcement—were also thoroughly corrupt. My wife and I were invited to a White House state dinner for Yeltsin in 1994, and my wife was seated near one of Yeltsin's top ministers; quite fairly, she wondered how a Russian politician, making $12,000 a year or so, could afford diamond cuff links. So many of the "democrats" became corrupt because they just could not resist temptation. Under Soviet rule, there were fewer temptations; moreover, the regulator was external and strong, even brutal. When the rules of the game changed, it turned out that the moral regulators within the individual had atrophied; when the external regulator was gone, all hell broke loose. And no one had more opportunities for greed than politicians. The state was still in control of every goody imaginable: licenses, natural resources, construction, and, not least, the biggest property redistribution in the history of the world. According to Yuri Boldyrev, who was briefly the government's chief investigator into corruption, the decay in state and public institutions now "goes beyond the limits of the imagination." For his troubles, Boldyrev was soon forced out of office.

A ten-page report drafted by police and security ministries and submitted to Yeltsin in 1993 described how senior military officers who were based for years in the former East Germany have been involved in huge embezzlement schemes. The officers set up their own companies to buy food and liquor, transported as military supplies, and then sold them on the free market in Poland and Russia. Sales were estimated at a hundred million Deutsche marks—$58 million. In another case, Air Force Major General Vladimir Rodionov and his deputy Colonel Georgi Iskrov were charged with using military aircraft for commercial flights and keeping the proceeds—a case that was not especially spectacular, but completely typical.

Yeltsin could not deny what was before everyone's eyes. He admitted in a speech to the heads of the central and regional law enforcement agencies that two-thirds of all commercial and financial enterprises in Russia—and 40 percent of the individual businessmen—were engaged in some form of corruption. He added that in 1992, $2 billion had simply "disappeared" from the budget of the Ministry of Foreign Economic Relations. Even the anti-mafia investigators in Moscow were suspect. In October of 1992, an Interior Ministry chief was arrested for taking a bribe. A subsequent search of his home found nearly $500,000 in cash in his house.

Law enforcement, too, was a bitter joke. Mobsters often had more troops and more powerful weapons than the police. Army officers and recruits, desperate for cash, were only too glad to sell guns, rocket launchers, and grenades to the highest bidder. And at a time when nearly everyone was impoverished—including police, jailers, and judges—the likelihood of successful prosecution was minuscule. Vladimir Rushailo, the chief of Moscow's organized crime unit, said, "Even if we manage to jail an influential member of the mafia, his fellow bandits immediately unleash a campaign pressuring victims, witnesses, judges, public assessors. And they do this quite freely. Clearly, the criminals are much more inventive than the lawmakers."

The level of unashamed corruption in the presumably "democratic" government and the lack of Russian identity for the state and its people were the most dispiriting themes in post-1991 Russia, and they helped make Zhirinovsky possible. Zhirinovsky could point at the Kremlin and, with great success, say that the path of pro-Western policy was the path of criminality and humiliation. It was time, he said, to establish Russian greatness, Russian values.

The conflict between a Westernizing and a nationalist impulse had deep historical roots and played on emotional urges deep inside nearly every Russian. Some Russian thinkers, like Herzen, understood that the typical Russian is both attracted and repelled by Europe and the idea of Europe; a push and pull in his self-consciousness is a critical component in the Russian national character. In his essay on Russia in the 1840s, Isaiah Berlin describes the phenomenon as a combination inferiority and superiority complex:

> To some degree this peculiar amalgam of love and hate is still intrinsic to Russian feelings about Europe: on the one hand, intellectual respect, envy, admiration, desire to emulate and excel; on the other, emotional hostility, suspicion, and contempt, a sense of being clumsy, de trop, of being outsiders; leading, as a result, to an alternation between excessive self-prostration before, and aggressive flouting of, western values. No visitor to the Soviet Union can have failed to remark something of this phenomenon: a combination of intellectual inadequacy and emotional superiority, a sense of the west as admirably self-restrained, clever, efficient, and successful: but also as being cramped, cold, mean, calculating, fenced in, without capacity for large views or generous emotion, for feeling which must, at times, rise too high and overflow its banks, for heedless self-abandonment in response to some unique historical challenge, and consequently condemned never to know a rich flowering life.

This conflict played on every Russian's relationship to history, the way he understood events as distant as the Tatar invasion, the imperial expansion, the advent of Peter the Great, the intellectual debates of the mid-nineteenth century; it is a debate played out in the texts of Dostoevsky and Turgenev, Herzen and Belinsky, Solzhenitsyn and Sakharov.

In Zhirinovsky's vulgar rhetoric, one could hear the echoes of a distinct Russian sense of pride, and injury, the notion that had it not been for Russia's defense against one foreign invader after another—Napoleon's armies, the Nazis—Europe would not exist. There was also the notion of the Russian empire as a bulwark against further invasions. After the fall of Constantinople in 1453, Moscow became the center of Orthodoxy, the "third Rome," and in the four centuries to follow, the empire expanded at a rate of fifty square miles a day: the Urals, Siberia, the Baltic lands, the Crimea, Catherine the Great's westward expansion into Poland, Belarus, and Lithuania, the nineteenth-century move into Finland, Georgia, Azerbaijan, Daghestan, Armenia, Bessarabia, Moldova, Central Asia.

During the perestroika years, Gorbachev's admirers, at home and in the West, would compare him to Peter the Great, for just as Peter opened up Russia to the West and sent his elite abroad to educate themselves as Europeans, Gorbachev ended a long, dark period of xenophobia and confrontation with the West. But less well known in the West was that there were hundreds of Russian intellectuals in the perestroika period who feared and loathed the West. Zhirinovsky would be their farcical but very real embodiment; their sense of injury went back to the nineteenth-century historian Nikolai Karamzin and his rejection of Peter's ultra-modernism. In the late eighties and early nineties, nationalist-oriented booksellers on the streets of Moscow almost always had Karamzin's works available. His rhetoric seemed almost contemporary:

Imitation became for Russians a matter of honor and pride. . . . it must be admitted that what we gained in social virtues we lost in civic virtues. Does the name of a Russian carry for us today the same inscrutable force which it had in the past? No wonder. In the reigns of Michael and his son, our ancestors, while assimilating many advantages which were to be found in foreign customs, never lost the conviction that an orthodox Russian was the most perfect citizen and Holy Rus' the foremost state in the world. Let this be called a delusion, yet how much it did to strengthen patriotism and the moral fiber of the country! Could we have today the audacity, after having spent a century in the school of foreigners, to boast of civic pride? Once upon a time we used to call all other Europeans infidels; now we call them brothers. For whom was it easier to conquer Russia—for infidels or for brothers? Whom was she likely to resist better? . . . We became citizens of the world but ceased in certain respects to be citizens of Russia. The fault is Peter's.

Karamzin wrote that Russia had been a great state for a thousand years and yet "we are constantly told of new institutions and new laws as if we had just emerged from the dark American forests."

With its peculiar combination of xenophobia and expansionism, the rhetoric of Karamzin's *Memoir on Ancient and Modern Russia* was like a refined and intellectual version of *The Last Thrust to the South*. When Zhirinovsky talked about the need to reign supreme among the Muslims and Asians, it evoked, in a vulgar way at least, Dostoevsky's famous Slavophilic line "In Europe we were hangers-on and slaves, whereas we shall go to Asia as masters." Westernizers, Dostoevsky said, were "destroyers of Russia, enemies of Russia"; "a Russian who has become a genuine European cannot help but become at the same time a national enemy of Russia."

Zhirinovsky's rhetoric of rebuke was only a grotesque version of the worldview of the nineteenth-century Slavophiles. ("We must pacify the south so that there are vacation centers, camps, sanatoria and preventive treatment centers there on the shores of the Indian Ocean and the Mediterranean Sea.") Grotesque, but symptomatic. Zhirinovsky was far from alone. Most people understood that the pain Russians were now enduring—the economic collapse, the political deadlock, the ecological time bombs—was for the most part the legacy, the falling bricks, of a toppled regime that held its subjects in contempt and regarded the ways of the outside world with total suspicion. Even under the best of circumstances, the job of moving Russia into the modern world, of bringing some stability to its economy and creating a normal political system, will take many years. Many people, especially those with a memory and an education, knew that. And yet the leaders of the growing alliance of former Communist Party chieftains and Great Russian nationalists were able to heap the blame on those who did the most to bring down the Bolshevik regime. In Moscow, one had only to leaf through a stack of newspapers and journals to hear the voices of post-imperial fury and nostalgia in full throat.

"We have destroyed all our foundations of human morals, we have destroyed Great Russia," Boris Govorin, a top government official in the Siberian city of Irkutsk, told the newspaper *Russki Vostok* ("Russian East"). In the rhetoric of the Red-Brown—that is, communist-nationalist—opposition, Russia was an occupied country controlled by a "treasonous" government that took its orders from the White House, the World Bank, and the International Monetary Fund. For some, the list extended to "the Judeo-Masonic conspiracy."

"What is happening now is an extension of the old feeling about the rest of the world that 'they may not love us but they fear us,' " Sergei Kovalyov, Sakharov's protégé, told me. "But now we are not terribly feared. We are a Third World country, and everyone knows it. And this knowledge brings on terrible psychological pain, not merely because of the poverty involved but also as a matter of pride. Suddenly, Russians have to see where they really stand in the world. And it is awful, and so they try to imagine a great past and make of it a new politics."

————

And yet the national question was not just one for extremists and kooks. The question of identity—What is a Russian?—touched everyone, including the most committed liberals and former liberals. Russia was groping for identity in foreign policy, in its spiritual life, in its history, its symbols and holidays. This was a country in which there was no national agreement on whether the defeat of the coup in 1991 was a good thing or a bad thing, or whether the Revolution of 1917 was a good thing or a bad thing; this was a country in which millions of people still celebrated the old Soviet holidays (May Day, Revolution Day) and nearly everyone was oblivious to the fact that the Yeltsin government had declared a holiday for the passage of the new constitution. Who exactly was a Russian? Did Russian mean being a citizen of the Russian Federation, or was it a matter of blood? Was a Jew Russian? A Chechen? A Yakut? What about Russians living abroad—in Ukraine, Estonia, or Kazakhstan?

Like most Westerners and reporters, most of my friends were educated Muscovites, urbanites who had benefited greatly from the political and economic reforms of the Gorbachev and Yeltsin years: they traveled, they earned money, they read what they wanted, wrote what they wanted. They would never have dreamed of voting for a communist or a nationalist, much less Zhirinovsky. But as time went by, even these Western-oriented liberals could not bear the lack of Russian identity. For years they wanted access to Western pop culture and Western goods, but now that they had those things they felt a little ashamed, humiliated. Where were the decent Russian movies or Russian clothes, what did Russia produce? What was this country they had longed for?

My friend Sergei Ivanov, a Byzantine scholar who taught at Moscow State University, said that he did not regard Russia with the same sense of opposition and alienation with which he regarded the Soviet Union. Where once he had rooted for the Czechs to beat the Soviets in hockey as a kind of small retribution for the invasion of 1968, all that had changed. "One used to oppose the state because it was opposed to the interests of the individual," he said. "Now, why oppose the state? I used to root for Washington against Moscow in the realm of politics. But for all my reservations about Yeltsin, I cannot do that now. I am what you would call a liberal democrat but I am against the eastern expansion of NATO. I am angry with Estonia's treatment of ethnic Russians—and this is after we all adored Estonia for opposing the Soviet Union. I am concerned about Russian speakers in 'Ukrainian' Crimea. I wonder why Russia was not invited to the celebration of Normandy. I wonder why the U.S. is so crazy about Russia selling a nuclear reactor to Iran when the U.S. is so eager to trade with awful states, China included. Why hasn't the Jackson-Vanick amendment been repealed? Why does Freedom House grade the Balts higher than Russia on the human rights scale?"

As a historian, Sergei also made it clear that the leaders of Russia had not thought through what exactly they were building, what they were in charge of, what they had inherited.

"I am no imperialist, but one has to admit that Russia has always been an empire," he said. "It was never a nation-state. Ivan the Terrible married a Circassian woman. Princes of Russia boasted of their Varengian, not Slavic, blood. Russianness is a matter of belonging to an empire. Russianness has no real role models or heroes. Peter the Great splits the population. He is a symbol for Russia's Choice, but not for someone like Solzhenitsyn. Maybe you could say Pushkin is alone in this. He is a hero to everyone. But there are also no shared values. We have no national holidays. What is Independence Day? No one remembers when it is. We still have the 7th of November off from work, as if we're celebrating a revolution we all agree was a total disaster.

"This is all a question of narrative. We have not agreed upon a national narrative. No one can write a textbook for schools. It's a postmodern situation: we mock all attempts to create a Russian narrative. The French can say, *Vive la République! Vive la France!* How long will Russia have to wait before we can say such things without complexes?"

CHAPTER 4

THE EXILE

On June 23, 1992, Yeltsin signed a presidential decree: "On the Removal of Restrictive Classifications on Legislative and Other Acts That Served as the Basis for Mass Persecutions and Violations of Human Rights." That act brought Aleksandr Solzhenitsyn's enormous secret file (or at least part of it) into the public domain. It revealed the actual voices of the Politburo, their paranoia and stupidity, Yuri Andropov's eagerness, as the head of the KGB, to get rid of the "hooligan" in his midst, and Leonid Brezhnev's constant wavering as general secretary, his desire to have the problem disappear without international repercussions.

The documents are a window on the remarkable attention the Kremlin leaders paid to one man; no one knew better than they did just how potentially damaging literature could be to their hold on power. While the world talked of a stable and monolithic superpower, Solzhenitsyn, solitary and possessed of an almost inhuman courage, wrote of the regime's wretched history and its inherent instability. In these documents, the leaders are overheard struggling with the problem of what to do with Solzhenitsyn: Can he be seduced? Silenced? Can we win with propaganda or must he be imprisoned?

One of the earliest documents in the collection, a wiretap of Solzhenitsyn's apartment in 1965, is among the most revealing. At a time when the height of dissent would have been a call for a reformed socialism (the Prague Spring had not even taken place yet), Solzhenitsyn goes on, in his table talk, about the "serpent" Lenin, "a man totally without principles." More than thirty years ahead of his time, he seems clairvoyant as he talks about the Soviet regime, its detachment, its precarious grip on power: "This is a government without prospects. They have no conveyor belts connecting them to ideology, or the masses, or the economy, or foreign policy, or to the world communist movement—nothing. The levers to all the conveyor belts have broken down and don't function. They can decide all they want sitting at their desks. Yet it's clear at once that it's not working. You see? Honestly, I have that impression. They're paralyzed."

And not only that. Solzhenitsyn, supposedly an ardent Russian nationalist loath to give up an inch of imperial territory, goes on at length about the inevitable and rightful crack-up of the Soviet Union:

"I'm amazed that liberal Russian people don't understand that we have to separate from the republics; they don't understand that we have to face this. . . . Liberal people. I tell them it's all over for the Ukraine, it has to go. . . . And how could there be any question about the Caucasus, the Baltics! On the very first day, if you want—whoever wants to leave, for God's sake, do so!"

Solzhenitsyn proved utterly fearless. While working on literary projects that could easily have brought on a penalty of death, he openly taunted the regime for daring to harass him. Here he is in 1971 writing a letter to Andropov expressing outrage at the way his dacha has been searched:

For many years I have borne in silence the lawlessness of your employees: the inspection of all my correspondence, the confiscation of half of it, the tracking down of my correspondents . . . the spying around my house, the shadowing of visitors, the tapping of telephone conversations, the drilling of holes in ceilings, the placing of recording equipment in my city apartment and my country cottage, and a persistent slander campaign against me from the platforms of lecture halls when they are put at the disposal of officials from your ministry. But after your raid yesterday I will no longer be silent.

The Politburo could no longer tolerate such a man. On the morning of January 7, 1974, the leadership of the Communist Party of the Soviet Union convened to draw up battle plans against a grave threat to communist ideology and power—a writer and his manuscript. Leonid Ilyich Brezhnev, the general secretary of the Party, sat at the head of the conference table and opened the meeting. "Comrades," he began, "according to our sources abroad and the foreign press, Aleksandr Solzhenitsyn has published a new work in France and in the U.S.—*The Gulag Archipelago.*"

By now Brezhnev's health was beginning to fail. He worked only four or five hours a day, his burden lightened by frequent naps, massages, saunas, snacks, and round-the-clock attention from his doctors. His speech was slow, slurred. "I am told by Comrade Suslov," Brezhnev went on, "that the Secretariat has taken a decision to develop in our press a debunking operation against this work by Solzhenitsyn and its appearance in bourgeois propaganda. No one has had a chance to read the book, but its essential contents are already known. It is a filthy anti-Soviet slander. We have to determine what to do about Solzhenitsyn. By law we have every basis to put him in jail. He has tried to undermine all our ideals: Lenin, the Soviet system, Soviet power, everything dear to us. This hooligan, Solzhenitsyn, is out of control."

Andropov, the chief of the KGB at the time, and a future successor to the Party throne, did not wait long before offering his recommendation. He was, by far, the most intelligent of the Politburo members and it is plain from reading the minutes of the Politburo session that Andropov's was the decisive voice. He, more than anyone else, understood the threat Solzhenitsyn's work posed to the regime. When Nikita Khrushchev approved publication of Solzhenitsyn's *One Day in the Life of Ivan Denisovich* in 1962 as a way of discrediting the Stalin era, a great cultural thaw began, one that so unnerved the communist leadership that they eventually called it off, banned Solzhenitsyn from print, and, in 1964, "retired" Khrushchev "for reasons of health." But Solzhenitsyn's literary mission, the process of giving voice to the tens of millions of victims of Soviet terror, went on secretly, even collectively. Much of *Gulag* was based on the

hundreds of letters and memoirs that former prisoners mailed to Solzhenitsyn after *One Day* was published. Andropov had an intuitive sense that
this new work could do as much, in its way, to undermine Soviet power
as all the nuclear arsenals in the West.

"I think Solzhenitsyn should be deported from the country without his
consent," Andropov says, according to the Politburo minutes. "Trotsky
was deported in his time without getting his agreement. . . . His *Gulag
Archipelago* is not a work of literature—it is a political document. This is
dangerous. Everyone is watching us to see what we will do with Solzhenitsyn, if we will mete out punishment to him, or if we will just leave him
alone. I maintain that we must take legal action and bring the full force of
Soviet law against him."

At this there is a full-throated chorus of "*Da!*"

Andropov fuels the already evident anger of the other members with
terse descriptions of Solzhenitsyn's "impudence," his meetings with foreign correspondents, his brazen flouting of Party control over literature
and publication abroad. (The manuscripts of *Gulag* and other works were
microfilmed by the Solzhenitsyns in Moscow and smuggled by their
friends and contacts to publishers in the West.)

Nikolai Podgorny, the president of the presidium, is furious, indignant
at the prospect of a righteous response abroad to any suppression of Solzhenitsyn. "In China there are public executions!" he says in complaint.
"In Chile the fascist regime shoots and tortures people! In Ireland the English use repression on the working people! We must deal with an enemy
who gets away with slinging mud on everybody."

"We can send Solzhenitsyn away to Verkhoyansk to serve his sentence
up beyond the Arctic Circle," says Aleksei Kosygin, the Soviet premier
and a "liberal" in the eyes of many foreign analysts. "Not a single foreign
correspondent will go visit him there, because it's so cold!"

No matter what we do, Brezhnev says, the Solzhenitsyn affair will pass.
The regime is unshakable. "In our time we did not worry about acting
against the counterrevolution in Czechoslovakia," in 1968, he says. "We
did not worry about throwing out Alliluyeva"—Stalin's rebellious daughter, Svetlana. "We survived it all. And I think we'll live through this. . . ."

As the general secretary droned on, the object of the Politburo's fury
was at work, writing in a small extra room of a friend's dacha in the vil-

lage of Peredelkino, about a half hour's drive from the center of Moscow. As he had since his prison days, Solzhenitsyn wrote in a tiny scrawl and in small notebooks, the better to conceal his notes and manuscripts in case of a search. After a day's work, he would go to the garden of the dacha and burn his extra drafts.

Solzhenitsyn had always been an avid listener to foreign radio stations on shortwave, and when he heard the news that *Gulag* had been published abroad, he allowed himself just a moment's satisfaction and then went back to his writing table. Remarkably, he was able to shut out the world —the world of the Politburo, of denunciations, of censorship—and worked fourteen to sixteen hours a day. While his wife and three young sons stayed at their apartment in downtown Moscow, Solzhenitsyn was spending six days a week in Peredelkino as a guest of the family's close friend Lydia Chukovskaya, the author of a short novel about Stalin's purges, *The Deserted House*. In Peredelkino, the light was better, there were no children, no phone calls, to distract him.

"Aleksandr Isayevich slept and worked in an extra room and kept a pitchfork near his bed, as if that would protect him against an attack," Chukovskaya told me many years later at her apartment in Moscow. She recalled how solicitous he was of her, how reluctant he was to bother her in her own work. Sometimes Chukovskaya would wander into the kitchen and find a note taped to the refrigerator door: "If you are free by nine, let's listen to the radio together." Sometimes Solzhenitsyn would go outside for a walk, but never through the village. Instead he paced back and forth across the dacha's small garden. When Chukovskaya asked him if he ever grew bored wearing the same tracks in the turf, he said, "No, I got used to it in jail."

"Wherever Solzhenitsyn happened to dwell and wherever fate cast him, he never for a moment ceased to be the absolute master of his own life," Chukovskaya once wrote. His working schedule was broken down not by the hour, but by the minute. "A long chat (except about work, or the creative process) would have been relaxation, idleness—and Solzhenitsyn and idleness are two quite incompatible things. It was as if, at a certain moment (I do not know why or when), he had sentenced himself to imprisonment in some strict regime camp, and was now rigidly enforcing that

regime. He was convict and guard rolled into one, and his own surveillance of himself was, perhaps, more relentless than that of the KGB."

Not only was *Gulag* now out in the West, it was also being read in Russian over Radio Liberty, ensuring even greater outrage in the Kremlin.
But despite the sensation, Solzhenitsyn did not sense quite how precarious his, and his family's, situation had become. He was not completely
naive: on New Year's Day 1974 he had drawn up a list of possible reprisals
the regime might take against him, a list that included imprisonment, internal exile, and even murder, but he thought a press campaign and petty
harassment the most likely punishment. He had no idea that the Party
was now choosing among the most draconian options.

On January 14, *Pravda* printed a long commentary, "The Path of a Traitor," that denounced Solzhenitsyn as anti-Soviet, pro-Nazi, a "defector to
the camp of the enemies of peace," and a decadent tool of the West who
owned "three cars and retained a Swiss lawyer." After that classic piece of
disinformation ran, abusive phone calls began to plague Natalia Solzhenitsyn in Moscow and her husband in Peredelkino. "We won't leave that son
of a bitch above ground much longer," one caller said. Others threatened
to poison the writer's food, harm his children, or kill him. But Solzhenitsyn somehow thought this would be the end of it, that he would go on
writing and living in Russia. On February 7, he wrote in his diary, "Fore-
cast for February: apart from attempts to discredit me, they aren't likely
to do anything, and there will probably be breathing space."

On that same day, Andropov sent a top-priority memo to Brezhnev
saying that the West German chancellor, Willy Brandt, was willing to accept Solzhenitsyn as an exile. They had to act quickly before Brandt
changed his mind or Solzhenitsyn got wind of the plan, Andropov advised. "There will be costs," he added, "but unfortunately we have no alternative. The unlawful acts Solzhenitsyn has already committed have
inflicted on us costs more profound that those which will come up
abroad in the case of expulsion or arrest." Andropov began mapping out
a minute-by-minute plan to arrest Solzhenitsyn and hustle him out of the
country before he or his family had a chance to react.

On February 12, 1974, in late afternoon, Solzhenitsyn was arrested at
home and locked in a cell at the Lefortovo Prison in Moscow.

The next day, Solzhenitsyn was charged with treason and stripped of his citizenship. KGB guards shuttled him to Sheremetyevo Airport and put him in an otherwise empty forward cabin of an Aeroflot jet bound for Frankfurt. The plane had been delayed on the ground for three hours in Moscow, the passengers were told, because of "the fog."

For eighteen years, between 1976 and 1994, a sign had hung outside the Cavendish General Store in southern Vermont:

NO DIRECTIONS TO
THE SOLZHENITSYNS

Ever since the family moved from Zurich to Vermont, in the summer of 1976, the residents of Cavendish—all 1,355 of them—were vigilant in protecting the privacy of their Nobel Prize winner. When the state's Republican congressman, James Jeffords, came to visit, he had to explain at length his station in Washington before anyone would help him find the Solzhenitsyn house.

In late 1993, not long after the October events and Zhirinovsky's triumph in the December elections, the Solzhenitsyns invited me to their house in Cavendish. They had decided, at last, to return to Moscow the following spring. The day before I was supposed to come up to the house, I wandered around the village where the Solzhenitsyns had lived for so long in isolation. The people in town seemed only amused that they were about to lose their celebrity resident. "They say the family is moving back to Russia come May," the counterman at the general store told me. "I'm thinking of taking down the sign and seeing what it'll get at Sotheby's."

Cavendish was in a deep freeze when I arrived in town. The bed-and-breakfast places in the area were filling up, mostly with skiers heading to the slopes in Ludlow, the next town to the west. That evening I ate dinner at a local restaurant, a professional football game blaring on screens in every corner. As I watched John Madden work the telestrator, it seemed odd that just a couple of miles away Solzhenitsyn was in his workroom, writing. Certainly it was not strange that a writer lived here—after all, what better place than Cavendish to fulfill a writer's fantasy of escape and quiet?—but this was Solzhenitsyn, a survivor of the camps, who knew nothing of John Madden, or Beavis and Butthead, or *Private Parts,* who spoke little English and couldn't care less. It haunted me to know that just up the road, in the hills, was the man who wrote this sentence (in *Gulag*) about the inability of the comfortable to imagine the capacities of evil:

If the intellectuals in the plays of Chekhov who spent all their time guessing what would happen in twenty, thirty, or forty years had been told that in forty years interrogation by torture would be practiced in Russia; that prisoners would have their skulls squeezed within iron rings; that a human being would be lowered into an acid bath; that they would be trussed up naked to be bitten by ants and bedbugs; that a ramrod heated over a primus stove would be thrust up their anal canal (the "secret brand"); that a man's genitals would be slowly crushed beneath the toe of a jackboot; and that, in the luckiest possible circumstances, prisoners would be tortured by being kept from sleeping for a week, by thirst, and by being beaten to a bloody pulp, not one of Chekhov's plays would have gotten to its end because all the heroes would have gone off to insane asylums.

Solzhenitsyn's exile in America remained, to the last, an astonishment. Living in what must be the most serene state in the union was a Russian whose destiny was singular, and, at the same time, nearly identical to Russia's. Born in 1918, just one year after the revolution, Solzhenitsyn was a captain on the East Prussian front during World War II, and survived; he was arrested in 1945, for making jokes in letters to a friend about Stalin, "the man with the mustache," and was then sentenced to a total of eight years in the gulag, a prisoners' research center, and "perpetual" internal exile in Kazakhstan—and survived; while he was still in Kazakhstan, he survived a case of stomach cancer that doctors assured him was terminal; and, despite the best efforts of the Politburo, he not only survived his battle with Soviet power, he prevailed. Now, after twenty years in exile, he was returning home. Solzhenitsyn would die in Russia, not a pariah but a free man. Was it too much of an embarrassment in the age of irony to think that his homecoming was somehow biblical?

The next morning, I steered off the main street in Cavendish and headed up Windy Hill Road and past the power lines, past a graveyard, past the trailers and the rotting tractors and the handsome vacation houses, to the fence around Solzhenitsyn's property, his mythic barrier against the world. In Russia, and even in the West, the legend was that the fence was huge, forbidding, even electrified, as if it guarded a prison camp. When he first moved to Cavendish, the *Washington Post* headline was "Solzhenitsyn's Barbed-Wire Freedom." The fence turned out to be nothing much, a flimsy chain-link job. Any self-respecting rabbit could have dealt with it. After moving in, Solzhenitsyn came to a town meeting and apologized to his neighbors for getting in the way of snowmobilers and hunters—"I am sorry for that and ask you to forgive me, but I had to protect myself from certain types of disturbances." Before he left the meeting Solzhenitsyn said he didn't expect he would be bothering them for long. "The Russian people dream of the day when they can be liberated from the Soviet system," he said, "and when that day comes, I will thank you very much for being good friends and neighbors and will go home."

The driveway wound past a brook, now frozen and banked with snow. Farther down a slope there was a pond, a small waterfall, a tennis court. Solzhenitsyn had always dreamed of having a court, but it seems he found fifteen minutes of play quite enough. His wife, Natalia, used to make fun of him for wanting to play such a "bourgeois game," and his sons long ago nailed a proletarian basketball hoop over the garage door.

"Thank goodness you found us," Natalia Solzhenitsyn said in Russian. "I thought you might have gotten lost."

"I did, a little."

"Well, it happens all the time."

"The birches here," I said, "look Russian."

"But they aren't, really," she said. "The birches here are fat, even a little gnarled. In Russia they are tall and thin and straight."

Natalia Dmitriyevna is a handsome woman, part Russian, part Jewish. She began her professional life as a mathematician, but when she married Solzhenitsyn in 1973 (both had been married once before), she became absolutely vital to his work and existence. She became, in fact, his assistant, his editor, his mediator with the outside world, his lion at the gate. She is a woman of fierce energy. In the days between his exile and her own, she managed to smuggle his entire archive, a vast trove of papers compiled over decades, from Moscow to Zurich. She raised four children and ran the household with the help only of her mother, Yekaterina Svetlova.

Thanks to the vigilance of Cavendish and Natalia Dmitriyevna, Solzhenitsyn wrote undisturbed, adhering to the same schedule every day of the year. He woke at around six, had a cup of coffee, and began. There was a lunch break in the afternoon, and he stayed at his desk until late in the evening. He wrote, ate, and slept, and that was about all. For him to accept a telephone call was an event; he rarely left his fifty acres. Home was all he needed. When the family bought the house in 1976, they soon built a second next door, a three-story "working house." In bad weather, Solzhenitsyn did not even have to go outside to get there. The houses were connected by a long concrete tunnel and a common basement. The main house was comfortable, yet unspectacular; it looked like a modest ski lodge, filled with light, but the furniture was absolutely ordinary, functional; the floors were carpeted in plain, almost industrial, colors. Since Solzhenitsyn's books had been published in over thirty languages, the family was quite prosperous, though they funneled all the royalties from *Gulag,* by far his top-selling book, into a fund used to aid political prisoners and their families. The fund, which Natalia ran, "is far richer than we are," she said.

There was something frenetic, yet peaceful, about the Solzhenitsyn household. Everyone had a job to do, and everyone did it with efficiency and evident pleasure. Upstairs, Natalia had her own office, where she ran what was, in its essence, a literary factory. She set type for Solzhenitsyn's latest works on an IBM composing machine and then sent the typeset pages to Nikita Struve in Paris, where he managed the Russian-language YMCA Press. Struve had only to photograph the set pages, print them, and bind them. Natalia set all twenty volumes of Solzhenitsyn's *sobraniye sochinyeniy,* his collected works. Only now that Solzhenitsyn had completed his series of immense historical novels, *The Red Wheel,* was either author or amanuensis able to concentrate on the move back to Moscow.

The children were also very much a part of the Solzhenitsyn enterprise. When the sons—Yermolai, Ignat, and Stephan, and their half brother Dmitri Turin—were small, they began the day with a prayer for Russia to be saved from its oppressors. They went to local schools, and when they came home in the afternoon their father gave them lessons in mathematics and the sciences (Solzhenitsyn had been a schoolteacher in Russia), and their mother tutored them in Russian language and literature. Until the boys began leaving home for boarding schools and college, they, too, helped with literary chores, setting type, compiling volumes of Russian memoirs, translating speeches. Now they were spread across the world. Yermolai, after two years at Eton, went to Harvard, where he studied Chinese and had a part-time job as a bouncer at the Bow & Arrow, a Cambridge bar. When I visited, he was living in Taiwan and working in trade. Ignat was studying piano and conducting at the Curtis Institute of Music in Philadelphia and had performed around the world to spectacular reviews— including the triumphant concerts with his father's old friend Mstislav Rostropovich in Russia on the eve of the October tragedy. Stephan was at Harvard, majoring in urban planning. (Dmitri, Natalia's son from a previous marriage, died of a heart attack not long after my visit.)

Ignat and Stephan were home for winter vacation, and I asked them if their father ever stopped working.

Ignat smiled slyly. "No, he's never said, 'Today I'm just gonna chill out, take a jog, and blow off this *Red Wheel* thing.' Not one day."

"Chilling out," Stephan added, "is not exactly his thing."

"So fine. Why can't the West get over this?" Ignat said, growing more serious. "Why is his working all the time such an annoyance? Why is it so bad that he lives in Vermont and not the middle of Manhattan?"

"They assume he must be weird," Stephan said.

Natalia led me to the working house, where Solzhenitsyn was waiting. While he was writing *The Red Wheel,* he often stayed for many days straight in the work house, replicating the way he would hole up for weeks and months at various dachas in and around Moscow before his exile. The first floor had its own Russian Orthodox chapel, with skylights and icons, and there was also a library of books and documents Solzhenitsyn gathered for use in *The Red Wheel*. Sometimes he worked on the third floor, where there was a skylight, but in winter the room was frigid. We met in his main work area on the second.

Even physically, Solzhenitsyn seemed a figure out of time. He had a nineteenth-century face: a Tolstoyan beard, narrow blue eyes, thinning, swept-back hair. In recent years his face had grown more lined, he had gained weight, yet he just looked at ease in an old brown cardigan and plaid Pendleton shirt. We sat across from each other at a small table where Solzhenitsyn had prepared himself for our talks with a set of small files of handwritten notes and a few volumes of his collected works sprouting bookmarks. I asked him if he had read the new Politburo documents describing how the leadership had decided on his exile.

"It is strange but we did not foresee this last step," Solzhenitsyn said with a sly smile. "My wife and I had become so impertinent. We felt that nothing would happen to us and we would manage once more to stay on our feet. The pressure had reached such a high level, but even so, various friends came to our place and said, 'You know, it's extraordinary, there is such tension all around, and yet here there is peace and quiet and the children are falling asleep.' So, yes, in this instance my intuition failed me."

Where Solzhenitsyn's intuition proved keenest was in his prediction upon arriving in the West that his books would surely be published in the Soviet Union and, what was more, that he would himself return to a liberated Russia. In the depths of the Cold War, he told Malcolm Muggeridge on the BBC: "In a strange way, I not only hope, I am inwardly convinced that I shall go back. I live with that conviction. I mean my physical return, not just my books. And that contradicts all rationality." It was a firm and intimate belief that even contradicted Solzhenitsyn's dire analysis of Soviet ruthlessness and Western accommodation. Before moving to Vermont, the Solzhenitsyns lived for almost two years in Zurich, and friends in Europe remember thinking that the exile was indulging in delusions when he spoke of inevitable return. "When I met with him in Zurich just after he was exiled, in the very first conversation we had, he said, 'I see the day when I will return to Russia,' " Nikita Struve had told me in Paris. "It seemed crazy at the time to me, but it was a real conviction, a poet's knowledge. He *sees*. The man *sees*."

"It's true. In my heart I sensed that I would return," Solzhenitsyn was saying now. "All of us in prison in the forties were certain that communism would fall. The only question was when. Perhaps I even exaggerated the danger of communism, perhaps even consciously, to inspire the West to stand more firmly. But remember: countries were falling to communism one after the other."

Ignat, who was at his father's side, smiled at this last remark, as if remembering something, fondly. (In fact, he was. Later he told me how when the boys were small, newly arrived in Vermont, their father sat with them on a boulder on their property and told them that the rock was really a flying horse and that when the time was right it would fly them all back to Russia.) "I always trusted Aleksandr Isayevich's feeling, his intuition, that we would return," Natalia Solzhenitsyn said. "He has this uncanny ability to see certain things that I do not and most people do not. It is not mystical. There is just a certain level of profundity that sets him apart. But I have to admit there were times when my own faith weakened. In the early eighties, when there was a new wave of arrests, when Andropov came to power, things looked very grim. Our own communications with Moscow became more tenuous as correspondents and diplomats became more wary about taking in mail. These were dark times, and it was very hard to believe that we'd be going home. I was losing faith."

That faith only gradually returned in the mid-1980s, as the Soviet Union began showing some signs of reform under Mikhail Gorbachev. But even then it was not easy. Although glasnost flourished in 1988 and early 1989, Solzhenistyn's works were still excluded from the process. At the time, when I asked Yegor Ligachev, the most powerful conservative in the Politburo, why the leadership had so far refused to publish Solzhenitsyn, he grew angry, every bit as fierce as Andropov had been twenty years earlier about the writer's cutting portrait of "everything dear to us."

"We have sacred things, just as you do," Ligachev said.

But it was not just a question of the conservatives. Even the self-described liberals in the leadership could not easily endorse the publication of Solzhenitsyn's books. At one point, the editor of the venerable literary journal *Novy Mir,* Sergei Zalygin, thought he had the tacit approval of the leadership to publish Solzhenitsyn and printed an announcement on the back cover saying that the process would begin in future issues. In the middle of the night, the printers got a "stop work" order from the Central Committee and the covers, at great expense, were torn off more than a million copies of the magazine. The Politburo's ideology chief, Vadim Medvedev, told a press conference soon after that Solzhenitsyn's works were impermissible since "they undermine the foundations on which our present life rests." It was only in late 1989, when the regime had clearly lost its hold over society, that Gorbachev let Zalygin go forward. Solzhenitsyn insisted that *Novy Mir* begin with *Gulag*.

Solzhenitsyn did not return to Russia at the first opportunity, mainly because he did not see how rushing home, and jeopardizing the chance to finish *The Red Wheel,* would help anyone. Instead, like the rest of the world, he followed the fall of the Soviet Union in the press and on television.

"In August of 1991 my wife and I were incredibly excited to watch Dzerzhinsky's statue taken down outside the KGB building. That, of course, was a great moment for us," he said. "But I was asked at the time: Why didn't you send a telegram of congratulations? You know, I felt deep inside that this was not yet a victory. I knew how profoundly communism had penetrated into the fabric of life. Afterward, for two years, we tap-danced about, and what were we doing? What was Yeltsin doing? We forgot everything else and fought each other. The same is true even now. All is in decay. It's too early to celebrate. Why was I silent about Gorbachev for several years? Thank God something did begin! But everything that began was done wrongly. So what do you do? Celebrate or weep? What can you say? I could not have gone over there and had a glass of champagne with Yeltsin in front of the parliament, the White House. The heart is not yet joyful."

Solzhenitsyn did finish the fourth and final installment of *The Red Wheel* in late 1991—the series runs to over five thousand pages—and I asked him (against the evidence) if exile had depleted his language and imagination.

"The thing is I came to the West when I was fifty-five years old," he said. "I had had an amazingly rich and varied experience of life. As a writer I did not need any addition to this experience but rather the time to process it. Purely for my work, the eighteen years in Vermont were the happiest of my life. Simply put, over eighteen years, I have not had one creative drought. Seven days a week, three hundred sixty-five days a year, without holidays or vacations, I worked, and that's all there is to it. Such conditions from this point of view, in terms of books and writing and just day-to-day life, I have never had before and will never have again. This was the richest period of my creative work.

"The loss was the pain inside me, the separation from the homeland, from its spaces and people, from interaction. Raising children as Russians in the West was extremely difficult, and it is only thanks to Natalia Dmitriyevna that we have been able to do this, because one usually becomes engulfed in the country in which one lives. So this was our loss. Now when we are about to go back to Russia we hope to recover from this loss, but not in the sense that the pain will go away. In fact, the pain will only increase because of the horrifying circumstances in Russia. One might have thought that after the fall of communism Russia would encounter serious problems. But it was hard to imagine that with leader after leader, and year after year, everything would worsen continuously. We are faced with incredible hardship for years to come. I am sure I will not have the chance to work so calmly again. I know that I will be torn apart by people's tragedies and the events of the time."

I asked Solzhenitsyn about his Russian and how he felt, living in Vermont, with his language. In addition to his political fears, did he harbor this personal and literary fear, too?

"I'm not worried," he said. "I have always been surrounded here by Russian manuscripts and I write in Russian. I studied English and German as a schoolboy but I have not been able to study them further since coming to the West. I do read in English and German, but I was not able to develop my conversational skills. If I need to read letters in those languages, or articles, I do it. I was constantly immersed in the Russian language, and," he said, gesturing to the woods and the fields of snow outside the window, "we really have a piece of Russia here. Once, my wife and I traveled across the country from the Pacific to the Atlantic, then by myself to conduct research, the Midwest mostly. But I simply could not allow myself the time to take a trip around America just to get to know the country. I had only two choices: to write *The Red Wheel* or not. To write it I had to give it my full attention. Maybe if I were not returning now to Russia, I might change my lifestyle on account of finishing the *The Red Wheel*. But now it is time to go back to Russia. There simply was not the time. One cannot encompass everything. Our history has been so hidden. I had to dig so deeply, I had to uncover what was buried and sealed. This took up all of my years."

In terms of the effect he has had on history, Solzhenitsyn is the dominant writer of the twentieth century. Who else compares? Orwell? Koestler?

And yet when his name comes up now, it is more often than not as a freak, a monarchist, an anti-Semite, a crank, a has-been. One afternoon in Cavendish, I was in the kitchen with Natalia and Stephan and I asked if Solzhenitsyn planned on making any public appearances, any speeches, before leaving Vermont for Moscow in the coming spring.

"Who would ask him to speak in America?" Natalia said. "Who in America wants to hear him?"

"Face it, Mom," Stephan said. "It hasn't worked out here."

Solzhenitsyn chose to live in Vermont not out of an overwhelming allegiance to the United States, but, above all, because of its *prostranstvo,* its size and space. In Paris, Solzhenitsyn's friend and publisher Nikita Struve told me, "Aleksandr Isayevich went to America so he could live far from the world—the world, not in the religious sense, but in the most ordinary sense. You could never do that in Switzerland or France. When everything is close together like that anyone can just drop by and knock on the door, ring the buzzer. In Vermont, it's not so easy. He lives, and has always lived, like an *otshelnik,* a hermit. Like a monk. No one has ever done this to quite the same extent. People said Gogol was crazy when he didn't go out. But look, great writers are almost always considered crazy. Great writers are a different sort of people."

I told Struve what he already knew: that Solzhenitsyn's reception in the United States had been troubled from the very start. "Americans do not generally live with fences around their homes, and Americans want you to live like they do," Struve said. "There are always people—in America, in Russia—who think of Solzhenitsyn as a superman, too, and that bothers them. There are always a lot of people who resent it when there is someone in their midst who is higher than they are. The man in question must be crazy, because he doesn't come out and live among them. He lived in America as if it were always foreign. And this Americans didn't like. He lived in Vermont, but it was his special Vermont. He didn't have to 'get to know' the West. He never went about making himself into a great 'Western thinker.' That is not his business. He didn't travel that much, either. That just was not his job in life. Solzhenitsyn was at war against Soviet power—the pen against power. This was his literary work, and he fulfilled it absolutely."

Early in his exile to the West, Solzhenitsyn accepted invitations to speak to the AFL-CIO in New York and Washington, at the Hoover Insti-

tution in California, and, most notoriously, at the 1978 Harvard graduation ceremonies. In those speeches he excoriated the West not only for
weakness in its negotiations with the Soviet Union but for a general cultural and civil collapse. To him, the rot of Western life was evident in billboards and tabloids, in the lyrics of rock music and the anti–Vietnam War
movement. He delivered those perorations in an elevated, angry, almost
Grand Inquisitor–like tone, a tone rarely heard in the West. Here he was,
in a typical pitch, at Hoover:

> Freedom! To fill people's mailboxes, eyes, ears, and brains with com-
> mercial rubbish against their will, with television programs that are
> impossible to watch with a sense of coherence. Freedom! To force in-
> formation on people, taking no account of their right *not* to accept it
> or their right to peace of mind. Freedom! To spit in the eyes and souls
> of passersby with advertisements. Freedom! For publishers and film
> producers to poison the younger generations with corrupting filth.
> Freedom! For adolescents of fourteen to eighteen to immerse them-
> selves in idleness and pleasure instead of intensive study and spiritual
> growth. . . . Freedom! To divulge the defense secrets of one's country
> for personal political gain. . . .

Somehow it was all too fierce and sarcastic, too impolitic. Solzhenitsyn was not Sakharov; this was not a lovable man. He gave Americans
little reason to relax or to admire themselves. The attacks came from
high and low, and they were endless. Jonathan Yardley wrote for *The
Miami Herald* in 1974 that Solzhenitsyn was a "not-very-thinly-disguised
Czarist." Writing the next year in *The Guardian,* Simon Winchester referred to Solzhenitsyn as "the shaggy author" and the "hairy polemicist"
and declared that the author has become "the darling of the redneck population." There was this headline in the *Daily Mirror* in 1976: SOLZHE-
NITWIT. Writing in *The Sunday Times,* Alan Brien reviewed the essay
"Letter to the Soviet Leaders" with total disdain: "Is Aleksandr Solzhenitsyn a crank? His open, unopened letter to the Soviet Government bears
a superficial resemblance to those lengthy screeds which flop on the desk
of every journalist from time to time, even down to the passages under-
scored and printed in capitals, full of contradictory assertions, obsessive

fears, Falstaffian escalations of statistics." And on it went, year after year. As recently as 1993, *The Boston Globe*'s former Moscow correspondent Alex Beam published an opinion piece under the headline SHUT UP, SOLZHENITSYN.

Some Russian émigrés came to resent Solzhenitsyn as well, partly because he showed them no great sympathy and urged them to stay in the Soviet Union. His exile, he argued, was unique because it had been forced, as if dozens of dissidents had not been given a choice between departure and brutal punishment. In his novel *2042,* the comic novelist Vladimir Voinovich, who was then living in exile in Munich, portrayed a Solzhenitsyn-like figure as a cross between the Ayatollah Khomeini and a Russian holy fool. "At a certain point," Voinovich told me, "Solzhenitsyn's quality of being uncompromising in his struggle against the system became something else. I began to notice an atmosphere of authoritarian impulses even in his work and certainly in his demeanor. I defended him, but after a while I got the impression that after he had written anything or said anything you either had to fall in line and agree or you were an enemy. He could be so unjust, unceremoniously casting people out of his circle for some slight, usually imagined. Also he is said to be a prophet, but what sort of prophet would have been predicting the triumph of communism over the West?"

Vassily Aksyonov, an émigré novelist who is far more sympathetic to Solzhenitsyn, said that the prickly relations with the outside world should have been predictable. "Solzhenitsyn's greatest problem is his isolation," Aksyonov said. "Look at J. D. Salinger. People assume that because Salinger has holed himself up in the country and made an obsession of that isolation, he must be crazy. The same with Solzhenitsyn. He is like some sort of owl up there in the woods. And so even though people can be unfair, he is also to blame for the negative myth. The couple of times I have seen him on television, it turns out that he is a perfectly normal, truthful person. He is not a living monument."

One of the absolute low points of Solzhenitsyn's reception in the West came at the highest levels. For a while, in 1975, President Ford considered inviting Solzhenitsyn to the White House. In the end, however, he and his advisers thought better of it. His secretary of state, Henry Kissinger, sent a memo through his executive assistant George Springsteen to Ford's national security adviser, Brent Scowcroft, saying, "Solzhenitsyn is a notable writer, but his political views are an embarrassment even to his fellow dissidents. Not only would a meeting with the President offend the Soviets but it would raise some controversy about Solzhenitsyn's views of the United States and its allies. . . . We recommend that the President not receive Solzhenitsyn." When I called Ford in Colorado in 1993 to ask about the incident, he spoke blandly about the need to avoid offending the Kremlin during sensitive arms negotiations. "It's the old never-ending conflict between foreign policy concerns and domestic political concerns," Ford said. "As a matter of principle, we made the right decision." But it seems he was rather less measured about it at the time. According to his former press secretary Ron Nessen, Ford called Solzhenitsyn "a god-damned horse's ass" and said the author wanted to come to the White House merely to inflate his lecture fees and publicize his books.

No one enjoyed Solzhenitsyn's dismal clashes in the West more than his former tormentors. In a memorandum to the Council of Ministers dated January 4, 1976, KGB chief Andropov wrote gleefully about Solzhenitsyn and "the fall in interest in him abroad and in the USSR." Andropov admits in the memo that the KGB helped promote, through its agents and contacts, "material useful to us" condemning Solzhenitsyn and his "class-based hatred of the Soviet power." Andropov was pleased to report that the compromising material, much of it insisting that Solzhenitsyn was an anti-Semite yearning for a return of the czars, "has brought about a reevaluation of his personality and has successfully brought up, and strengthened, doubts about the reliability of his distorted 'work.' "

What the KGB failed to point out was that Solzhenitsyn's reception was actually varied. In Europe, especially in France, the publication of *Gulag* and the exile itself in 1974 immediately changed the intellectual landscape. Suddenly a generation that had grown up under the thrall of Jean-Paul Sartre's brand of leftism and a continuing romance with Marxism-Leninism now turned to the avatar of anticommunism. Largely thanks to Solzhenitsyn, the *nouveaux philosophes,* former Marxist thinkers like André Glucksmann and Bernard-Henri Lévy, assumed an intellectual authority in France. Perhaps the American landscape did not change as markedly as it had in France because it had lived under fewer illusions about the nature of the Soviet regime. Orwell, after all, had been published and absorbed, and anti-Stalinist redoubts, the *Partisan Review* most of all, did much to obliterate lingering fantasies about the Soviet Union even among former communist sympathizers. But the American intelligentsia, especially on the left, was not entirely convinced of the accuracy of all Solzhenitsyn had reported, or, at least, had not focused on it sufficiently, choosing instead to concentrate more on the war in Vietnam or its dalliances with Castro's Cuba. Susan Sontag, who would shock an audience of left-wing intellectuals and activists at New York's Town Hall in 1982 simply by equating communism with fascism and suggesting that the *Reader's Digest* may have been more accurate than *The Nation* in its assessment of communism, quite honestly says she was taken aback by Solzhenitsyn and *The Gulag Archipelago*.

"It was January 1976—I remember the time precisely because I was still sick with cancer—and I was having a long conversation with Joseph Brodsky," Sontag said. "We were both laughing and agreeing about how we thought Solzhenitsyn's views on the United States, his criticism of the press and all the rest, were so deeply wrong. And on and on. And then Joseph said, 'But you know, Susan, everything Solzhenitsyn says about the Soviet Union is true. Really. All those numbers—sixty million victims—it's all true.' Until then I must have felt that it was an exaggeration or one-sided somehow. I don't really know what kind of inner reservations I had. But at that moment, something gave way."

Brodsky told me, "I was not surprised really that Susan had been so shocked. Maybe I found it revolting and idiotic. But I have a theory of why these things don't seep through, and that is a theory about self-preservation, mental self-preservation. Western man, by and large, is the most natural man, a mental bourgeois, and he cherishes his mental comfort. It is almost impossible for him to admit painful or contrary evidence. Plus, when you add in the phenomenon of geography, which was very real until recently, and add into it the particularity of Soviet reality, even just the difficult names—when you add all that in you have a considerable barrier, a mental fence that was constructed especially by the Western left. It was mostly among the intellectuals, the educated classes. I was in Ann Arbor in the early seventies and a woman was cleaning my place. She saw my Russian books and she asked me, 'What kind of system do you have over there?' I tried to explain, this way and that, and she cut me off. She said, 'You mean tyranny?' And that was that. So, you see, sometimes education results only in obfuscation."

The history of willful obfuscation regarding the Soviet Union has a long and painful history among some of the most revered intellectuals of the century. The desire to wish away the catastrophe of the Soviet Union makes for a depressing psychological portrait. "We cannot afford to give ourselves moral airs," George Bernard Shaw declared, "when our most enterprising neighbor (the USSR) . . . humanely and judiciously liquidates a handful of exploiters and speculators to make the world safe for honest men. . . . Mussolini, Kemal, Pilsudski, Hitler, and the rest can all depend on me to judge them by their ability to deliver the goods and not by Swinburne's comfortable notions of freedom. Stalin has delivered the goods to an extent that seemed impossible ten years ago; and I take my hat off to him accordingly."

While such stupidities became less common with time, many intellectuals on the left still remained hesitant to denounce the Soviet Union. The reasons were various, but perhaps the most important was the liberal aversion to join ranks with anticommunism as a movement. Joe McCarthy was repellent, and so, too, was the senator who greeted Solzhenitsyn most emphatically, Jesse Helms. Often the leading anticommunists were so harebrained in their rhetoric or repugnant in their positions on other issues—race and the war in Vietnam being but two—that there was no way the left could find a common language with them. What remains a wonder is how resistant the left was to the figure of Solzhenitsyn. Oddly enough, Solzhenitsyn's children, as bridges between their father and the American world they grew up in, understand as well as any scholar the barrier that developed between the writer and his newfound land.

"My father spent his entire life fighting the communist system, and, understandably, there was no relativity involved: they were evil and that was that," Yermolai told me. "It was a question of a battle to the death that was black-and-white and requiring courage. Having gone through the Western system, through the Vermont schools and Harvard and all the rest, I guess I've been inculcated with the more relative way of things, leaving a door open for merits to both sides on issues.

"But you should know that it wasn't like my father was some kind of anti-Western ogre at home. It's true, we didn't watch television that much when we were young. Nothing like the national average. But I remember watching the '86 World Series with my mother, the Mets and the Red Sox, and we listened to rock 'n' roll, all the usual things."

My visit to the Solzhenitsyns made them immediately less alien to me. It somehow humanized the father to see Ignat's room, with hand-drawn emblems of the New York sports teams on the wall, or to hear Stephan mimic a *Saturday Night Live* shtick to his mother's indulgent incomprehension. Even when it came to the attacks on Solzhenitsyn, the sons were good-humored, ironic, American.

"I suppose in the age of political correctness we should all feel emotionally victimized," Ignat said.

At lunch in the kitchen, Solzhenitsyn himself reminded me of a gruff uncle put upon by a chaotic world. He sat at the head of the table and took delight in announcing the day's news from Russia, which he monitored on a shortwave radio, and then gave his commentary. ("Isn't it about time Yeltsin cracked down on crooks?") When he was done harrumphing, he forked his way through a plate of fried cutlets, beet salad, and potatoes, excused himself, and returned to the work house.

Back in the study, I asked Solzhenitsyn about his relations with the West. He knew they had gone wrong, and he had no intention of making any apologies for himself. "Instead of secluding myself here and writing *The Red Wheel* I suppose I could have spent time making myself likable to the West," he said. "The only problem is that I would have had to drop my way of life and my work. And, yes, it is true, when I fought the dragon of communist power, I fought it at the highest pitch of expression. The people in the West were not accustomed to this tone of voice. In the West, one must have a balanced, calm, soft voice; one ought to make sure to doubt oneself, to suggest one may, of course, be completely wrong. But I didn't have the time to busy myself with this. This was not my main goal."

I mentioned that I had recently heard a lecture in New York given by Solzhenitsyn's biographer, Michael Scammell, and that, at the end, all the questions from the audience boiled down to "Why doesn't Solzhenitsyn like us?"

The notion that he is "anti-Western," he said, is wrong and "arose out of the inordinate sensitivity and superficiality of Western correspondents. My speeches to the AFL-CIO in 1975—and I would not take back a single word of them—were built in the following way: one speech versus the communist state and the second against communism as an ideology. Both of them were absolutely correct. I said there: do not help us. Fine. But at least don't help dig our graves. Immediately, on the next day, the press was in an uproar, saying that Solzhenitsyn wants to destroy détente and go to war with the Soviet Union. Never in my life did I ever call for liberation from the West. Nor did I ask for the West to fight for our sake, or even help. I said only, just do not help our executioners. They asked about détente. I said, Yes, I am for détente, but only so that all cards are on the table. Otherwise, what really happens under détente is that you are being deceived. For example, in the speech to the unions I noted, please understand, you are being deceived. There are still POWs in Vietnam. They will not be released because they were tortured. The whole Washington press corps had a great laugh at my expense. What a stupid thing he has dreamed up! Everything has been counted up and is in order! And now we see today that they say not everyone was returned, but back then they laughed. You see, the whole atrocity of communism could never be accommodated by the Western journalistic mind. I spoke based on my experiences in the gulag.

"Most Americans understood what I was saying, even if the press did not. The press did not understand because it did not want to and because I had criticized them. But how can I not criticize the press? How can the press aspire to true power? No one elected it. How can it aspire to an equal level with the three branches of government? The people in the press can be either scoundrels or good, it's all a matter of chance. The press does play very often a positive role. In Russia today the press is unraveling what our criminal oligarchy is up to. Even though most of the Russian press depends on the government for financial support, there are still excellent articles. How can one not value the press? But there must not be abuses and in relation to me there have been staggering abuses."

It was a curious thing: Václav Havel was almost universally admired, even loved, in the West; Solzhenitsyn was not. And yet Havel's essays and letters show an admiration of, and an affinity for, some of Solzhenitsyn's greatest obsessions: the need for a spiritual dimension in politics, a need for the East to see Western capitalism and democracy with a clear eye, without romanticism. I mentioned to Solzhenitsyn that part of his problem might be one of his glaring differences with Havel: while Havel reveled in Western pop culture and wrote affectionate paeans to the Rolling Stones and Frank Zappa, Solzhenitsyn called pop culture "manure."

"Well, these things, after all, are the pits of Western culture," he said. "This is not to the credit of the development of Western culture. This is the image I use: that it is manure that flowed under [the Iron Curtain] and it influences the unformed, the youth. They have no idea what thinkers or writers there may have been in the West. They just hear rock and roll and wear some sort of T-shirt with something on it. This is dangerous for the younger, unprotected part of the population. Maybe they'll develop badly. They need to be protected. Our youth is in terrible straits."

The charges that hurt Solzhenitsyn most in the West were anti-Semitism and authoritarianism. There exists even now a lingering suspicion that Solzhenitsyn's critique of secularism in the West and his Russian patriotism are somehow a combustible combination, one that spells trouble for Jews and other non-Russian minorities. The charges are preposterous; nowhere does Solzhenitsyn support a theocracy or fundamentalism, and yet they persist. (In the Soviet Union, the Kremlin's charge was that he was actually a Jew—"Solzhenitsker"—and a bourgeois counterrevolutionary.) The most comprehensive set of accusations was published in the American Jewish magazine *Midstream* in 1977. There an émigré named Mark Perakh charged Solzhenitsyn with, at best, a thoughtless attitude toward Jews. He noted that in the second volume of *Gulag* all the camp commandants shown in a full-page gallery of photographs were Jewish and that in *Lenin in Zurich,* the evil "genius" supporting Lenin was Parvus, a German Jew. (Solzhenitsyn, for his part, says the pictures in *Gulag* were the only ones available at the time, and that the historical characters in *Lenin in Zurich,* Parvus included, are portrayed accurately and according to reliable records and witnesses.) Even the late Irving Howe could not abide *August 1914* because he found it dismissive of Jewish concerns, namely the pogroms in southern Russia and Ukraine. "Something of the brutality of the commissars has rubbed off on you, I'm afraid," Howe wrote in an essay. "It did not seem so in *The First Circle* or *Cancer Ward.* What has happened to you? . . . The answer is that his zealotry has brought about a hardening of spirit, a loss in those humane feelings and imaginative outreachings that make us value a work of literature, regardless of the writer's political position." Howe was far from alone in disliking *August 1914*—the critical consensus is that the novel is not up to the standard set in the early novels or in *Gulag*—but it is unclear how he comes to his charges. His argument is summary and weak, and he seems, above all, aggrieved that Solzhenitsyn turned out not to share his affection for socialist principles.

"In the magazine *Midstream* I was charged with anti-Semitism because nowhere in *One Day in the Life of Ivan Denisovich* did the word 'Yid' appear!" Solzhenitsyn said. "The word doesn't appear and therefore I am an anti-Semite! The author is sure that in the camps there was no more urgent question than the Jewish question. He thinks they all sat around and condemned Jews all day and said 'Yid.' Well, in this book no one uses the term, so I must be hiding the facts—and why would I do that unless I was an anti-Semite? Meanwhile, in reality, there were informers being knifed, there were uprisings against the authorities, there were murders with machine guns spraying all around! There were no more than five or six Jews in the whole camp! The same thing with the accusation of czarism, that I want to return to the past. There is not a single passage that has been shown me saying that I want to return to the past, that I want priests in power, a theocracy.

"Anti-Semitism is a prejudiced and unjust attitude toward the Jewish people as a whole. My own work has no such attitude. The press has said, 'Please make such a statement.' But there exists in this country the presumption of innocence. Why should I suddenly come forward with a statement that I am not an anti-Semite? It would be as if I were to make the statement that I am not a thief, that I have not stolen anything. If I am accused of actually stealing from someone then I would come forward and deny it. So, if somebody were to show where specifically I exhibit an unjust or prejudiced attitude toward the Jewish people, if they would show me one such quotation in my work, I would gladly defend myself. But nobody has ever pointed out such a passage and yet I am still asked to make the statement that I am not an anti-Semite."

Solzhenitsyn made no farewell tour of the country he had lived in for eighteen years, but he did make the rounds in Western Europe. He stayed with Nikita Struve in Paris, met with Pope John Paul in Rome, and said his farewells to old friends in Switzerland and Germany. The trip to Europe was mostly personal, but there were two public speeches, one in Liechtenstein, one in France, that gave a good sense of Solzhenitsyn's current thinking and of a distinct shift if not in his views, then in his emphases and his tone.

At the International Institute for Philosophy in the village of Schaan, Solzhenitsyn rehearsed many of his old themes for the people of Liechtenstein: the failure of the West to recognize the scale of evil in the Soviet Union, the lack of an ethical dimension in politics since the rise of secularism. But even if he sounded much like a preacher, there was less fire and brimstone than there had been at Harvard sixteen years before. Gone was the old, astringent tone, gone were the scathing images and sarcastic phrases. He called for a saner, more limited role for modern technology, a search for a spirituality that would allow men and women to move beyond self-absorption and a fear of death. A pleasant, almost New Age modesty had leavened his rhetoric. Small is beautiful. Man is lost without belief.

A few weeks later, on September 25, 1994, in the town of Lucs-sur-Boulogne, Solzhenitsyn spoke to a crowd of thirty thousand people gathered to commemorate the massacre of ninety thousand Frenchmen by the revolutionary Jacobin government between 1793 and 1795. It was a remarkable event, probably the most important public appearance Solzhenitsyn had made since Harvard. At the podium, he attacked violent revolution, all attempts to remake a society at one bloody moment. The uprising at Vendée and its brutal suppression were, he said, parallel to the Bolsheviks' slaughter of peasant uprisings in Tambov and in western Siberia in the early 1920s.

"That every revolution," Solzhenitsyn said, "brings out instincts of primeval barbarity, the sinister forces of envy, greed, and hatred—this even its contemporaries could see all too well. They paid a terrible enough price for the mass psychosis of the day, when merely moderate behavior, or even the perception of such, already appeared to be a crime. But the twentieth century has done especially much to tarnish the romantic luster of revolution which still prevailed in the eighteenth century. As half-centuries and centuries have passed, people have learned from their own misfortunes that revolutions demolish the organic structures of society, disrupt the natural flow of life, destroy the best elements of the population, and benefit only a few shameless opportunists, while to the country as a whole revolutions herald countless deaths, widespread impoverishment, and, in the gravest cases, a long-lasting degeneration of the people. . . .

"I would not wish a 'great revolution' upon any nation. Only the arrival of Thermidor prevented the eighteenth-century revolution from destroying France. But the revolution in Russia was not restrained by any Thermidor as it drove our people on the straight path to a bitter end, to the abyss, to the depths of ruin."

Later, when I met with Solzhenitsyn, I asked him why he had been so sweeping in his judgment. Was the American Revolution, too, a catastrophe?

"No," he said. "By revolution I mean a violent overthrow of power in a particular country that claims human lives. Such revolutions have occurred in France, in Russia. The word 'revolution' is applied to any change today. That is not what I mean by revolution. The American Revolution, to me, was not a revolution. This was a national liberation—like Italy liberating itself from Austria, like the unification of Germany in the nineteenth century. I condemn revolution because it undermines the strength of the nation, instead of allowing evolutionary development."

In this, Solzhenitsyn would soon hear ringing agreement from an ally in the Kremlin, Boris Yeltsin. The government's Commission for the Rehabilitation of Victims of Political Repression issued a report condemning Lenin and the Bolshevik suppression of the Kronshtadt Rebellion of 1921. The sailors of Kronshtadt, who had initially supported the Bolsheviks and a socialist system, staged demonstrations calling for fair elections, a representative parliament, and other reforms repugnant to the new regime. The communists declared war on the "counterrevolutionary conspiracy" and crushed the uprising with mass executions, deportations, and jailings. The chairman of the commission, Aleksandr Yakovlev, declared that Kronshtadt proved that Bolshevik terror was Lenin's singular contribution to Russia. Stalin, he said, "was just the Great Continuer of Lenin's Task. It all began under Lenin."

In Vermont, Solzhenitsyn kept his own counsel, preferring to work on his literary projects. In his only major American interview after the rise of Gorbachev, to *Time* magazine in 1989, he held fast to one ground rule: there could be no questions about politics in the Soviet Union, the better to avoid any signs of undue euphoria or discouragement. Then, in 1990, Solzhenitsyn published his long essay "Rebuilding Russia," first in the newspapers *Komsomolskaya Pravda* and *Literaturnaya Gazeta* and then in foreign languages. Much of the essay was prescient, calling for an end to the Soviet empire and the evolutionary development of democracy. But in that essay Solzhenitsyn remained reticent about the great personalities of the past seven or eight years in Russia. Why, I asked him, did he think the Soviet Union finally collapsed?

"I can say I was the first person to predict the Soviet Union would collapse and that this was necessary," he said. "Not only did Gorbachev not want to hear about this, President Bush and other Western leaders also said the Soviet Union must remain intact. For me it had been clear for many years. Ever since I was in prison, it was clear to all of us that communism could not stand on its own. By an irony of fate, communism, which is based on the theory that the economy is the basis of all human activity, collapsed for economic reasons. Its economy was completely absurd. It could survive only with an iron grip. When Gorbachev first tried to ease the iron grip, the process of collapse accelerated. Gorbachev did not have in mind the negation of socialism. Even when he came back from captivity after the attempted coup in August 1991, he said once again that our 'choice' was socialism. By no means did he intend to part company with socialism. He wanted only to rearrange things slightly and give the nomenklatura economic influence. There were clearly dirty economic transactions going on. Under Gorbachev, the debt more than quadrupled. The country never saw that money.

"Gorbachev imagined he would give glasnost to the Moscow intelligentsia, and, with its help, and with the help of the press, he would tame the extreme conservatives in the Party. But glasnost immediately spread to the whole country and on to the nationalities question. The nationalities question sprang up everywhere, and the most extreme chauvinistic points of view developed. He could not cope with that. He was short-sighted. He could not imagine where all this would lead. In general, Gorbachev and his circle were locked into a Marxist ideology and they were shortsighted. For example, in Eastern Europe. He could not foresee what would happen. He wanted to replace their Ligachevs with their own Gorbachevs and leave it at that. But as soon as he touched something, all of these velvet revolutions happened right away."

Solzhenitsyn gave almost no credit to Gorbachev, insisting that his motivations were all ones of either expedience, necessity, or cynicism. But what of Gorbachev's decision to withdraw from the arms race and end the Cold War?

"This was not cynicism," Solzhenitsyn said. "He really understood that the country was in such a difficult economic situation that to sustain the tension of the old rivalry with the West was no longer viable. The Cold War was essentially won by Ronald Reagan when he embarked on the Star Wars program and the Soviet Union understood it could not take this next step. It had nothing to do with Gorbachev's generosity; he was compelled to do it. He had no choice but to disarm."

In contrast to his denunciations of Gorbachev, Solzhenitsyn was generally supportive of Yeltsin and even issued a statement of support when Yeltsin ordered the storming of the rebellious parliament.

"I both support Yeltsin and I criticize him," Solzhenitsyn said. "I support him because—well, Gorbachev was not sincere in all his pronouncements, while Yeltsin was. Yeltsin truly decided to cut off ties with the Party. You might have seen on TV in 1990 how he walked out of the Party congress with everyone sitting down looking at him as if they were wolves. And in August 1991, when he read his pronouncement from atop a tank, he acted courageously again. One cannot even compare him to Gorbachev. Yeltsin truly wanted what was best.

"But immediately after August 1991, Yeltsin committed a series of mistakes, and very serious ones. In September 1991, he could easily have dissolved the Supreme Soviet, dispersed the local soviets, closed down the Communist Party, and nobody would have dared to object. There was such a surge of enthusiasm then! Everyone wanted this done, but he did not do anything. And so two years later—in October 1993—he was forced to carry on this horrifying carnage in Moscow. In 1991, he could have done it with clean hands.

"Secondly, there is his indifference to the twenty-five million Russians now living abroad. He made no statement about this. God forbid we should have some sort of war for this as in Yugoslavia, but as a politician Yeltsin should have said, 'We take note that there are twelve million Russians in Ukraine, seven million in Kazakhstan, and in all negotiations we will always remind you of this and will seek a political solution to this question.' But he did not do this. He simply said, 'I accept all the borders,' and let it go at that. It was Lenin who established these false borders, borders which did not correspond to the ethnic borders. They were set up in such a way to undermine the central Russian nation as a conscious punishment.

"So it has turned out that twenty-five million Russians all of a sudden live outside Russia. This is the biggest diaspora in the world! The leaderships of Ukraine and Kazakhstan both are extremely shortsighted. They have taken upon themselves a task which culturally cannot be worked out. For example, in Kazakhstan they will have to turn those Russians into Kazakhs. So what do they begin to do? They begin to rename villages. They make it a criminal act to speak out against the exclusivity of the Kazakh language. In Ukraine they are eliminating Russian schools. . . . Everyone who takes the Ukrainian military's oath of allegiance is asked the question 'Would you fight against Russia?' "

In the past two years, the Russian army had meddled consistently in the "near abroad," the former republics of the Soviet Union, in a clear attempt to reestablish at least some of the power Moscow lost with the collapse of the union. Did Russia really have the right to send troops into Tajikistan, Armenia, Azerbaijan, and Georgia the way it had? I asked.

Solzhenitsyn raised his finger as if preaching to a large crowd. "Interference in Georgia or Armenia and Azerbaijan? God forbid!" he said. "This sphere of influence, this military presence, is a remnant of imperial thinking. It must not be there. Of course, there is also a technical explanation. Why has Russia conducted itself this way? After the breakup of the USSR, Russia found itself with no protected borders. You could do anything you like, bring in anything back and forth across the borders:

drugs, radioactive materials, arms, and so on. And so, in panic that the borders could not quickly be fortified, Russia decided to protect the old borders. But we must restructure, adjust. We must stop insisting on the right to take actions in the breakaway republics."

Finally, I asked about the two most pressing problems in Russia: the collapse of the economy and the advent of a powerful opposition force dominated by hard-line nationalists, neofascists, and communists.

"Yeltsin's economic mistakes are enormous," said Solzhenitsyn. "Yeltsin felt the need to adopt any reform as soon as possible. We had Yegor Gaidar, a theorist who sat in his office under the influence of the International Monetary Fund, which itself exhibited total ignorance of the situation in Russia. Gaidar adopted a policy thinking that once prices were freed you would solve everything because competition would begin and then the prices would stabilize and fall.

"This is why the people, desperate and not knowing how to express themselves, expressed themselves the way they did in the December elections. They said, in effect, 'Anyone, but not you!' . . . It was not a choice *for* fascism, and it is not a choice *for* communism. I receive letters saying, 'We feel thrown out into the cold. No one needs us. We cannot in any way influence what is happening.' This is not democracy. We have an oligarchical merger of communist nomenklatura and the shadow economy. Our people have no influence."

Solzhenitsyn said that Zhirinovsky himself was a "clown."

Hitler was also a clown, at first, I said.

"In terms of being a clown, Zhirinovsky even outpaces Hitler," Solzhenitsyn said. "I've never encountered this level of unending lunacy. It is a joke at every step of the way. Now, more importantly, people speak about the danger of fascism in Russia. For me, the term 'fascism' is more appropriate than 'national socialism.' National socialism is based on racism, and without racism national socialism is inconceivable. That is its basis and its theory. Racism, as a state policy, is possible only in a very homogeneous country such as Germany, not in a multinational country like Russia. The danger is not in fascism, as many say it is, but is rather that it is possible to come to power merely on slogans refuting current policy."

During our conversation, Natalia Dmitriyevna joined us. I mentioned that when I had been in Moscow a couple of months before I had been disturbed to hear about how the city police had carried out wholesale arrests against Armenians, Azerbaijanis, and Chechens under the pretext that they had, collectively, reduced the capital to rampant crime. It was even more disturbing to read polls in *Izvestia* showing that the overwhelming majority of Muscovites were all for the arrests. Somehow the Solzhenitsyns did not see the issue as a matter of civil liberties.

"You know, this question is first of all a criminal question," Solzhenitsyn said. "The Caucasians created a real mafia, and in the Moscow and St. Petersburg regions they have monopolized the arms and restaurant trade."

"I saw this with my own eyes," said Natalia, who had been back to Russia twice since the ban on them had been lifted. "It is monstrous. There is nothing national about it. It's a criminal situation in Moscow when every father fears for his daughter walking at night. These people are all armed to the teeth. They occupy every market. I saw myself how the Russian old women from the Moscow suburbs who try to sell some radishes or green onions have to work outside the subway stations because they have been driven from the markets. Every market stall has to be bought for a huge sum, and of course none of these women could afford that. They have completely taken over life in Moscow, and I'll be the first to applaud if they are driven out—not because they are Chechens but because they are bandits. They have behaved like an occupying army which conquered the country."

In *The First Circle,* Solzhenitsyn made the famous remark that in a tyranny, a real writer is like a second government. Whether it was Pushkin, Tolstoy, or Herzen under the czars or Akhmatova, Pasternak, or Mandelstam under the Bolsheviks, the role of the writer in Russia had been outsized. But if all goes well in Russia, that kind of artificial authority will, happily, vanish.

"When I said that a writer is like a second government, I meant this in the context of a fully totalitarian regime," Solzhenitsyn told me. "And indeed one can see today, in the newly published documents of the Politburo, that they were concerned with my personal fate as seriously as if I were a whole state. In this sense, there was no exaggeration. But in a free society, this formula no longer applies. Moreover, literature, like so much else in Russia, is now in a state of terrible degradation. At the moment, literature means very little. And yet I still hope that my books might help serve moral goals. I still hope to be useful in some way. I cannot write simply to be able to say, 'Look how cleverly I have crafted this.' I refuse to see literature as amusement, as a game. I think that you ought not to approach literature without a moral responsibility for every word you write."

Solzhenitsyn's approach to literature, as a reader and as a writer, is as antimodern as some of his political positions. In our talks, he was disdainful of some of the contemporary writers in Russia now who tend to look for inspiration to, say, the sexual narratives of the Marquis de Sade or the formal play of Italo Calvino more than they do to Russian realism. He cannot abide experimentalism for its own sake or pure pleasure as a literary end. Even Vladimir Nabokov, to Solzhenitsyn, was ultimately a disappointment.

"I don't take anything away from his artistic force," he said. "I nominated Nabokov for the Nobel Prize, although he didn't receive it. But at the same time I am grieved that Nabokov, who came from a family which so avidly participated in the affairs of Russia, who could have written so much and compiled even more material on the Russian Revolution a long time before me, well, I am grieved that he washed his hands of it and busied himself only with literary successes. I am pained by this. I do not understand it. I do not understand how this is possible.

"As it happens, I do not like *Lolita* at all. It seems to me in bad taste. But he has some fine novels like *Invitation to a Beheading* and many others; I rate him very highly. But I don't like *Lolita* because it is an unworthy play on sexuality, in my opinion."

Over the years, a loose critical orthodoxy has evolved about Solzhenitsyn's own collected works. *One Day in the Life of Ivan Denisovich* is the undisputed masterpiece. *The First Circle* and, to a lesser extent, *Cancer Ward* are important works not only of political comment but of realism; it's as if, in the land of socialist realism, Solzhenitsyn took a debased form and gave it life. *Gulag*, too, is generally considered a masterwork, but of *what* is less clear. Of memoir? Political analysis? Documentary prose? No matter. The three volumes of *Gulag*, like *One Day*, will endure.

Solzhenitsyn said he sees his own work differently from nearly everyone else in the world. In 1937, when he was still a convinced communist, he dreamed of writing an epic history leading to the October Revolution of 1917. He even began making notes and writing early sequences that he used, decades later. *The Red Wheel* has been the obsession of Solzhenitsyn's writing life. As his politics changed (especially in prison, where his labored defenses of Marxism, he said, "shattered like glass"), so changed *The Red Wheel*. Eventually, he came to believe that the October Revolution, celebrated in Bolshevik mythology as a popular revolt, was actually a coup d'état carried off in circumstances of complete chaos. More important, he felt, were the historical events beginning with World War I and climaxing with the February Revolution, the overthrow of the czar, and the short-lived replacement with the doomed provisional government.

"When I began to study the February Revolution, I understood, first of all, that it is the central event of modern Russian history," Solzhenitsyn said. "I came to understand its weaknesses, its flaws, and how it was already doomed to result in October. Doomed. I understood this because by April 1917, Lenin was already laughing at it. Everything lay at his feet. He could have tried to seize power earlier—and he did, in July. So gradually, my emphasis shifted in time to February. Then I realized that to explain the February Revolution, I had to explain how czarism and society had developed by that time. And so I retreated and retreated all the way to the end of the nineteenth century, even though I was rebuked in the West for admiring the czar and for calling for a return to the past. The émigrés, meanwhile, chided me for writing an insulting book about the last czar, Nicholas II. But the truth is, I described him as he was. I do not praise him or rebuke him. I simply portray him as he was."

So vast is the project, so numerous are the characters, that one could more easily summarize *War and Peace* than *The Red Wheel*. In fact, Solzhenitsyn is engaged in a polemic with Tolstoy in his novel, insisting that individual personalities, like Lenin, the czarist minister Pyotr Stolypin, and various others, are absolutely critical to the course of events. Tolstoy, in the chapters that end *War and Peace,* professed his belief in a more determinist view of history, one bereft of great men.

The Red Wheel is formally quite different from anything Solzhenitsyn has written before. Alternating with the historical narrative are long biographical set pieces, newspaper clippings, and other experiments that borrow from sources as varied as John Dos Passos and Tolstoy. But perhaps most striking to Russian readers is Solzhenitsyn's language, his use of Russian words that had fallen into disuse. For many years, Solzhenitsyn made it his business to compile such words, even assembling a privately printed dictionary with thirty thousand entries. Even though Solzhenitsyn has been using such language ever since *One Day in the Life of Ivan Denisovich,* it is the language, more than the formal experiments or even the sheer immensity, that seems to trouble the Russian writers who have read all or part of *The Red Wheel.*

"The language is not at all appropriate," said Vassily Aksyonov, the author of *The Burn* and many other novels. "It's very strange to be reading a conversation between imperial guards and they are talking like two peasants. In *The Red Wheel,* Solzhenitsyn is at his best only when he is writing about something that he knows absolutely, that he is close to. The sections on Lenin are great. But there is so much that is uneven. His descriptions, for example, of Russian village life are false, and his writing about old Petersburg society is also not a success. It's too far from him."

Joseph Brodsky was even more critical: "What Solzhenitsyn has done overall is tremendous, but I am not a complete champion. I can't approve of his stylistic endeavors. He is a writer with natural gifts and talent. But I think he suffers from this desire, widespread in the twentieth century, that a Russian writer should have his own distinctive style. Solzhenitsyn had reasons to doubt that he was in possession of such a commodity despite the grace of *One Day in the Life of Ivan Denisovich.* In a sense, he went shopping for a style and he wound up with two things. First, he wanted to tap the dictionary. He forged or coined words that have Slavonic roots but which are not really Russian. There is Russian grammar and to a certain extent vocabulary there, but it's Slavic, not Russian. More importantly, in *The Red Wheel,* he decided to enliven things because of the extraordinary threat of monotony. And so he is relying on the sort of filmlike technique in Dos Passos, with headlines and documentary material all spliced in. Sometimes it seems there is more scissors and paste than actual scribbling, if you know what I mean. It seems grotesque to my eye. It reflects a groping for a style. It's as if he sees Proust with his style

THE EXILE | 151

of elaboration, Beckett's dead-end style, Andrei Platonov's cul-de-sac syntax, and he knows he needs something to call his own."

When I summarized such criticism for Solzhenitsyn, he seemed more intrigued than dismissive. "My language is this," he said. "There is a river flowing along, and you can take water from the surface, or you can probe more deeply and take from a lower stream. I take from the lower streams of the river of our language. In Russia, because of the general decline of Russian culture, there is a general decline in the language. If you now say to a Russian words like 'briefing,' 'establishment,' 'consensus,' everyone will understand. But as for Russian words, they will ask, 'What is this?' They are losing the Russian language. It is because our people are now losing the richness of their language and snapping up Englishisms that my language seems somehow strange. Of course it would be a lot easier to write more simply, but I don't need this. I am trying to rescue the old richness of the language. There is a layer nearby the day-to-day language which is dying off for lack of common use. That's the layer which I am trying to rescue. On this point, Brodsky is not correct. I don't try to reach for incomprehensible words or Old Slavonic, and I don't make up any words. I take from what exists. When I compiled and published this dictionary I gave examples of usage by twenty or twenty-five Russian authors. This is the responsibility of the writer. Without this the writer is pale and flat and then he has nothing."

The Red Wheel, which Solzhenitsyn finished in 1991, comprises four immense volumes running to over five thousand closely printed pages: *August 1914, November 1916, March 1917,* and *April 1917.* Because public interest in Solzhenitsyn was still high when Farrar, Straus & Giroux published *August 1914* in 1972, it sold well. "We were right behind *Jonathan Livingston Seagull* on the *Times* best-seller list," said Roger Straus, the publisher. "We sold hundreds of thousands of books." But Straus said that when he publishes *November 1916* sometime in the late nineties he expects to print no more than twenty or twenty-five thousand copies. "The truth is," said Straus, "I'd consider myself lucky to sell that. The interest is just not there anymore." Solzhenitsyn's French publisher, Claude Durand of Fayard, said the same: "The young just do not know who Aleksandr Solzhenitsyn is." In Russia itself, the publishing industry, like the rest of the economy, is in a state of free fall, and *The Red Wheel* languishes, incomplete. Solzhenitsyn is resigned to thinking that the books that he considers the centerpiece of his work will not be read properly and completely until the next century.

In the meantime, many of the Russians and non-Russians who have read at least part of the books have expressed disappointment, even boredom. "The everyday response is based on a kind of tiredness," said Alexis Klimoff, a professor at Vassar who has translated several of Solzhenitsyn's books and admires even the late work. "One of the problems of reading *The Red Wheel* is time. It's thousands and thousands of pages which are, if you wish to make a serious judgment, meant to be read together. It's physically exhausting and it's unlikely that people have the opportunity to do it. It becomes a matter of 'Oh hell, life is too short.' Which is true enough. But it is irresponsible in some fundamental sense."

The critics who have read *The Red Wheel* sympathetically measure it against *War and Peace,* often finding that Solzhenitsyn is better at war, Tolstoy at peace. The two works differ, too, in that Solzhenitsyn wants his work to stand as reliable history, a definitive account of Russia's chaotic march toward the rise of Bolshevism. "The fact is that Tolstoy's work on *War and Peace* was not very similar to mine on *The Red Wheel,*" Solzhenitsyn told me. "I won't compare the two works themselves but rather their respective aims. Lev Tolstoy wrote in the 1860s about the events of 1812. So, approximately, fifty years after the fact. But in that time Russian society itself had hardly changed. There was an aristocratic Russia that still existed; everyday life was much the same. Therefore his task was easier in this sense because he was describing the same world at an earlier stage. He could easily have transported the people of his world into his novel, because it was much the same circle. I started in 1937, but really seriously began writing in 1969, and from 1969 to 1917 is about the same time difference, but I wrote, I can say, about an entirely different world, a new planet. Prerevolutionary Russia and then the Russia in which I have lived were cut off from each other. They were different worlds. I had to transport myself into a country that no longer existed. So I did not have the chance to transport today's people into the books."

Not long before I visited the Solzhenitsyns, I had driven to the village of Troitse-Lykovo on the outskirts of Moscow. The main road out is the Rublev Highway, a kind of golden pathway for the Kremlin elite, past and present, who have their dachas west of the city. On Friday afternoons, black Chaika limousines roar along the highway, often seizing the empty middle lane—the "Kremlin" lane—the better to start the weekend a few minutes early. Aleksandr and Natalia Solzhenitsyn had hired Russian contractors to build a house in "dacha-land," on the same site, as it happens, where the fabled military strategist of the Stalin era Marshal Mikhail Tukhachevsky once lived. The Solzhenitsyns razed the old wooden house and designed a V-shaped brick house. The plans called for a working wing, with room for archives, a library, and research assistants, as well as a "living wing" with six bedrooms and various living areas. A high wooden fence painted grass-green surrounds the ten-acre property. The house would not be ready for the Solzhenitsyns' arrival that spring, and they were resigned to living in an apartment they own downtown.

When I lived in Moscow, from the beginning of 1988 to the end of 1991, most intellectuals began to realize it was inevitable that Solzhenitsyn would be published and would return home. The right-wing editors of journals such as *Nash Sovremennik* ("Our Contemporary") were hopeful, figuring that Solzhenitsyn would present a nationalist alternative to Andrei Sakharov and the more Western-oriented radicals. Many of the liberals were terrified. Vitaly Korotich, who was the editor of the reformist magazine *Ogonyok* ("The Little Flame"), told me that it was entirely possible that Solzhenitsyn would come to Moscow as an "Ayatollah Khomeini." The publication of "Rebuilding Russia" in 1990 was an enormous letdown for the right and a relief for the reformers: the essay was anti-empire and pro-democracy. Russians and non-Russian reformers said the piece showed traces of Solzhenitsyn's distance, his difficulty in grasping events he could only see on television or read about in the press, but, in all, there was relief.

In the days before Solzhenitsyn's return, opinions in Russia about him were emotional and mixed. A poll taken in St. Petersburg showed that 48 percent of the respondents would like to see Solzhenitsyn as president of Russia, despite his desire never to hold office. Only 18 percent picked Boris Yeltsin. But in more rarefied circles, among intellectuals especially, a more ironical attitude toward Solzhenitsyn had formed, one that ranged from indifference to mockery:

"Solzhenitsyn is late. Developments have accelerated way ahead of him. He must realize he is coming back to a world that is utterly foreign to him."

"He should have come back when the communists were driven out. Where was he? He has nothing to say anymore. This *Red Wheel* of his is the work of a graphomaniac. I tried to read it and fell asleep every time."

"Maybe if he'd come after Sakharov died in December '89. The reaction to Sakharov's death, the outpouring, was an indication of how much one honest man meant in those days. But the time for a single heroic figure has passed. Solzhenitsyn's authority is based only in the past."

"I suppose he'll come back and play the role of Tolstoy, the great writer who gives us all advice, the prophet who accepts visitors and wears a great beard. The beard is very important in this role."

Solzhenitsyn, for his part, was well aware of the range of attitudes that awaited him. His wife had been back three times. His sons had also been to Russia. Some Russians had even sent letters to Cavendish telling the writer what they had heard and what they themselves felt about his return home.

"Many await my arrival with hostility," Solzhenitsyn said. "There are those who weep for communism and who consider me its main destroyer, the main person at fault. Some fanatics are literally saying they want my neck. Secondly, the mafia understands that if I wasn't going to make peace with the KGB, I certainly would not with them. Third, there are those who believe in myths—for example, that I will return and become the head of Pamyat or head of the right wing. They cannot understand that I want nothing to do with power or any political position. Finally, there are the powers-that-be themselves. I do not avoid critical comments. In Europe, or with you here today, I do not avoid criticizing today's authorities or the current reforms and how they are being conducted. I speak out sharply and will continue doing that. I will not be amazed if I am denied access to television after a while.

"In other words, life will not be easy in any respect. But I am going because I have fulfilled my literary duty and now I must try to fulfill my duty to society to whatever extent I can. How it will turn out, I don't know."

In our time together Solzhenitsyn insisted several times that he had no interest in politics, that he would never run for political office or accept an appointment of any kind. I asked him if he would play the sort of role Sakharov did in the late 1980s, a moral compass for a country that is adrift.

"My role can only be moral," he said. "What other role can I have? But the situation is changing very quickly. Many years have passed since Sakharov's death. In fact, there is no guarantee that Sakharov would have remained as influential and as admired as he was. The situation is changing so quickly and it is difficult to say how much my moral efforts will resonate and be successful. The fact that my books have not been read, this also interferes a lot. You can't get them. People say, 'Who's Solzhenitsyn? Oh yes, he's the guy they kicked out, he did something long ago.' But there are no books. This makes it very difficult."

As I was getting ready to leave Vermont, I thought that one of the most remarkable aspects of Solzhenitsyn's journey was that he was going to be able to finish it. From the moment his plane landed in Russia that coming spring, his life would be complete. As a writer, too, he had finished all he had wanted to, restoring the memory of the Soviet holocaust, giving voice to the lost. Now his literary old age would take on a Tolstoyan pattern; in his last years, his great novels done, Tolstoy worked on much shorter fiction, honing valedictory stories like "Hadji Murát" and "Alyosha the Pot" to perfection with ten, fifteen, twenty drafts.

"There is no sense at my age in beginning a big project," Solzhenitsyn said. "But I am very interested in the short form and I am beginning to work in it again now. It's not just a question of age. I began with short stories, but the task ahead was always first my novels, then *Gulag,* and then *The Red Wheel,* and I had to fulfill those tasks. Finally, I have the chance. Now I will replenish my impressions of life in Russia, of today's Russia, and I will definitely write short stories. For the moment, while I am still in Vermont, I am working on stories using materials from the twenties and thirties, because I cannot write about today's Russia without personal impressions of it. I remember well these things from my youth. And then having finished *The Red Wheel*—this huge beast now felled—there are many loose ends left over and it is unclear what to do with them. I have a mountain of leftover material that has to be sorted out."

The Solzhenitsyn house in Cavendish was filling up with packing crates. There were a few brand-new American Tourister extra-large suitcases in the guest room. The Solzhenitsyns were not selling the Cavendish house, preferring to keep it, at least for now, as a base for their children. The boys all said they intended to move to Russia, to be of use to Russia, though not right away. Only the center of the household had almost put America behind him.

"It's almost as if we no longer live here," Solzhenitsyn said. "In spirit, we have already gone. I await different trials and different tasks. I am ready for this and I thank God I have the strength for now. Naturally, I have been following intensively what has been going on in Russia, and I am well informed. But the meetings with specific people and learning about their specific fates, that still awaits me. The specific situations at particular cities, at farms and factories, that awaits me. I will need, first of all, a period of reacquaintance to get a sense of the lower depths of life in Russia. I have to take careful note of it, the way an artist would, of today's situation and the people's mood."

Was he returning with any optimism at all?

"If it took Russia seventy-five years to fall so far, then it is obvious that it will take more than seventy-five years to rise back up," he said. "A hundred or a hundred and fifty, we can guess. It is very difficult to find a country in modern history systematically destroyed for as long as seventy-five years. And it is important to remember that they destroyed selectively, not just anyone, but those who were the most intelligent, those who might protest, those who could think on their own, the life force of the people."

"But, of course," Natalia said, "it will be a happy day, returning. Even now it is as if a terrible weight has been lifted from us. Just the knowledge that we will finish our lives in Russia is a great relief. When I was back I got pleasure just from being surrounded by the Russian language. I remember being in the metro and hearing that banal voice: 'Careful! The doors are closing. . . . The next stop is . . .' But it was in Russian! Just to pass stores that say *moloko* and *khleb* instead of 'milk' and 'bread.' The pleasure in that!"

It was getting to be time to go. Natalia had fed us all one last time. Ignat played a Schubert sonata. Natalia loaded me up with files, clippings, and a Christmas cake to take home to my family. We all agreed to meet again, in Moscow. As a final question, I mentioned to Solzhenitsyn that I remembered his speech in Liechtenstein when he said that modern man, by putting himself at the center of the world, fears death because death becomes the end of all things. Now that you are seventy-five, don't you fear dying? I asked him.

"Absolutely not," he said, his face lighting up with pleasure. "It will just be a peaceful transition. As a Christian, I believe there is a life after death, and thus I understand this is not the end of life. The soul has a continuation, the soul lives on. Death is only a stage, some would even say a liberation. In any case, I have no fear of death."

"And where will you be buried?" I asked.

"I've made a preliminary choice," Solzhenitsyn said. "Maybe I'll change it later, but I have one in mind. It's in central Russia and I invite you to come there after I have gone."

CHAPTER 5

MOSCOW, OPEN CITY

By the time I visited Solzhenitsyn in Vermont, I no longer lived in Moscow either. I visited three, four times a year, usually for a couple of weeks at a time, sometimes a month. This way of seeing was not the same as if I were living there, but it made the changes in the city all the more startling to me; the effect was much like making periodic visits to friends and each time being shocked by the seemingly freakish growth spurts of their children. On one visit the streets would be lined with makeshift kiosks selling everything from shampoo to beer; a trip or two later, and the kiosks had disappeared and the old state-run stores—for so long the empty, forlorn symbols of central planning—had been turned into bustling places of business: the kiosk pioneers had become small businessmen. I would drive through one neighborhood and wonder when had all those green-glass office buildings gone up; when had the neighborhood started to look like Dallas? And when did this neighborhood, with its exquisite small offices and residences, begin to look like Helsinki or Copenhagen? Just as I had grown used to the idea of a scattering of McDonald's restaurants downtown, a "drive-thru" appeared. Suddenly an enormous new cathedral on the Frunze Embankment was competing for skyline attention with the towers and domes of the Kremlin itself.

To be in Moscow in the 1990s is to be taken by surprise on a daily basis. Street names change, erasing honors given seventy-odd years ago to dubious Bolshevik warriors; thanks to a befuddled city planner with too much time and power, the flow of traffic takes a new direction; fortunes are made and, all too often, spirited out of the country to banks in Zurich, Nicosia, and Vaduz; gangs form, recapitulating, in their way, the history of young people in the West: hippies, punks, grungers, skinheads, metal heads, Tolkeinites; a gay bar opens down the street and features a "transvestite night"; the Lubavitcher Hasidim set up a synagogue and lobbied the government to try to take possession of a trove of manuscripts stored away for decades in the damp corners of the Lenin Library; the Lenin Library becomes the Russian State Library; a neighboring apartment building is cleaned out by mafiosi who have decided to "privatize" the place; the involuntarily gentrified are told, not asked, to accept an apartment so far from the center of town that it might as well be in the center of Minsk. The changes reach to the simplest level: there are no longer any lines, but there are more homeless living in underpasses, train stations, city parks. Car prices have soared but the number of car owners—and hence the level of traffic—soars too. In Moscow only the weather is more or less the same as it was.

In 1991, it was obvious to everyone that the collapse of the Communist Party, and then of the Soviet Union itself, would transform politics. What we could not imagine was the astonishing speed with which it would also transform the city and the texture of everyday life. As the old regime collapsed I had only the slightest intimations of the changes to come. In mid-August 1991, my family was scheduled to fly home to New York for the last time, ending my stint in Moscow for *The Washington Post*. (My wife reported for the *Post*'s rival, *The New York Times*.) The flight was scheduled for August 18, a Sunday. A few days before, I interviewed Aleksandr Yakovlev, who had been Gorbachev's closest aide throughout the perestroika years, although now he had been shoved aside as the reactionaries in the Communist Party asserted themselves in the Kremlin. We met at City Hall, where Yakovlev ran a government commission looking into the atrocities in the Soviet past. It was a quiet summer morning, a day off for most people, and he greeted me and some colleagues from the *Post* wearing baggy khaki trousers and a short-sleeved shirt. Dacha clothes. Yakovlev talked about many things that morning—the chaotic process of perestroika, Gorbachev's achievements and failures, the "great mist" of the future—but it was a mostly rambling conversation, a reflection, a riff, and yet, just before we were getting ready to go, Yakovlev said, as if it were an aside, that "forces of revenge" within the Party and the KGB were preparing a putsch.

I didn't know what to make of his comment. The next day, at a picnic with some Russian friends on the Moscow River, we talked about Yakovlev's prediction of an "imminent" coup d'état. Words like "coup" and "putsch" were common currency in Moscow political talk; so much so that every time one politician made a move against another, "coup" and "putsch" would be trotted out as the nouns of choice. Every time Gorbachev was about to face a plenary meeting of the Central Committee, *tout Moscou* predicted apocalypse. (And not without reason: the Central Committee had openly turned on Gorbachev.) Yakovlev certainly had his sources of information, but he also had his political motives. Maybe he simply wanted, yet again, to tar his reactionary opponents with the "coup" brush. In Russia, a coup seemed farfetched, my friends and I agreed. The Soviet Union was struggling, but this, after all, was not a banana republic. And 1917? Well, that was something else—not quite parallel.

"But I'll tell you one thing," I said, in the plummy tone of one rehearsing his valedictory. "Check out Moscow in a few years and there will be shopping malls everywhere."

"*Ti soshol s uma,*" said my friend Sergei. "You've gone nuts."

"Oh, you're right!" Sergei's wife, Masha, said mockingly. "Downtown will look just like Fifth Avenue. Be sure to visit!"

So that was the consensus: no coup, no shopping malls.

A couple of days later, one prediction went sour: there were tanks parked not a hundred yards from my front door. The coup was on. (Thankfully, it was over sixty-odd hours later.) Less earth-shattering to political historians, perhaps, is the fact that the second prediction—"the shopping-malls vision," as my friends dubbed it on the spot—came true far more quickly than I had imagined. Capitalism may have crept slowly, erratically, dangerously into provincial cities like Tambov, Stavropol, and Vologda, but in Moscow, the capital and the traditional city of the Russian avant-garde, the signs of money were everywhere: advertisements, billboards, neon, foreign goods, and, yes, shopping malls. As late as 1989, a foreigner or a native Muscovite who wanted to buy most Western goods either ordered them from foreign catalogs and had them shipped or got on a plane. By 1996, Tver' Street, one of the main boulevards radiating from the Kremlin, had sufficient shops to sate all but the most jaded plutocrat. As late as 1990, a ballplayer in search of a decent pair of basketball shoes bought them on the black market, abroad, or not at all. By 1996, Nike and Reebok had outposts in Moscow, and for the summer Olympics, the main sponsor of the Russian Olympic team was no longer the Communist Party of the Soviet Union, but rather the executives of Reebok.

The rule of class and privilege is now no different in Moscow from what it is in Paris or Vienna, Los Angeles or Amsterdam. Money walks. If you have money nowadays in Moscow, you can taste it all: lobsters flown in from Maine, salmon from Scotland, caviar from Azerbaijan, lamb from Auckland, pineapple from Hawaii. Visitors to Moscow in the seventies remember well the dreary ritual of eating at restaurants offering shoelike "cutlets" and bonelike "chicken." Now there is every cuisine imaginable—even Russian if you look hard enough. I waited years for the arrival of Chinese food in Moscow—I even traveled thousands of miles east to Khabarovsk, mainly because I had heard you could get a decent kung pao chicken there—but now . . . One night at a Chinese place not far from my old apartment, I asked for hot and sour soup but was informed by the waiter that this was a *northern* Szechuan restaurant, not southern, and would I consider one of a dozen other soups? None, as it turned out, was any worse than the best of Mott Street in New York.

If you have money in Moscow, you might be invited to a party and meet a television executive in his twenties who will tell you, deadpan, "When I was a diplomat in Rangoon I was bringing socialism to Burma. Now I'm the guy who brought *Santa Barbara* to Russia!" If you have money in Moscow, you might have slapped down a $3,000 annual membership fee near the Dynamo soccer stadium to join a short-lived gentlemen's club where the highlight of the evening was a rat race, featuring real rats sprinting through a neon-lit maze. The rats were taught their ironic run by the former trainer at the great Durov Animal Circus. (The race, I should add, did not begin until a dwarf dressed as an eighteenth-century page rang the bell.) If you have money in Moscow, you might live in a gated mansion outside of town and send your kids to boarding school in the Alps; you also might meet your end in a contract hit, blown to smithereens by a car bomb, ignited, of course, by state-of-the-art remote control.

Everyone is looking for a taste of "the sweet life." Hundreds of women in Moscow have quit their low-paying jobs as teachers, doctors, and engineers and have taken to selling cosmetics for Avon, or Mary Kay. (A pink Cadillac in modern Moscow would not be out of place; there are now dealers in town for Porsche, Mercedes, Saab, and BMW.) The Communist Party newspaper *Pravda* is dying, but a hipper version called *Pravda Pyat* ("Pravda Five") has started publication in search of "left-leaning" souls of Generation X. Venerable literary monthlies like *Novy Mir* hang on, mostly thanks to the largesse of the American financier George Soros, but a former Maoist from Holland, Derek Sauer, is making a fortune with a Russian-language edition of *Cosmopolitan*. Exams in Scientific Socialism are, of course, no longer required in universities, and business schools are filling up as soon as they can be opened. On Marshal Rybalka Street, a producer named Aleksei Karakulov runs a school for children whose ambition it is to become supermodels. Parents pay $60 a month to send their kids, ages four to fourteen, to Model Show. There is a market for all this. Propaganda has shifted from the ideological to the corporate: in today's Moscow, the faces of Claudia Schiffer and Cindy Crawford are nearly as ubiquitous as Lenin's once was.

Not long ago, Moscow's imperious and all-powerful mayor, Yuri Luzhkov, complained of a bad social life. He had no place to go out, poor dear. And so a club was created for him, named, appropriately, Magisterium. One wonders, however, why the mayor had complained. Surely he would have found a good time at the Silver Age Club, where the evening's highlight is an auction for a single long-stemmed rose. (The rose rarely goes for less than $1,000.) The owner is planning to open a new club on Lubyanka Square within firing distance of KGB headquarters. He has announced a fervent desire to have party games; he said he would hold mock arrests and serve dishes like "brains of the enemy of the people."

Before the great political and economic changes of the late eighties and early nineties, the most remarkable feature of Moscow was its astonishing drabness: its lack of color; its lack of restaurants; its lack of foreign goods and foreign culture; the absence of billboards, neon, and commercialism of any kind. More often than not, places of business carried soul-defeating names like "Restaurant," "Bread," "Wine," "Clothes," or, more specifically, "Clothes Store No. 14." The most radiant objects in the Moscow skyline were the ruby-red stars shining above the Kremlin towers.

For the urban intelligentsia, the greatest pleasure and novelty of pere-stroika was not the publication of forbidden literature—much of it had been circulating in underground, samizdat editions—but rather the seemingly more banal process of getting a visa and a ticket and going abroad. In the seventies, Russians on flights abroad were either carefully selected by Party committees or were emigrating; it was near impossible just to go somewhere. By the late eighties, Aeroflot flights especially were filling up with people escaping the drabness of Moscow and the even more dreary provincial cities. There were students going to study in Prague or Paris; parents going to Brighton Beach to visit their émigré sons and daughters whom they had thought they would never see again; nascent businessmen on "fact-finding" junkets to New York; retired art professors going to Rome and Florence to see, for the first time, the paintings they had been dreaming about all their lives.

When this wave of travel began, the Russian travelers at Sheremetyevo Airport were positively giddy with the novelty of it all. They were con-fused about customs declarations. They packed as if they were going over-land to Sumatra—and returned loaded up with VCRs, washing machines, stereos, everything they could manage. By the nineties, however, many Russians going abroad became as accustomed to the idea of travel as any New York banker with two million miles on his frequent-flier account. It was the miracle that seemed to accompany any liberty: it seemed impos-sible, and unnatural, that travel had once been all but forbidden. (On the other hand, poorer Russians discovered that travel was expensive; even trips "abroad" to Ukraine, Kazakhstan, and the rest of the former republics of the Soviet Union became for them all but impossible.)

Russians are still traveling, but the hungry urgency is gone. The sense that it could all end—that freedom was a raised window just waiting to slam shut once more—has diminished. Even the most hardened commu-nist and nationalist politicians at least pretend that they have no intention of caging in the population should they come to power. There is also the sense, for Muscovites, that they no longer live in a barren outpost of civilization. The great jumble of political conflict, economic upheaval, and cultural shifts summarized in the word *transition* can be intensely painful and bewildering. It is also intensely interesting. Every yearning and joke that characterized the period before Gorbachev was linked somehow to the dreariness of life, its lack of excitement, stimulation, and possibility. The Brezhnev years were known as "the period of stagnation," not merely for economic and political reasons, but also because of the shabby texture of life, its lack of promise. Now there is no place on earth more future-directed, more interesting, than Russia.

There are other cities in Russia that have, each in its own way, joined this process of transformation—St. Petersburg, Nizhni Novgorod, Yekaterinburg, Khabarovsk, Vladivostok—but the center of it all is still Moscow. There really is no second place. Even St. Petersburg, with its historical role as the window to the West, cannot compare. More than 80 percent of the country's capital is in Moscow. The banks, the foreign businesses, the political actors, the cultural and intellectual institutions, the information and communications centers, the trends in fashion, language, and popular culture—all of it is centered in the capital. In some provincial cities, a single natural resource can transform the lives of the top layer of the population—oil in north central Russia, nickel in Norilsk, gold in Yakutia—but the deepest transformations are in Moscow.

"You cannot understand Russia just by understanding Moscow," the reform politician Grigory Yavlinsky once told me, "but without understanding Moscow you can't understand the future."

The leaders of the Soviet Union were determined that the capital of their revolution live in a historic void. The mythology and ideology of bolshevism required the destruction of all previous myths and ideologies. In 1918, Lenin decreed that all czarist monuments had to be replaced by monuments dedicated to "the liberation of labor." Those churches that were not leveled by an order of the Kremlin and the wrecking ball were either left to decay or were transformed into stores, or warehouses, or public toilets. Renaming streets has always been a part of revolutions—

the French found this even easier than toppling heads into baskets—and under the Bolsheviks, street names resonant of monarchy or commerce were immediately renamed. Meat Trader's Alley, for instance, became Kirov Street. Under the Bolsheviks the streets were gray but the names were red: Red Army Street, Red Warrior Street, Red Beacon Street, Red Guard Street, Red Guard Boulevard, Red Guard Lanes 1, 2, 3, and 4, Red Barracks Embankment, Red Barracks Street, Red Cadet Lanes 1 and 2, Red Proletariat Street, Red Student Lane, Red Dawn Street. Just about the only indignity spared Moscow came when the sycophants in Stalin's Politburo suggested that Moscow be renamed Stalinodar. Even Stalin thought that might exceed propriety.

The transformation of Moscow in the nineties is not merely about money. There has been an attempt through the manipulation of symbols in Moscow to prove to Russians and the world that the country has reentered history, that it is determined to define its future through an understanding of history far richer than the one offered in the standard Stalinist textbooks. Moscow City Hall had a special office in charge of renaming streets or, better to say, *re*-renaming. Kirov Street is Meat Trader's Alley again; Kalinin Street is New Arbat Street; and Gorky Street is Tver' Street once more. The process of re-renaming is so widespread that no one knows where anyone is going—a fairly apt metaphor for just about anything in post-Soviet Russia.

The first "new master" of Moscow was Yeltsin himself. In 1987, when he was the head of the city's Communist Party Committee, his historical renewal plans seemed revolutionary. He helped convert the Old Arbat district into a pedestrian mall, and in no time there were small restaurants, street musicians, art peddlers. He also opened up the more distant park, Izmailovo, as a kind of outdoor arts and crafts bazaar. The more substantial changes, however, came after the decline of the Party. The city's post-Soviet mayors—first the economist Gavriil Popov, and then, beginning in 1992, Yuri Luzhkov—indulged what can only be described as a rebuilding mania. The city administration, with the help of a new breed of bankers desperate for access to cozy relations with Luzhkov, combed through the history of the city in search of churches, monuments, and buildings to revive. In 1990, Popov decided at once to shut down the House of Scientific Atheism and to rebuild the Kazan

Cathedral on Red Square. The next year, after the coup, many of the toppled statues of the Bolshevik icons—Dzerzhinsky, Kalinin, Lenin— were carted off to the grounds of the New Tretyakov Gallery and scattered around the grass. The area is now known as the Garden of Sculpture of the Epoch of Totalitarianism.

One of the institutions in town that has marked well the speed of historical change in Moscow has been the Museum of the Revolution on Tver' Street. Before Gorbachev came to power in 1985, the museum was the repository of objects tied to 1917, Year Zero, the most glorious of all events in the official Soviet past. When Gorbachev tried to amend that official version of events in 1987 and 1988 with an official version of his own, the museum changed accordingly. In his attempt to find an alternative to Stalinism, Gorbachev rehabilitated one of Stalin's greatest enemies, Nikolai Bukharin, the theoretician whom Lenin had dubbed "the favorite" of the Party. After his execution in 1938, Bukharin's name was unmentionable, except as a prime example of an anti-Soviet wrecker and conspirator. But in 1988, Bukharin became the official object of affection. He represented, at least to Gorbachev, an alternative to Stalin and Stalinism. The Museum of the Revolution set up an exhibit of his letters, his clothes, even his modest landscapes.

The Bukharin fad, like Gorbachev's yearning for a "reformed socialism," proved short-lived. By the mid-nineties, the Museum of the Revolution had been transformed as utterly as Moscow itself. In the lobby, where it had once been possible to buy volumes of Marx, Engels, and Lenin, there was now a shop that sold *The History of Liberalism in Russia, Memoirs of the Whites in the Civil War,* stamps from Uganda, a stuffed Mickey Mouse, Solzhenitsyn's *How to Reform Russia,* baseball and basketball trading cards, and Lego sets. Another shop acted as a trading post for communist-era junk: propaganda posters, Komsomol pins, Party banners, Lenin busts, Stalin busts, war medals, a complete set of Brezhnev's ghostwritten memoirs. Sacred objects were now kitsch. Old Russians battered by the high cost of living came trooping in with these things hoping to sell them for a few thousand rubles; ironic Russians of the middle and upper classes, to say nothing of souvenir-hungry tourists, snatched them up. A young man with a ponytail named Aleksandr Fomin ran the shop and told me that sometimes he ran across posters from the twenties that he sold through the Sotheby's auction house.

"I don't collect any of this stuff myself," he said. "Who could stand to look at it?" He said he was twenty-nine. "After all, I practically grew up in the new times. To me, this is just business."

Upstairs, in the museum proper, the exhibits on Soviet history have about them a sense of rueful irony. A propaganda picture of the happy masses ("Thanks to the Party for Our Happy Childhood!") hangs next to a picture of slum children in an industrial city. There is a vigorous-looking picture of Brezhnev that ran on the front page of *Pravda* (it was probably doctored by the editors) and then a picture of Brezhnev plain: senile, decrepit, clueless. Nothing is missing here. History is recaptured: the camps, the stampedes at Stalin's funeral, the repression of artists and writers, the brutalities of industrialization and collectivization, the extraordinary triumph of the war. Perhaps only one figure is consciously slighted: Gorbachev, still so hated in Moscow, merits only one tiny display case.

In his otherwise thin and unrevealing book *Moscow, We Are Your Children,* Moscow's mayor, Yuri Luzhkov, tries to paint a glorious vision of the city's past. Using photographs, paintings, drawings, and old maps, Luzhkov describes a Moscow as grand as Rome, Paris, or London, a city rich with commerce, event, character, and architecture. Just as Stalin was determined to create a new Moscow by destroying remnants of the pre-Soviet past, Luzhkov set out to create a new Moscow by rebuilding many of those same places. At an astonishing rate, Russian workers and workers hired from abroad rebuilt or restored the Bolshoi Theater, the National Hotel, Resurrection Gate at the entrance to Red Square, the Tretyakov Gallery, the Moscow Zoo, Gorky Park, and dozens of other sites. The outer Ring Road, once known as "the Road of Death," is now decently lighted and as smooth as any ordinary highway in the West. Nineteenth-century houses that had once been homes of wealthy merchants and then fell into disrepair are now headquarters for Russian and foreign businesses. An enormous (and, alas, grotesque) war memorial has opened on Kutuzovsky Prospekt: in the end, the complex will include a church, a mosque, a synagogue, and a fountain, lit red at night, the better to evoke the bloodshed of the war. Outside the Kremlin gates, Manezh Square has become a vast pit filled with construction equipment; the plan is to open an underground mall that will include six levels of offices, stores, banks, and parking. The city has also announced plans to build SITI, a financial center modeled on the City of London.

While the story of Yeltsin into the mid-nineties was one of moral and physical decline, Luzhkov's reputation in Moscow is like that of Richard Daley at his peak in Chicago: everyone assumes, rightly or not, that he uses less than ethical means to achieve positive ends.

The reasons for Luzhkov's popularity are not hard to fathom. In September 1991, the Moscow leadership issued a decree allowing the conversion of state housing into private property, meaning that, for a nominal sum, Muscovites suddenly owned their apartments. That also meant people could buy and sell apartments; brokerage firms suddenly appeared to handle the new market. In 1993, with his aide Larissa Piyasheva, Luzhkov also managed to privatize more than 90 percent of Moscow's retail shops and 70 percent of all restaurants and service outlets. Foreign businesses stream into the capital in search of new markets: McDonald's; Goldman, Sachs; Dannon Yogurt; Pizza Hut; Baskin-Robbins; Nina Ricci; Estée Lauder; Benetton; Christian Dior; Yves Rocher; Siemens.

Luzhkov, who was born in 1936, grew up in Moscow when it was, for nearly everyone, a poor city. Although he is quick to describe the glories of old Moscow, he also says, "I don't want to idealize our life. If we even begin to discuss the conditions of our everyday lives, it will be just awful." His family of six people lived in one room with no running water, indoor plumbing, or gas. Luzhkov was trained as an engineer and worked in chemical plants before joining the city administration under the old regime. When Gavriil Popov appointed him to a top job in 1990, members of the Moscow City Council asked him whether he was a democrat, a communist, or, perhaps, an independent.

"I have always been loyal to one platform and will remain loyal to one platform: the *administrative* platform," Luzhkov declared. In 1991 and 1993, at Yeltsin's moments of most severe crisis, Luzhkov proved himself loyal; but otherwise he was positioning himself outside the ideological debates of national politics. He was a builder. He got things done. (Never mind exactly how.) If the moment required a little nationalist bluster, he would provide it.

Above all, Luzhkov intended to bring as much money and activity into Moscow as he could. He recognized, he said, that "businessmen who come to this different country soon realize they have come to an entirely different galaxy"—a galaxy without guarantees or rules of the game. After a power struggle with members of the Yeltsin government, Luzhkov won the right to establish the rules of the game in Moscow. Operating almost independently of the national government, he acts as the economic overlord of the center of Russian wealth. Luzhkov determines who will get what property. Luzhkov determines tax rates. Luzhkov creates the look of Moscow, its skyline, its street life, its rate of change. The Russian press rarely dares to criticize Luzhkov, not least because he is so popular. Even Daley in his time was not as dominant.

"Luzhkov is the most natural creature of this Russian transition," said Sergei Stankevich, who had served as deputy mayor under Popov. "Luzhkov is a fish very much in the water. This is a time when the market exists but under the strictest supervision of the state. He is father, administrator, supervisor, boss. He encourages those private initiatives which are ready to cooperate with him. He is honest—in his understanding of honesty—and does not betray his own people. Of course he created the necessary guarantees for himself, but this is one of the rules of the time. Still, he deserves respect."

———

The most visible and resonant instance of historical reconstruction in Luzhkov's Moscow is the Cathedral of Christ the Savior. No construction project has embodied more of the grandiosity and hypocrisy of the resurrection of Russia than the rebuilding of a cathedral that had been looted and dynamited at Stalin's order in 1931.

The story of the Cathedral of Christ the Savior is, perhaps, the most telling instance of magical realism, Russian style. After the defeat of Napoleon in 1812, Alexander I signed a manifesto ordering that there be a contest among architects to design a cathedral commemorating the great victory of the Russian people and the people's gratitude to God for the preservation of Russia. The cathedral took decades to design and build—it was not consecrated until 1883—but when it was finally completed it was, if not the most beautiful of churches, certainly the most grandiose. There were five gold domes, the highest of which was as high as a seventeen-story building. There were fourteen bells in four separate belfries—their combined weight was sixty-five tons. Twelve immense doors opened into the church. The cathedral contained 177 marble panels describing the heroic battles with the French. The artists included Vereshchagin, Sedov, Surikov, the most famous in Russia at the time. The combination of these battle scenes and traditional icons was intended to merge the history of the church and the history of Russia. On Christmas and Easter as many as fifteen thousand people squeezed inside the cathedral—all carrying beeswax candles—and soloists from the Bolshoi Theater would sing the holiday chants and hymns. Although the Assumption Cathedral on the Kremlin grounds was far older—it was opened in 1475—the Cathedral of Christ the Savior quickly took on an enormously important role in the iconography of Russia itself.

"It might not have been the most exquisite of churches, but even non-believers like me used to go there, if only to be with our friends and congregate in the park area outside," Lev Razgon, a famous writer and camp survivor, told me.

One afternoon, I visited the construction site on the Frunze Embankment—the precise location of the original church. Crews were working around the clock. There was a small exhibition hall on the grounds. The focus of the little museum was a television and videotape player that played, over and over, the history of the cathedral's rise and fall. Along with a fifth-grade class out for a field trip, I took a seat and watched. The narrator, in a grave March of Time voice, described how in the early twenties, as Lenin's campaign against the church went into high gear, services at the cathedral were ordered stopped. Nearly 95 percent of the churches in the city were "smashed, liquidated." Priests were jailed, executed, or, at the very least, co-opted by the state. One priest, the narrator said, had his tongue cut out and his eyes scooped from the sockets. He was shot and left to burn on a pile of manure. "Such was the state's struggle against the 'opium of the people.'"

I watched the schoolchildren around me as they heard the narrator read one of Lenin's secret telegrams to his lackeys: "Now when there are cannibalism and corpses in the street we must expropriate church valuables. Don't hesitate to kill any resisters. The more reactionary clergy we shoot now, the better: it will mean less resistance for decades thereafter." The October Revolution, the narrator said, "was intent on shouldering aside all previous history." The children watched, still and absorbed. I couldn't help but think that just a few years before, Soviet schoolchildren learned lessons of history quite opposite to this one.

The film cut to pictures of churches being dynamited and burned, to peasants forced not only to give up their icons, but to smash them in the streets before smiling troops of the secret police. The decision to destroy the Cathedral of Christ the Savior—akin to Mussolini flattening St. Peter's—was made in secret, and by July 1931 secret police operatives and young Komsomol workers began the process through a gigantic looting operation. Working in shifts, around the clock, they wrenched huge slabs of marble off the walls, cut down the bells from the belfries, cut down the crosses, the icons. Nearly a thousand pounds of gold leaf was stripped from the domes. The sound of picks and axes and jackhammers was unceasing. Some of the materials ended up as benches in subway stations, as the facades to new bureaucracies like the Central Planning commission; a few objects were preserved in museums like the Antireligious Art Museum on the grounds of the Donskoy Monastery. Eleanor Roosevelt managed to acquire the iconostasis and then donated it to the Vatican. Priests who tried to protest the looting were executed.

Vladislav Mikosha was a young cameraman at the time. One morning, with only minimal explanation, he was ordered by Kremlin authorities to make a record of the scene of destruction. "Wonderful marble sculptures were dragged out of the cathedral with ropes around their necks," he recalled. "They were thrown off high places and into the mud. Arms, legs, and angel wings broke off. . . . Gold crosses were ripped off the cupolas with the help of tractors."

Finally, on December 5, 1931, demolition experts set off a series of dynamite charges to finish the job. As Timothy Colton recounts in his history of Moscow, the first two attempts to topple the main structure failed. According to an account published in 1989 in *Literaturnaya Rossi-aya*, "believers in the crowd let out that the Lord had heard their prayers and would not let the church be destroyed." The third blast, however, did the job. The Cathedral of Christ the Savior was now mere rubble. It took five months of drilling and pile driving and eighteen months of carting and clearing to get rid of the forty million bricks that had been a church.

Needless to say, anyone protesting the destruction of the cathedral within the Soviet Union was silenced in the most obvious ways. A couple of demolition workers who refused to take part in the destruction of the cathedral were sent to labor camps. Any protests from outside the country were met with disdain. Lev Perchik, the head of the City Planning Department under Stalin, said in 1934, "We still sometimes hear timid voices complaining about the undue severity of our surgical methods. Such claims only amuse us. No one has identified a single demolished building which should have been saved; it is easy to find dozens more which must be demolished. We cannot reconstruct a city like Moscow without a surgeon's scalpel."

Stalin's intention was to replace the Cathedral of Christ the Savior (an archaic symbol, for him) with a monument to Lenin so enormous that it would tower over the greatest symbol of modernity at the time, the Empire State Building. For Moscow, this building would embody the permanence and the genius of the regime: it would be its Pyramids, its cathedral at Chartres. Just as the czar had initiated a design competition for the cathedral, Stalin initiated one for what would be called the Palace of Soviets. And as the Terror began, as hillsides and riverbanks and city dumps and village compost heaps became the secret grave sites of countless thousands of kulaks and "wreckers" and "conspirators" and "enemies of the people," Stalin identified the glorious shape that would now stand on the Frunze Embankment. He selected a design that can only be described as a Tower of Babel with Lenin on top. Boris Iofan's design was, in fact, eight meters higher than the Empire State Building, a spiraling confusion of stairs and columns and height, and the Lenin he envisioned at the top would be so huge that it would be three times the size of the Statue of Liberty—Lenin's index finger alone would measure six meters. To make room for a surrounding plaza—"the largest plaza in the world," naturally—the nearby Pushkin Museum of Fine Arts would simply be lifted and moved to another neighborhood.

Stalin's design to erase the old gods of man and establish bolshevism as the reigning faith—this precise attempt to destroy one temple and erect a new one on the old, holy ground—came to the most pathetic and banal of ends. Workers managed to build a foundation for the Palace of Soviets by 1938—that peak year of the purges—but they soon discovered that the area was cursed. There were dozens of natural springs on the grounds, and the foundation soon became an enormous, stagnant pool. What was delayed by water would soon be put off indefinitely by war. Stalin's attention was diverted to more immediate needs. The steel used in the palace foundation was torn out and used for railroads. For years, the Palace of Soviets remained nothing more than that: a reeking pool surrounded by a wooden fence.

After Stalin's death in 1953, Khrushchev thought at first he would go ahead and finish the palace; after all, he was no less interested than Stalin in surpassing the United States as the citadel of industrial modernism. But when it became clear that any construction even remotely as big as Iofan's design for the palace was impossible, Khrushchev simply converted the construction site into what it had been for years: he ordered the construction of an outdoor heated swimming pool, "the biggest in the world."

The new masters of Moscow are, in their way, no less pretentious, no less interested in self-aggrandizement, than the old ones. There is something unseemly about the spectacle of lifelong apparatchiks like Yeltsin and Luzhkov, once so faithful to the Leninist faith, now acting as the disciples and building agents of Christ.

And yet, all cities are the result of the vanities and the haphazard tastes of their masters. Moscow could do worse than have a mayor who wants, at once, to rebuild the old and give free rein to the new. The cathedral project will cost $300 million at the very lowest estimate and will result in a near-exact replica of the original. Building began on Orthodox Christmas—January 7—1995, and should be completed by 1997, the

850th anniversary of the city. The money is coming from the state and private donations. Bankers, like Mikhail Smolensky of Stolichny Bank, are more than eager to act as the city's Medicis. Their sense of self is burnished and their access to newly privatized properties is made, courtesy of a grateful mayor, a great deal easier. Smolensky told me he had donated the 422 kilograms of gold necessary to coat the cathedral's domes.

"But you're Jewish," I said.

"What difference does that make?" he said with a smile infinitely indulgent of my stupidity.

Luzhkov, for his part, has declared the project "sacred" and his chief of staff explained why: We want the fact of reconstruction to be symbolic of Russia's re-creation. We want our society to get together and be reborn as a great nation. The whole idea of rebuilding the church unites us."

After watching the film and looking over some of the relics from the original cathedral, I met with one of the Orthodox priests, Father Mikhail Ryazantsev, who ran the little museum and was preparing for the cathedral's opening. The immense cost of the project was well worth it, he said, because Christ the Savior would turn out to be an essential "working" symbol of the new Russia.

"The re-creation of the cathedral is a matter of historical justice," he said as the flock of children flowed by us. "After years of forgetting and the oblivion of our history since 1917, we are now coming back to our roots. We are recovering the memory of our ancestors who thought it was necessary to commemorate the memory of those who defended Russia in 1812 and to honor God, who truly saved Russia from the invading aliens. The people who say that all this money should go straight to the poor don't realize that the people who are donating money do not provide this choice. Nor does it rule out helping the poor in addition to this."

Father Mikhail showed me a huge book in which visitors to the museum had written their comments about the reconstruction of the Cathedral of Christ the Savior. There were numerous odes to Christ (for his mercy) and Mayor Luzhkov (for his beneficence). There were no complaints so far as I could see.

"Lord Jesus Christ, forgive and pardon us. . . ."

"We are grateful to Luzhkov."

"He who destroys, dies. He who builds will live forever."

"My greatest dream is coming true. Dear Yuri Mikhailovich, let the Lord God grant you long life. Russia is being resurrected."

"Man does not live by bread alone. Such a cathedral will be in the souls of all of us. Honor and glory will be ours."

The idea and the symbolism of rebuilding the Cathedral of Christ the Savior and so many other monuments ruined during the Soviet period has not escaped criticism. Since television and the printing presses are controlled either by the state or by bankers, who depend on their friendly relations with the state, one does not frequently hear criticism of such projects. But modern, implicit censorship has nothing like the power of the old Soviet variety, and contrary opinion is never entirely stifled. The most coherent critical voice on the rapid transformation of Moscow is that of Aleksei Komech, the director of the Institute of Art Studies. Komech works in a lovely nineteenth-century mansion on one of the side streets of old Moscow not far from the Kremlin. The building is—rather pointedly—unrestored, and it is just fine for Komech.

"The annihilation of landmarks is rather rare nowadays, but we are still losing something because the construction interests are determining the character of the city," Komech said. "Charm is being lost." s The new Tretyakov Gallery "looks like a big industrial enterprise." The project to turn Manezh Square into an underground mall "is a madhouse." The Resurrection Gate on Red Square "is a dead architectural piece." The new statue of the great war hero Marshal Zhukov "is the worst statue ever." And the neo-Mediterranean mansions, or *kottedgi*, springing up as housing for the nouveaux riches on the edges of the city are "appalling." In general, "historical Moscow is disappearing before our eyes," he said. "The mayor is very authoritarian and has uncultivated tastes. In 1989–1991 it was fashionable to take the public's advice. Now it is very different: let them speak, but we will do what we want. There is an incredible search for the grandiose: the Cathedral of Christ the Savior, the war memorial, the Manezh underground mall. Pretentiousness prevails."

Komech said that Luzhkov, Yeltsin, and other officials are too eager to create new signs and symbols—"it makes them feel like new people." They have dispensed with a distinctively Moscow style and replaced it with a mélange of styles that could just as easily be mistaken for Vienna or New York "with a Moscow facade."

When I asked about the Cathedral of Christ the Savior, Komech assumed an expression of offense and sadness.

"What can I do?" he said. "When it is completed and decorated inside, its ugliness will be evident to all. There are no artists to replicate what was there in the first place. The Orthodox Church will not tolerate a new style, either. As someone said on Radio Liberty, how is it possible for Ilya Glazunov"—a nationalist artist who is scheduled to paint icons—"to do a cathedral when all his people look like communists?"

Moscow's architects and artists, Komech said, are selling themselves out "for a piece of candy," for quick cash. "They act like prostitutes," he said. "We used to think the stick was more efficient than the carrot. But we were wrong. I was at a meeting with the deputy mayor of Moscow in charge of construction and the architects. The deputy mayor acted just like a general secretary of the Communist Party. The architects all got up and went on about how lucky they were to have this government which cares so much for Moscow."

Just as the ordinary people who had written in the cathedral's guest book were unanimous in their praise of the cathedral, the Moscow intelligentsia—a skeptical lot—were nearly unanimous in their opposition. But most were less stern than Komech; they tended to be sweetly amused more than angry.

Leonid Parfyonov, a popular television host and documentary filmmaker, smiled brightly when I asked him about the new cathedral towering over downtown Moscow.

"To some degree I agree with Komech," he said. "This is a junk copy of a Russian original that was never much good in the first place. It's also disgusting to watch former members of the Central Committee act pious and more religious than the patriarch himself. This is a cathedral being built by men raised in an era of Romanian furniture sets thinking they are Louis XIV. And yet there is vitality, real life, in all this. This is an aesthetic built on illegal money and faux Orthodoxy and tawdriness. But what else is there? This is our life as it is! To get angry at this is to be angry with life itself. Maybe it would be better to have Nabokovs and great aesthetes all around us, but that is not the life we really have. So there is some charm in this vitality. Let's get angry at the prime minister, Viktor Chernomyrdin, for making himself one of the richest men in Russia, but not because he is incapable of acting with the style of a sixth-generation Rockefeller. Chernomyrdin is a simple boy from Orenberg who got average grades in school."

The new Moscow is a city of money; more specifically, a city of money tied to government. It is nearly impossible to make a fortune without an extremely close relationship to the Kremlin or City Hall or both. The conversion of properties from absolute state ownership to private hands—surely the biggest land grab in the history of the world—looks fitful, chaotic, incomprehensible from outside. From inside, it is a rather logical system, one built not on law or equal access, but rather on personal access to state power. Access can be acquired in a variety of ways: election, friendship, bribery, barter.

In the winter of 1995, an American diplomat in Moscow, Thomas Graham, outraged the Russian Foreign Ministry when *Nezavisimaya Gazeta* published his article about the various oligarchies (or "clans," as he called them) that control Moscow and the country beyond. Graham's article cited a "Moscow group" centered around Mayor Luzhkov and various banking and real estate interests; a Kremlin group of Westernizers like Anatoly Chubais, who ran the country's privatization program; the military-industrial complex directors who, with the help of various conservatives in the Kremlin, pressed for subsidies and higher defense spending; and the heads of the oil and gas industries, which had the support of Prime Minister Chernomyrdin. After the article appeared, the Russian Foreign Ministry put on a fine and punctilious show of outrage—diplomats, they sniffed, were not supposed to take such critical analyses public—and the U.S. State Department responded by acting suitably chagrined. Graham, of course, kept his job. To have fired him would have been lunacy. Not only was he one of Ambassador Thomas Pickering's most valuable intellectual assets in Moscow, he was also right. I spoke with numerous Russian politicians—Mikhail Gorbachev, Andrei Kozyrev, and various communists among them—and all of them accepted the article as a fair assessment of the new arrangement of power. One could quibble with certain details—Kozyrev, for instance, said that one had to consider that political and economic power was no longer as "Moscow-centered" as it had been under Soviet rule—but no one objected much to the term "oligarchy" or to the map of power that Graham had drawn. "An intelligent piece of work," Gorbachev said. "I'm not sure I could have laid it out better myself!"

The symbol of the "Moscow group" is the new cathedral. The symbol of the richest of the oligarchies, the oil and gas group, is a thirty-four-story glass-and-steel skyscraper on the southwest edge of the city. In its own secular way, the headquarters of Gazprom is itself a cathedral.

There is no private company in Russia—or, quite possibly, the world—that compares to Gazprom. With control of one-third of the world's gas reserves, one million acres of land, over 365,000 employees, and interests in dozens of other businesses, Gazprom has annual revenues estimated by Western industry analysts at $20 billion to $25 billion and profits of $6 billion. If it were to be ranked by the Global Fortune 500, Gazprom would be second in profits, behind only Royal Dutch Shell. Gazprom is responsible for 5 percent of the entire Russian economy and is the country's biggest taxpayer, pouring $4 billion annually into the state. In fact, Gazprom does not pay nearly the amount of taxes it should.

When other resource-based industries, including the oil industry, were privatized in the early nineties, the government made sure to break them up and create potentially competitive companies. The gas industry, which had been run by Chernomyrdin during the Gorbachev era, remained a monopoly. The government retains 40 percent of the stock in Gazprom but gives the company relatively free rein, so much so that critics charge that with Chernomyrdin running economic policy, Gazprom is untouchable and is allowed to avoid or defer billions in tax payment.

Gazprom resembles a state as much as it does a business. Not only has it branched out into banking, shipping, construction, farming, and other businesses, it also has a vast social program for its employees that includes insurance, recreation, hospitals, and retirement facilities, as well as its own farms to provide food. For executives there are private planes, vacation homes, and various other means of Western-style coddling. As successful as Gazprom has been, its ambitions are unquenched. The chairman, an old Chernomyrdin protégé named Rem Vyakhirev, wants to build a gas pipeline between western Siberia and Western Europe, a project that would cost at least $40 billion. Yevgeny Yasin, Yeltsin's economics minister, is one of the few top-level officials to challenge the Gazprom hegemony, saying that the corporation has gone beyond the scrutiny of the state. But then he asks plaintively, "Should you slaughter the milk cow while it is still giving milk?"

Chernomyrdin has undoubtedly proved a friend to Gazprom. On a flight to Siberia with Vyakhirev aboard, Chernomyrdin wished his friend a happy birthday by toasting him with a glass of vodka: *"Za vas, za nas, i za gaz!"* he said, a rhymed toast meaning "To you, to us, and to gas!" Chernomyrdin sternly denies that he holds shares in Gazprom or benefits in any way from its activities, and yet many critics, including the former finance minister Boris Fyodorov, say that the prime minister holds a 1 percent share in Gazprom. If that rumor is true—and it is the common currency of Russian politics—Chernomyrdin ranks among the wealthiest men in Russia. The estimated value of Gazprom runs between $400 billion and $900 billion based on gas reserves alone; there is no account of how much the other business properties are worth.

Even the most ardent Western supporters of Yeltsin's early economic liberalization programs cannot abide the power of Gazprom. Jeffrey Sachs, who is hated by Russian communists and nationalists for his role in helping design post-Soviet economic policies for Moscow and Warsaw, says that natural gas resources were simply stolen from the Russian people and that the industry ought to be renationalized. Anders Aslund, the former Swedish diplomat who worked as an adviser to the Russian government in 1991 and 1992, compares Gazprom to Standard Oil before the American government decided to break it up. But Gazprom is even more powerful, Aslund told David Hoffman of *The Washington Post*. "John D. Rockefeller was not the president, but Chernomyrdin is prime minister." Of all the elegant knickknacks in Vyakhirev's office at Gazprom, one above all denotes his true power: a cream-colored telephone that is connected directly to the office of Viktor Chernomyrdin. His explanation is thoroughly American, a robber baron's explanation: "What's good for Gazprom is good for Russia."

One afternoon, I visited one of Yeltsin's closest aides in the Kremlin, Giorgi Satarov. I had known Satarov since he was an obscure academic. In those days, he was willing to speculate about Yeltsin's penchant for swinging between democratic and authoritarian ideals, the erratic course and complicated nature of the new Russian state, but now, as he sat with a seignorial air in his Kremlin office, he was in no mood to concede that Gazprom or the oligarchic structure of Russia was in any way dangerous or even inappropriate.

"Do you know a country where economic interests do not play a political role?" he said. "In the history of the United States there were certainly moments in which one or another economic oligarchy became stronger. Sometimes they were related to railroads or cotton or the military industry. In any system, somebody can become temporarily stronger. Here, Gazprom has become stronger under these rather unstable conditions. If you look at your history cold-bloodedly, you'll see that the same was true at certain points for the power of the slave owners and then the industries of the North, then the railroads. Our situation now, if you like, is a perverse one. In a more general sense, the government continues to be a participant in the economic game. Chernomyrdin's being a descendant of a certain economic group is just a consequence of that."

The rapid transition from communism, a system in which all were, as Joseph Brodsky put it, "equal in poverty," to one in which the world is rife with both opportunity and unfairness has been delicious for the lucky and skillful few and a shock to nearly everyone else. It takes cunning, flexibility, privilege, and youth to move quickly enough to find a silken niche in the new world. Suddenly an outwardly classless society has fractured into classes of radically different experiences and levels of wealth, and the result has been a Russia filled with resentments and envy. Even the intellectuals who dreamed for decades of an open society now feel a hollowness inside. The old life in which books and conversation were central has given way to one in which friends are so busy making a living that they have little time for reading, writing, or each other.

"Before the fall there was a uniformity to life," my friend the playwright Aleksandr Gelman told me. "Everyone was more or less equal. Everyone lived more or less okay, or equally badly, but no one was rich. Everyone dreamed about freedom, and this united them. People could recognize each other, who they were, with just a couple of words. This created a certain ambience, a quality of human relations. It wasn't always wonderful, but it was *familiar*. Suddenly lots and lots of artists and composers and writers began to live quite badly. There was no support for them anywhere. Perestroika was quite a blow. So they rented out their apartments and lived in their dachas. Their lifestyle changed. The fact that people had to depend on something like the largesse of George Soros was humiliating. They didn't become opponents of democratic reform, exactly, but this discontent grew. And so now freedom is associated not with joy entirely, but with a depressed state. Even normal people who are for change have some sense of anxiety. It doesn't matter that we dreamed about freedom for so long. The initial joy subsided. It's like 1917 when there was initially this hope for a new Russia of justice for the masses or the limited expectations after the Twentieth Party Congress in 1956 when there were hopes of a more humane socialism. This freedom that we have now has no limit or perspective. After all, what are we really dreaming of now? That in thirty years we will live as well as they do in Finland? These are realistic and pragmatic hopes, but they are not inspiring dreams. The typical Russian man wants society to have grand goals, and there is an absence of that now."

In Moscow especially, but in other big cities as well, political jokes have given way to New Russian jokes. For example:

One New Russian says to another, "I just bought the most fantastic tie in Paris. It cost three hundred dollars!"

"Oh really?" says the other proudly. "I just bought the same tie for *four* hundred dollars!"

And so on. These jokes, so often told by people of superior education and declining incomes, portray the New Russian as loaded, lucky, and preposterously crude. The jokes are much like those that used be told about oil sheikhs and their vulgar new mansions in Beverly Hills and Bel-Air. There is also an air of perishability about the New Russian of legend and fact. Not long ago I heard about the owner of a health club in Moscow who was desperate for new members because so many of his old members had been rubbed out in mob hits. It sounded like the beginning of a joke, a fable, but it was a fact, reported in the *Financial Times*.

The infantry of the new Russia—the midlevel businessmen, to say nothing of the midlevel mobsters—are too often worthy of the stereotypes and jokes. Three gold chains are always better than one. These New Russians are a presence everywhere from the coast of Cyprus (where there is, in effect, a mansion community of Russians eager for sun and tax shelters) to the Negresco Hotel in Nice (which has seen so many visitors from Moscow lately that the management has added a Russian menu at its restaurant).

But the true barons of Moscow business—the men who own the banks, the media outlets, the import-export firms; the men who ride to work surrounded by security cars and measure their personal fortunes in the tens and hundreds of millions of dollars—these New Russians have caught on quickly to the Western folkways of big money. At least in their glossy annual reports, these barons have tried to ape the etiquette of noblesse oblige. Banks like Stolichny and Menatep have acquired major art collections and make sure to provide high-profile loans to museums. Other businesses donate to the theater, the opera, the ballet. Even Gazprom, which seems impervious to the outside world, has bankrolled a new edition of the works of Aleksandr Pushkin.

Andrei Bystritsky, a sociologist and a commentator for the newsweekly *Itogi,* told me that the "dirty secret" of modern Russia is that it really ought to be grateful for the initiative and energy shown by the young and the middle-aged, for no matter how vulgar or dishonest the New Russians may seem, they are "practically our only hope." Russia, unlike the early United States, cannot depend for its development on seemingly unlimited intellectual and moral resources—especially not in politics. "Boris Yeltsin is not Washington or Madison or Hamilton or Lincoln, and as a result we have tremendous drift and human casualties," Bystritsky said. "I don't always approve of biological theories of culture, but it is important to remember that we wiped out the best and the brightest of this country and, as a result, we sapped ourselves of intelligence and energy."

Ironically, one of the most skeptical voices about the vibrant and chaotic culture is that of the man who initiated the freedom in the first place. Gorbachev retains a priggish—call it Leninist puritanical—view of advertising, of consumer society, of wealth in general. "I think that a lot of what's happening is really inappropriate," he told me one morning at his office. "It's the immorality that I regret the most. Those who led this democratic process led a gigantic purge of everything that had been accumulated in this society for decades. They twisted everything in knots. Those who campaigned against privileges now build themselves gigantic palaces. They snatched up property. They have been like pigs at the trough. I am shocked by this. And for the Russians, this excess of American advertising—well, it's not all negative, but there is so much excess. In the first years after 1991, television was flooded with American and foreign movies. Russian culture was driven underground. This couldn't help but cause resentment. Let me tell you, people have had enough thrillers. They began to get nostalgic so now on Channel 6 there are old Soviet movies like *The Tractor Operators*. People love them. They got sick of soap operas and wallowing in melodramas from Mexico and Brazil. There is a return to the old. It's because people are sick of the twists and the jerks in their lives. I imagine France went through the same thing."

Unlike most Muscovites, I admire Gorbachev, but it is easy to see that he is, in many ways, a man of his generation. He is stricken with the regrets of one who is optimistic in the abstract but unable to accept the concrete manifestations of the new age. As Grigory Yavlinsky once told me, if many people were afflicted by a deceptive euphoria in 1991, there are even more now who suffer from an "anti-euphoria." They mistake transition and change for apocalypse. The older the man or woman, the more likely it is that they suffer from anti-euphoria.

For younger people, like Leonid Parfyonov, the television commentator, it is perfectly natural that Moscow has become an international city and, at the same time, distinctly Russian.

"That initial inferiority complex is gone and now there is a kind of sense of wholeness," Parfyonov told me one day over lunch at a restaurant called Twin Pigs. "People now think, 'Okay, so they live well in the West. And we can visit when we want. But we like it here better. We're a tougher people and life here is interesting now. We'll spend New Year's Eve watching a Grundig television and drinking Absolut vodka—the new national drink—and eating American salmon and French cheeses. But we'll sing our songs. Russian songs. That is who we are now in Moscow. We are a city of everywhere.' "

CHAPTER 6

THE BANKER, THE PRESIDENT, AND THE PRESIDENT'S GUARD

Until the collapse of the Soviet Union, Taganka Square was known in Moscow and in the empire beyond as a nexus of the avant-garde. The Taganka Theater, led by its principal director, Yuri Lyubimov, dared to put on politically barbed productions of, say, *Boris Godunov*, designed to delight the audience and infuriate the regime. Lyubimov finally wearied of the political intrigues and attacks orchestrated against him by the Kremlin and went into exile in 1984. He could not return to the Soviet Union until 1988, when the more liberal faction in Mikhail Gorbachev's ruling Politburo won a furious battle to grant the director a visa. With the fall of communism, Lyubimov came and went as he wished, staging productions in Moscow, Tel Aviv, and New York.

As a symbol of the new age, the Taganka was replaced by another building on the square, the Moscow Commercial Club, a plutocrats' watering hole modeled on the pre-Bolshevik redoubt, the English Club. For the first generation of post-Soviet tycoons, the Commercial Club was their Racquet Club, a self-conscious attempt to flee the all-are-equal-in-poverty egalitarianism of the old regime. The more exclusive the better.

The industrialist who ran the club, Vladimir Semago, counted himself a member of the small social-democratic wing of the Russian Communist

Party, but his notion of after-hours activity seemed closer to Edwardian London than to Moscow in the twenties. The club, he said, would soon be a "closed society with permanent members"—proletarians need not apply. It was definitely swank. There were three luxury restaurants, a casino, and a series of meeting rooms on the premises. No rising damp, no filth in the corner, no curious smells, nothing Soviet. It was a bad idea to show up in anything less formal than a suit—a foreign suit.

On the winter night I visited in 1995, the occasion was the presentation of a glossy new almanac of entrepreneurs, *The Birth of the Russian Business Elite*. Dozens of BMWs, Mercedes-Benzes, Jeep Cherokees, and Lincoln Town Cars were lined up at the curb. Well-dressed men and their sable-swathed women negotiated the icy sidewalk and headed for the entrance; their bodyguards, pistols and machine guns bulging under their jackets, were left to freeze outside. It was five degrees below zero. The guards wore no hats. Before ringing the security buzzer, I checked the club's address to make sure it was the right place. There it was—2 Bolshaya Komunisticheskaya Ulitsa, that is, 2 Big Communist Street—the right place.

I was visiting the Commercial Club on the off chance that the most powerful and mysterious member of the new Moscow elite, Vladimir Gusinsky, would show up. It was hard to slap a familiar analogy on Gusinsky. The Russian J. P. Morgan? The Russian Citizen Kane? No one tag did the job. Gusinsky was one of the few businessmen listed in the new almanac as *super-elite*. Of all the magnates in Moscow, he was the one everyone knew by name. As a pioneer in commercial banking and real estate, Gusinsky was a forty-one-year-old first-generation capitalist living in a jungle world with few rules or restraints. He was also Russia's first and biggest media mogul, and, as a result, deeply embroiled in Kremlin politics. He owned a controlling interest in Russia's only independent commercial television channel, NTV, as well as a leading liberal newspaper, *Sevodnya* ("Today"), and the news radio station Ekho Moskvi (Echo of Moscow). Since he traveled in a business world rife with mafiosi (in 1994, fifty bankers were executed in Moscow alone), Gusinsky protected himself as if he were a head of state. Of the twelve thousand people in his employ, over a thousand were members of a privately trained security force. Like many of the moguls in town, he lived in a walled-in mansion compound outside of town that featured security measures worthy of Fort Knox. His cars were all bulletproof. He took his vacations in Spain and Portugal and flew there in a private jet, a British Aerospace 700. When he came to New York on business, he stayed at the suite he kept, year-round, at the Carlyle Hotel. His son was in a boarding school in Switzerland.

Gusinsky was not universally adored. Human rights activists and nearly everyone else found it curious that one of his leading analysts was Filipp Bobkov, a former deputy chairman of the KGB, an odious figure who began his KGB career under Lavrenti Beria in 1945 and, in the Brezhnev era, created the infamous Fifth Directorate, which waged war on dissidents. "Mr. Bobkov and his colleagues are engaged in questions of security," Gusinsky once said, waving off all concerns. "We'd be ready to hire the devil himself if he could give us security." Russian critics also said that Gusinsky was far too close to—and profited overmuch from—the mayor of Moscow, Yuri Luzhkov. The headquarters of Gusinsky's bank—called MOST—was located in Luzhkov's headquarters; it was as if Citibank were inside Gracie Mansion. A large part of the city of Moscow's bank account was in the coffers of MOST.

Until the Gorbachev era, Vladimir Gusinsky was no one special. Like Lyubimov, he was a theater director, but he had little of Lyubimov's wit or daring: an unsuccessful director, barely a presence. As would one day become clear, Gusinsky's true talents were in making connections, calculating costs and benefits, taking risks—in other words, he was a natural businessman in a country where business was prohibited. His talents would have to wait for their historic moment.

Gusinsky was born in 1952, the year before Stalin's death. His mother's family had suffered under Stalin; his grandfather was a businessman who lost everything under the Soviets and was shot during the purges; his grandmother spent a decade in a labor camp. Gusinsky's mother and father were, like all Jews at the time, victims of the ordinary discrimination of the era.

"I lived in an apartment of mostly working-class families, went to school, and like all boys in school was defined by my ethnicity, and whoever felt like beating me up and so on—well, I got used to fighting," Gusinsky told a reporter on a business trip to Washington. "My father explained to me what this thing 'Jew' is, and that I needed to defend my Jewish heritage as necessary, and sometimes this led to fisticuffs. When I finished high school, it was my dream to study physics and mathematics. I applied to the Moscow Physics-Engineering Institute in the theoretical physics department. I was warned by everybody that I'd never get in. Jews weren't being taken at this particular college at this particular time. But I am a determined person, and I applied anyway—and I didn't get in."

As a young man, Gusinsky served in the army, took classes in theater, and drove a cab. He hung around theaters, helping out with sets, costumes, and properties. He directed only rarely. To support himself, he worked as a kind of street merchant for a while, trading, buying, and selling goods. He would have to wait a while longer before his taste for business would be a matter of ordinary life.

In 1987, Gorbachev introduced a series of tentative decrees permitting, for the first time in a half century, some of the trappings of business activity. The Communist Party sanctioned foreign investment and a form of limited private enterprise known as *kooperativi*. Cooperatives had been a vestige of "late Leninism," the brief period in the early 1920s of the New Economic Policy when the state relaxed its war on small business and private farming. (After Lenin's death, in 1924, Stalin obliterated cooperatives, and private initiative, in business or in the countryside, became a crime against the state.) Under Gorbachev, cooperatives sprang up everywhere: suddenly there were snack bars, video salons, tiny manufacturing outfits, button makers, dry cleaners. The cooperatives were, for as long as they lasted, Gusinsky's real theater.

To generate some early capital, he tried whatever he could dream up. In one scheme that brought in some initial profit, Gusinsky leased a glassware factory at night and produced drinking glasses—one of the thousands of products hard to find in Russia. He had even grander plans. Working with APCO, then a division of the Washington-based law firm Arnold & Porter, Gusinsky began a joint venture that operated as a consulting firm. With the help of his American partners, Gusinsky advised foreign clients on potential markets in the Soviet Union. For, say, $10,000 or $20,000, he might advise a Western food chain where and how to build a hard-currency grocery store to service Moscow's foreign community. Though his political opponents have accused Gusinsky of every sin imaginable, there is no proof that he was, or is, guilty of any wrongdoing. But his enemies made assumptions. Even in the relatively innocent days of the late eighties, there were hardly any rules governing the nascent business world. The easiest corners to cut were taxes (most Russians dodged the collector) and currency regulations (trading dollars for rubles on the black market was easy and highly profitable). That was the world he lived in.

From the start, Gusinsky showed a flair for entrepreneurial myth-making. Like many American pioneers of business, he knew the value of a charming starting-out story. Nearly all Russians believe that the name of his bank and holding company—MOST—is meant to mean "bridge," as it does in Russian. It does not. One afternoon, in 1988, when Gusinsky was visiting his American partner, a lawyer named Marjorie Krauss, he was amazed to see on the streets of downtown Washington people lining up to remove greenbacks from a small computer stuck into the wall. Gusinsky, who still wore a bumpkin look of awe, listened as Krauss explained the concept of an automatic cash machine. Gusinsky inspected the machine.

"MOST," read one of the decals near the machine.

"What a convenient country America is!" said Gusinsky.

Not long after, Gusinsky split with his American partners and developed his commercial bank. He bought up dozens of properties around Moscow to refurbish and then sell at many times the original price. He also introduced something unknown in Russia: the credit card. One of Gusinsky's first advertisements read, simply, "What a convenient world!"

During perestroika, Gusinsky began cultivating friends in the Soviet Cultural Fund (run by Raisa Gorbachev), in the Ministry for Foreign Economic Relations, and, soon, in Moscow City Hall. The connections were at least as important as the talent. By the mid-1990s, Gusinsky was worth as much as $50 million. That hardly made him the richest man in Russia—the hills of Cyprus and the beaches of the Costa Brava were already populated by Russian entrepreneurs richer than Gusinsky—but when his media and political influence were thrown into the equation, he was certainly one of its most powerful private citizens. He meant, at once, to keep his secrets and be noticed. In 1994, he celebrated the fifth anniversary of the bank with a reception at the Metropole Hotel. Champagne, pâté, caviar. The party cost $200,000. As the guests left the hotel,

each was given a silver-plated clock . . . .
saw on the cash machine in Washington . . . .

Meanwhile, the cocktail party at the . . . .
where I was hoping to find Gusinsky, was a bu . . . . .
ple stood around, talking, but still wondering wh . . . .
sians like a spread. This was no spread. The chan . . . . there. Rus-
hors d'oeuvres spongy and damp, as if the caterer had . warm, the
businessmen for Episcopal bishops. . . . . Russian

Here and there was some shop talk, political talk, vacation . . .
tone of it, the blithe, moneyed shimmer of it, was all new to me. . . . . The
in Moscow, I had been at diplomatic dinners, Communist Party rec . . .
tions, factory cafeterias, kitchen-table debates—the familiar rituals of
the old regime—but never this. Russian entrepreneurs? A historic instant
ago, such people simply did not exist; had they tried, they would have
been locked up in a psychiatric ward or in jail for their efforts.

While I tried to overhear the talk and check out the Italian suits and the
English shoes, I remembered a conversation I'd had in Moscow six or seven
years before with a young journalist named Vladimir Yakovlev. He was in
his mid-twenties then, the grandson of a KGB man, the son of a prominent journalist who had written a dozen books on Lenin and then took
over as editor of *Moscow News*. Yakovlev, who used to come to my office at
The Washington Post to hustle a makeshift translation service of the daily papers, told me he was starting up a newspaper called *Kommersant*—"a kind
of *Wall Street Journal*" for a country that barely knew what a stock was.

"I'm starting a newspaper for a class that doesn't exist yet," he announced. I thought he was mad.

When I talked to Vladimir's father, he said simply, "I'm not a hardened Leninist anymore, but I have to be truthful: I don't understand my
own son."

Now, the class that Vladimir Yakovlev had envisioned—property owners, big businessmen—existed. *Kommersant* itself brought in millions, and
its founder became a first-generation Ochs, a leading member of the
club, though with all his wealth, Yakovlev had become a recluse, a believer, it was said, in Eastern religious practice.

Evidence of the new class was no longer confined to a few streets or
hotels as it had been at the start. Now it was everywhere: the billboards

*ᴇsᴜʀʀᴇ*ᴏs and the Cherokees; the new stores and *television* all over town; the pull-out business section in *restaurants sp*...*ons* called *kottedgi* that make sections of suburban *Izvestia; the* ᵣ patches of Westchester; the foreigners roaming *Moscow* l lobbies and ministries looking for the next nugget *around* t like. You saw the new rich in first-class lounges in air-*from* th ienna to Los Angeles or on the Concorde from New York *ports* ᵢn. They went on shopping raids to Paris and the duty-free *and* ʝ ᵢn the United Arab Emirates. They did their best to look like the *hav* ᵣnational business set. They tapped away on PowerBooks. They were ᵢᵣ ʝrever whipping out the cellular phone. But they were also fledgling rich. Sometimes the trips abroad induced a pang of class anxiety, as if they were not quite getting this being-loaded thing right. Could you wear the Armani suit without a tie? Was the Vuitton luggage too much? To remedy their insecurity, the Russians invented *Domovoi,* a kind of *Town & Country* primer for the plutocracy. Just as historians will comb through back issues of *Pravda* to study the communist era, future scholars will find *Domovoi* essential to understand the new rich at century's end. I picked up a few issues and read articles on how to treat your maid; the splendors of Gianni Versace; advice on planning your summer vacation abroad; where to get the proper furniture for your new dacha; where the best private schools are; how to evaluate high-end stereo equipment; where to shop in Tokyo; how to care for your pedigreed hounds; what's going on in Verona, Milan, Karlstad, New York, Leipzig, Geneva.

Now at the Commercial Club, the cocktail chatter began to fizzle. "We'll be in London to see the children," I heard one banker say.

"Why don't you fly over with us?" said another.

Then some more silence.

Near the drinks table, a very rich man stood with his very tall, very young girlfriend, saying nothing. She wore a skirt not much wider than a belt and smoked a cigarette that looked like a needle. She seemed cubist and dangerous: dominatrix of the duty-free shopping binge. No one bothered to stare.

Finally, the businessmen were given copies of the almanac, and they quickly turned to see how they had been described. They need not have

worried. The editors gave them the same fawning descrip
lywood press agent peddles to *People*.

Just before the reception broke up, a buzz whipped ar

"Gusinsky's men."

"I thought he was out of town again."

"He's come straight from the airport!"

"Where was he? London?"

"Who knows?"

"Gusinsky . . ."

I shouldered my way to the anteroom, where a homely man in aviator
glasses and a ratty plaid shirt stood smiling. The best-known businessman
in Russia looked, at least on this occasion, like Mr. Weekend, pulled from
his BarcaLounger. He was surrounded by grown men in suits paying
homage.

"Volodya!"

"Privyet!"

As they fairly swooned before him, Gusinsky took one man, drew him
close by the elbow, and brought him into his confidence. The man kept
nodding as Gusinsky spoke softly in his ear. Then the next courtier and
another whispered exchange. After a half-dozen such encounters, I finally made my way to Gusinsky, introduced myself, and asked if we could
meet sometime. He said sure and gave me the name of someone to call,
and yet he said it all in that mock-agreeable tone of voice that usually
means no, nice to meet you and all, but no, don't count on it.

Out on the street, Gusinsky's caravan—a string of sedans and jeeps
stuffed with armed guards—was more impressive than any of the others.
His drivers kept the engines running. His guards looked more alert, more
anxious.

For good reason. On December 2, 1994, in one of the most bizarre
political episodes of the post-Soviet era, one that underlined all that is
chaotic and strange in Moscow, armed men dressed in crisp fatigues and
black ski masks followed Gusinsky's cars from his brick dacha in the elite
Uspenskoye region outside the city to his headquarters in City Hall. All
along the road from the wooded outskirts to the center of town, both

eyed each other warily. The paramilitaries rode in unmarked cars. They wore no identifying patches or symbols on their fatigues.

Once the nervous cortege arrived at City Hall, the same paramilitaries, still without identifying themselves, began to interrogate Gusinsky's guards. Witnesses said they were blunt and threatening. Finally they left. The MOST security people thought they would likely return.

At around 5:00 P.M., the mysterious troops did return to City Hall, and now they were far more aggressive. Armed with Kalashnikovs and grenade launchers, they ordered several of Gusinsky's drivers and guards to lie facedown on the snow-covered parking lot and stay there for nearly two hours. The soldiers roughed up the head of the MOST security team and a few others badly enough to send them to the hospital with broken ribs and other injuries.

From his office upstairs, Gusinsky called Yevgeny Sevostyanov, chief of the Moscow regional branch of the Federal Counterintelligence Service (FSK)—the successor to the municipal KGB. Gusinsky demanded to know who was harassing his people and why. Sevostyanov sent some of his own men to the scene to investigate. At City Hall, Sevostyanov's FSK officers discovered that the armed men were members of an elite corps—the guard assigned to protect the president of the Russian Federation, Boris Yeltsin. After a long discussion, troops on both sides quietly left the scene.

It did not take long for Gusinsky's people to understand what had happened. The commander of the presidential guard, General Aleksandr Korzhakov, was Yeltsin's most intimate friend. In his memoir, Yeltsin credited Korzhakov with absolute loyalty. He even thanked him for saving him from bouts of depression. "Aleksandr Korzhakov, my chief of security, and I have been inseparable since 1985 when I moved to Moscow," Yeltsin wrote. "When I was kicked out of the Politburo in 1987, they also fired all my guards. Nevertheless, Korzhakov remained with me. He called and, just like that, asked if he could come over and keep guarding me, without pay. . . . On our days off, I sometimes visited him in his quaint little native village outside Moscow, which he affectionately called 'Buttermilkton.' There wasn't enough room for us in his small cottage, so we set up a tent outside, and went fishing and swimming in the river. To this day, Korzhakov never leaves my side, and we even sit up at night during trips together."

Now, as Yeltsin grew more and more isolated and his aides more aggressively hostile to the press, it became harder to know what was happening in the Kremlin. But it was clear that Korzhakov was a leading member of the "party of war" advising Yeltsin to abandon democratic niceties and use the "iron hand" to impress an electorate grown weary of chaos and cynical about the prospects for a liberal society. It was this "party of war"—Korzhakov included—that urged Yeltsin to send troops to Chechnya and that would later try to get him to call off plans for presidential elections in 1996. Korzhakov's presumption was extraordinary. As chief of security, he had no official political function other than the safety of the president, and yet he obviously influenced policy. At one point, he sent an urgent letter to the prime minister, Chernomyrdin, demanding a change in policy on oil exports.

Even before the December 2 raid, Korzhakov was known to despise Gusinsky. He had denounced Gusinsky as corrupt and a threat to political stability. Naturally, on the night of the raid, Korzhakov was not about to tolerate interference from a third party like the FSK. Two hours after sending his men to find out what was going on at City Hall, Sevostyanov was fired from his post by direct order of the president—yet another blow to reform. Sevostyanov had been appointed in 1991 precisely because he came from outside the security forces; he had even worked alongside Andrei Sakharov in the pro-democracy movement.

In the aftermath of the raid, Korzhakov kept up the pressure. The next day, he tried to arrange press coverage that would cast Gusinsky in a damaging light. In a statement relayed to the wire services, Korzhakov claimed that his men went to MOST to investigate the possibility that the bank had helped engineer a temporary collapse of the ruble in October 1994, known as "Black Tuesday." (Gusinsky, for his part, said he made just $40,000 speculating on currencies that day.) One notoriously pro-Kremlin news program, *Nota Bene,* eagerly broadcast the official version of events, but most other outlets did not. Gusinsky's own media outlets—NTV, *Sevodnya,* and Ekho Moskvi— were critical of the raid, but they were not alone. *Izvestia,* which had evolved since the collapse of communism into a remarkably authoritative newspaper, published a front-page article saying that Korzhakov, as the president's bodyguard, had assumed enormous and inappropriate political authority. Such abuse of power, the article suggested, "could bring on a police state" in Russia.

Not long after the raid, I visited Igor Malashenko, a clever graduate of the old Central Committee apparatus who now ran the day-to-day oper-ations of NTV. (His office, naturally, was also in City Hall.) Malashenko said the incident had to do with a growing fear in the Kremlin that Yeltsin was doomed to lose the 1996 elections. Gusinsky gave hundreds of thou-sands of dollars to several of the pro-democracy parties for the 1993 elections, but as Yeltsin's ratings had fallen, Kremlin advisers were con-vinced that Gusinsky would put his money and media outlets behind Luzhkov or Grigory Yavlinsky, the leader of the democratic opposition party, Yabloko. "They're just terrified," Malashenko said.

Another entrepreneur close, but not beholden, to Gusinsky told me that the incident was intended as a public show of strength. "MOST was too tightly tied to the Moscow government," he said. "It was a sign from Yeltsin to Luzhkov: 'Be careful. I'm the boss. You work as my employee. You are not an independent figure.' "

The raid, as it turned out, might have been predicted. Two weeks be-fore it happened, the slavishly pro-Kremlin newspaper *Rossiskaya Gazeta* published a bizarre (and unsigned) assault on MOST headlined "Snow Is Falling: Will the President and Government Fall?" The front-page article attacked Luzhkov and his supporters for pretending not to launch a pres-idential campaign but, at the same time, scouring the provinces for po-tential votes.

"Secret service sources contend that the campaign to elevate Luzhkov to the presidency was launched, first of all, by the MOST financial group and several other banks close to the Moscow government," the article said. "It appears that MOST Bank was the kingpin behind 'Black Tuesday' when it raked off the equivalent of one year's profits by manipulating $14 million on that day.

"Now, the MOST group has its sights set on the pinnacle of power," the article went on. "That is how one may interpret the reshuffle in top gov-ernment circles following 'Black Tuesday.' For this purpose, the MOST group is gradually 'taking over' the most influential media outlets, begin-ning with such mouthpieces as *Sevodnya,* NTV, etc. . . . And so, plenty of capital has been accumulated and the media have been bought. What next? Next comes the 'shaping' of public opinion, the spreading of rumors, fanning up hysteria and simply the dissemination of outright lies."

The article accused Filipp Bobkov and other ex-KGB figures working at MOST of "compiling files" on competing presidential candidates. "Doubtlessly, these 'security people' draw information from mafia structures which 'call the tune' when it comes to the question of giving support to Mayor Luzhkov." With MOST in the forefront, the unsigned article concluded, a "moneybags party" intended to seize power in Russia.

Gusinsky denied the charges in *Rossiskaya Gazeta*. In an interview with the popular weekly *Argumenti i Fakti,* he said the Kremlin simply could not get used to the fact that there were now new centers of influence. "The attack on MOST began when we invested for the first time in mass media," Gusinsky said. "They all began looking for a plot." And as for the idea that the mayor had his eyes on the presidency, "Luzhkov does not pretend to great power," he said. "Believe me. We're friends."

Gusinsky's public bravado masked a private anxiety. Not long after the attack, he went with his wife and young son to the airport to catch a flight to London, where they kept an apartment. Gusinsky nearly missed his flight when he was delayed, unaccountably, by security police at the airport. Finally, they left, and when Gusinsky returned a few days later, his family was not with him. It was safer for them in London, he felt.

In mid-December 1994, when the Russian army began to shell the Chechen city of Grozny and Gusinsky's television station showed the most gruesome and damning footage, the conflict between the Kremlin and the tycoon resumed. There was talk that Yeltsin's Security Council was considering banning NTV from the air. Gusinsky's people said that all of it—the attack on MOST, the war in Chechnya, the threats—was a pretext for establishing early on a state of national emergency and the suspension of the 1996 presidential elections.

In the anxious period between Yeltsin's triumph over the pitiful coup attempt in August 1991 and the collapse of the Soviet Union on Christmas night, interested parties—old apparatchiks, young entrepreneurs, mafiosi—all began to wonder about the new world that was so obviously on the horizon. What would be the new arrangement of power and property? Or, as Russians have been saying for centuries, *Kto kogo?* Who beats whom? Who benefits?

In early December 1991, with the dissolution of the union just days away, thirty of the biggest organized crime leaders in the empire held a summit meeting at a dacha outside Moscow. These men, known as *Vori v Zakonye* ("Thieves in Law"), descend from a mob legacy in Russia that dates back to the seventeenth-century highwaymen and Cossack robbers who, before setting out on raids, sometimes killed their own wives and children to prevent them from falling into enemy hands. Over the centuries, Russian mafiosi developed codes of almost monastic discipline. There was, above all, an absolute insistence on keeping aloof from the state, with its czars and general secretaries. Mobsters who fought with the Soviet army in the Great Patriotic War were scorned when they returned from the front; at home and in the gulag, they were branded scabs and beaten. Under the Bolsheviks, these mobsters controlled innumerable markets: car sales, spare parts, cigarettes, food distribution. Where the official mafia—the Communist Party— failed as a producer or marketer, the underground moved in. Even in the last year of communism, 1991, the shadow economy was the most efficient distributor of goods and accounted for over $60 billion in revenues.

The mobsters who gathered for that meeting outside Moscow that December saw opportunities in the collapse of the Soviet Union, but they also knew it would bring chaos, decay, uncertainty. Many Communist Party bureaucrats prepared themselves for the coming fall by turning themselves into private businessmen. They became consultants, rainmakers, men who could use their influence and access to bureaucratic power to cash in. Even some of the members of the would-be junta in 1991—a group pledged to the maintenance of a communist system—went into business as bankers or industrialists after their coup failed. It turned out, though, that the Thieves in Law had an even keener sense of the post-Soviet future than the politicians. The collapse of the Communist Party and its imperial control over the economy—over prices, production, wages, over everything—would lead to an economic free-for-all unprecedented in modern history, for without a Communist Party there would be no way to impose discipline.

The land of the police state turned into what Russians call *bespridel:* anarchy, lawlessness, unchecked greed. The temptations now were enormous. There were resources like oil and gas to be sold off, money to launder, currency games to play, territories to control. Because the stakes were so high, the world of the mafia became wildly competitive and brutal. The old spheres of influence in cities like Moscow were now battlefields, with groups from Georgia, Azerbaijan, and Chechnya fighting with Russians, Jews, Ukrainians. Mob hits became commonplace: shootings, stabbings, car bombings. In a feverish search for new markets, some of the *Vori v Zakonye* set up overseas branches. One of the thirty who gathered at the dacha, Vyacheslav "the Jap" Ivankov, a godfather from the eastern port city of Vladivostok, went to the United States, where the FBI quickly became obsessed by him; he was finally arrested in New York in 1995.

Westerners had a good sense of the increased visibility and menace of the mafia; they saw films of the young thugs and their molls in spandex miniskirts strolling through the casinos of Perm or Volgograd; they saw the photographs of police checking out a murder scene. The images, however, represented the most obvious ills of post-Soviet economic life. There were also the would-be legitimate businesses trying to operate in a wild landscape made even wilder by a vast bureaucracy that remains in place and, in countless instances, wants its taste of the profits. It was this shadowland of business anarchy and government corruption that was harder to understand and see—and was at least as important.

The moral ambiguity of business relations in Russia had become, for those who lived it, a given. Ask a banker, a politician, or a human rights worker whether this or that businessman is honest, and you will get the same shrugging answer: in the standard sense of the word, honesty does not—*cannot*—exist in Russian business. Tax rates are so confiscatory that no one can pay in full and stay open. The legal system simply has no provisions for many of the most ordinary aspects of business. Laws on bidding procedures or conflict of interest barely exist, providing infinite room for mischief.

The government is still the unavoidable factor in economic life and bribery is normal in business life, a given. Under both czarist and Soviet rule, bureaucrats always took bribes and accepted certain privileges as their due. But there were limits. In Gogol's *The Inspector General,* the mayor fires the police chief not because he stole, but because he stole more than his due. The Communist Party, in its time, also enforced well-understood standards on greed. The general secretary got this much meat, his deputy a bit less, and all the way down the line. Grab too much, step too far outside the given order, and you would be stalled in your career, fired, even sent to jail. As a way to set down a marker of discipline within the Party, Gorbachev even engineered the arrest in 1988 of one of the most notoriously greedy members of the Brezhnev regime—a former militia official, Brezhnev's son-in-law, Yuri Churbanov.

Now there are no such limits. "It's as if everyone has privatized or marketized himself," Mikhail Leontiev, the economics columnist for the newspaper *Sevodnya,* told me one day at his office. "Army officers in charge of a tank division, judges who rule on corruption cases, bureaucrats who control licenses—anyone with something to 'sell' now acts as if he were in private business. The situation here is worse than it is in Colombia. There is no border between the legal and the illegal."

But to consider all business in Russia as organized crime is not quite right either. Gusinsky, for example, spoke of his contempt for both the mobsters and the bureaucrats with whom they did business. Gusinsky and his peers are also immensely proud, even vain, about their role in creating wealth for ordinary people and, in general, helping to turn Russia into a normal country. "In his time, one great American said, 'What's good for GM is good for America,'" Gusinsky told a Russian reporter. "In any country there exists five percent of the population who provide work for the other ninety-five percent and develop the economy."

Igor Bunin, director of the Center for Political Technology, has studied the behavior of businessmen in post-Soviet Russia, and he told me one day at his office that in his wide experience of interviewing and polling businessmen, three-quarters of them consider themselves legitimate, and yet the same number say that bribery is habitual and, for better or worse, a necessary part of commerce. To ask the average businessman whether he has paid bribes is considered somehow childish, prudish. He will issue a routine denial, for the record, and then cast you a scathing look. "Pay bribes?" the look says. "How could I stay in business otherwise?" It's as if you had asked him if he cheats the rain by wearing a raincoat.

The "privatized" bureaucrat demanding cash for a signature was the least of a tycoon's worries. Russian bankers, especially, often felt the threat of violence, even of contract killers hired by organized crime figures or rival bankers. "Ten to fifteen thousand dollars and you are gone," one financier told *Moscow News*. "It's simple and not expensive as prices go now. Why don't killers demand a hundred or two hundred thousand dollars for our lives from their employers? Because they risk practically nothing: they shoot, throw away the pistol, and disappear. If the militia caught them even every other time and murderers were the subject of show trials, then the number of people fond of shooting would decrease. In any case, the price of a businessman's life would rise sharply, for real risk would require real money. You will agree that not everyone, even very rich people, could afford to pay hundreds of thousands of dollars for a contract killer."

One afternoon, I went to see Aleksandr Yakovlev, the owlish Communist Party intellectual who was Gorbachev's closest liberal adviser, and asked him what he and Gorbachev imagined they were getting into in 1987 and 1988 when they first began to relax the restrictions on private enterprise. Could they have envisioned a new Russian rich and a world of chaos?

Yakovlev shook his head. Ordinarily, he liked to make a display of his sagacity, but even he could not say with conviction that he had predicted the new breed. "We never even thought about such people," he said. "It was impossible to plan for such a thing. I never even thought businessmen, as you understand them, would develop in this country. I had high expectations for cooperatives, trade groups. We never thought it would be so explosive. It was supposed to be *evolutionary*. But, well, what can I say? Business is good. Let the strongest and smartest survive. After all, these people are the locomotives of reform. The government tries to portray itself that way, but have you ever met a government bureaucrat who was a locomotive of anything? He's only a brake."

Yakovlev was one of the leaders of a tiny social-democratic political party, the Movement for Democratic Political Reform. One of the cofounders was Gavriil Popov, a former professor of economics at Moscow

State University who was elected mayor of Moscow as a democratic reformer in 1990 and resigned two years later. Popov was still close to his former number two, Luzhkov, and, like Gusinsky, had an office in City Hall. Moscow journalists often described Popov as rich and shady, but they were no more successful in proving their case against him than they had been against Luzhkov or Gusinsky. Round and friendly, Popov resembles Winnie the Pooh and knows it. When I asked him if he ever benefited monetarily from his position, he smiled and tucked his chin. "Oh, of course not," he said, still smiling.

When the conversation did not concern his own days as mayor, Popov described the business world with a kind of amoral insouciance. He didn't have a bad word to say about anyone, including one notorious huckster named Sergei Mavrodi who lured thousands of Russians to "invest" in his fund, MMM, that turned out to be nothing more than a pyramid scheme—one that eventually collapsed, ruining countless ordinary people.

One of the ways that Gusinsky and other entrepreneurs grew rich was to buy newly privatized properties—office buildings, apartment houses—at absurdly low prices, fix them up, and resell them at prices that are now beginning to surpass those in New York and Tokyo. The key, of course, was to have an inside track on the original bargain-basement offerings. In 1992, the height of the privatization landgrab, Yuri Shchekochikin, a prominent investigative reporter for the weekly paper *Literaturnaya Gazeta,* wrote about MOST's purchase of more than one hundred buildings in Moscow from the city. He claimed that after MOST bought one unfinished building at city auction, the municipality used the proceeds of the sale to renovate an office block and hired as its contractor none other than MOST. Outraged, Shchekochikin wrote about the way leading businessmen, working in conjunction with city politicians, have "behind the smokescreen of democracy and our victory in August 1991 . . . divided up Moscow into spheres of influence, and have already sold one another the best parts of the capital." He went on, "We have three types of capitalists in our city. There are entrepreneurs who have been given the chance to make real money, thanks to the changes in the system, and there are criminals who launder their dirty capital in legitimate business. But the first and the second types are mere kids in comparison with our *biznesmeni* in the official structures of power. They,

in disguise, are the true masters of Moscow." Yeltsin, who was then extremely close to Luzhkov, quickly rose to the mayor's defense.

A better defense than Yeltsin's word is the pathetic lack of restraint on
business practices and the enormous importance of personal business
contacts between developers and bureaucrats. "To become a millionaire
in our country it is not at all necessary to have a good head and specialized knowledge," said Pyotr Aven, former minister of foreign trade and
now the president of Alpha Bank. "Often it is enough to have active support in the government, the parliament, local power structures and law-
enforcement agencies. One fine day your insignificant bank is
authorized, for instance, to conduct operations for budgetary funds, or
quotas are generously allotted to a company which is in no way connected with production for the export of oil, timber, and gas. In other
words, you are appointed a millionaire, as someone put it very aptly."

When I asked Popov about the situation, however, he shrugged.
MOST had its headquarters in City Hall, it had a large share of the city
account, it did real estate deals with the city. Wasn't there a problem
there? "Someone like Gusinsky is an entrepreneur in league with the bureaucracy, and I don't think there's anything criminal about that," Popov
said. "Under present conditions, a private entrepreneur cannot handle a
big business on his own." In fact, Popov said, what spoke best for Gusinsky was that he, unlike many who made fast profits in the earliest wave of
Russian business, had not left the country. "Gusinsky has tied himself and
his family to Russia," he said. "He cannot leave. That Gusinsky is active in
politics is not unique, but the scale and the degree of his personal involvement are."

Few Russians shared Popov's laissez-faire sanguinity. Tens of millions of
people felt ripped off by these new masters of the Moscow universe. They
did not believe any of this wealth would trickle down to them, and they
were ready to believe any charge, any rumor. The poor were not alone in
this. The sense of visceral alarm in Moscow about the rise of the new rich
spread across the political spectrum. A conservative like Aleksandr
Solzhenitsyn and a liberal like Yuri Afanasyev, the former leader of the
Democratic Russia movement, both said that from the ashes of totalitarian
communism had risen an oligarchic system in which politics were played
out according to the economic interests of bureaucrats, entrepreneurs,

and mafiosi. The late Len Karpinsky, a columnist for *Moscow News,* who was in the forefront of the reform movement, questioned whether the fall of the old regime had not led to something even more pernicious. "If the bureaucrat continues to be pivotal to the system," he wrote, "we may well find ourselves living under 'nomenklatura capitalism' whose despotism will not be inferior to the planned socialist system." A few scholars could point out that, historically, other economies in time had developed rules of the game, limiting the more violent and primitive manifestations of early capitalism, but Russians had a right to ask how and when.

It was not always easy to meet Russian entrepreneurs and harder still to get them to talk freely about their work. They were, for good reason, security-crazed in all respects and, as a result, not eager for anything more than the most cursory publicity. Like most American businessmen, they concluded that journalistic scrutiny—whether of their bookkeeping or their personal lives—was an invitation to disaster, especially when they were so deeply resented. Still, there were opportunities to buttonhole members of the new elite. In early 1995, Gusinsky and several other powerful business figures organized a one-day Congress of Entrepreneurs at the Hall of Columns—the site of Stalin's funeral—and MOST doled out passes to the press.

By early morning, the hall was filling up with businesspeople from all over the country: oilmen from western Siberia, gas and chemicals executives from the Urals, bankers from everywhere. One speaker after another made the same series of points: No matter what the rest of the country, or the world, might think, the new wave of Russian entrepreneurs craves a legal order. Chaos is bad for the country and bad for business. The fetish for security, the epidemic of bribery, is not the fault of business but of the government's unwillingness to take the offensive against organized crime and get rid of bureaucrats in its own ranks. Businesspeople, they argued, can generate a middle class, but not without a working legal order. Without a middle class there will never be any stability or prosperity in Russia.

In the hallways, some of the richest people in Russia stood around kibitzing. There I ran into one of the great converts of the era, Svyatoslav

Fyodorov, a renowned eye surgeon who had been a member of the Communist Party Central Committee under Gorbachev and now is a Moscow tycoon and would-be politician. He still ran his huge clinic, but he had also moved into real estate, investments, and God knows what else. To some degree, Fyodorov looked as he had in his earlier incarnation—crew cut, slightly Asiatic eyes, tugged-down mouth—but he also wore the best suit this side of Savile Row: a navy cashmere number, cut just so. Before I could ask a question, he relieved himself of an angry set piece.

"This country needs a Franklin Roosevelt, a government of revival and reconstruction," Fyodorov said. "Look what he faced in 1933: the collapse of society, isolationism. Roosevelt created the economic conditions for recovery. With our intellectual capacity, we could do the same thing. Surely our capacities here are at least what they were in the United States in the 1930s. The government now is playing the role of the destroyer. The present government is simply bankrupt."

After Fyodorov finished and drifted off down the hall toward the dining hall, I met Irina Khakamada, one of the leaders in parliament of the pro-business-and-democracy movement, the Party of December 12th. Khakamada, who is in her late thirties, asked what sort of things I had been hearing about modern Russian businessmen, and as I described my conversations with various Moscow intellectuals, most of whom played key roles in the perestroika movement and now see only disaster and oligarchy, she rolled her eyes.

"Ridiculous!" Khakamada said. "It's just ridiculous! Most people in the country feel that businesspeople do nothing more than fleece Russia, that they're responsible for Black Tuesday, that they're all mafia, thieves, to blame for everything. This generation of the sixties is especially like that. They are so accustomed to battling the system. They never learned the value of wealth. To them, it's all foreign. It's just too easy to write off every business as mafia."

But I also talked with several businessmen who, in the interest of stability, of course, wanted to set aside the complications and niceties of democratic procedure in favor of a "transitional authoritarianism." Their preferred models were invariably South Korea, Singapore, and Chile. At the Congress of Entrepreneurs, I met Kakha Bendukidze, a rotund Georgian-born scientist whose success has been so enormous that he bought 25 percent of one of the biggest industrial plants in the country, Uralmash in Ekaterinburg. Bendukidze was also general director of an oil investment firm, NIPEK, that employed seventy thousand people. When I met him he was thirty-eight—not terribly young for a Russian entrepreneur.

"To begin with," Bendukidze said, "it's hard to compare Russian business to American or English business. It's much more like the first generation of Carnegies, Rockefellers, or Rothschilds. But there is also a strict difference because things developed in Russia a lot differently than in America in the late eighteenth and nineteenth centuries. Here we have no generations. We have people who themselves change from year to year. But we do have many of the same problems. They had criminals, lies, everything we have today. It's very similar. The Rockefellers cut pipelines and all the rest. The difference is that all of this is happening in a quite developed country like Russia. Rockefeller established an economic structure, while we here are dividing up a preexisting one."

Had the dividing-up led to an oligarchy in Russia? I asked.

"It would be *nice* to have an oligarchy in Russia," Bendukidze said, laughing. "Civil society is the only basis for economic development. So, in the meantime, we must create substitutes for civil society. Oligarchy is a substitution for civil society. It's better than monarchy. It's not exactly totalitarianism. It would be nice to have a General Pinochet to help us, but we don't have a General Pinochet. You see, historically, you can't develop an economy without occupation or dictatorship when there is a ruined economy. Look at Korea, Taiwan, Singapore, Japan. What we do not need is elections. We generally are not ready to elect the people who need to be elected. Remember what Professor Probrazhensky says in Bulgakov's *A Dog's Heart*?: 'If people can't keep their own hallways clean, how can they elect a parliament?' Unfortunately, I don't know who our General Pinochet is or could be. Yeltsin is better than what might come next, though. Who can be sure of a smooth transition? Can you be sure that the next person will not be even less successful than Yeltsin? I fear a more radical person, a crazy nationalist."

Then I asked the expectable, liberal question: Wouldn't the suspension of elections simply push democracy further into the future, making it even more of an illusion than it already was?

"Democracy is not an illusion, unfortunately," Bendukidze said. "There are moments in history when you can push history too far. Look at the success of the National Socialist Party in Germany in 1933. They came to power through democratic procedures. But if there had been an anti-democratic power in Germany, it would have been better for the German people."

Bendukidze's brand of politics—support for a Russian Pinochet leading to democratic capitalism—would have been unspeakable a few years ago for anyone calling himself a democrat or a liberal. Now it was common currency. As 1996 approached, more and more executives feared elections and called for their cancellation.

I even discovered that this point of view had its manifesto, an article called "State and Market" published in the December 1994 issue of *Novy Mir*. The author was Mikhail Leontiev, the economics columnist for *Sevodnya*—a Gusinsky property. "Gusinsky doesn't share my politics but he lets me write what I write," Leontiev told me. "But look, we cannot afford democracy at the moment. We don't have a normal people; bandits are in charge. We need a period of sanitation or, rudely speaking, a *chistka*—a purge. Those who are capable of doing this should do it. We'll need five to ten years to prepare society, to create a working economy, to feed people and destroy their desire for marginals, like Vladimir Zhirinovsky, in politics. People have to understand what a democracy means. This is a sick society. You cannot have the patients running the madhouse."

It was one thing to listen to a fascist like Zhirinovsky rave about reconquering the old empire, quite another to hear someone like Leontiev, who had just a few years before postured as a liberal full of optimism about a Russian democracy, rave about the need for a "purge" and a "temporary suspension of democratic procedures." There is no doubt that in Weimar Germany and modern Algeria democracy did open the way to danger, but what was the guarantee that "limited" authoritarianism would not lead to even greater danger? What would Andrei Sakharov have thought of all this? Sakharov's moral presence, his judgment, had never been replaced. Leontiev, incidentally, had run for a seat in the Duma. His campaign slogan was "The Only Good Thief Is a Dead Thief." He lost.

———

In an ambiguous political world, Gusinsky was, perhaps, the most ambiguous figure of all. As a media tycoon, he served an invaluable function, undermining the government monopoly of television. Gusinsky also kept his distance from his media properties; in one case, his newspaper, *Sevodnya*, published a scathing commentary on a Kremlin economics official that probably cost MOST a fortune in potential business. Some of his journalists, whom I've known since long before the rise of Gusinsky, said their boss had given them such a free hand that they were not even sure he was reading *Sevodnya* or watching NTV.

Gusinsky boasted that by creating jobs he was helping to create a middle class and a civil society. As the historian Richard Pipes points out in *Russia Under the Old Regime,* "Russia's inability to produce a large and vigorous bourgeoisie is usually seen as a major cause of its deviation from the political patterns of western Europe, and of the failure of liberal ideas significantly to influence its political institutions and practices." The threat of fascism is rooted in national humiliation and economic uncertainty; a nation of prosperous merchants, farmers, and computer programmers—a middle class—is not likely to vote a fascist into the Kremlin.

At the same time, Gusinsky was elusive about his business and disingenuous about some of the people he employed—namely General Filipp Bobkov. When Gusinsky felt he was under unfair attack, he lashed out in the courts—or his lawyers did. He sued *The Wall Street Journal* for running a column about MOST's employment of ex-KGB men—he dropped the case after winning an agreement from the paper to run a lengthy correction—and he has threatened to sue several Russian media outlets. When I asked Yegor Gaidar, the former prime minister, if Gusinsky was, perhaps, a Russian Carnegie—a fairly innocuous question, I thought—he preferred to keep quiet. "Mr. Gusinsky is a living person," Gaidar said. "He can sue me if he doesn't like the comparison."

Judging by that first meeting with Gusinsky at the Moscow Commercial Club, I didn't think he would sit for an interview. But perhaps because he felt under attack and in need of public attention, I was finally able to meet him. Gusinsky's people told me that at such-and-such time

I should go to the main door at City Hall—the same door where Comrade Korzhakov's troops had assembled on December 2. It was, from the first, an unsettling experience. MOST's advertisements around Moscow were meant to reassure the customer, to bring him slowly into the new world of compound interest and credit cards. One billboard showed a plant breaking through the soil. The caption read, "A Natural Phenomenon." Yet there was something unnatural, or unnerving, about MOST headquarters. I saw dozens of young men in fatigues, rifles slung over their shoulders. They slouched in armchairs and couches and, like mesmerized children, watched cartoons on television. A peculiar army. One of Gusinsky's press representatives took me to the elevators and on up to MOST's offices on one of the higher floors.

Upstairs, the scene was even more bizarre. In the late eighties, in the first flush of private business, secretaries usually dressed like streetwalkers and executives dressed like John Gotti. But this could easily have been a suite on Wall Street: well-dressed executives and secretaries were walking with obvious purpose and talking in whispers; everything was buffed, sleek, quick, secure. I waited for a few minutes and then was taken into Gusinsky's office. This time, he was decked out in a well-tailored suit and stood taller than he had at the party: in business mode. From the start, he was disarmingly, self-consciously open, as friendly as could be. His office had a panoramic view of Moscow, and yet the interior seemed intended to resemble some other office—an English broker's office, perhaps. We sat on couches and armchairs around a coffee table. I put out a tape recorder; so did Gusinsky's press representative. I began by asking Gusinsky about his ambitions as a businessman, beyond money or influence. Did he see himself as a Russian Henry Ford?

"I am in this first generation of entrepreneurs, and there are already second and third generations formed, each with its own attitudes," Gusinsky said. "The speed of the movement turned out to be extremely fast. People came with different backgrounds and outlooks. It's all a huge, roiling mix. It's not acceleration so much as a preset speed set at a fantastically high level. The first wave began with people who were one hundred percent creations of the system. Many of them tried to make some quick money and then hide it all. They were scared of Soviet banditism. Their mentality was very closed, especially in the first years of the cooperative movement. At that time, people thought they were building something like 'society with a human face,' as if personal goals, like making some money for yourself and your children, were not sufficient. The truth is that personal goals are normal motivations. These people cloaked themselves in a new ideology. Many of them came out of the Young Communist League. Some emerged from the old black market, which essentially became legalized. And there were people from the Soviet system who showed some new energy. I would say about eighty percent of that first wave that made some money went abroad—the nouveau riche money wave, I call it. They left because they didn't trust the state. They didn't think things could last. But those who did stay are now in key positions. . . .

"I myself was related to the Ministry for Foreign Economic Relations. Our cooperative was under their auspices. In those days everyone needed a government patron to 'raise' you. The essence of entrepreneurship was to establish a good patron—just as it is in any bureaucratic system. My patrons from the ministry now work here with us."

And the second wave of business?

"The second wave is the toughest and most criminalized," Gusinsky went on. "They were people who came to the market on a wave of aggression. Now we have to reap the fruits of their criminal activities. We feel it, and you feel it too in the West. These are tough, criminal people. Some of the people who emigrated left because of these criminals. I know many people who said to themselves, 'Why should I risk my life and the lives of my family? I'd rather leave.' "

The third wave "is different," he said. "It is perfectly legal. These are young people who came to the fore in the last two years. They are fearless and are not involved in criminality. They are normal people, well educated, full of energy."

I said that all I'd been hearing in Moscow—including from his friend the former mayor Gavriil Popov—was that under current conditions, there was no clear line between legal and illegal business. What did honesty mean in Russian business?

Gusinsky assumed an expression of indignation. "It's exactly the same difference between honesty and criminality that exists in the United States," he said. "Please, understand this. Criminal business is based on the gains of illegal business. It's not about decreasing taxes. It's about avoiding taxes entirely. It's about extortion. Isn't this the case in New York? It's not a purely Russian thing. In Russia, this wave has been much bigger than anywhere else because democracy is for all—for normal citizens and for gangsters alike." Gusinsky said that the only reason he has had to hire so many security personnel was "to oppose these organized signs of the criminal world."

"To talk about 'clean' and 'dirty' is stupid. It's Popov's theory that there is reciprocal penetration of government and business, and, as a result, everyone becomes dirty. The government takes bribes and the businessman gives them. But this society is not based on a few lies. It's based on unlimited government lawlessness. . . . There is an unequivocal understanding that the only way you can really defend yourself against the lawlessness is through an investment in politics. Our thinking would be different if our only goals were to make money and emigrate. Then we wouldn't care. We would just give bribes, corrupt some more bureaucrats, and do as we please. This is why in the December 1993 elections all the big business structures began to invest, to finance politics. The politicization of Russian entrepreneurship is a diffuse mechanism aimed against Russian lawlessness. It's not because we want to become politicians. We are forced to politicize because it serves our interests—not so much the interests of our individual companies, but the interests of all who want to live an ordinary life, for all who want to live and not be attacked as we were on December 2. In that case they just pushed people's faces in the dirt and the snow and beat them with rifle butts, all to show who's the boss. Today there are various ways of defending yourself. I choose a civilized way of doing it. . . .

"It is impossible to deal with the state now. There is just no judicial power. . . . The tax police come and they make their private income based on what they confiscate. It's a government racket when an army or police force feeds itself by robbing money from the people."

But how, I said, was it possible to be so righteous when a former KGB general like Bobkov was among his top advisers? What exactly were his ties to the KGB and its successor agencies?

Gusinsky smiled. "My ties to the KGB are like the ties of any American corporation to the CIA, any big organization in which high-ranking specialists are employed," he said. "I assure you, if a company gets into a foreign market, it will hire specialists, workers from intelligence, people who used to investigate that country. This is normal. Where does a person like William Colby work? Or where do people who worked for the National Security Agency or the FBI or the CIA work now? The same here. Bobkov makes it possible to analyze things. He is an analyst."

Gusinsky said that about twenty of his employees were former KGB and none of them worked in the security division. "Our security comes from the police or young people who served in the army," he said.

But why such a huge security force? Did he really need eleven hundred people?

"The government does not fulfill the most basic functions, like the minimal insurance of security," Gusinsky said. "They are simply unable to do it. In some cases this happens in the West. Big companies everywhere can have their own security companies, just as they do their own analytical services. It's just that our security service is a little bigger than some others. Our security service works for MOST and is also hired out to clients. This, too, is a commercial activity. Look, all the banks have them, and they usually range from two hundred to eight hundred people. It's a sign of the times. Either you pay the gangsters or you defend yourself."

Gusinsky talked for a while about his media properties and the distance he keeps from them. In fact, he appeared willing, to a remarkable degree, to let NTV, Sevodnya, and Ekho Moskvi go their own liberal way.

"The press cannot be entirely free," Gusinsky said. "I don't know how it is in the United States, but if the executive editor of The New York Times gets a call from someone, a 'friendly request,' to refrain from printing something for the sake of national interests, the editor will sometimes comply, I think. This is not a matter of a ban. It's normal behavior.

"Freedom of information is the main thing to a journalist, but an editor in chief is less a journalist than he is a politician. Dmitri Ostalsky"—the editor in chief of Sevodnya—"has to understand what is going on around him in the world. He should not limit the flow of information, but he does have to think about the trends of his paper's operation. I don't tell Dima, 'Do this,' 'Don't do this.' If I ever tell him that, it will be the end of the newspaper. What we do is talk and I explain to him how I understand things and, should he continue to press in the same direction, what the consequences might be. Then the decision is up to him."

I was still curious why, with all his interests in banking and real estate, Gusinsky bothered with media properties. NTV, for example, was a $15 million investment. Igor Malashenko, who ran NTV for Gusinsky, had told me that television has turned out to be an "incredibly profitable" business and they could expect to make money on Gusinsky's investment "very soon." Nevertheless, there was no guarantee that the Kremlin would let that happen.

"Media is business and NTV is good business," Gusinsky insisted. "Now, newspapers—newspapers may not be such good business for the time being, but it is foolish to start something today and expect that it will make money tomorrow. Russia has great potential as a print market."

A secretary performed the trick of serving coffee and tea, cookies, and candy without interrupting her boss. Gusinsky raised one eyebrow to indicate gratitude, and then she was gone. The only time Gusinsky seemed to abandon his attempt to be charming, the only time he got testy, was when I raised the issue of his difficulties with the Yeltsin government and its hostility to him.

"Something is going on in the Kremlin, but we don't know what it is," he said. "The Kremlin is a black box and we don't know what's going on inside it, but we can tell that something is wrong. We begin to see that a person with power can begin to say to himself, 'Why do we need elections? Maybe we won't win. What then? It is me who is leading the country on a democratic path. What if the communists happen to win? So let's arrange it so that there are no elections.' Such is the temptation, the temptation to preserve power. Not only the president, but his circle. The number one person exists, but his behavior is formed by his circle.

"Until this very last moment, we have supported Yeltsin and all the other democratically inclined movements. The Stolichnii and Menatep banks have, too. In fact, nearly all the banks have. This is the way it used to be, but now is the moment of truth. Our support will depend on a lot of things. Everything will depend on the behavior of the president himself.

"We are now in a situation when people are afraid again to speak openly in their own offices, afraid that they are being bugged. People are afraid to speak on the telephone. The fear of the 1980s has returned—this totalitarian consciousness of being watched. They are testing people's loyalty. You can take bribes, you can give bribes—as a rule, no one cares—what is of greatest concern is loyalty to power."

Was the attack on December 2 a message from the Kremlin? I asked.

Gusinsky leaned forward in his chair and frowned. "There are easier ways of sending a message," he said. "This was a demonstration that a time of unlimited lawlessness is coming. Six months or a year ago I would have thought we'd move ahead very quickly—Russia's potential is great—but now I can't say this. I'm not so sure if we'll proceed much further. There can be no economic progress without democratic freedom, and no democratic freedoms without institutions of a free market."

Gusinsky started looking at his watch. His press people started looking at their watches.

One last question. What sort of advice would he give to foreigners who wanted to come to Russia and do business?

This time, Gusinsky smiled, but there was still no amusement in his expression. "A very simple piece of advice," he said. "Be very careful. Russia is a country with huge potential. But one has to be very careful."

As it turned out, no one would have to be more careful than Vladimir Gusinsky. In late January 1995, as the Kremlin was waging its assault on Chechnya, it reopened the front against MOST. NTV's coverage of the war was, evidently, too candid. Yeltsin kept silent on the matter, but his trusted guard and friend Korzhakov lashed out. Under the pretense of announcing that he had "never taken part in politics," Korzhakov gave a blatantly political interview to *Argumenti i Fakti* in which he accused MOST of protecting "criminal commercial structures" and "frightening the people with talk of a 'police state.' "

"The threat to society does not stem from the Security Service," Korzhakov said, "but from those people who arrogantly and casually strut around the center of Moscow with weapons in their hands in full view of the mayor's office, from the same financial mafia that is breeding a new generation of politicians and striving to set up a 'pocket' government of people who are buying up state bureaucrats and pursuing their own selfish interests at the expense of the motherland."

The publicity about Korzhakov's own involvement in politics came only after December 2, he said, and the source was "a flock of geese and highly placed people linked with them." Korzhakov made it clear that the "geese" were Gusinsky's, and then added, "I will mention, by the way, that hunting geese is an old hobby of mine."

Three days later, another paper, *Nezavisimaya Gazeta* ("The Independent Newspaper"), ran a front-page story under the triple-stack headline

THE **MOST** GROUP EXPECTS MORE UNPLEASANTNESS
GENERAL MAJOR KORZHAKOV ANNOUNCES
GOOSE HUNTING SEASON HAS OPENED

The news, for MOST, was ominous:

A well-informed source at the Kremlin has told *Nezavisimaya Gazeta* that one of the Russian special services will soon take measures aimed at weakening the position of Vladimir Gusinsky in international and Russian banking circles. It is expected that as a result there could be a discontinuation of links between European financial establishments with MOST Bank, pushing aside major foreign and Russian clients, massive withdrawals of deposits and refusal of interbank credits.

Investigations reflecting negatively on the activities of the MOST Group and its connections among politicians, businessmen, bureaucrats and "force structures" are being prepared for publication in newspapers and videotaped television pieces. After public opinion has been worked up, the Prosecutor General's Office will sanction the arrest of highly placed officers for corruption and abuse of office and of various financiers for buying the cooperation of law enforcement organs.

It has become known that Vladimir Gusinsky, who is living outside the country at the moment, has been placed under the control of the Russian secret services abroad. There is an investigation under way of his private bank accounts, which belong to him by rights of private real estate property in the West.

In conclusion, the article said the government would try to get the British to extradite Gusinsky and might even appeal to Prime Minister

John Major to do so: "And after that, Lefortovo Prison and a show trial on Moscow's financial genius."

While *Nezavisimaya Gazeta* did not reveal its Kremlin source, Gusinsky showed every sign of believing the report. He told the paper from England that he planned to sue the president's bodyguard. "We believe," Gusinsky said, "that what Mr. Korzhakov said constitutes a physical threat aimed at the leadership of MOST."

Gusinsky also told the paper, by telephone from England, that he would stay abroad "for a little while." He hoped to return sometime soon.

CHAPTER 7

RESURRECTIONS EVERYWHERE

As it is often said in Russia, Tolstoy looked precisely like "Tolstoy." Lev Nikolayevich played the role of the Great Russian Writer so exquisitely that his beard, that magnificent silver nimbus, was as serene and perfect in its way as the harvest scene in *Anna Karenina*. He was a prophet, teacher, nobleman, peasant, and holy fool. Pilgrims would come to Tolstoy's estate at Yasnaya Polyana, and if they were fortunate enough to receive an audience they would ask questions as if to a priest: What is the nature of sin? What is the meaning of my life? How can we go on?

The phenomenon in Russia of the writer as moral authority and political truth-teller intensified with the advent of bolshevism. How could it not? Part of the brutal messianism of the regime was to turn writers into "engineers of human souls," and those who rejected the role met predictable ends. They rapidly became official pariahs (or corpses) and unofficial martyrs. Osip Mandelstam's summation of the leadership's obsession with literary authority would become the epitaph to a perverse culture: "Poetry is respected only in this country—people are killed for it. There is no country in which *more* people are killed for it." Beaten, sick, half mad, Mandelstam died in the camps; his final offense to Stalin had been to write a poem comparing the Great Mountain Eagle to a cockroach. In the Soviet Union, poets named the animals.

The history of opposition in the Soviet Union has been largely a matter of literature, a legacy that began with Dostoevsky's prescient vision of revolutionary fanaticism in *The Devils* and ended with the barbed wire and mass graves in Solzhenitsyn's *The Gulag Archipelago*. Real literature, not the lying, Kremlin kind, was holy. In an empire where honest clergy were killed or oppressed, where every church and synagogue was infiltrated by informers of the secret police, the secular parishioner knelt before the poem, the story, the novel. Illegal onionskin manuscripts were passed hand to hand as sacred texts. Even as the oppression dwindled under Gorbachev, the myth of the Russian writer lingered. As late as 1991, I would go to readings in Moscow and hear audiences ask poets and novelists the old Tolstoyan questions: What is the meaning of life? How should we live it?

Few Western writers were immune to the myth. For decades they came to Moscow (and other Eastern European capitals) as if in search of foreign authenticity. If they were lucky enough to break free of the miserable conferences and tours set up by the hacks at the local "creative unions," they would spend one of those magical evenings around a battered kitchen table with a Russian writer, sharing the vodka and the potato salad, the speculation and the irony. It was a kind of talk they could find only rarely as dinner-party warriors in Manhattan, Cambridge, or East Hampton. Saul Bellow's *The Dean's December,* John Cheever's journals, Philip Roth's *The Prague Orgy,* and even John Updike's story "The Bulgarian Poetess" all have about them this sour whiff of wet wool, sweet cigarette smoke, and urgent conversation. They all fell in love a little. None of these writers was foolish enough, of course, to want to trade places with their mythic counterparts, but there invariably came a moment when they found themselves wondering, painfully, why democracy necessarily meant a marginal place for serious writing and totalitarianism an impossibly exalted one.

Solzhenitsyn, like Tolstoy, was well aware of his own beard, his own legend. He planned for himself, in the spring of 1994, a homecoming that had about it the self-conscious air of the Great Russian Writer act-ing out the climactic chapters of his own mythic biography, his longest, his *essential,* text. He never let on to me when I visited him in Vermont, yet he had long ago devised the route of his return. Instead of flying di-rectly to Moscow, he would fly to the Far East via Alaska and work his way west slowly by train. The homecoming was literally a production, underwritten and filmed by the British Broadcasting Company. And as Solzhenitsyn arrived in Vladivostok at the end of May to begin his jour-ney, the younger writers of Moscow and St. Petersburg were watching the event on television with a measure of interest—but more with be-musement, even disdain.

Flying first class on an Air Alaska flight from Anchorage to Magadan, the center of the Kolyma camps in the old gulag system, Solzhenitsyn turned to his wife, Natalia, and wondered aloud what sort of expression he should wear as he came down the stairs and stepped on Russian soil for the first time since his forced exile in 1974. (The intimate moment is a highlight of the subsequent BBC documentary.)

"It would not do to smile," Solzhenitsyn said.

"But gloomy?" Natalia said.

"No, girl, no," he decided. "Thoughtfulness." That would be the ex-pression. Minutes later, he came down the stairs, an expression of thoughtfulness dangling from his brow. Not gloomy.

In the coming weeks, Solzhenitsyn traveled through Russia by train. He and his family rode in a specially equipped car, rather like visiting roy-alty. In each city and village, he gathered complaints, met with people, gave speeches. In Moscow, the reaction to the spectacle was withering.

"Until now," Vitaly Tretyakov wrote in *Nezavisimaya Gazeta,* "only the sun has dawned over Russia from the east. Everything else has come from the west. Now there is a second: the sun and Solzhenitsyn. . . . History will tell us whether Aleksandr Solzhenitsyn is a man of genius as a liter-ary artist. It is indisputable, however, that he is a genius at arranging his place in history." Another critic, Grigory Amelin, said Solzhenitsyn was "shamelessly outdated" and mocked his "Hollywood beard." Even some of Solzhenitsyn's greatest admirers were at least embarrassed by the grandiosity of his arrival.

For these younger critics and writers, the myth of the Great Russian Writer, the martyr and saint, was as much a part of the Soviet past as the Five-Year Plan and Lenin's Tomb. Amelin even had the punk audacity to write, "In Moscow he'll be received like a demigod, but who needs him? No one. . . . Solzhenitsyn is a spiritual statue, he is like a hat stand in the lobby, displaying a vast arrogance, sprouting prophetically—but in the end, he is moth-eaten."

Amelin's fury betrayed the anxiety of the mediocre before the superior. (His metaphors were worse than moth-eaten. Hat stands sprouting prophetically?) But even if Solzhenitsyn had played a significant, even singular, role in the months to come—and, alas, he did not—his heightened status had about it the feeling of anachronism, a closing act. With the fall of the old regime, the role of the writer and artist in Russian society had changed, probably forever. Suddenly the writers who had seemed so essential politically during the Gorbachev period—the novelists, poets, and critics who won seats in the Soviet parliament and dominated the liberal-minded press—disappeared from public view and were faced with the prospect of their own diminishing importance.

In St. Petersburg, I met with Aleksandr Kushner, a leading poet in Russia and a contemporary of Joseph Brodsky. As young men, the two used to call on their own idea of the Great Russian Writer, Anna Akhmatova. Kushner writes in a high, classical style and does not think much of the self-proclaimed postmodernists and avant-gardists who have begun to dominate the various literary magazines. We had a drink at one of the latest manifestations of luxury capitalism in the city, the Grand Hotel Europe, where rooms are no cheaper than they are at the best hotels in New York or Paris. Kushner looked around, more amused than embarrassed by the sight of foreign tourists and local mafiosi. When I mentioned that it seemed that serious writers were becoming marginalized in Russia, as they were in the West, Kushner nodded and sighed, as if in happy relief.

"The writer in Russia was for so long like an uncrowned prince," he said. "Even an unpublished poet had a place of respect. Now this is gone. Why? In those days literature was the one real door open to people of a certain kind. Now there are lots of doors to walk through. You can go into business, play on the Israeli soccer team, play for a New

York hockey team, make your fortune in Greece, or even go into politics if you should choose. At the same time, literature in the eyes of many people has lost its exceptional importance. Literature will always have a place, as it does in America. Marginal, but important. Small but beautiful. Of course, if a monster, a fascist, like Vladimir Zhirinovsky is ever elected president of Russia, literature might have to assume its old role. But for now, no."

Ludmilla Petrushevskaya, a celebrated Moscow playwright and prose writer of Kushner's generation, told me she not only welcomed the new, seemingly reduced status of the writer, she had prayed for it. Her family had been "drenched" in politics since the nineteenth century and she wanted nothing more than to see that obsession end. "Maybe I hate politics because the first time I ever attended an interrogation was when I was in my mother's womb," she said. "In my family, there were Decembrists and then Party members as early as 1898. Some of them ended up in the basement of Lubyanka or in the camps. So I loathe politics. That is innate with me. I always wanted to be an unremarkable, quiet person. I wanted to live my own life, to wake up in my own bed. In childhood I woke up anywhere but: I lived on the streets, and later in an orphanage. I don't like waking up in train stations or on park benches. I want to be a private person and be left to write.

"Even as late as 1985, everything of mine was still banned. Now it's the mid-nineties and everything has been allowed for quite a long time. So how has the situation changed? It's very funny. Because of the explosion of what I call 'mafia realism'—the junk crime fiction that is so popular—all the bookstores are filled with stories about gangsters, or books for gangsters. And what do gangsters love to read? They love to read about love and how-to books about overcoming impotence. Or they don't read and just watch videos. Or maybe they don't even have the time for that. The mafia are very busy people, after all. But I don't worry about all this. Finally, I can go my own way. I waited a long time for my readers, and my readers, what few of them there are, waited a long time for me. I hope I give them something—but not prophecy."

In Moscow, I also visited a writer who, unlike Kushner or Petrushevskaya, was young enough to have grown up able to read the Western avant-garde. Vladimir Sorokin, the author of seven books of fiction, is widely known as Russia's most scandalous writer. One of his stories begins as a socialist-realist parody of a familiar scene: an old man describing to a young boy the Nazi blockade of Leningrad. The story then spins out of control, ending with the old man's rape of the boy. The assault on the conventions of socialist realism are nearly as brutal as the assault on the boy. Sorokin's understanding of the Great Russian Writer was ironic; the figure had become for him just another icon, there to demolish or cherish depending on the story at hand.

"In the first place, I think the myth was formed as the result of deep crisis, especially in the Russian Orthodox Church, and the writer gradually substituted for the priest," Sorokin told me. "Paradoxically, even while this myth is dying here, it persists in the West. Not long ago I was in Zurich and gave a reading. After I'd read some rather brutal, grotesque scenes having nothing whatever to do with politics, the audience had a chance to ask questions. One young man got up and said, 'We've come here to a recital of a Russian writer seeking hope, because Russian literature is the last preserver of hope.' I had no idea what this man meant! For me, literature is a game. I said, 'I'm afraid you've come to the wrong place for hope.' The poor guy. He'd have been better off going to a church."

———

Long before Lenin had a chance to seize power and cast his first uncooperative writer into exile, he sketched out a manifesto of socialist culture, *Party Organization and Party Literature*. "In sharp contrast to bourgeois custom," Lenin wrote in 1905, socialism would reject commercialism, careerism, and individualism in favor of literature serving the Communist Party and the proletariat. The writer would be the "cog and screw" in the social machine. "It will be a free literature because it will serve not some satiated heroine, not the bored 'upper ten thousand' suffering from obesity, but millions and tens of millions of workers, those people who make up the best part of our country, its strength and future." Not for him the "aristocratic anarchism" of Tolstoy or Dostoevsky; better the model of Nikolai Chernyshevsky's crackpot idealism in *What Is to Be Done?* (a book satirized in Nabokov's novel *The Gift*).

The organization that came to stand for the officially sanctioned literature was the Soviet Writers' Union, a guild created by the Communist Party in 1932 and patrolled by the KGB. Mikhail Sholokhov, a loyal union man and one of the most dubious winners of the Nobel Prize in the history of the award, once summed up the spirit of the official literary soul under socialism: "I write at the bidding of my heart, and my heart belongs to the Party." Sholokov used the authority of his Nobel and his position in the union to denounce Solzhenitsyn and other writers of independence. So willfully blinded was the union leadership to the idea of real literature that in 1979 it awarded its highest award, the Lenin Prize, to the Party general secretary, Leonid Brezhnev, for his trilogy of memoirs. Brezhnev's literary gifts were positively Reaganesque. But unlike Reagan, who produced an audiotape of his memoir, *An American Story,* thereby assuring the world that he had at least read part of his ghostwriter's work, there was no such guarantee from Brezhnev.

Using the manipulative trick that Russians call *knut i pryanik,* the whip and the gingerbread, the union managed to combine the power of ideology with the power of the purse. With Party funding, the union presidium ladled out, or withheld, the petty privileges of Soviet life to its membership. The degree of submission determined everything: the size of a writer's apartment, the site of his vacation (ah, to get the good rooms in Pitsunda!), the quantity and freshness of his food parcels, the frequency of his travels abroad, the pressrun of his latest book, the quality of his medical care, and the pomposity of his funeral. For as long as the presidium met at 52 Vorovsky Street—a mansion said to be the model for the Rostov house in *War and Peace*—members in good standing could drop by the Central House of Writers, the "club," around the corner and eat subsidized salmon sandwiches, drink subsidized coffee, buy subsidized books, and get a subsidized haircut. The union provided, and the union took away. It was the source of rage, gossip, intrigue, and fear. To be expelled from the union—a select group, to be sure—was to be barred from everything, including the possibility of publication.

By the early 1990s the club was a sorry place, an empty symbol of a miserable past. Not only had it lost all its power, its subsidies were gone. No one could afford the sandwiches. The café was, decidedly, half empty. Even the talk was sad, a little desperate. There was an air of deflation and complaint. Pathetically, some of the worst apparatchiks of the union now protested that they, too, had been dissidents in their way, that they, too, did their best in secret to stretch the bounds of the permissible. One morning I had a cup of coffee at the café with Vladimir Novikov, a critic of modest reputation who had been the second man in charge at another institution of Soviet literature, the Gorky Literary Institute. Novikov said he knew everything had changed, "and probably for the better," but his voice was anything but joyful. "After the collapse of the coup in August 1991, the unions started splitting and collapsing," he said. "And as they have disappeared they have left a lot of writers wondering about some very mundane things. Their financial survival, for one thing. Their spirit, for another."

At the height of the Gorbachev period, the literary world lived in a state of prolonged euphoria. Not only had Gorbachev sanctioned the publication of popular fiction like Anatoly Rybakov's *The Children of the Arbat* to help fill in the "blank spots" of Soviet history, he also allowed the various monthly magazines, the "thick journals," to publish the true classics of an era: Akhmatova, Platonov, Tsvetayeva, Bulgakov, Pasternak, Zamyatin, Grossman, Osip and Nadezhda Mandelstam, and finally, in 1990, Solzhenitsyn. At first, the ruling Politburo argued for hours over whether it would sanction the publication of this novel or that selection of poetry; finally, it handed the decisions over to the editors themselves. From late 1987 into 1989, everyone on the metros and buses seemed to be reading the same thing at the same time. One month it was *Doctor Zhivago*, the next it was *Life and Fate*. It was a civic, as well as literary, explosion.

For centuries, these intellectuals and their forebears had been a kind of shadow government, a moral prod to the czars and, later, the Communist Party. When Pushkin stood up to Alexander I or Sakharov to the general secretary, they were asserting a belief in the power of truth and the individual against a brutal system. Perhaps the apotheosis for the liberal intelligentsia came in 1989, when one intellectual after another was elected to the Soviet legislature: at its first gathering, Yuri Karyakin, the Dostoevsky scholar, called for Lenin to be removed from his tomb and buried in the ground; a short-story writer, Nikolai

Shmelyov, outlined the rot of the Soviet economy; a novelist, Yuri Shcherbak, described the horrors of Chernobyl; an Olympic weightlifting champion who became a writer, Yuri Vlasov, denounced "the underground empire" of the KGB. It was a moment in which words could not have had greater meaning.

But the moment passed. Politics after 1991 was less about ideas than interests; literature became a more private matter and writers were no longer in the thick of public life. While one might have predicted this development, it came as a shock to the men and women, mostly middle-aged and older, who thought their great victory would lead them somewhere, anywhere, else.

One afternoon, I went to the ramshackle offices of *Znamya* ("Banner"), which had been one of the leading literary and political monthlies in the Gorbachev years, to see the deputy editor, Natalya Ivanova. I had been visiting Ivanova as a reporter on and off for years, and had never known her to be so pessimistic. At first, I thought the reason for her pessimism might be the fate of *Znamya* and the other literary monthlies. Where once they sold a million or more copies, in the late 1980s, now they sold no more than eighty thousand or so. Where once the best-seller lists were filled with titles by Solzhenitsyn, Orwell, and Brodsky, they were fast becoming litanies of what Bulgakov called MASSOLIT. Pulp fiction, self-help, all manner of triviality. Larisa Vasilieva, a Russian pop historian, made a fortune with *Kremlin Wives,* a look at the seamy world of political boudoirs in the communist era. Rex Stout became the most popular foreign novelist in the country. "People want a little pleasure," one novelist, Viktor Yerofeyev, told me. "If they have to read about one more concentration camp, they'll die."

But Ivanova was worried about more than the statistics of culture. It was inevitable, she realized, that once the regime fell, the abnormal importance (and popularity) of serious literature would fade. "We can all accept the idea that the only people reading now are the ones who read for nonpolitical reasons," Ivanova said. "Now you see the rise of advice columns, personal ads, Harlequin romances. Well, that's okay. What is unexpected is the general degradation of culture and of the intelligentsia itself. Its dominant position is now held by this new class of so-called businessmen, and they have no class at all. This new bourgeoisie is made up mostly of speculators stealing from the country."

Ivanova showed me the galley proofs of an article of hers called "Double Suicide," which she was getting ready for publication in *Znamya*. It was an angry piece, in which she accused her fellow artists and fellow thinkers of being more interested in "the course of the dollar" than in "moral problems," of bowing humbly before a new and vulgar image of what the Bolsheviks used to call "the shining future." Where once the Russian landscape had been littered with one kind of propaganda—"We Are Marching Toward Leninism," etc.—television, radio, and the newspapers were now filled with propaganda of a different kind: advertisements for unaffordable Western luxuries, fantastic commercials geared toward lives that hardly exist. One minute, you were *Homo sovieticus,* surrounded by the aggressive blandness of communism; the next minute, you were watching a Slavic bimbo in a bikini sucking on a maraschino cherry and telling you which casino to visit. There must have been, for many people, something profoundly irritating about ads for investment funds or American cat food in a country where most citizens were living in what Westerners would recognize as poverty. A year or two of exposure to American-style commercials had produced what decades of communist propaganda could not: genuine indignation against the excesses of capitalism. The intellectuals were bewildered by it all and proved incapable of providing moral guidance. "People struggled for a new life, and it turned out that this life deceived them," Ivanova said sadly.

It was also dispiriting that for the young there was just no sense, no prestige, in pursuing intellectual careers. At Moscow State University, it was suddenly a cinch to gain admission to the humanities departments; everyone wanted to learn business and finance. The endless ethereal conversations around the kitchen table, the wonderful no-show jobs at academic institutes, the big audiences for poetry readings—that world was dying out. The political scientist Andrei Kortunov remarked to me, "What we had under Gorbachev and for the years before was like the ecological system in Australia before the English brought their dogs and rabbits. We had this weird, authentic, original kind of culture. The intellectuals were even a privileged class. But when the English came, with their dogs and rabbits, the ecological system decayed. I suppose we need to go through this period of consumerism and pop culture, just as they are doing in Poland and Czechoslovakia. The question is whether Russia will ever be able to preserve even part of the old ecology—its distinctive intellectual character."

One night, over dinner at the luxurious Kempinski Hotel, the journalist Leonid Radzikhovsky laughed when I asked him about the lost world of the Russian intelligentsia. "I am a cynic maybe, a realist," he said, "but there is no more moral authority in Russia. Russia is a country in the stage of primitive accumulation of capital. Look around you, at this restaurant. What will dinner cost? At least a hundred dollars, right? An average Moscow salary for at least a month. In the nineteenth century, there were landlords and peasants and no thought of mixing them. But now everyone thinks he has a right to have dinner at the Kempinski. And everyone wants it. This is *all* anyone thinks about. People don't think about novels or plays or poetry. If it is true that everything in America is about dollars, it is even truer now in Russia. This is a hungry country, and it wants to be fed."

The specter of money had become the dominant factor in cultural life. Opera singers, musicians, conductors, dancers, and artists were leaving the country in record numbers—not for the freedom, but for the irresistible fees. Soviet books and magazines had once been so heavily subsidized by the state that they were practically free. No more. Beginning on January 1, 1992, the government freed prices—literature included. Subsidies disappeared. State publishing houses found themselves struggling to survive. They had to buy paper, pay authors, and print books all without the help of the Communist Party. The new wave of independent publishers also could not afford to work on a false economy. Faced with the soaring prices of books and bread, people had to choose bread.

"People need every ruble they have to survive. Books cost a fortune. No one can afford to subscribe to everything the way we did a few years ago," Alla Marchenko, an editor at the monthly journal *Novy Mir,* told me. "Money even influences the young writers and what they write. It has to. For the first time, really, young writers have to ask themselves, 'Is this material commercial enough?' Or, 'Maybe I should forget this and become a banker?' It used to be that a writer could live off his honoraria. A poet could even get by for a month publishing a block of poems in the magazine. Now we pay one hundred thousand rubles for an entire novel—less than fifty dollars. The money is just symbolic now. You go to the Central House of Writers these days and it is practically empty. They look like dogs sniffing around for money as if it were a piece of meat."

Dying, too, were the vast literary institutes where intellectuals earned a living wage at state expense simply by occupying an office and thinking great thoughts about Pushkin or Dostoevsky—or drinking coffee, as the case often was. "These institutes were set up as a kind of literary mirror of the scientific establishment and its well-funded effort to build the atom bomb," a prominent young critic, Andrei Zorin, told me. "No one taught. No one produced much. And they all got the little salary necessary to get by in the Soviet Union. This was considered the best possible place to live and work, a heavenly paradise. And soon it will be gone, all gone."

After so many years of being the center of political and cultural attention, many writers and artists faced the prospect of losing an audience forever. Their fruit is no longer forbidden or delicious; it is usually just left alone. "It is terribly sad, even tragic," Zorin said. "These people were brought up under Soviet censorship and with the idea that they were the conscience of the country, that their books would be published in gigantic editions, and everyone would read them. There is an old saying: 'Be careful what you struggle for, you will probably get it.' The interesting part of it is that the liberal writers were warned. The right-wing nationalist writers all said that when a free market came the only thing anyone would want to read or publish would be trash. Liberals, including Andrei Bitov, who was one of the very best of the sixties generation, said, well, that was all right, they would always have one hundred thousand readers or so to buy their books. They were sure there would always be an audience to listen to them. Now look!"

Bitov, the author of *Pushkin House,* adjusted well enough. He became a kind of literary godfather. He helped found *Solo,* the best of the new literary journals, and tirelessly campaigned for younger writers. And yet even some of Bitov's most sympathetic protégés admit that his own writing has suffered lately. "I've known Bitov for a long time, and I have witnessed his inner tortures," said Aleksandr Mikhailov, the young editor in chief of *Solo*. "During perestroika, when the opportunity was there to write however you wished, he could not write a single significant piece of any length. He was unable to resume a novel he had been working on for a long time. Finally, he finished it after ten years. It's called *Waiting for an Ape*, closing off a trilogy that began with *Birds: Or New Evidence of Men* and *A Man in a Landscape*. Well, he finished it, and to my great regret it proved a failure. He hopes this is not so, but he feels it is so. His mood is not very good. He is nostalgic for his old self, his self of the Brezhnev period. He understands that as a writer he was better then and his spiritual condition was more powerful and elevated than it is now. He feels the times passing him by. Not long ago he told me, 'You know, I'm already older than Lenin was when he died.' "

For all the anxiety and gloom among the middle-aged and older writers who thrived during perestroika and now found themselves disillusioned by a new world, there was a sense of takeover and exhilaration among the young (and the young at heart). In fact, the literary scene in Moscow was possessed of more optimism than nearly any other realm of life. Incompetence, conflict, and the specter of nationalism and neofascism haunted politics; brutality and greed distorted economic life. But in literature a vital aesthetic revolt was under way. One did not need a beard or a prophetic voice to play. A new generation of younger and middle-aged prose writers—Petrushevskaya, Tatyana Tolstaya, Vladimir Makanin, Zufar Gureyev, Oleg Yermakov, Viktor Yerofeyev, Yevgeny Popov, Aleksandr Terekhov, and many others—won increasingly wide audiences. The rise of a Russian Booker Prize also created some excitement and competition in the literary world.

Even before Gorbachev came to power, there had been a broad range of unofficial writers interested in a form of dissidence more aesthetic than political. Having gleaned some of the tenets of postmodernism from foreign texts and their friends in the art world, Dmitri Prigov, for example, and others used the artifacts of their surroundings—the orthodoxies

of socialist realism, the symbols and language of official Soviet culture—
and made them the raw material of their art and comedy. Prigov, who is
now in his fifties, remained a star of the avant-garde and a godfather to
scores of younger writers. Like Joseph Brodsky's lyrics, Prigov's poems
and short prose pieces are barely translatable. But while Brodsky is difficult mainly because of his rhythms and syntax, Prigov presents a problem
mainly of reference and comedy. A reader who did not spend much of his
life being force-fed the peculiarities of Soviet Newspeak—Novoyaz—
would have trouble reading Prigov. As a performance artist, however,
Prigov began to cross the borders of comprehension. His dramatic readings and bizarre stagings brought his wordplay into broad relief. Even as
late as 1986, Prigov infuriated the authorities when he went around
Moscow pinning on trees little slips of paper that had on them bits of
pseudo-Soviet wisdom. Residents would find the following on random
birches:

"Comrades, the faces of children and kittens remind us of eternity.
Dmitri Aleksandrovich."

Or: "Citizens, if you trample the grass and destroy the bird's nest, how
will you be able to look your mother in the face? Dmitri Aleksandrovich."
"Citizens, a tree is innocent and pure. It doesn't have a premonition of
evil. Dmitri Aleksandrovich."

The KGB did not appreciate the joke and sent Prigov to a psychiatric
hospital for a couple of days before his friends rescued him. Though he
was among the last psychiatric prisoners under the old regime, Prigov
had almost nothing to do with politics in the usual sense. He did not
draft petitions, write about prison camps, or organize demonstrations.
There was nothing about him that spoke of the Great Russian Writer. A
friend of mine in Moscow said she once saw Prigov when he appeared
on a stage filled with other writers at a somber evening commemorating the victims of the labor camps. She said she had rarely been so embarrassed for anyone. "He tried to avoid it, but Prigov couldn't help
being a little funny," my friend told me. "He just didn't know how to behave in that sort of situation, the sort of situation that another kind of
writer lives for. We saw Prigov afterward and it was hard to look him in
the eye."

Like the avant-gardists of the twenties, Prigov appropriated anything and made it his own. He was just as ruthless with the classics of Russian and Western art and literature as he was with the language of the old Politburo. In *An Action for Fifty-five Minutes,* Prigov and the poet Lev Rubenshtein recited *Hamlet* and Chekhov's *Ivanov,* respectively, while a paranoid-seeming critic ripped apart various texts. An alarm clock hidden under stacks of old newspapers called the performance to a halt. When I met him, Prigov was preparing a "samizdat edition" of Pushkin's *Yevgeny Onegin,* "Lermontovizing" it by replacing all the original adjectives with "insane" and "unearthly." To get at the essence of Lenin, Prigov wrote a series of sonnets "about electrification," which are meant to be recited—"Crazily! Ecstatically!"—while one pianist performs the *Appassionata* and another the *Moonlight* sonata. Prigov was also "working on" Volume One of Stalin's collected works, "Lermontovizing" it by adding a series of "romantic adjectives in all the right spots," as he described it to me.

I met Prigov at his apartment on the outskirts of Moscow and found him to be a ceaselessly funny man whose conversation was no less a performance than his art. When I asked him about the Prigov version of Stalin, his eyes lit up with glee. "When you substitute these romantic adjectives, the speeches become a magical mantra," he said. "It turns out this was the main message of Stalin's speeches in the first place. It's a natural deconstruction of the inner meaning of what was going on."

Everyone in Moscow who knew Prigov liked him enormously. Even the artists and critics who found him too frivolous, a matter more of chic than of art, invariably called him a friend. He was remarkably free of intrigue or dark resentments; he was unfailingly generous to younger writers. In fact, his impish wit, slight frame, and goggly glasses made him seem a "younger writer" himself.

As a young man trying to support his art, Prigov worked as a hack sculptor. "I made the gigantic bunnies and bears you see kids climbing on in playgrounds," he said. "These were great works, and I always fulfilled my plan." As a poet, Prigov also set himself a plan, Soviet-style. "I shall write ten thousand poems!" he once declared, and then went ahead and did just that. Part Derrida, part Monty Python, he set about playing with the verbal stuff of Sovietism. He was first published, abroad, in 1975 in the Paris-based paper *Russkaya Misl'* ("Russian Thought"). Unlike the Great Russian Writers of the day, Prigov was, as he says, "widely known in narrow circles."

"In those days, to the outside world, the status of an unofficial or dissident writer seemed to be taken up by Solzhenitsyn, Vladimov, Sinyavsky—all the names you know, the political and social writers," he said. "The dynamics of reader reaction were imperceptible, like a needle not showing on the charts, beyond perception, like a fish talking. But after a while I started giving readings: fish-reading readings. Then gradually I was perceived. People became indignant, disgusted. A few were delighted. My circle of people was a kind of aesthetic opposition. By using Soviet language and cliché we created an aesthetic. Deconstructing one language, we created other languages. And believe me, the powers were no less disgusted by our offense than by the attempt of the dissidents to create an opposition in their own, more traditionally elevated literary language. But, as you see, in the long run, my circle, my sort, turned out to be in opposition not only to Soviet power, but to the dissidents as well.

"Our position was to deconstruct any attempt to create a myth or any grand theory. We were out to deconstruct the figure of Lenin, but also the figure of Solzhenitsyn. They can all be responded to as pop figures. In the last years of Brezhnev, the authorities began doing something truly bizarre. They began looking for adjectives to describe, officially, for propaganda purposes, the nature of our great socialism: 'real socialism,' 'completed socialism,' 'built socialism,' and all the rest. They put everything aside to find the solution. What was the proper adjective? Inside our magical culture, this was a completely logical act. They had to find the true secret name and as soon as it was pronounced, the object begins to serve you. It was a wonderful case of concentrating reality in a tiny concept, a little piece of language. It was a tiny formula of culture, and I was very aroused by this.

"In everyday life, one would attend Komsomol meetings, a football game, school, where you were spoken to in a particular, magical official way; but elsewhere you spoke in the lingo of a separate life. In this respect the culture spoke in a sacred language. There was real schizophrenic quality to this life. The first desire was not a practical one, but to overcome this schizophrenia. You had two possibilities. Either escape to a world of culture and dreams or pick up the language of everyday life and bring it to the culture. The second position was our position.

"The mystic Meister Eckehart once said that an angel in hell flies in his own little cloud of paradise. These slogans were like little angels in hell, fleshless, but with tremendously suggestive, Platonic qualities hanging in the air. It was clear that this kind of thinking, though, was as heretical for dissidents as it was for the communists. For dissidents, their ideas were interpreted not as real ideas but as a discourse equal to communist ideas."

I asked Prigov how his aesthetic had been affected by the sudden disappearance of Soviet power—and with it, Soviet rhetoric.

"The end of Soviet power just changes my range of powers," Prigov said. "The liberals now become characters, too. I work the mainstream, as always: homosexuals, liberals, feminists. By the way, I will have written twenty thousand poems by the year 2000. Right now I'm up to eighteen thousand five hundred."

Before leaving, I asked Prigov about the scene now, and he, like nearly everyone else in town, quickly and happily announced the diminished position of literature in Russia.

"Literature is no longer very prestigious," he said wryly. "Young people with a lot of energy have gone off into other adventures. The structure of culture will change. As it has elsewhere. Art that can make its way into the market will atract people. Avant-garde art will become a marginal pursuit. This is a transitional moment. There are still a lot of people around who find literary activity important; of course, they are visionary sorts and unpractical minds. This is neither good nor bad. In every society, functions are redistributed according to the needs of the people."

———

Many writers of the sixties generation simply vanished from the scene, unable to adjust to the new air. The playwright Aleksandr Gelman, for example, did well abroad with his plays but said that he still found that the

"Shakespearean battles" of politics—Gorbachev versus Yeltsin, Yeltsin versus the parliament, etc.—had eclipsed anything that his own dramatic writing could provide. "I'm trying to find my way and my audience again," Gelman told me.

But one writer of that generation who made the adjustment rather easily was the satirist Vladimir Voinovich. In the Brezhnev era, Voinovich wrote a mock epic, a classic, about his quest to acquire a slightly bigger apartment. In *The Ivankiad,* there was more truth about late Sovietism than in a thousand issues of *Pravda.* Voinovich had emigrated to Munich and still spends about half the year there, but after 1991 he was given a spacious apartment in downtown Moscow and reentered the absurdities of Russian life, his customary material.

I asked Voinovich what he had found particularly absurd since his return. Voinovich, who has Asiatic eyes and a huge shock of white hair, grinned widely at the mention of the absurd—his favorite subject, his meat.

"One of the great absurdities is all my old neighbors who were *communyaki,* apparatchiks in the Central Committee, or whatever. Now they act as if it—meaning the Soviet Union and all it meant—never happened. Suddenly there are a lot of gentry around and everyone was always a Christian believer. Another absurdity is when people, with their ingrained Soviet habits, march on to capitalism. The Party big shots and the KGB people were, of course, the quickest to adjust. They betrayed their so-called ideals in a flash. Meanwhile, the 'democrats' still act like the old Soviet leaders. They have to adjust to a new life, but their ways of behaving, their bearing, their relations with other people, are the same as they always were. They were raised to behave a certain way. Yeltsin acts like the general secretary of the Communist Party. You see, very few people understand that they are living in history. Under Brezhnev, everyone thought that life would stay the same for a thousand years. They couldn't imagine it being different."

While Voinovich thrives on the absurd contrast between the old regime and the new, a younger writer like Aleksandr Terekhov uses the present realities of provincial life as the material for novels of the grotesque like his *Rat-Killer.* Terekhov is boyish, barely thirty, and utterly believable when he says that his generation of writers "never really lived without freedom. For us, freedom is no great accomplishment. Of course, we read all those stories that started coming out with glasnost some years ago, but we never felt that extra charge on our skin, the thrill of the forbidden."

Terekhov grew up in the Tula region, three hours south of Moscow. His hometown was called Stalinogorsk and then the name was changed to Novomoskovsk. "I am a provincial boy," he said. "I found out about Solzhenitsyn, Sakharov, and homosexuals all at the same time—when I got out of the army. Before that I was interested in nothing much but soccer. Like a normal Russian philistine, for me the rest of the world hardly exists. I am almost sure Bill Clinton exists, and I suppose there is a Statue of Liberty, but as for the rest, I sincerely doubt it. And this is true for almost anyone living in Russia.

"My goal is to write about Russia after it has collapsed into freedom. My theme is not Moscow, but the provinces, which are more typical of life in Russia. For this society the hardest thing is the lost sense of the truth. In the provinces, the Party organizations are singular and are all the same people: the prosecutors and the bureaucrats are all the same as they were before 1991. But while communist ideology limited the stealing, these people are now all unashamed and grab up everything they possibly can. So people see this and they despair. What chance do they have? And so they drink themselves to death, never seeing any hope. Only the former communists have any influence in these towns. The villages are very rough for anyone who makes any money. Everything is transparent. You cannot just disappear the way you can in a big city. If you've built a new building and have a BMW and yet live, allegedly, on one hundred and fifty dollars a month, everyone will ask out loud, 'Where did he get the money?' And everyone knows. They despise these people with money. The sense of injustice is intense. There is a strong desire to destroy democracy and at least create an appearance of justice. The provinces are very bleak and violent. Moscow, by population, ranks only seventy-fourth in violent crime. In the provinces people will simply disappear. They're never found. People cannot quite fathom why, in order to reach democracy, people must be killed in the streets. Anyway, this is what I try to capture in my work. I wonder if I can really do it."

Just as the Bolsheviks tried to invent a new jargon of Soviet man, the coming of capitalism in Russia and the fall of the old regime helped create a new language that became the source of fascination and creativity for the younger generation of writers and critics. The linguistic break was as severe and shocking to the older generations as anything since 1917. One of the first things Solzhenitsyn complained about upon arriving in Russia was the rise of foreign words like "voucher." (It did strike me odd, however, that when I asked his wife, Natalia, how she negotiated Moscow traffic, she said, "*Speeduyu!*") Suddenly the more conservative writers sounded like the hoary members of the Académie Française whining about *franglais*.

"The revolution in language is absolutely marked," Irina Prokhorova, the editor of the *New Literary Observer,* told me. "I spent three days at the White House during the coup in August 1991. There were old people there who spoke obscenely, and yet it was very natural. For three days, I, too, spoke that way. Then I realized that people needed a revolutionary rhetoric but the old clichés had been spoiled by the old propaganda. Cursing was the only medium now possible in the search for a new expressive language, a new ideological rhetoric. Now Zhirinovsky is on the scene and his language is interesting to analyze. He's the most contemporary because he found the most adequate way to speak to people. It's not his economic policy that people are interested in. He uses a combination of colloquial speech and a cynical attitude. He may be a clown but he is liked precisely because of his obscenities, his rudeness. He found something in mass psychology. At the same time, Yeltsin has no language. He can't find it. He still sounds like a Party man. He lacks this instinct for a new language, of what to say and how to say it. In this way, Zhirinovsky is a postcommunist populist, a man of new mentality. And while we laugh, he gains popularity all the time. He proclaims his newness not as a communist or as a dissident. He is not associated with anything.

"Zhirinovsky aside—he is truly dangerous—this change and interest in language is all good. It helps flush out the old-style Newspeak. It is also really rich soil for a new generation of writers. I don't say we've found our new Russian James Joyce, but the new language does help in explaining our new realities."

In Moscow, I found that it was Vladimir Sorokin who had become most notorious in trying to capture those new realities. Sorokin was thirty-eight, a large, lumbering man with a soft, hesitant voice and long rock-star hair. The only one of his seven novels to be published in English was *The Queue,* a work about a line (for what is unclear) written completely in dialogue. We are not told who is speaking, but it soon becomes clear who is falling in love with whom, what is being sold, and the agonies and banalities of Moscow street life. Sorokin also caused a sensation in Moscow with his story "A Month in Auschwitz," a dark parody of Turgenev's *A Month in the Country,* the poems of Aleksandr Blok, and much else as well.

Sorokin lives on the outskirts of Moscow in the last dilapidated housing development before the immense forest begins. I asked him how he developed his approach to parody and prose, in general.

"Well, my material was official literary language at first, and then I began using the literature of the nineteenth century," Sorokin said. "Literature for me was pop material the way a Brillo box or a soup can was for Warhol. This discovery for me was like the discovery of the atom bomb for some world power. And judging by the response of the critics, it was almost as dangerous. I suppose what makes me different from a normal writer is that while a normal writer has his own unmistakable literary style that he can be recognized by—Joyce and his style, Nabokov and his, Kafka and his—I am not at all like that. Sure, Sasha Sokolov will never write like Kurt Vonnegut or vice versa. But I don't have my own style. I grab one and then I make it my own. I try to make it new. I derive great pleasure from this. I don't pick up a writer's concrete style, but rather a language of certain tendencies.

"In the late seventies I put out a collection of stories called *The First Subbotnik.* It had a whole section of typically socialist-realist stories. Industrial short stories. Country lyrics. The routine at a regional Party committee. I even wrote my preface according to the given formula. It was like any collection published by a provincial publisher in Kaluga. Every story began in an absolutely ordinary way. The better part of the story was totally in synch with the canon of socialist realism. At some point, however, the characters would become lost. They were like puppets whose strings had suddenly been cut. And then I would begin to write according to noncanonical laws and do strange and terrible things to my characters. To me it was reminiscent of the insect who lays eggs on a caterpillar. The caterpillar would crawl on, not noticing. After a while the larvae would crawl out and the worms would eat the caterpillar up from inside. This was what I was trying to do to the literary corpus.

"I have a novel called *Marina's Thirtieth Love* in which the whole process goes in reverse. It starts out as a quasi-erotic novel. The heroine, by all Soviet standards, is the incarnation of evil—a nymphomaniac, a lesbian, a kleptomaniac who gets erotic pleasure from stealing. She mixes with dissidents. At home she keeps a portrait of Solzhenitsyn, and she prays to it as if it were an icon. She is even convinced that Solzhenitsyn is the only man with whom she can reach orgasm. Then her fate begins to change, and so does the language of the novel. She is a teacher of music. She meets a man who looks like Solzhenitsyn, but he is a Party secretary at a factory. She gets involved with him and things begin to change. The novel ends with her getting rid of her old life. She goes to work at the factory and becomes a real shock worker of socialist labor. At this point, the novel becomes a typical Russian novel of the salvation of the hero, like Tolstoy's *Resurrection*. By the end, the language is pure socialist realism and dissolves into a gigantic fake quotation from the newspaper *Pravda*."

Although Sorokin had written quickly and prodigiously nearly all of his adult life, he soon discovered that he had come to a kind of stopping point in his career, for even while the literary scene was thriving in its new smaller-scale mode, reality itself was confusing. "For two years I've been more or less silent. Since the novel *Four Stout Hearts* came out I haven't been writing," he said. "Probably this is connected not only with fatigue—I've written seven novels—but also with the change in language. It's an interesting time to be alive. One myth has been destroyed—the myth of communism. It's been displaced by a new myth, the myth of the market. You may have noticed two or three years ago the streets of Moscow filled with people standing on the streets selling things. Everything. They were not beggars. It didn't mean they were starving. It was typical for Russia, the materialization of a myth. Earlier the Russians materialized the myth of European romantic communism, and they tried sincerely to implement it. Now the idea of the market is perceived literally: go on the streets and sell! This new myth has already enveloped the country, and it demands its own language. This language is actively displacing the old language of socialist realism. This is true on television, in the press, on the street, and in literature. There is a real invasion of this new language, a new mentality. Even though it is a slow process, it is still a new country. All my returning émigré friends say as much. It's not just a matter of the exteriors—the ads, the kiosks selling Western goods—it's about a mental change as well.

"For me," Sorokin went on, "this is one of those times in Russia when real life is even more vivid than literature. But when things settle down again, when things freeze up, the writers will be called for. This is a time of wakefulness. There will come a time when we will yearn for dreams. Writers are the suppliers of dreams."

Solzhenitsyn completed his triumphal *tour de l'horizon* and arrived in Moscow on July 21, 1994. When his train pulled into Yaroslavl Station, rain poured down on the crowd of well-wishers and reporters who had gathered to meet him.

As Solzhenitsyn came to the door, there was no room for him on the platform. The mayor of Moscow, Yuri Luzhkov, barked at the crowd, "Get back, back! If you don't get out of the damn way, he'll *never* come off that train."

Finally, Solzhenitsyn descended, and over the din of shouted questions, he gave his verdict to the rain-soaked mob.

"I have met many wonderful people through this long journey," he said. "Students, farmers, factory workers. People who live in slums, doctors and teachers who work without pay for their fellow countrymen. I hope I can start today to bring their message to the ears of the leaders in Moscow. Our country is collapsing. I never thought the exit from communism would be painless, but nobody would have thought it would be this painful."

Solzhenitsyn went on in this way for a while, and the crowd thinned and cleared.

In the coming months, the Solzhenitsyns stayed at an apartment downtown while workers struggled to fix up their house in the woods outside the city. He kept his promises: he avoided presidential and Duma politics, he started no movements, made no alliances. The only major public event was a speech to the Duma in October. The speech itself repeated his by now familiar themes—the economic humiliation, the falling birthrates, the corruption of the government, the indifference of the West. What was remarkable about the occasion was the way the majority of deputies, faced with this heroic figure, either ignored him (some even slept) or showed their derision.

Several months later, I met with Solzhenitsyn at the apartment where he lived when he was arrested in 1974; he now used the rooms as a headquarters for his charity fund. When I brought up the Duma speech, he waved his hand and assumed an expression of disgust.

"I knew how I would be received in the Duma," he said. "They could barely gather a majority to receive me. So when I came out in front of them I could see that they could barely pay attention, quite intentionally. One would tap away on a computer, another would laugh, another would walk out. I laughed at them to myself because I knew this was being shown on television to the people."

Solzhenitsyn enjoyed the praise he got from his fans, but he was also well aware of the derisive laughter. When he started making biweekly fifteen-minute appearances on television, he was mocked as a "talkshow host." He did not enjoy this. Surprisingly, the meeting that had gone best had been in the Kremlin.

"When I met Yeltsin, my goal was to relate to the president everything I had seen and all the conclusions I had made along the route to Moscow," Solzhenitsyn said. "If it had been possible to meet for five hours, I would have talked for five hours. It was important to me to relay my ideas, not to check on his condition or his attitudes. As for my attitude to Yeltsin, listen: I began studying 1917 long ago and I can understand all the characters acting in that drama, all the secret mechanisms and maneuvers, all the psychological drives. I think it is inconceivable for me or anyone else to understand so fully the current political situation."

Jokingly, I told Solzhenitsyn that he had held out on me when we met in Vermont. I asked what he had been thinking when he planned the trip home.

"The idea of coming back from the east was born right after I was expelled in 1974. It was right then that I told my wife—and she remembers it well—I had seen so little of Siberia. Siberia is a huge continent. I wanted to begin with Siberia, to merge with Russia's body, so to say, to cover its space, but slowly, slowly, taking the longest path there is. There was no other way to enter. When I happened to be in Canada in 1975, I took an express train that went coast to coast. I remembered that and thought that this was the way I'd like to return home—and even then, as I've told you, I was sure I'd be going back home.

"To come immediately to Moscow would have been an entirely different matter. It would have meant locking ourselves into Moscow and away from the rest of Russia for months. We would have been simmering in the Moscow atmosphere, which is not the atmosphere of the rest of Russia. For decades, Moscow was raised and maintained differently from the rest of Russia. I didn't want to find myself, right away, in something like a trap, an ideological one. Step by step, through these huge territories of Siberia, in the regional centers and villages, I saw an enormous number of people. I came to Moscow enriched by an encounter with the real Russia. If I had come straight to Moscow I would still have had one foot in Vermont."

In Solzhenitsyn's eyes, his trip across Russia was a complete success. He dismissed his Moscow critics, he dismissed the BBC's irreverent documentary. For him, it was a triumph and there was nothing more to be said. After holding meetings in various towns and cities, he recalled, "I would say to anyone who wants me to sign books, I won't leave until I do. I would sign and look them in the eye. Someone would say, 'Thank you for existing.' Or 'Thank you for coming back.' Everyone said that: 'Thank you for coming back.' Sometimes I would stay doing this for more than two hours. Then there would be flowers. What could I do with all these flowers? So I gave them away to people, to old camp inmates or to the young women."

Rather gently, I thought, I suggested that his opinions had not changed one bit from the period before his return. Did he really learn anything crossing Russia?

"By the time I arrived," Solzhenitsyn said, "I was ready to assess what was actually going on. At that time there was nothing strange or surprising except the spiritual potential of the people. They are still alive, not suppressed, still able to get on their feet and create a strong country. My wife and I feel we have come to our place, to Russia, and here is where we belong."

CHAPTER 8

THE BLACK BOX

The Russian leadership gave up its control of newspapers partly out of a sense of moral obligation and partly out of the discovery that print no longer had the power it once had. Compared to the Soviet era, when *Pravda* was a primary means of propaganda, newspapers had become a boutique industry. Newspapers were now free, various—and mainly unread. With the collapse of Soviet-era subsidies and distribution systems, newspapers and journals fell to a fraction of their old circulations. Also the prices were prohibitive; what had once cost three kopecks now cost several hundred rubles at least—almost a dollar. Newspapers were a relic, a specialty item. *Izvestia,* for example, transformed itself from a propaganda sheet into a serious, authoritative newspaper; but now its circulation was a tenth of what it had been. Papers of the liberal elite like *Sevodnya* and *Nezavisimaya Gazeta* were quoted constantly by the foreign press, and yet they had a circulation of just 100,000 and were almost never available outside Moscow.

Nearly all Russians were getting the vast majority of their information from television. And because people could no longer afford to go regularly to the movies or the theater, they also depended almost solely on television for entertainment. Even more than in the United States and other TV-possessed countries, television in Russia was the center of attention. Working adults watched three hours a day and even more on weekends. The phenomenon had enormous political importance. Not for nothing did the battles of August 1991 and October 1993 in Moscow, and Lithuania in January 1991, focus on the main broadcasting centers. To seize the Kremlin, everyone knew, one first had to seize the airwaves. After the "events" of October 1993, Yeltsin closed a few hard-line communist and nationalist papers—nearly all of them had advocated popular uprisings—but within weeks he let them all reopen. Yeltsin did not need the stain of censorship on his already bloodied image; censorship was simply not worth the trouble.

After the fall of the union, the Russian government maintained a controlling interest in the two biggest stations: Channel 1, or "Ostankino," which reaches all of Russia and the former Soviet republics, and Channel 2, or "Russian television," which reaches all of Russia. There were other stations with less range; the most important and independent, by far, was NTV.

The editorial idea for NTV came from Igor Malashenko, a clever man in his forties who had worked in Aleksandr Yakovlev's office at the old Central Committee and then held a series of high-ranking positions in state television. Unlike the former dissidents who had come to political prominence under Gorbachev and then were washed away in the 1990s, Malashenko was a man of his time, skilled in the art of bureaucratic battle, interested in making money and a name for himself but, at the same time, linked to what remained of the liberal political forces. He wanted to do right by Russia and, above all, right by Igor Malashenko.

Malashenko joined forces with a well-known broadcaster, Yevgeny Kiselyov. Kiselyov, like so many young Russian star journalists, learned his craft in a way unrecognizable to his Western colleagues. He began, in fact, as a teacher of young spies. The son of an aviation engineer, Kiselyov studied Persian at Moscow State University and worked in Iran and then in Afghanistan during the war as an army interpreter. For three years he taught Persian at the KGB's academy for young recruits. Then, in 1984, he took a job with Radio Moscow's Persian service. In 1987, he moved to television, first on the Ostankino station and then on Russian television. When the KGB was threatening the Baltic states in 1990 and 1991 and the Kremlin was demanding friendly reports, Kiselyov and several other broadcasters made big names for themselves by refusing to bow to censorship. After 1991, Kiselyov and many others in television began to think that the country had to have at least one independent station. Too many reporters and producers had been forced out of their jobs for the sin of giving a balanced picture of the war between Yeltsin and the Khasbulatov parliament.

Initially, Kiselyov and Malashenko were thinking only about a single program, a weekly independent newsmagazine show modeled, more or less, on *60 Minutes*. The show would be called *Itogi*—"Wrap-up"—and would feature sophisticated interviews and features about the news of the preceding week. To get funding they approached Vladimir Gusinsky at MOST, who had already shown an interest in the media by backing the newspaper *Sevodnya* and the radio station Ekho Moskvi. They met at MOST's headquarters in the mayor's office. After Malashenko and Kiselyov unspooled their plan, Gusinsky answered with a shocking plan of his own.

"Face it," he said. "You'd better start an entirely new station, not just a show. Be realistic. If *Itogi* is truly independent, they won't let you operate on a state-run channel."

Together, they devised a more ambitious plan. Gusinsky was willing to put up $15 million, partly in credits and partly as an initial investment. They would try to buy five or six hours a day on Channel 4, a station which had for many years been a kind of cheap dumping ground. The mix of bad entertainment and third-rate talk shows was getting no advertising revenue and dismal ratings. The state might be eager to sell airtime and reap a percentage of the advertising profits. Russian businessmen and the state were both for the first time discovering the delights of selling broadcast minutes for piles of money; under the Soviets, only Gorbachev permitted advertising, and it was primitive and minimal. NTV, with a mix of high-quality news and high-gloss entertainment, would enrich all concerned.

In even the most liberal period of Soviet rule, such a plan would have been unthinkable. Independent news? The political risk to the men in power was too great. But the times had grown more fluid, more complicated and unpredictable. Even though Yeltsin craved supportive coverage on television, he also had other interests: government income, the appearance of a free press. In December 1993, the government agreed to let the new station broadcast on Channel 4.

Naturally, critics wondered why NTV should be any more independent than the other stations. They were right to wonder. There were commercial interests in Russia now: what would prevent Gusinsky from using and manipulating the station to his advantage? The answer, of course, was absolutely nothing. There were no fairness laws to keep anyone in line. Press criticism appeared in the various elite magazines and newspapers but had minimal influence. The deputy director of MOST, Sergei Zverev, said, "We do not try to influence programming in the slightest, but it is natural that when we organized a television company, we chose people who share our views."

NTV was an immediate hit: a commercial success with its movie schedule and a *succès d'estime* with its news programs and the Sunday-night magazine show, *Itogi*. As the host of *Itogi*, Kiselyov quickly became the most visible and best-known journalist in the country; everyone with the least interest in politics watched *Itogi*. NTV's evening news introduced a new style: more open, more Western than any other in the history of the state. The announcers were younger versions of their American cousins: cool, objective, a little ironic, exquisitely dressed. The footage shown of Yeltsin was, if anything, irreverent; if he was looking particularly old or infirm or even tipsy, NTV was quick to show it.

In fact, differences among the three evening news programs described the various stages of Russian development that seemed to be occurring in the society all at once. I spent a morning with Vsevold Vilchek, codirector of the Russian Commission on Radio and Television Policy, talking about those differences. Vilchek was not a young man—he was in his sixties, old enough to remember the early development of Soviet television as a propaganda tool. And he had traveled enough to know how the French, the Germans, the Americans, even the Chinese used the medium.

"If you flip around the three key stations—Ostankino, Russian TV, and NTV—you will get a picture of our strange world," Vilchek said.

"Ostankino, with its somber announcers and rather official-style news, is oriented toward the current system of power. It creates out of our realities an image of the world that 'proves' the stability of today's regime. It might criticize the regime once in a while, but it is really relaying the regime's rather light self-criticism. Russian TV's news program, *Vesti,* is a bit better than Ostankino—it is less official—but the ratings show that it is losing its audience because it is combining the very subjective with the official.

"Then there is the NTV news. If you watch it, you can understand that it is being backed by a certain group of businessmen in moderate opposition to the government. The program itself may not be very engaged—it is distanced in the American or European style—and yet it reproduces a certain image of the country and the way it should be, perhaps sometime in the future. The image is of a richer, freer, more colorful, European Russia. Even the announcers, with their good suits and slangy, up-to-date language, seem like people from a new and different world. They are disconnected from the entire Soviet experience and culture. They pretend that they come from somewhere else, Russian-speaking France, perhaps. They are ironic, irreverent. In the end, NTV provides a picture of the world that keeps the viewer within the framework of democratic ideas, though it doesn't necessarily support the president.

"The experience of these three stations is like taking a walk in Moscow. You can walk on some central streets and notice that things are being fixed up, they are prettier than they were before. At the same time, you can walk to places, whole neighborhoods I'm afraid, that are just reeking junkyards. Everything coexists side by side. The three channels, consciously or not, represent that."

The great test for NTV, and for all the television stations, was the war in Chechnya. In December 1994, Yeltsin ordered tens of thousands of army troops to bring down the region's rebellious local government and its president, Dzhokhar Dudayev. Readers of *The New York Times* and viewers of ABC's *World News Tonight* learned of the brutality of the war: the botched assault in Grozny in the snows and mud of winter; the slaughter of thousands of civilians throughout the province; the ferocious protests against Moscow; the bombardment of nearly every building in the city's downtown; the denunciations of Yeltsin by old allies like Yegor Gaidar.

And yet in Russia, a viewer accustomed to getting all his news from the main channel would have seen precious little of this.

While bodies were littered all over the streets of Grozny, Ostankino described the battle in terms not much different from those the Newspeak Soviet television had used to describe the Afghan war. Ostankino portrayed the Russian army as a friendly force come to liberate the local population from its evil local leaders and guerrillas.

NTV's depiction of the war in Chechnya was as fine and courageous as any I'd ever seen in the West. Although the station's producers were working with just a fraction of the reporters and resources available to Channels 1 and 2, NTV provided stunning reportage from Grozny as well as analytical pieces from Chechnya and Moscow. NTV's reporters set up camp in Chechnya and stayed there, month after month, at a time when reporters were being killed regularly. Kiselyov and the other members of the NTV team were not naive about the potential consequences of their broadcasts, but just as the war started, Foreign Minister Kozyrev assured Kiselyov personally that the station would keep its license no matter what; the West would not tolerate any blatant manipulation of the news. Kozyrev's assurances, however, would turn out to be meaningless.

Yeltsin, for his part, kept his distance from NTV and the press as a whole. In the Gorbachev era, he had been extremely available, especially to reporters he had gotten to know in 1987 and 1988. Even I, a foreigner, had the chance to interview him several times; once I sat with him in his office in downtown Moscow as he accepted visits from ordinary citizens; he enjoyed behaving like a czar and didn't mind my watching the performance. But now he was practically invisible. He withdrew and felt no more obligation to explain himself or his policies to the public than the Romanovs had.

"Yeltsin became impossible to interview," Kiselyov told me when we met in the midst of the Chechen war. (A burly man with a thick mustache, Kiselyov tried to affect a surface cool, but the pressures on him were obvious. His desktop featured a huge bottle of antacids.) "I interviewed him once during the war with the White House," he went on. "All the questions had to be submitted ahead of time—that was the precondition for the interview. Naturally, Yeltsin's staff prepared a draft of every answer, and I even got a copy of that a half hour before the meeting. But Yeltsin was still more nervous than I was. He fiddled with a pen, he expressed dissatisfaction with the things on the table. Yeltsin just doesn't like the press anymore at all. I have heard from some of his circle that he is very television-shy. To appear on television for him is always a bad idea. He avoids it."

The night before I met with Kiselyov, I had watched him on *Itogi* trying valiantly to interview the prime minister, Chernomyrdin. The more Kiselyov prodded, the more the minister acted like an unjustly pestered beast. He fairly grunted his monosyllabic replies and then cut the interview short.

"What can I say? This mentality shows that all the talk about a civil society and rule of law is all for outside consumption, a public relations effort for the West, no more," Kiselyov said. "Inside, we still live by the ethics of the nomenklatura. One of the laws of this system is that the system of power should be a black box. Sure I could have asked a probing question about his involvement in Gazprom and all the profits he makes. He wouldn't have thrown me out of his office, but I would have become his enemy. That would be the case in the United States or Britain, too, but here it is much more complicated. We are in a vulnerable situation. We have to think about the future. There are still powerful enemies, and if it comes to a bad situation there are those who would shut down NTV. Chernomyrdin and I were playing a game known to everyone. I had to ask questions and he had to avoid them. Unfortunately we are all still very survival-conscious. That's the hidden agenda, always."

For an American journalist the idea of having to submit questions in advance is (or should be) a violation of independence. But the Russian journalists felt they had to play by those rules; their freedoms seemed fragile, impermanent. If one needed any proof that Kiselyov was speaking the truth about the predicament of journalists in the new Russia, then it certainly came on December 14, 1994—the day Sergei Nosovyets, an officer in Yeltsin's press department, called Igor Malashenko for a chat. Nosovyets did not mince words. The president had seen NTV's coverage of the first days of the war, he said, and he, Nosovyets, was warning Malashenko that NTV might lose its broadcast license.

"Sergei Anatolyovich, is this an official warning?" Malashenko said.

"Yes, it is," came the answer. "It is official."

The next day, Kiselyov and Malashenko were "invited" to a meeting with Kremlin officials for what was announced as a briefing about the war. The meeting was scheduled for the White House, which was now being used as the headquarters for the government ministers. (The legislature was relocated to the old State Planning building near the Kremlin.) When the two NTV partners arrived at the appointed meeting hall, they saw that some of the leading generals and ministers in the government were arranged at a head table. They wore the sour faces of men who had eaten a bad meal. The invited journalists sat at little desks facing the head table. The atmosphere, Kiselyov thought, resembled a classroom, and the journalists were the naughty students—and the NTV journalists the naughtiest of all.

The generals began the session by lecturing the journalists on the cruelty of the Chechen rebels. They read extracts from obviously faked wiretaps of conversations between the Chechen president, Dudayev, and his supporters; in the conversations, Dudayev seemed to be encouraging gratuitous cruelties: torture, beheadings, etc. "They told us they were authentic, real counterintelligence material, but they had the ring of fakes—like two KGB officers play-acting in a movie," Kiselyov said.

All the ministers kept mentioning NTV, saying their reporting was especially pro-Chechen and anti-army. At one point, Yeltsin's most intimate aide, his chief of administration, Viktor Ilyushin, said, "Look, we don't have a set of rules. If we did, we'd know who is right, who not, who deserves a license, who not." And every time NTV was mentioned, Aleksei Ilyushenko, the prosecutor general, made grim theatrical faces.

"He wanted to show that NTV had angered him deeply," Kiselyov said. "They all realized that after a week or so of the war they needed help. We were showing all kinds of gruesome material. Now they were hinting about illegal satellite dishes and the rest."

At one point, one of the ministers asked, "From a legal point of view, can we shoot down the transmitter?"

Another said, "Well, TV is not really paying us. We can shut off transmitters."

Finally, the deputy prime minister, Oleg Soskovets, dropped all pretenses. "This will all end soon! Don't think this will go on forever. NTV is, in fact, MOST, and MOST gets its money from the Moscow city budget. There could be a decision to withdraw Moscow's money from MOST and it will all end."

Malashenko turned to Kiselyov and whispered, "You know, this feels like the mid-1980s again, if not earlier."

The two men left the session knowing that if NTV simply ignored the warning, there could well be no more NTV (to say nothing of Gusinsky's entire financial operation). Kozyrev might have given them a different, more comforting signal just a few days before, but the truth was that Kozyrev was losing influence while the hard-line "party of war" was gaining.

"So we had no choice. We started to pace ourselves for a while," Kiselyov told me. "There was a tactical retreat, a feeling that if we do not show, at least on the surface, that we've reacted to government criticism, then they will take decisive measures against us. We could not risk doing otherwise."

For a couple of weeks, NTV softened its coverage. There were fewer corpses on the air, fewer interviews with bereaved Chechens. The news show even broadcast a report of the infamous "snipers in white stockings." The KGB had been putting out a ridiculous story that the Chechens had hired from the Baltic states a team of female snipers who, for some reason, wore white stockings. Everyone I knew who had been to Chechnya (myself included) thought the story a fake. "Snipers in white stockings" was a code phrase for the absurdity of the Kremlin's lies about the war, and yet, for at least a while, NTV put such things on the air.

"It's easier for Americans to stick to principles of professionalism and objectivity than it is for us," Kiselyov said. "They do not need to choose among communism, fascism, and democracy of God knows what stripe. We are still in that state. Life could take any course imaginable, and under such conditions it is hard to remain impartial in the Western manner."

NTV's retreat, however, was tactical and temporary. Soon the coverage toughened up. Malashenko and the rest, with their insiders' instinct for the government bureaucracy, had a sense of when to pull back and when to resume. If the Kremlin's reaction (or nonreaction) to their broadcasts was any indication (and nothing else really counted), Malashenko's timing was exquisite. NTV kept its license and the country saw the war in Chechnya on television, saw it gruesome and plain—the first "living-room war" in Russian history.

———

The Kremlin's wavering attitude toward television, its desire (all at once) to control it, liberate it, and profit from it, was a curiosity for everyone— including those in the top ranks of the industry. I had known Eduard Sagalayev, the head of the new commercial channel, TV-6, for several years. Under Gorbachev, he had run the main news program, *Vremya*. He knew from the inside how closely Gorbachev monitored his own televised image; both Gorbachev and his wife, Raisa, used to call the *Vremya* studios repeatedly before a broadcast dictating everything from scripts to camera angles, all to make the general secretary look like a "new man," a vigorous, intelligent leader not to be confused with his geriatric predecessors. Sagalayev watched the Yeltsin people with pity and amusement. They had neither the will nor the ability to match Gorbachev.

"Yeltsin's image-makers are amateurs," Sagalayev said. "These are his real loyalists, but they are people who have no notion of public relations. But Yeltsin is to blame as well. He likes to make all decisions by himself, even decisions to appear on television when he is not in the best of shape. In Berlin"—at an occasion in 1994 when Yeltsin was clearly in his cups and decided to steal the baton and conduct a local military orchestra— "one of his people tried to guide him away from the orchestra. Gently. But Yeltsin shoved the poor guy thirty meters down the street. Of course, this all ended up on television. Needless to say, there were inten- sive discussions about the incident afterward." On another trip, Yeltsin's plane landed in Ireland, where he was to have a brief meeting with the leading members of the government. Yeltsin, however, was so drunk— "incapacitated," his press people said—that he was unable to carry off this bit of simple diplomacy. The Irish waited on the tarmac. No Yeltsin. The incident, which was an international scandal, got only brief mention on the state-run television channels.

In his new incarnation, Sagalayev did not have to bother with such political matters. TV-6 mostly showed old Soviet and Western movies. They paid little for the films, and ratings were good enough so that Sagalayev and his commercial backers were making a pile of money. TV-6 had started out as a joint venture with Ted Turner, but Sagalayev said he balked at the arrogance of his Western partners. "For an equal amount of dollars, they wanted to control the entire operation," he said. "All we had to do was produce the programs. They treated us like idiots. Also we ran into what Gorbachev used to call 'the human factor.' For the first time in our lives we encountered, face to face, American haughtiness, a feeling on their part that American culture and technology are incomparable. The situation reminded me of an American businessman who goes to the Ivory Coast and for a few beads wants to buy everyone's labor. Some things were totally amazing to me. One American manager came to me and said, 'I had a Coke in the fridge and now it's not there. Warn your people not to take anything or I'll call the police.' I had to hold myself back from slapping him in the face. Our Russian staffers have a tradition of sharing. Of *course* one of my people took the drink, but he did it in a perfectly natural way. He would just as soon give one, too."

The partnership with the Americans collapsed, but TV-6 did well all the same. Mainly, it fed the popular appetite for junk. The only show Sagalayev produced with any real editorial zing was the sensational *Scandal of the Week*. The afternoon I visited, the obvious candidate for that week was a hilarious incident in which Ivan Rybkin, then the speaker of the Duma, refused to carry humanitarian aid back to Russia from abroad because he said the plane was already overloaded; in fact, news reports said, it was loaded with furniture he had bought for his own use.

Sagalayev and I were having a fine time gossiping about Rybkin and his furniture. He had already received a string of calls on his *vertushka*—a special phone line connected to the various ministries, a holdover from the Soviet era. Clearly, Rybkin and his aides were nervous that the furniture case was going to end up on *Scandal of the Week*.

While we were chatting, Sagalayev's cream-colored phone rang. The *vertushka*. I couldn't hear both ends of the conversation, of course, but from Sagalayev's questions it was clear that Rybkin's furniture was at issue.

"Is it true?"

"Was it a furniture set?"

"It's just not a *Dutch* furniture set? I see."

"Was it for the KGB?"

"Well, maybe we won't do it, Viktor. We'll see."

Sagalayev hung up the phone and flashed a knowing grin. "Viktor," it turned out, was one of Rybkin's aides. Sagalayev was not eager to share with me the details of the conversation, except to say, "I know how to talk to these people. It's many years of experience. I calm them down first, tell them it will be okay. But then I don't even bother talking to the reporters for the program. I let them go ahead with what they're doing. In thirty minutes I'll call back and pretend I talked to the producers. Later, Rybkin will call Viktor in and give him a raise and everyone is happy.

"So, you see," he went on, "little has changed since the days of Saltykov-Shchedrin. I think it was he who said, 'If I was awakened in the middle of the night and asked, "What is going on in Russia?" I would say, simply, "In Russia, they steal." ' You see, in Russia everything is done more or less openly, and public opinion—public outrage—is just ignored. People all understand that their fate is in the hands of the people above them. Bribes come in the millions of dollars, and few deny themselves the indulgence. What the press says hardly matters anymore."

When I first came to Moscow to live and work in 1988, the dominant show—the most innovative show—on television was called *Vzglyad,* "View." It was the ultimate perestroika-era program, full of interviews with KGB men and drug addicts, ex-dissidents and first-generation millionaires; there were rock videos, daring commentaries, even men without ties—a first for the traditionally stuffy Soviet airwaves. The show attracted 140 million viewers (more than half the Soviet population) on an average Friday night and featured stories like the one about a man who lived in a one-room apartment with his pet horse. There was also quite a bit of political criticism, much of it aimed at the Communist Party and the military. In one segment on the Afghan war, *Vzglyad* showed footage of a Soviet helicopter pilot hit by enemy fire. His voice turned hysterical and then, suddenly, very somber. "Farewell, farewell," we heard him saying, and then there was a thud and the screen went dark. Cut to footage of blood and wreckage on a road and then an Afghan merchant begging for mercy. Then cut to a young Soviet vet who said, "The Afghans think we are oppressors. I am a soldier and did what I was told to do. But the paradox is that I don't know what we were doing there, or if we should have been there at all."

The show's humor and informality, its daring and youth, were new to Soviet television—so much so that at times it disappeared from the air, victim to a wavelet of Kremlin censorship. As the show faded, the young well-connected men who shared the screen as cohosts went their various ways. Aleksandr Lyubimov, whose father was a retired KGB general, stayed in the news area, producing programs and hosting talk shows. Artyom Borovik, whose father was also well connected to the old Soviet regime, edited a tabloid crime and scandal magazine called *Sovershenno Sekretno* ("Top Secret") and, with his fluent English, appeared occasionally on *60 Minutes.* Lyubimov and Borovik both made fortunes in their ventures. After I'd had dinner with Borovik and his wife, Veronika, one night, they gave me a lift back to my apartment, all the while apologizing for the lack of legroom in the back of their new BMW.

The real star in the group was the one with the most humble beginnings—Vladislav (or "Vlad" to his friends and viewers) Listyev. On *Vzglyad,* Listyev had been "the smart one" (in the same way that John Lennon was "the smart Beatle"). But his next project was neither modest nor smart. He became the host of a perfect emblem of postcommunist Russia: an imitation of the American game show *Wheel of Fortune.* While *Vzglyad* was banned for a while in 1990, Listyev decided to make some money with a game show. He called it *Polye Chudes*—"The Field of Miracles." The show looked exactly like its American progenitor—slick host, bimbo hostess, roulette wheel, hysterical contestants, etc. The only difference, at first, was that the prizes were of a more earthbound and domestic order: toaster ovens, for example, not sports cars. With time, of course, expectations blossomed and so did the prizes. Sports cars replaced toaster ovens.

Listyev had been a star, especially among the urban intelligentsia; now he branched out into popular stardom of the sort never seen before in Russian television. After Yeltsin, he was the most famous man in the country—and probably the most popular. "Vlad was criticized a lot for selling out his bravery for a game show, for leaving politics," Lyubimov said. "He had seventy percent of the audience, the highest-rated television show ever. When there is a war raging in Chechnya, of course there is an interest in politics. But we experienced, in general, the rise of a normal people, people who prefer entertainment and sports to constant news shows on the air."

In addition to launching a version of *Wheel of Fortune,* Listyev also imitated two other American shows: the audience-participation routine of *The Phil Donahue Show* and the one-on-one style of *Larry King Live.* For his talk show, Listyev even imitated King's look, wearing suspenders and no jacket. The two shows, *Chas Pik* ("Rush Hour") and *Tema* ("The Theme"), made Listyev even more popular; now he was everything to everyone: showman, shrink, inquisitor.

As a businessman, Listyev was just as smart. He started a few popular children's shows and became extremely active in the advertising end of the business. Although he lived modestly by the standards of the "New Russians," no one doubted that he was making millions, even tens of millions, of dollars in commercial television. "Russia does not really make anything anymore, but television made millions," said Artyom Borovik. "We're making money, literally, out of air."

Listyev's biggest source of income was his production and holding company, VID. In the last days of Soviet rule, Listyev and his partners created VID to produce their own shows; they also expanded, investing in construction, real estate, and other ventures. When programs were allowed in 1991 to gather their own advertising and sell airtime, VID did that, as well; and since Listyev's programs were the most popular in the country, his ad rates were extremely high. A one-minute ad on "Field of Miracles" cost $40,000—an unheard-of sum in Russia.

Vlad's reputation as a businessman was beginning to equal his reputation as a showman. In November 1994, Yeltsin issued a decree transforming Ostankino, the largest state-controlled channel, into a semiprivate holding company called ORT. The state held on to 51 percent of the shares and sold the rest to the carmaker Logovaz, Aeroflot Airlines, Olbi, Menatep Bank, Gazprom, Inkom Bank, and several others. That consortium, in turn, hired Listyev to be the general producer of ORT. One of

Listyev's first acts as an executive was to declare a moratorium on all advertising until he was able to straighten out the rather murky and corrupt system at ORT.

"I know a lot of people at Ostankino and how much they are making," Listyev said in an interview before he took over the job. "With every year they are making more and more, including illegal funds. What is Ostankino today? It's a great colossus being pulled back and forth between the state and private firms and individuals."

"Lots of cash was moving around at the time," said Leonid Parfyonov, the popular TV host and producer. "There was waste and tremendous corruption and abuse by those who worked for the programs. It was never a secret. And I don't really blame them. The system was absurd, and the question was, why wait? They played the game offered to them. All Russian business began with cash, and television was no exception. Someone would go abroad and buy the Mexican soap operas and give them to Ostankino under the condition that the advertising would be his. The serial might have cost ten thousand dollars and the commercials would bring in thirty thousand dollars a minute. This was not something extraordinary or condemnable in the Russian situation. And it's nothing compared to the export sales of copper, oil, the sale of arms.

"You see, one main characteristic of the new Russia is to take advantage of every situation as it presents itself to you. No one waits. No one lets things develop or simmer. No one wants to miss a single second. After all, there is no absolute guarantee that the opportunity will be there again tomorrow. The rich in this country are hungry. They want to go on and on, growing and growing, eating and eating. The gambling spirit is a different psychology. A few people made some money, bought a castle in Scotland, and disappeared. But most of them didn't. They are here."

Parfyonov was one of Listyev's closest friends. As we ate lunch together one day at a hotel in downtown Moscow—Parfyonov was wearing an Armani silk jacket; he was just back from the Cannes Film Festival—I said that I could not account for Listyev's special appeal. Why was he, more than anyone else, the star of Russian television?

"Vlad Listyev was a replica of various Western models," he said, "but you cannot succeed here if you merely imitate Phil Donahue or Larry King. That would get you no more than a five-percent rating. You must understand that television here is more important than in the United States. Mass television here is even less intellectual than it is in the States. We don't watch to gain knowledge. We watch to acquire stereotypes, I would say. Or types. The old stereotypes of the communist era are obvious: tractors, communal kitchens, the good word of the general secretary. Now the new stereotypes are, say, blacks can be our friends, a wife can be unfaithful, give some pocket money to poor kids, gambling is okay—new values, in other words. This country has no entertainment, no leisure industry. No one reads much anymore. There is little religion except customs or fashion. Television substitutes for all of these things. Listyev was a conduit for new ideas, of a new form of life. In this, he was invaluable."

What was the stereotype of Vlad?

"The most persistent stereotype of Vlad inside the trade and among many millions was of a man with a well-deserved success," Parfyonov said. "The success of most New Russians is assumed to be ill-deserved, the result of some sort of crime or shenanigans. Now Vlad was wealthy, but no one begrudged him his wealth. If he got one dollar from everyone who loved him in Russia he would have been richer by a couple of hundred million dollars. Listyev was the embodiment of a Russian dream. He was handsome, young, not embarrassed to say he drank a bit at one time. But he was ours. It seemed he had the formula for the new Russia, a clear and simple formula."

———

Vlad Listyev feared assassination. All over Moscow and throughout Russia, businessmen had been getting shot, knifed, even blown up by car bombs. This was one of the preferred ways of settling business disputes, unpaid loans, property squabbles. The courts were irrelevant, by far the least developed institution in the new Russian state. Better to hire an assassin and a bodyguard. "I myself thought of buying a Kalashnikov or a pump-action shotgun," Listyev told the magazine *Sobesednik.* "Then I realized it was silly."

On March 1, 1995, two gunmen murdered Vlad Listyev on the second-floor landing of the stairs outside his apartment. He was shot once between the shoulder blades, once in the head. The photograph of him sprawled dead on the concrete steps became as well known in Russia as the Zapruder footage of the Kennedy assassination is in the United States.

Squad cars and ambulances descended on Listyev's building on No-vokuznetskaya Street as soon as neighbors found the body. The news shot across the country almost instantly. Broadcasters on the evening news announced Listyev's murder with the sort of gravity and sobriety accorded to the passing of a king. At the Ostankino offices, reporters and staffers absorbed the news not only as a personal loss, but as an assault. "Who is next?" said Lena Sarkisan, a reporter. "We are living in a country of terror." Although the police had no suspects—and to this day there have been no arrests—everyone was convinced that the murder was something of far greater moment than a robbery gone bad. People used the word "assassination."

Before the day was over there were dozens of theories floating around town: a contract had been out on Listyev because of his plans to fire people at ORT and revamp the advertising system; the government wanted to intimidate the press and make an example of Listyev (the army was already suspected of murdering a reporter at the newspaper *Moskovski Komsomolets,* Dmitri Kholodov, after he broke a story about corruption in the army); someone didn't like his politics (though he didn't seem to have any); he owed a lot of money to someone dangerous; there were jealous women in his past.

The short answer was, no one knew anything. The instant the news of Listyev's death became public, he became a martyr; but a martyr of what exactly depended on who you were, what resentments and suspicions most haunted you. In the evening, while the police still worked the crime scene at Listyev's building, snow began to fall. Hundreds of people, many in tears, came to the Ostankino complex on the north edge of town and stuck long-stemmed carnations into the fence of the broadcast center, tribute to their fallen video god. The television executives ordered a halt to regular programming; instead the screen showed Listyev's face. A video icon. The sudden, solemn shift in programming was reminiscent of the way the communists used to honor a fallen general secretary with repeated playings of "Träumerai."

Eduard Sagalayev, who had known Listyev from the beginning, told me he was sure that money—big money—was behind the killing. "When people are threatened with losing their fortune, when their well-being is threatened, they'll take, shall we say, *steps,*" he said. "The price is stable enough and there is no shortage of potential killers—what with the high rate of unemployment and a lack of training for the young.

"It is hard to describe how deeply people felt about Vlad. People became disillusioned with the role of the voter. They felt they could no longer influence the course of events and the economy. They transferred their emotions from politics to personal problems and popular figures. The vacuum in people's lives was being filled by television, videocassettes, and a nostalgia for the good old times. Unfortunately neither the president nor the government is interested in people's personal lives. There is an almost declared hostility: the massive corruption of the leadership, all in complete view of the people. Vlad appealed to the broad audience at a very low intellectual level, to a people who have very little opportunity for small pleasures, for movies or concerts. In the provinces, there is just no opportunity. During Soviet times, there were clubs, but all those developed into businesses, offices, stores, or just faded away. All that is left is television, and he was its embodiment."

Sagalayev's theory was far from eccentric. Yegor Gaidar, who had been Listyev's guest on various shows, said that it was clear that Vlad had "crossed paths with someone whose income is based on television, with someone who got rich and is getting rich with the help of commercial and political ads on television."

It is unlikely that there will ever be an arrest. There will be speculation. According to a report in the December 30, 1996, issue of *Forbes,* secret documents from the organized crime unit of the Moscow police show that Listyev believed he was a marked man trapped in a complicated battle between two businessmen with huge vested interests in ORT: Sergei Lisovsky, the advertising mogul, and Boris Berezovsky, the automobile magnate, who owned around a third of the stock in ORT. Listyev, the report said, "was caught between two ruthless characters. He paid with his life." Both men denied any involvement in the murder. Both men would become heavily involved in the Yeltsin reelection campaign.

————

There had not been a display of public grief in Moscow as enormous as the Listyev funeral since Stalin died in 1953. Even Andrei Sakharov's funeral and memorial services in December 1989 could not come close. Sakharov had been the hero of a broad sector of society, but mainly it was the urban intelligentsia that stood for hours on line in the cold to see his body and wish him farewell. Listyev's appeal was broader. Everyone knew his face, his voice, and very few had disliked him.

In the morning, Ostankino scheduled an official memorial service in its main auditorium. Yeltsin arrived at the broadcasting compound in his Chaika limousine. He got out of the car and walked slowly, stiffly, to a side door. His bodyguard, Aleksandr Korzhakov, walked at his side. Before he walked into the building, Yeltsin donned a mask of grief. Inside, he walked onstage together with Yakovlev.

"A tragedy has occurred," Yeltsin said, reading from a stack of cards, "a tragedy for Ostankino, a tragedy for all journalists and for all Russia. This was a murder by bandits, a murder of one of the most talented of our people. This is not the first time a journalist has been killed."

Then Yeltsin tried to repeat one of his best-known rhetorical ploys: he begged forgiveness of the people, just as he had after so many other crises. "I stand before you as one leader to blame, one who has not done enough to prevent banditry, crime, corruption, bribery." Yeltsin bowed his head. Then, as he was leaving the stage, he stopped and stood before a huge video image of Listyev onstage. The president bowed to the image and then walked off into the darkened wings.

———

A Mercedes hearse carried Listyev's body to a church on Yeleseyevski Lane. His widow, a dark-haired young woman with black sunglasses and a mink coat, stepped out of a limousine and walked to the church. All around were crowds: in the streets, in the church; there were even people sitting in the branches of the trees. After the service, tens of thousands of people lined the streets to wave to the funeral cortege and say good-bye to Vlad Listyev. Tens of millions more watched on television. The next morning, in *Moskovski Komsomolets*, Aleksandr Minkin drew this conclusion from the Listyev murder: "Democracy does not protect people from killers," he wrote. "It protects society from concentration camps."

CHAPTER 9

YELTSIN'S VIETNAM

"If you pick the flowers, you could explode," Mayerbek said.

"What?"

"If you go off the road and into the field, there are mines. Russian birthday presents. Step on one, you might explode."

Twenty miles by mountain road from Grozny, the Chechen capital, I felt safe enough to get out of the Zhiguli, a banged-up tuna can of a car, and take a short walk. Apparently not. I backed out of the field of lilies and high grass, one soft step at a time.

"Better," Mayerbek said. "Much better. Now maybe let's get back in the car and get going."

A Chechen in his mid-forties, Mayerbek had been working as a driver-fixer since the civil war in the Russian Caucasus began in December 1994. He was a handsome man with an unfailing sense of humor. He had needed that humor. After saving his money for years, he had remodeled a four-room apartment in Grozny, but now the apartment building—and much of the city—was charred rubble. Russian bombing raids in the first weeks of the war leveled the central neighborhoods; old men who fought in the Soviet army against the Nazis said that Grozny looked no better now than Stalingrad after the war. When Mayerbek talked about his apartment he called it a "four-room ashtray." He was just grateful that his family had survived. After more than a year of fighting, more than eighty thousand civilians and soldiers had been killed in Grozny and in the villages of Chechnya—quadruple the Soviet losses in Afghanistan. Mayerbek's family were now living with relatives in Sochi, on the Black Sea, and he was supporting them by driving reporters around the war zone. The pay was considerable—upwards of $200 a day—but so was the risk. He had already been rammed by an armored personnel carrier; every so often, Russian troops shot at journalists and declared the incident a "mistake."

We climbed back into the car and headed on to Grozny. There was a nine-o'clock curfew, and missing it would not have been the best idea. The fighting had tailed off lately, but even now snipers came out after dark. The Russian soldiers, in their panic, shot back, sometimes raking apartment buildings with machine-gun fire to keep everyone inside and scared. After dark, inside was where we wanted very much to be.

Earlier in the day, I had flown from Moscow to Sleptsovskaya, in the neighboring republic of Ingushetia. (The Grozny airport was under Russian military occupation and closed to ordinary Aeroflot traffic.) On the flight, I read one of Tolstoy's last stories, "Hadji Murát," which is set in the Caucasus in the nineteenth century. The story opens with a scene of summer, when "there is a delightful variety of flowers—red, white, and pink scented tufty clover; milk-white ox-eye daisies with their bright yellow centers and pleasant spicy smell; yellow honey-scented rape blossoms; tall campanulas with white and lilac bells, tulip-shaped; creeping vetch." Rarely is Tolstoy so excessive, so pungent, and yet from the moment Mayerbek and I started driving along the rutted roads from Ingushetia east into Chechnya it was clear what had swept the old man away. The hills are as wild and knobby and green as Scotland's.

The road to Grozny was alive with village commerce. We passed sheep and shepherds. We passed herds of goats, bell-clanging oxen, a pack of wild dogs. We passed a holy man kicking a cat. We passed ten-year-old boys selling plastic bottles of gasoline, young women selling Snickers bars and cans of German beer. If you wanted a grenade, you could undoubtedly have bought that, too. Ever since the Soviet Union collapsed and the army left behind a huge cache of arms, buying grenades from street vendors had been as easy as buying lemons: $3 a grenade. We passed a few mosques, and houses that were as big as mosques. These were the ornate brick mansions of the *vozdushniki,* the "air people"—so called because it seemed as if they had made their fortunes out of thin air. Their houses were called "castles in the air." Perhaps a few had come by their fortunes honestly, but throughout the Caucasus, and especially in Chechnya, there were wealthy men who had made millions of dollars trading in arms and narcotics and working bank scams. We passed many cars like our own—Soviet models of putrid color, dust-furred, battle-bashed—but many more that were foreign luxury models: BMWs, Mercedes-Benzes, Range Rovers, and Lincoln Town Cars. Airmobiles.

Now that the shelling had moved to the south and Russian troops controlled Grozny, there were surprisingly few military checkpoints on the way to the capital. The ones we saw were manned not by the eighteen- and nineteen-year-old boys who had been the cannon fodder of the first winter assaults but by hardened-looking troops in their twenties and thirties—contract soldiers in the Interior Ministry's special forces, the OMON. Five miles outside Grozny, we pulled up to an OMON outpost: a couple of tanks, troop trucks, a long trench, a communications van. The soldiers were dressed in preposterous Rambo outfits: headbands, mirrored shades, sleeveless muscle shirts, bandoliers, belts packed with hunting knives. Some soldiers had the sorts of tattoos you see in Russian prisons and in the mobs: finger tattoos, wrist tattoos, pectoral landscapes, dorsal abstracts. Some wore earrings—big hoop earrings, like pirates. The OMON soldiers were not averse to harassing, and occasionally shooting, whoever seemed to irritate them. During the day, they were calm, even bored, drinking the warm beer and vodka they bought or stole at the roadside stands, but by nightfall they were often raging drunk and scared of their own shadows, and then they were a menace. Lee Hockstader, a friend of mine from *The Washington Post,* was riding around one night and was pulled over by the OMON. The soldiers poked rifles in his stomach and made him lie down in a muddy ditch. It crossed Lee's mind that this night might be his last. Then he did something remarkable. Taking note of the soldiers' mercenary garb, he told them that, believe it or not, he had once interviewed Sylvester Stallone—a total lie. In fact, he went on, you could even say that he and Sly were—well, good buddies.

The soldiers wanted nothing more than to look like their movie hero—
they had seen all his movies on video—and now they melted at the sound
of his name. "You know Sly?" Lee had uttered the secret password. The
soldiers dragged him to his feet. Suddenly, they were curious, even
friendly: "You *really* know Sly?" By the time the night was over, Lee was
sharing a bottle and some food with his new friends, and when his nerves
had settled he was up and on his way, back to covering the war.

Mayerbek drove past a sign welcoming us to Grozny; it was riddled
with bullet holes. Grozny is a sprawling city, the biggest in the Caucasus.
The population had been 400,000 before the war, but now it had
dropped to less than 100,000. The Chechens, in great numbers, had gone
to stay with relatives. Most of the people stuck in the city were ethnic
Russians who had no place to go. So Russian planes were dropping bombs
mostly on families of helpless Russians. Even now, corpses and assorted
body parts littered the streets of Grozny. Sometimes people would collect them and bury them in mass graves around town. Sometimes dogs
got there first.

We passed an old Soviet propaganda sign reading "The Army and the
People Are One" and then some post-Soviet graffiti: "Allah Is with Us"
and "Liberty or Death" and "Death to Yeltsin." Then came the first sign of
the winter assaults—a huge oil tank that had been bombed and had then
burned for days. Now it looked like a gigantic plastic cup that had melted
in the sun. Evidently, the Russians, in their quest to "disarm illegal military formations," found it necessary to destroy a multimillion-dollar business. "In Russia, a fly lands on your nose, you get rid of it with a shotgun,"
Mayerbek said. We drove on into the center of town.

"There's your hotel," Mayerbek said after a while, pointing to a heap of
rubble. "The Frantsuzsky Dom"—the French House.

The center of Grozny—a city center as big, it seemed to me, as Balti-
more—was an utter ruin. Block after block, street after street. Every
apartment building in sight. The Chekhov Library. The art museum. The
oil-and-gas institute. Mosques and churches, hospitals and schools, a cognac factory, a nursing home, the sports stadium, the indoor arena. Gut-
ted, destroyed—all of it. More than forty thousand Russian troops had
invaded in mid-December '94, and then, on New Year's Eve, Russian air-
craft and heavy artillery had let loose a relentless storm of firepower on

Grozny. It is hard to imagine the intensity of the barrage except to say that at the height of the shelling of Sarajevo there were thirty-five hundred detonations a day, while in Grozny the winter bombing reached a rate of four thousand detonations an *hour*. By spring, the Russian army had chased the Chechen leader, General Dzhokhar Dudayev, out of the city and south, into the hills. (A year later, the Russian army would home in on his satellite telephone transmissions and, in the midst of an ostensible cease-fire, bomb Dudayev's headquarters, killing him and several aides.)

The destruction of Grozny was appalling, utterly senseless. Even Mayerbek, who had been shuttling in and out of the city for months, let the car slow to a crawl and stared out the window, still shell-shocked. You looked at the city and could not quite believe it possible. What's more, this unholy scene, this rubble, was a fair representation of what had become of the Russian president Boris Yeltsin's promise as a man of democratic reform. No matter what good he had done in the past ten years, he could not undo this. He could fire all the ministers he wanted, but it would not lift the blame from him. Mikhail Gorbachev badly marred *his* immense reputation when, in January 1991, KGB troops advanced on the television tower in Vilnius and killed fourteen people. How many were killed in Chechnya? And for what? Yeltsin could not skirt judgment. As Lev Razgon, a writer and a former political prisoner, said, "Dudayev was a psychopath, but Yeltsin is to blame." Or, as the playwright and commentator Aleksandr Gelman wrote in *Moscow News,* "Stupidity now reigns in Russia."

Sergei Kovalyov, a former political prisoner who was working as the Russian human rights commissioner, spent many weeks under fire during the war; he charged his own government with war crimes, including the beating and torture of Chechen prisoners in holding cells called filtration points. He and aides from the human rights group Memorial interviewed people who had not only been beaten at the filtration points—I met many such people—but also tortured in ways worthy of the old KGB. Sometimes the torturers used dogs, whose bites tore away chunks of flesh; or soldiers shot exhaust fumes into hoods placed over prisoners' heads; or they strangled the prisoners with barbed wire; or they shocked them with electrodes attached to a powerful generator. "They put the bare wires on people's necks and sometimes on their genitals," Kovalyov said. "I saw the marks left by this torture from electrodes. They remain afterward. It's like a burn, not with the blisters from a typical burn but, rather, with a dry scab. The top layer of skin is burned away." The Russian government denied the reports of mistreatment. Although Kovalyov may not have had all the facts, his record for truth greatly exceeded that of the Russian government. Kovalyov had been nominated for the Nobel Peace Prize; no one was likely to nominate Boris Yeltsin.

The Military Prosecutor's Office received dozens of complaints from Memorial and other human rights groups, but no one expected anything more than a few symbolic convictions. Kovalyov said he was furious at the human rights violations in Chechnya, but not shocked. "I knew these people before, in places like the Interior Ministry police, and they cannot change suddenly," he said. "What's a few years? At the start, they swore there would be no more inhuman persecution, especially for political reasons. They swore we were now becoming a law-abiding state. But it's the same people. That is the terrible thing. You cannot remake an entire country with words. History hasn't given us the same forty years that God gave Moses to wander in the desert."

The war has been cruel on even the pettiest level. In the days before New Year's Eve, when the bombing raids began, Russian soldiers went door to door throughout the city looting apartments for money and for carpets, furniture, clothes—anything they could sell in the open-air markets. In the villages, soldiers stole cattle and then slaughtered the animals for barbecuing. Sometimes they tossed grenades out of helicopters at cattle just for the sport of it. Sometimes they tossed the grenades at Chechens for the same reason.

Mayerbek navigated his way through downtown Grozny with care. The streets were badly rutted, sometimes cut off completely by a fallen bridge, a broken sewer main. Shell casings littered every street. Each day brought new reports of kids being killed or wounded while picking up abandoned ordnance or unexploded bombs. All over the city, there were signs tacked up reading "Mines." The most common sign on doorways was *Zdyes' zhivut lyudi,* "People live here"—an attempt (usually futile) to appeal to the sympathies of the Russian army.

"It's getting late, but let me show you one more thing before we get inside," Mayerbek said.

There were fewer and fewer people out walking along the streets, and those who risked the evening air were carrying rifles. Not far from the city center, Mayerbek pulled up to what seemed to be a small, fenced-in cemetery. There were hundreds of jagged tombstones.

"Chechen tombstones," Mayerbek said. "When Stalin deported our people to Kazakhstan, in 1944, the Soviets uprooted these gravestones and scattered them out on the road. They drove their jeeps over them, degraded them, and left them there. When the Chechens were allowed to come home, in 1957, they gathered up the tombstones, and when we were allowed we built this memorial." Many of the headstones were shot through with shrapnel, and a few were daubed with fresh white paint, crude graffiti. "*Na khui!*" the soldiers had scrawled. Or, roughly, "Fuck yourselves!"

The Chechen Republic is a tiny, landlocked parcel on the southwestern periphery of Russia, and even now to most of the world it seemed a second-order crisis spot, a geopolitical obscurity: Sri Lanka, Angola, Chechnya. In the Russian imagination, however, Chechnya is an obsession, an image of Islamic defiance, an embodiment of the primitive, the devious, the elusive. For more than three centuries, the czars and the general secretaries—and now a democratically elected president—have tried to obliterate the Chechens, first by war on horseback, then by deportation in cattle cars, and now by heavy artillery bombardment and carpet bombing.

When Yeltsin described Chechnya in the first days of the war as a "criminal" state, deserving the same regard as the Medellín cocaine cartel or the Golden Triangle in Southeast Asia, he was joining in a traditional Russian strain of rhetoric, a resonant demonology. In the mid-nineteenth century, while the czars' armies were engaged in what turned out to be a forty-year war with the great warrior of the Caucasus Imam Shamil, a Russian civil servant and scholar named Platon Zubov wrote, in a book on the northern Caucasus entitled *A Picture of the Caucasian Region and Neighboring Lands Belonging to Russia,* that the Chechen nation is "remarkable for her love of plunder, robbery and murder, for her spirit of deceit, courage, recklessness, resolution, cruelty, fearlessness, her uncontrollable insolence and unlimited arrogance," and that "the Chechens spend their life plundering and raiding their neighbors, who hate them for their ferocity." According to Zubov (and here he seems to speak for his regime and the regimes to follow), "The only way to deal with this ill-intentioned people is to destroy it to the last." In this, the czars did not quite succeed: they ended the war by declaring victory but allowed the Chechens to live in relative autonomy. Alexander II even paid Shamil a perverse compliment by not executing him; instead, the czar first exiled the legendary warrior to a provincial town in Russia and then let him spend his last days in Mecca.

Although the persistence of an independent Chechen spirit has always inspired Kremlin leaders to acts of war, it has also inspired Russia's poets to conjure up romantic images of bravery and spirit. In verse and prose, the Chechen becomes more of a trope than a man; he is nature itself—untamable, wild, raw. Pushkin, Lermontov, Tolstoy, and many lesser writers went to the Caucasus, and returned home to write about the resistance to Russian imperial power. The historian Marie Bennigsen Broxup writes that to Russian readers tales of daring and exotica in the Caucasus were as intoxicating as Kipling's tales of the imperial frontier were to the British. In "Hadji Murát," Tolstoy describes how Chechen villagers reacted to the destruction of their homes by Russian marauders:

The inhabitants of the village were confronted by the choice of remaining there and restoring with frightful effort what had been produced with such labor and had been so lightly and senselessly destroyed, facing every moment the possibility of a repetition of what had happened; or to submit to the Russians—contrary to their religion and despite the repulsion and contempt they felt for them. The old men prayed, and unanimously decided to send envoys to Shamil asking him for help. Then they immediately set to work to restore what had been destroyed.

Long after the czarist failure to crush the Chechens, Stalin tried to remove them from the map entirely. In the midst of the war with Germany, he ordered the mass deportation of the Chechens, and also of other small ethnic groups, from the Caucasus and the Crimean peninsula to Siberia and the wastes of northern Kazakhstan. Stalin charged the Chechens with collaborating with the Nazis, even though German troops had never penetrated the region's territory. On February 23, 1944—Red Army Day—Soviet secret service officers, driving American Studebaker trucks, rode into every Chechen town and village. Under the pretense of holding town meetings, local Communist Party officials were told to gather the people in the central village squares. When they arrived, the NKVD officers announced that everyone would be taken to trains for "transfer." There was little chance to escape. Soldiers held the crowds at gunpoint. In some cases, the NKVD gave women and children just time to pack a small bag; the men were locked up in barns. Old men and women deemed unfit to travel were shot on the spot. About half a million Chechens were herded into cattle cars. The trip took up to a month. There was often no food or water for days. When the journey was over and the Chechens climbed down out of the cattle cars, corpses that had been held upright for so long in the crush collapsed, some stiff with rigor mortis. That winter, temperatures were as low as forty below zero. The Chechens slept in unheated barracks. Ernest Ametistov, a member of the Russian Constitutional Court, who spent his childhood in the Kazakh city of Karaganda, said he remembered well the sight of the Chechen deportees as they came off the trains in his city. "I think such horrors become embedded, genetically, in the consciousness of a people," he said. The Chechens lived in exile for thirteen years, and were allowed to return to the Caucasus only after Stalin died and Khrushchev, in 1957, announced that it had all been a mistake.

The Chechens proved no less defiant in exile than they had been in battle against the czars' generals. In the third volume of *The Gulag Archipelago,* Aleksandr Solzhenitsyn recalls seeing, while he himself was living in exile, that the Chechens were the one group that utterly refused to submit to Soviet power. "The Chechens never sought to please, to ingratiate themselves with the bosses; their attitude was always haughty and indeed openly hostile," he wrote. "As far as they were concerned, the local inhabitants, and those exiles who submitted so readily, belonged more or less to the same breed as the bosses. They respected only rebels. And here is an extraordinary thing—everyone was afraid of them. No one could stop them from living as they did. The regime which had ruled the land for thirty years could not force them to respect its laws."

We spent the night at the apartment of Mayerbek's sister Natasha, on the outskirts of town. The bombs had wiped out the water and sewage systems. There was no electricity. On the way to Natasha's building, we passed some more castles in the air, and we saw that they, too, had been shelled: tin roofs split in half; brick walls with holes six feet across. There could have been no rational military reason to bomb so far from the center and Dudayev's administrative building, the presidential palace. The Russian generals who objected to the war—and there were many, even in the highest ranks of the Defense Ministry—went on television to point out the difference between the total destruction ("of our own people") in Grozny and the more surgical attack by American bombers against Baghdad, in 1991. In Grozny, I heard a lot of people, including Russian soldiers, say the same thing: "Our surgeons are of the meatball variety." (The metaphor was general. After he was out of office, Andrei Kozyrev would tell me that, yes, he had supported the war while he was foreign minister, "but I was under the impression that we would call in a surgeon, not a butcher.")

Natasha and her husband, Magomet, lived on the top floor of a nine-story building. Their windows looked out on a military base. We walked up the stairs (there was not a functioning elevator in town), and Natasha, a friendly woman who worked at the city telephone exchange, showed me around the apartment. She had a few souvenirs of the battle, the most impressive of which was a line of destruction (broken glass, pulverized wall) described by a mortar shell that had come screaming in through a window.

"We count ourselves lucky," Natasha said. "We were out. No one was hurt. But there is not a person I know in this city who hasn't lost a friend, family. I know one woman who lost four children in an afternoon."

Outside, the summer shadows lengthened. The apartment was half dark. Natasha put out a few candles. Her husband sat in a hard-backed chair. Magomet was eighty-one, a career military officer, and in the heat he was dressed in a sleeveless T-shirt and dark pants from an old uniform. As Natasha and Mayerbek and I talked about the war, Magomet would sigh heavily, not saying much other than "*Vot takiye dela,*" meaning, "Well, that's the way things are."

The candle flames shook a little in the breeze. We sat in silence. We were tired, and the air was hot and close. And then the old man began a monologue, about how his parents and his two brothers had died in the deportation to Kazakhstan, while he had been away at the front. We asked him to tell us more.

"Once, while we were on the front just before the storming of Berlin, two men from SMERSH came up to me and said, 'Did you know that your parents have been repressed?' I didn't, of course. They showed me documents saying that certain peoples—the Chechens, the Ingush— were bandits and had been sent to Kazakhstan. And then they looked at me, and one of them said, 'Do you think this is right?' So I said, 'Well, if they are bandits, of course it is right.' My friends and family had never done anything to betray Soviet power, but I believed these men. And they told me, 'You seem like a real officer, a man with dignity.' "

Magomet crossed the room and, holding a candle in one hand, sorted through a few photographs with the other. He dug out a curling picture of his first wife and their two sons.

"She died in the deportation," he said, sitting down again. "Here, these are pictures of my two sons. When I came back from the front, I had no idea where they were, whether they were alive or dead. Naturally, I couldn't come back to live here. I lived a long time in Moscow. I didn't find out my sons were alive in Kamchatka—eight time zones from here—until years later. So. That's the way things are."

Magomet had given the army more than fifty years of his life, and now here he was sitting in a city as flattened as the Berlin he had known as a triumphant soldier in 1945. Just a month before he told his story, Moscow had celebrated Victory in Europe Day. Among the soldiers who marched in Red Square in front of Yeltsin and President Clinton were (unbeknownst to Clinton) units that had participated in the destruction of Grozny. Magomet said that the parade had disgusted him.

"There is nothing to celebrate now. I don't know why they're celebrating in Moscow," he said. "We stormed Berlin, and it was awful. But in a city like this—our own city—the army killed children, killed women, killed everything they saw in front of them. Half of Chechnya is destroyed now. That's the way things are." As the candles burned down, Natasha served us plates of meat and sliced tomatoes. After it was completely dark outside, the shooting began. Tracer bullets sizzled across the sky, lovely and menacing. Later, in the distance, the shelling began. Hundreds of frogs bellowed in a swamp near the apartment. I was sleeping in a bed next to a window. Mayerbek suggested that we keep the shade drawn. "But we'll keep the window open," he said. "No use dying from the heat."

———

Yeltsin's rationale for the invasion was that General Dudayev, who had been the president of Chechnya since 1991, was running an outlaw state. This would be a little like the United States Army's bombing Brooklyn and Queens to take out the Gambinos. What's more, the rationale included depths of cynicism and racism. There was no more criminal city in Russia than Moscow itself (and presumably the air force would not be called out to level the Kremlin). Moscow was lousy with hit men and racketeers, millionaires who made their money out of protection scams, thugs who evicted old ladies from their apartments to "hasten privatization." There was a Chechen mob in Moscow, but it was just one clan of many that had turned the capital into a kind of criminal bazaar.

But Yeltsin, for all his failures, for all his fading powers of leadership and moral discernment, was an instinctive populist. He believed that he could hardly lose by demonizing the Chechens. And even though the majority of Russians were against the war, they showed no great impulse to demonstrate their sympathy with its main victims. The biggest protests numbered no more than a thousand people, and after a few months there were hardly any demonstrations at all. In Moscow, and in many other cities, people readily identify the mafiosi with, to use their euphemism, "people of Caucasian origin." More often, people from the region are lumped together as "Chechens" and, not infrequently, "black asses"—the Russian equivalent of "niggers." Yeltsin knew well that for many Russians the Chechens were nothing more than a tribe of "thieving niggers."

The Chechen regime—as opposed to the vast majority of the more than a million people living in the republic—was richly deserving of condemnation. Even after the Russian tanks and planes had reduced the republic to ruins and created a set of martyrs as inspiring as Shamil's warriors in the nineteenth century, I met many Chechens who despised

General Dudayev and held him as much to blame for the disaster as Yeltsin. There were many Chechens who believed that Dudayev was a fraud from the start—a tinpot dictator who exploited the enthusiasm for independence and Islam. Dudayev, who had served the Soviet Union all his life, suddenly began to sound like the reincarnation of an imam (as played by Peter Sellers with a fake mustache and a sidearm). After winning a highly dubious race for the presidency (several regions in Chechnya didn't even have a chance to vote), he took the oath of office with one hand on the Koran. Just before the Russian invasion, he asked the parliament to adopt the Sharia, the body of Islamic law. Few members seemed to mind that his dedication to Islam was as flimsy as it was newfound. According to various press reports, Dudayev's wife was a Jew from Estonia, and before the campaign he had never exhibited much interest in Muslim ways. Dudayev once told an interviewer that Muslims must pray three times a day. When he was told that, no, actually it's five times a day, he replied, "Oh, well, the more the merrier."

The political story of the Chechen disaster began with the euphoric days of August 1991. As the Soviet Union was collapsing, Dudayev left his military post in Estonia and came home to Chechnya to make a new career. Like every other republic in Russia, Chechnya had been run by Moscow and a local Communist Party administration. With the failure of the August coup and the dissolution of the Soviet Union four months later, the Communist Party leader, Doku Zavgayev, was unceremoniously tossed out and replaced by a chaotic crew of local politicians, all of them waving the new twin banners of Islamic nationalism and Chechen independence. "I suppose I'm lucky I wasn't killed," Zavgayev told me one afternoon in Moscow. "They said that I supported the August coup. That's a lie. But it didn't matter. I supported Chechen sovereignty, too, and that didn't matter, either." With the support of the speaker of the Russian parliament at the time—Ruslan Khasbulatov, himself a Chechen—Dudayev and his national guard captured key government and communications buildings in Grozny. They seized the local KGB building and ransacked the files, making of the event a kind of local Bastille Day.

Moscow, in the meantime, did not pay much attention. Yeltsin was preoccupied with his struggle to oust Gorbachev from power and the Soviet Union from existence. After that, he had to deal with a huge economic reform and his constant battles with the parliament. He was hardly spending his time on a minor region with a population that made up less than half of 1 percent of Russia's. The few Moscow politicians who bothered to pay attention to Chechnya gave their support reflexively to Dudayev; after all, he was making anticommunist noises and speaking up for the national rights of his people—a rhetorical gambit very much in fashion at the time. The democrats had exploited national feeling in the Baltic states, Ukraine, and elsewhere to destroy the old regime. In the late eighties, Russian democrats loved Estonians, for instance, precisely because the Estonians *hated* the Russian leaders of the Soviet Union. In 1990 in Kazan, Yeltsin encouraged the Russian republics to "take as much sovereignty as you can handle." So how bad could Dudayev be?

Disastrous, as it turned out. Chechen mafiosi in Moscow quickly saw an ally in Dudayev and awarded him a bulletproof Volvo station wagon—a car that had originally been intended for Erich Honecker before his fall from power. The mob proved to be the most prescient judge of Dudayev's character and intentions. All of Russia has seen the vast rise of organized crime since the collapse of the Soviet Union, but Dudayev managed to distinguish the region in this department, making of Chechnya what one Yeltsin aide, Sergei Shakhrai, called "a free economic-criminal zone." General Dudayev promised his people untold wealth. With its oil wells and pipeline, Chechnya would become another Kuwait, and kitchen faucets would spew milk and honey, he told them. Instead, Dudayev created Chicago in the twenties, but without the city services. While the more conventional economy failed—oil production, especially, languished—Chechen mafiosi engaged in some of the most spectacular criminal scams Russia had ever known. With Dudayev's police looking the other way (or, more likely, cooperating at every turn), Grozny became a center of illegal trade. The city's airport served as a hub for unsanctioned flights hauling contraband and outlaws. According to Kremlin figures, between 100 and 150 unsanctioned planes landed in Grozny from abroad every month, all with the cooperation of customs inspectors and other officials. The flights—from the Middle East, Turkey, Central Asia, and elsewhere—brought in huge amounts of narcotics and "duty-free" goods, and a succession of bandits in hiding. Mafiosi were also in the habit of robbing cargo trains traveling through

Chechen territory. Government officials enriched themselves by selling oil abroad and keeping the foreign-currency profits. Grozny also became a center for the production of counterfeit currency. Even more spectacular were scams, especially in 1992 and 1993, in which mafiosi used faked financial documents to win billions of rubles in "credits" from the Russian Central Bank. The government estimated that Chechen mafiosi, with the help of heavily bribed officials in Moscow, bilked banks in various parts of Russia of hundreds of millions of dollars.

Yeltsin and his defense minister, Pavel Grachev, in their planning for the war on Chechnya, could have had no illusions about the amount or the quality of the Chechen armaments. Ever since 1991, the Chechens had been pilfering arms from the army stockpile; in 1992, Moscow, rather than face the complicated military problem of trying to extract the arms from Chechen territory, simply left behind tens of thousands of weapons, creating one of the world's greatest arms bazaars. According to military sources, the arms cache that the Russians abandoned was sufficient to equip two tank divisions: howitzers, bazookas, machine guns, mines, ordnance. AK-47s, still among the most sophisticated and durable assault rifles in the world, cost about $100 in the outdoor arms market.

Dudayev showed no resistance to the criminality around him. He seemed to encourage it. He installed several of his relatives in key positions where bribe-taking was endemic—the managements of the main city market and the major banks, for instance. Many of his personal guards and flunkies were ex-cons who had been freed from prison in a general amnesty declared after the collapse of the Soviet Union. Dudayev's personal stake in all the criminal activity, however, is unclear. Chechnya's former head of secret services, Ibragim Suleimenov, claimed that Dudayev stashed millions of dollars in Swiss banks (but then there were precious few Russian ministers about whom one did not hear the same).

Dudayev's real ambition, it seemed, was to flout all direction from Moscow. Chechnya paid no taxes into the federal treasury after 1991. For some obscure reason, possibly having to do with his misbegotten ideas of Islam, Dudayev declared that girls need not go to school for more than three years or boys for more than seven. The schools emptied. He then proposed some public-works schemes that called into question his sanity: one such project was the building of a "water pipeline" to Saudi Arabia.

The situation in Chechnya was deteriorating so quickly that some Russian nationalists came to support Chechen independence not out of any great regard for the Chechens but rather out of frustration. Solzhenitsyn, for one, asked, in essence, Who needs them? Let them go.

For all the chaos in Chechnya, however, and for all the anxiety about the republic in Moscow, it was never a foregone conclusion that Chechnya was lost to Russia. As the economy in the region worsened, and the elderly failed to get their pension checks and workers failed to get their paychecks month after month, Dudayev's populist appeal began to fade. The contrast between the ordinary people (poor, by and large) and the "air people" supported by the regime began to grate.

And yet both Dudayev and Yeltsin headed inexorably toward conflict. Neither of them showed any predilection for diplomacy, each indulging instead his own eccentricities and excesses. Both wallowed in a demonizing rhetoric, the rhetoric of the nineteenth century. Yeltsin declared that there were only criminals in Chechnya, while Dudayev, in post-midnight interviews he gave at the presidential palace in Grozny, ranted on about his theory of what he called "Russism." "The symptoms of Russism are unparalleled cruelty, insidiousness, soullessness," he said. "There is a kind of satanic quality in its history, and they are taking it out on a small land like Chechnya."

Some of Yeltsin's aides were pushing for a peaceful political solution to the crisis. Three months before the war began, the Analytical Center of the Kremlin delivered a report to Yeltsin recommending that Moscow cut off all aid to Grozny and the regions of Chechnya most clearly controlled by Dudayev, while at the same time financing generously the regions in the north, where resistance activity was most prevalent. Then, the report said, Moscow would wait out the parliamentary elections scheduled for 1995 and see what happened: maybe Dudayev would be voted out; maybe the Chechens would see the advantages of forging a closer relationship with Moscow.

"The report was well thought out, but the president was not inclined to listen," Emil Pain, one of the few liberal analysts still left in the Kremlin, told me one afternoon. "It was clear whom he was listening to."

Yeltsin was increasingly shutting out men like Pain and taking the counsel of his conservative "power ministers" and drinking buddies—

Defense Minister Grachev, Interior Minister Viktor Yerin, Deputy Prime Minister Oleg Soskovets, Nationalities Minister Nikolai Yegorov, and the counterintelligence chief, Sergei Stepashin—and, perhaps most of all, his bodyguard, Aleksandr Korzhakov. In a Kremlin that had come to resemble a Byzantine court, Korzhakov had thousands of troops at his command and was the lackey closest to Yeltsin. Officials like Yeltsin's chief of staff, Sergei Filatov, said they knew that Kremlin telephones were tapped, and it was said that Korzhakov even tapped the phone of the prime minister, Viktor Chernomyrdin. Yeltsin even revived the element of Rasputin-like black magic: one of Korzhakov's top KGB deputies, Giorgi Rogozin, read astrological and cabalistic charts for guidance in arriving at Kremlin policy decisions and made sure that the president's bed was pointed in the "right"—north-south—direction, the better to absorb "a favorable energy field." Another Kremlin aide, Leonid Smirnyagin, told me, "A Byzantine court is not a bad metaphor: we have an aging sovereign and a clique of Praetorian guards obsessed with security."

Yeltsin was also well aware that Russian nationalist sentiment had festered since 1991. Politically, he could not tolerate a fracturing of the Russian Federation. Zhirinovsky's startling victory in the December 1993 elections and the growing strength of the Communist Party (with its added element of nationalist ideology) put great pressure on Yeltsin to act. "The invasion was a direct response to the ascendance of Zhirinovsky and the communists," said Emil Pain. "The crisis came at a time when every group that had taken up arms—the Ossetians, the Abkhazians, the people in Karabakh—had, in effect, won. That trend had to stop somehow. It was a question of statehood, of sovereignty."

In the late summer of 1994, Stepashin convinced Yeltsin that he could pull off an operation in Grozny that would unseat Dudayev with a minimum of bloodshed. The anti-Dudayev forces—led, in the main, by former aides who had broken with Dudayev over issues of money and power—would do all the dirty work, he assured Yeltsin. Stepashin's agents in the Federal Counterintelligence Service (FSK), the domestic division of the old KGB, formed a plan to supply the opposition with arms and seize Grozny in a surgical coup d'état. Taking no chances, Moscow sweetened the deal for the opposition, offering $1,000 each to Chechen recruits.

At the last minute, most of the Chechens pulled out of the operation, yet on November 26 the FSK went ahead anyway, using Russian troops. The mission ended in disaster. Dudayev's forces, which had been preparing for much larger assaults, easily defeated Moscow's troops and paraded prisoners before television cameras. Yeltsin looked foolish.

"He was utterly humiliated, and that could lead only to disaster," Pain said. Kovalyov, Yeltsin's human rights commissioner, who was one of the most vocal opponents of the war, told me he thought that the president's own vanity was what led him to stumble toward war. "Psychologically, Yeltsin believes he is blessed with a singular gift, and this is reinforced by the people around him—the infallible ability to make the right decision in a time of crisis," Kovalyov said. "He also believes that there are certain knots—Gordian knots—that cannot be untied, and must be cut. And he has experience to go on: his victory over the coup in August 1991, his confrontation with the Supreme Soviet in October 1993."

Smirnyagin said he thought it was plain that Yeltsin, while still making all the key decisions in the Kremlin, had degenerated. Despite high blood pressure, Yeltsin continued to drink heavily, and, according to Kremlin sources, Korzhakov was the only man in the Kremlin "who could put his hand over Boris Nikolayevich's glass and say, 'Enough.'" There was no evidence that Korzhakov did this often. In late 1994, at least five top Kremlin officials sent Yeltsin a private letter begging him to cut down on his drinking; the president reacted only with anger. His behavior was frequently bizarre. On a riverboat trip near Krasnoyarsk, in Siberia, Yeltsin acted the high-handed czar, ordering one of his aides, Vyacheslav Kostikov, to be thrown overboard; when Kostikov was dragged back into the boat soaking wet, Yeltsin led the laughter. At other times, Yeltsin was morose and withdrawn. When Chechen rebels took more than a thousand hostages at a hospital in Budyonnovsk in June 1995, Yeltsin chose to leave the country for a meeting with Western leaders in Halifax, Nova Scotia. With President Clinton sitting next to him during a press conference, Yeltsin raged on about how General Dudayev had asked for asylum in Turkey—a statement with no basis in fact. Clinton watched the performance with bug-eyed wonder, as if he were sitting next to a crazy relative rather than the president of a nuclear power.

"The president is not the same person he was," Smirnyagin said. "If you watch footage of 1991, when he climbed up on that tank during the coup, he was a different man—a vivid personality, vigorous. Now, well . . . Later on, I think, he'll be assessed as a heroic politician who sacrificed himself in many ways for reform, but not now."

In the meantime, Kremlin sources told me, there should be no doubt that Yeltsin had the final word on every step of the Chechen war. He was no marionette. In private sessions with his Security Council after the disaster on November 26, his power ministers assured him that a quick, full-scale military invasion was the way to go. The operation would be over by New Year's, they said. In fact, Defense Minister Grachev bragged, the whole thing could be accomplished "in two hours by a single paratrooper regiment." Tragically, Yeltsin chose to believe him. On November 29, Yeltsin signed a decree setting the invasion in motion. Rather than rally political support for the operation, however, he kept the decree secret not only from the public but also from his parliament and the majority of his own advisers.

"A good chess player can see combinations ten moves ahead of time; a bad one can only work them out two or three moves in advance," Otto Latsis, one of Yeltsin's more liberal and less influential advisers, wrote in *Izvestia*. "The Russian government in the days of the Chechen crisis has been unable to foresee anything, even one move in advance."

"There was a complete degradation of statehood in Chechnya," Smirnyagin said. "But the sheer stupidity of the military intervention was that Dudayev was already on the way out."

All this was lost on Yeltsin. Ever since the collapse of the Soviet Union, he had struggled to define the Russian state: would it be based on Western models or would it follow, as the neo-Slavophiles hoped, a "third," or "special," path? For a brief period, he relied on the support of the people who had brought him to power—pro-Western liberal democrats, anti-communists—and in the euphoria of the moment he told the various regions to take "as much sovereignty as you can swallow." But after the December 1993 elections, which were remarkable for the astonishing success of nostalgic communists and Russian nationalists, Yeltsin recognized that he could no longer afford to appear to be an overtly pro-Western leader. If he was to regain the presidency in the 1996 elections, he had to appeal to democratic and nationalist constituencies. He would assert—or reassert—Russia's place in the world. Yeltsin toughened his posture in regard to the West and to any rebellious regions in his own country. He made noise about the expansion of NATO into Central Europe. He threatened the United States with a new "Cold Peace." As for Chechnya, Yeltsin was gambling that a quick victory would be a popular and relatively painless way to establish the imagery of a powerful new Russian state. "All the problems of Russian statehood are reflected in the Chechen crisis, as in a drop of water," Yeltsin said. Thus, he set the stakes.

———

Although Defense Minister Grachev boasted that the operation would take only a couple of hours, his own deputies in the Defense Ministry knew well that he was doing little more than dragging fresh meat to slaughter. By the time Grachev bothered to inform his top generals that army and Internal Ministry troops—a force of more than forty thousand men—would invade Chechnya in mid-December, they had barely more than a week to prepare for that action. The Chechens had been preparing for war practically from the moment they declared their independence, in the fall of 1991. For three years, General Dudayev had laid his plans. He created a presidential guard and an army built, in no small part, from hundreds of convicts let out of jail after the fall of the Soviet Union. These were men who had served first in the Soviet army as boys and later as mercenaries in Abkhazia and Ossetia; some were simply hardened thugs. As an air force general in Afghanistan, Dudayev had won a modest reputation for his tactical skills and his advocacy of carpet bombing. In Chechnya, of course, he could not hope to hold off the Russians by matching them in ordnance; instead, he planned a guerrilla defense of Grozny and then, inevitably, like so many Chechen fighters before him, a partisan war carried out in the south, in the foothills of the Caucasus. He also promised to "move the war into Russian territory"—a promise he made good on when one of his commanders grabbed dozens of hostages in Budyonnovsk, just north of Chechnya.

"Faced with a military problem like this, any rational army would have gathered its forces and set out a deliberate plan to overwhelm the enemy with a superior force," Pavel Felgengauer, the military correspondent for the Moscow newspaper *Sevodnya,* said. "Just look at what was done in preparation for the Desert Storm attack, in Iraq. But Yeltsin is notorious in his misperception of what an army can do, and Grachev was only too glad to feed his misperception. Unfortunately, our president believed you could order up a huge military operation as easily as ordering up a limousine."

The Russian invasion in mid-December turned Grozny into a slaughterhouse. The Russian force—undermanned, confused, and egged on by a president and a defense minister who insisted on a quick victory—trudged through knee-high mud and blinding winter fogs and was met by well-trained guerrilla forces. The Chechens were able to surprise and trap one Russian tank after another, by a hit-and-run strategy using three-man teams; snipers hid out in apartment buildings and picked off Russian soldiers; and small groups of Chechen troops crawled through a network of underground tunnels and conduits, rose up, and fired grenades into Russian forces. At the same time, Russian officers found themselves ordering attacks that had no grounding in common military strategy—attacks without reconnaissance, without reinforcement. One crack brigade, the 131st Maikop Motorized, was ordered to capture a series of roads and the railway station. It found that it had no backup, and had been simply led to its own destruction.

"Essentially, the Maikop Brigade does not exist anymore," Colonel Viktor Litovkin, *Izvestia*'s military correspondent, told me. "In general, there was a complete lack of coordination in the military. The forces that should have backed up the first echelons of attacking forces never did it."

One afternoon in Moscow, I met with Colonel General Eduard Vorobyov, who for many years was one of the most highly regarded military men in Russia. He was fifty-eight and trim, and, though he wore civilian clothes, he had an unmistakably military posture. We spent a few hours talking on a bench in the narrow park that divides the city's Boulevard Ring. It was a perfect afternoon, cool and bright—at the start of the white nights. Vorobyov, despite his studied calm and polite manner, did little to conceal his fury. At the start of the war, he had been asked to command the army invasion of Grozny. He refused and then resigned his commission.

Vorobyov was the unlikeliest of rebels. He attended the best military academies and rapidly made his way up through the ranks of the Soviet army; he was a platoon commander in the Carpathian Military District, led a tank force into Prague in 1968, commanded army contingents in Lvov, Yerevan, Ashkhabad. In Turkmenistan, he headed all training for troops going to Afghanistan. He led the evacuation of Soviet troops from Czechoslovakia in 1991. As first deputy commander of Russian ground forces, he served on the Moldovan border and, in 1992, in Tajikistan.

"Up until the last minute, I felt that there would be no use of force against Chechnya," Vorobyov said. "Clearly, force would not resolve anything. You only have to look at the way Russian generals struggled for forty years against the Chechens in the nineteenth century. I also thought—naively, as it turned out—that our leaders would never use their arms against their own people."

Vorobyov said that nearly the entire top command of the army had been shut out of the planning of the operation. Under Grachev's direction, Colonel General Aleksandr Mitukhin, the commander of the Northern Caucasus Military District, worked out the invasion blueprint. On December 5, the plan was basically approved, and on December 11 the war began.

"But guess what?" Vorobyov said. "There was no instant victory. Grachev's prediction was a fraud. Look, with respect to military training, Grachev never went above the rank of commander of a paratrooper division. He is nothing as a politician, either. And as a diplomat—well, people ought to blush on that score. This is a painful thing for me—to talk this way about the defense minister. No matter how bad our attitude may be now toward the word 'patriot,' I am still a patriot, despite the fact that our country has lost all its ideological bearings. I love our home, our country. If I criticize, it is because I want the situation to be better. The fact is, Grachev was appointed defense minister in the first place because he was loyal to Yeltsin during the August coup of 1991 and then, in October of 1993, he agreed to bring in the tanks. In any other circumstance, considering his skills, he would have been fired half a dozen times by now."

In mid-December, Vorobyov flew home from St. Petersburg to Moscow after a business trip, and the moment he stepped onto the tarmac he was told to call the chief of ground forces, Vladimir Semyonov.

"Do you have your field uniform with you?" Semyonov asked him.

Vorobyov said he did not.

"Well, it doesn't matter," Semyonov said. "It will be delivered to you. Don't go home. Go straight to Mozdok." A small city fifty-five miles from Grozny, Mozdok was the military command center for the Chechen operation. "You are to render assistance to the planners there."

Vorobyov arrived in Mozdok on December 17. For the next three days, he met with everyone who had any bearing on the operation: commanders, opposition leaders, even Cossacks.

"The political leadership wanted us to step things up, and to do this we had two options," he told me. "We could start a huge artillery barrage, which would have been very difficult because of the weather—it was terribly foggy, and visibility was zero. We would be shooting into the fog, essentially, destroying civilians. This is a terrible crime. Artillery also requires reconnaissance operations, but the weather made that impossible as well. The second way was a rapid ground invasion. But the troops we had were just not prepared for this. They were badly trained, they barely knew one another. The truth is, they would have needed a month, even three months, to prepare. To throw them into battle—which is what was done, finally—was a crime.

"On the morning of the 21st, I reported to the chief of the general staff, General Mikhail Kolesnikov, that the operation was badly thought out, a sheer adventure. The situation was absurd. I asked Kolesnikov to pass on my feelings to the minister of defense. In an hour, Grachev called me and asked me to take command of the operation. I said, 'But I have explained my feelings to Kolesnikov.' I said neither yes nor no. He repeated his request. And I repeated my reply. After a pause, he said, 'Okay, I'll fly to Mozdok today.' "

That evening, Grachev held a short meeting of the generals in Mozdok. At last, he said, "I'll take charge personally," and he appointed his first deputy and others to run various parts of the operation. To Vorobyov, Grachev said, "I am disappointed in you, Comrade Colonel General. I think you should submit your resignation."

"I did not sleep that night," Vorobyov recalled. "I was up all night in my bunk in the railcar we used as sleeping quarters. I had to think it through. Mind you, as a soldier, I am no pacifist. Had the preparations for war been adequate, I would have executed those plans without thinking twice. That is what I do. That is—*was*—my job. But Russia has lost in every respect in Chechnya: politically, militarily, morally. Russia has more than a hundred ethnic groups. Will it resolve all disputes through force?

"I reached the conclusion that without a decision of parliament, without a presidential decree, without proper military preparation, this was all an adventure. The defense minister bragged that he could accomplish everything in two hours, and when the moment of truth came, when things got complicated and he was confronted by his own words, things went out of control. I am sure the original plan was under the influence of these unwise words 'one brigade in two hours.' I began to think through the errors: our underestimation of the Chechen passion; the lack of military surprise; the dependency on air power in bad weather; the dependency on a phony opposition movement; the utter lack of preparation. My God, our tank troops went into battle without maps of the city!

"To think of all this was depressing, but I had to do what I saw fit. The next morning, the morning of December 22, I submitted my resignation. I remember the note almost exactly: 'By refusing the job of commander in Chechnya, I have disobeyed an order for the first time in my thirty-eight years as a soldier. Because of this, I cannot remain in office or command my troops. I ask to be dismissed from the Armed Services of the Russian Federation.' "

Vorobyov was smiling now and there was no regret in his voice. "The resignation was accepted, and here I am," he said. "A retiree looking for work."

———

Mornings in Grozny, I would go to the central market. During the winter bombing raids, the market had all but disappeared; every building nearby had been destroyed. But now the market had revived. The crowds were smaller, of course, because so many thousands were still living in the hills, but the place seemed ordinary enough—the bargaining, the hustle. The moment I took out a notebook and asked a middle-aged Russian woman a few questions, however, I was besieged by dozens of people, enraged, shouting.

"They bombed for months, and we lived in the basements like dogs!"

"God gave the Russians the atom bomb! If God had been so generous to us, the war would be different now!"

"A soldier just shot my nephew and threw him into a hole—simple as that."

"The soldiers are in the market all the time, drunk, red in the face—vulgarians! They steal everything and then stick a gun in our faces and say, 'So! You want us to pay, do you?' "

The anger was directed not only at the Russians or at Dudayev but also at the Clinton administration and its woefully late and pitifully restrained condemnation of the war. "During the Cold War, you Americans used to go wild over one or two political prisoners," one man said. "But when an entire city is wiped out there is hardly a word from you! Would President Clinton have come to Moscow for the V-E Day parade if Sakharov were alive and in prison?"

The people in the market, after months of living in basements and feeling the pounding of the bombs resonate in their guts and in the back of their skulls, had emerged not dazed but enraged. These were not the living dead of so many war stories. When they were not struggling to get enough water and food to make it through the day, they were talking about the war, about their anger at the Russians. And they were, to my astonishment, well informed. Considering that most of them did not have access to newspapers, or electricity for television, they knew what Yeltsin was saying about the war—that he was telling the West that this was not a war at all but rather a "police action" to "disarm illegal military formations." In every conversation I had in Chechnya—in the Grozny market, in villages, in refugee dormitories—I heard the voices of a population that would make out of its immediate suffering a lifelong politics of resistance and rage. No matter what could come of negotiations between the Kremlin and the Chechens, all that a settlement would do is paper over this historical civil war.

"I served the Soviet Union all my life," a young father named Robert Solgiryev said one morning in the Grozny market. "They sent me in to the Chernobyl cleanup three days after the reactor blew. I was there for half a year. When Yeltsin ran for president, I voted for him. Most of

Chechnya voted for him. In 1991, we thought he was a great democrat. And now he's betrayed us. His lies never end."

One of the most glaring of the official lies had to do with casualties. By early 1996, the Russian government had admitted to the deaths of only one or two thousand of its soldiers and, unofficially, about five thousand Chechen casualties; the human rights group Memorial, which kept observers in the region from the start of the war, said the figures were five times as high or more, with a total death count of at least thirty thousand. I went to the Central Cemetery in Grozny—the city's biggest by far— but that proved to be little help in solving the mystery. There were more than five hundred freshly dug graves there, and also one long open grave where seventeen bodies, blackened and mutilated, were left rotting in the sun. Dogs trotted up and down the rows of graves. The place stank of death, and flies buzzed and swooped in little clouds. A gravedigger came by and warned me that from time to time snipers fired on people visiting the cemetery. We stood behind a clump of trees and talked for a while. Before leaving, I asked him why there seemed to be so few bodies here. "The army takes its dead and wounded back with it, and the Muslims in Grozny tend to bury their own in family-grave plots or in the courtyards of their buildings," he said. "You're just seeing a hint of the dead." By the time the war seemed over in late 1996, Yeltsin admitted that eighty thousand people had been killed in Chechnya.

For the next couple of days, while the Russian army was still pounding Dudayev's positions in the hills, I went to see the Chechen opposition leaders in Grozny and the surrounding villages. In a search for political sanity, there was none to be found in Yeltsin or in Dudayev, and, it turned out, there was none to be found in the opposition, either. The men I met were, in the main, rapacious fools—killers some of them—who promised only to multiply the chaos. At best, they were Yeltsin's puppets, appointed by Moscow, despised in Grozny.

Mayerbek and I drove about a half hour out of town to the village of Tolstoy-Yurt, where Ruslan Labazanov, the self-proclaimed Robin Hood of the opposition, lived. Labazanov had once been Dudayev's bodyguard and tough guy, but then he split with his mentor for the usual reasons— disagreement over power and money. In the months preceding the war, he and a small band of armed Chechens had controlled several key villages in the republic. But Labazanov was as much a performance artist as he was a rebel, his act being that he took from the rich (the form of taking was left vague) and gave to the poor (the degree of giving was similarly unclear). Labazanov said he was all for free elections. He wanted Chechnya to be a democratic Islamic republic within Moscow's benevolent orbit. Splendid. Labazanov, however, was a former mobster and a convicted murderer (a subject he tended not to bring up), and his allegiance to the principles of Jefferson and Mill was hazy.

Tolstoy-Yurt was a small village in the hills outside Grozny, and it did not take us long to find Labazanov's house. Everyone in town knew him, and knew enough to stay away from him. He lived in a typical "air people" compound—a brick house surrounded by a high metal fence. We pounded on the gate. Two young men dressed in black fatigues and festooned with an incredible kit—machine gun, grenades, knives, pistols—answered. The arrival of strangers was not unusual. Even in the thick of the late-winter battles, Labazanov seemed to spend more time entertaining reporters and prowling around his compound than actually engaging in freedom fighting. In the courtyard were a Nissan jeep (with Dubai plates), a Lumina minivan, and a black Mercedes sedan—bulletproof, we were told. A huge Doberman paced nearby. A heavily armed dwarf led us up the stairs and into the house.

"Sit down here," the dwarf said, pointing to a few chairs around a kitchen table. The dwarf wore a bandanna and a bandolier. He had a kind face.

We sat down. For the next half hour, the dwarf and the guards passed in and out of the room, tossing quizzical glances at Mayerbek and me. Finally, Labazanov, attended by the guards, made his entrance. "Hello," he said grimly. "You may call me Ruslan."

Ruslan was built like a linebacker—powerful and squat—and he had worked out an excellent opposition-freedom-fighter look for himself: a full beard, mirrored sunglasses, a headband with an inscription in Arabic. ("I think it says, 'There is no God except Allah, no prophet but Muhammad,' " he told us.) He wore a massive gold Rolex, gold bracelets, and diamond-encrusted rings. He was fantastically well armed, and he lovingly described all his toys, like a little boy going through his box of Mighty Morphin Power Rangers: "This is my Israeli pistol. It can put you away from fifty meters. This is my marine knife. Look at the size of the blade." All this took about ten minutes. Then he asked, "Would you like to see a videocassette? It's a movie about me."

For the next fifteen minutes or so, we watched footage of dead bodies, burning bodies, and bodies with horrific wounds—all of it with a throbbing rock-and-roll soundtrack. I recognized some of the footage from coverage of the war that had been broadcast in Moscow. Then the film took a turn toward self-advertisement. It cut to Ruslan sitting in a room with various supplicants; they had come to him for help or money. One man faced the camera and said that he had lost everything in the war and only Ruslan had helped him. An old woman said much the same. Ruslan solemnly gave them rubles.

"You see," Ruslan said, turning off the television. "I have given help to six thousand people. Six thousand! Sometimes as much as two hundred thousand rubles!" About $44.

It would be pointless to quote the rant that followed. Suffice it to say that Ruslan gave his analysis of the political situation in Chechnya and in Russia in general. His guards nodded sleepily; they had heard this many times before—starting, no doubt, when he and they were in jail together. The story in Grozny was that Ruslan was in the pay of the KGB and/or the army, and that his men were his former cellmates. As he went on, my eyes wandered around the room, and after a while I spotted a slender yellow book by his telephone. The title was *Yids Are Killing Russia*. I picked it up while Ruslan was still talking, and started leafing through it. It was a standard-issue anti-Semitic tract—the sort of garbage that fascist teenagers sold from makeshift stands outside the old Lenin Museum, near Red Square. I interrupted Ruslan and asked him about the book.

"Oh, that?" he said. "It's just some interesting reading. Believe me, if Jews had done this war it would have been less bloody, more accurate. They are smart people. Israel is a small country, but very powerful."

Ruslan suggested that we talk about something else. He said he was twenty-eight years old and married. Soon one of his men served us lunch, and Ruslan ate in silence while watching a sitcom on television.

When he finished eating, he called his dog over—a three-legged dog—
and stood up in a way that made it plain there would be no dessert. "I
must get back to my work," he said. "We'll see you soon."

———

Stalin once said, "One death is a tragedy; a million deaths is a statistic." It
may have been for this strange Stalinist reasoning that to many Russians
and to many people abroad the destruction of Grozny seemed a statistic
and the massacre at the village of Samashky a tragedy.

Samashky, built by the Cossacks in the 1860s and then populated by
Chechens in the 1920s, had for many years been a prosperous village,
with good farming, a railway connection, and a working jam factory. It is
located about twenty miles west of Grozny, and until recently it had a
population of about fourteen thousand. On April 6 and 7, 1995, Interior
Ministry OMON troops, wearing black masks, ransacked the village's
central streets, tossing hand grenades into basements and firing at un-
armed women and children. Between a hundred and three hundred residents were killed, and there is no proof that any of the dead were
pro-Dudayev guerrillas; to the contrary, the evidence is that the guerrillas had left for the hills weeks before the attack. By the time the massacre
was over, the streets of Samashky were covered with the dead: a corpse
with its head split open like a melon; another corpse with all its limbs
blown off. The OMON sealed off the village completely—even from
Red Cross doctors—for three days thereafter.

Mayerbek and I had a hard time getting to Samashky. When we
reached the main checkpoint, about two miles outside the town, OMON
troops harassed us, saying that our car had to be confiscated. They said
that Mayerbek's registration was one digit off and was therefore "highly
suspect." We were detained for two hours, until one of the Samashky village elders, an old man with a Tolstoyan beard and a knit cap, talked the
soldiers into letting us visit. We spoke with the OMON captain for a
while, and he said that stories that he and his men were stealing farm animals and drinking were just lies. Over his shoulder I could see one of his
men slaughtering a goat in a trench. I assumed that the goat had not been
flown in from Moscow. Another soldier walked through the trench with
a case of vodka balanced on his shoulder.

For the next few days, Mayerbek and I shuttled between Samashky and a few surrounding villages where refugees from the massacre were living. Many of the houses were large and had well-swept courtyards, but along the streets where the massacre had taken place the houses were burned out. Only their brick walls and iron gates were still standing. Soldiers had aimed flamethrowers at the houses and tossed grenades through windows and doors. Invariably, they had found people hiding in basements, and in many cases they had thrown grenades into the basements—to "flush out guerrillas," the OMON captain had explained. Several witnesses described watching their spouses or their children lined up in the street and shot. Everyone talked about the look of wildness in the soldiers' eyes, their animal rage.

"I was home and hiding in the basement," a nurse named Fatima Kulkayeva told me at the local hospital one afternoon. "We were hiding, but we didn't believe that anything really terrible would happen. They had given the village elders a deadline for handing over two hundred–odd weapons—which, of course, no one had. When the elders turned over only a few guns, they told us it would be the end. How could Russians be so cruel? I have a seven-year-old boy and a six-year-old girl and my mother living with me. My daughter—I'd have to say that she has gone crazy since the attack. She was shaking, shaking for days, and even now she hears planes and the shooting. She gets crazy at night. I was not for Dudayev before, but I am for Dudayev now."

Time and again, the people in the village compared the attack to My Lai and the Russian soldiers to "your Lieutenant Calley." They remembered the My Lai massacre because it had once been a common refrain in Soviet newspaper reports about the war in Vietnam. "Your Lieutenant Calley was a Young Pioneer compared to these guys," one of the village elders said. "And in America, if I remember right, there was a trial about My Lai. Do you really think there will be a trial here? And who is qualified to judge?"

On my last day in Samashky, I met an old man named Aladdin Magamedov, a veteran of the war against Germany, who had come home only to be deported to Kazakhstan in 1944 with the rest of Chechnya. He had lost a leg to the Nazis, and then he lost much of his family to the Soviet regime during the deportation. He had survived all that. Now he sat outside the hospital on a bench. After the massacre, he said, he began having nightmares and fits of rage. He saw flashes of light, like silent gunfire. He told me this calmly, almost as if he were talking about someone else, or a memory. Everyone in town had seen Russian soldiers murder women, children, old people. No one would forget it. They would not forget this any more than they had forgotten the deportation under Stalin, the wars under the czars. "If they are going to destroy us all, I wish they would hurry up about it," he said finally. "At least we would suffer less." The old man stared out, shielding his eyes from the sun. Thousands had left the village. There was no sound there now except the wind in the trees and the noise of firing practice two miles away. I said good-bye and headed for the car.

That night, I stayed at the house of a rich man in Nazran, an hour's drive away: $40 a night in the middle of nowhere. A castle in the air. Mayerbek and I ate lamb cutlets and had a couple of drinks of vodka, and then we went to our rooms—big, high-ceilinged rooms. I lay down on the bed and thought about the old man in Samashky and about how he and so many others had talked of the Russians who invaded their village as creatures beyond—or beneath—hating. Their words, as I remembered them, struck an uncanny note, as if I had heard them before. It seemed too neat, it is true, but I *had* heard them. I pulled "Hadji Murát" out of my bag and started reading again the story I'd read days before:

The old grandfather sat by the wall of the ruined house cutting a stick and gazing stolidly in front of him. He had only just returned from the apiary. The two stacks of hay had been burned, the apricot and cherry trees he had planted and reared were broken and scorched, and worse still all the beehives and bees had been burned. The wailing of the women and the little children, who cried with their mothers, mingled with the lowing of the hungry cattle for which there was no food. The bigger children, instead of playing, followed their elders with frightened eyes. The fountain was polluted, evidently on purpose, so that the water could not be used. The mosque was polluted in the same way, and the Mullah and his assistants were cleaning it out.

No one spoke of hatred for the Russians. The feeling experienced by all the Chechens, from the youngest to the oldest, was stronger than hate. It was not hatred, for they did not regard those Russian dogs as human beings, but it was such repulsion, disgust, and perplexity at the senseless cruelty of these creatures that the desire to exterminate them—like the desire to exterminate rats, poisonous spiders, or wolves—was as natural an instinct as that of self-preservation.

CHAPTER 10

RESTORATION TRAGEDY?

The war in Chechnya was the most outrageous violation of the promise of 1991, a brutal and unambiguous sign that the Yeltsin government had driven itself to the point of political and moral disaster. Although the war was far from the government's only mistake, it was certainly the most vivid display of how arrogant and insular Yeltsin and his regime had become. By late 1995, the president's popularity ratings had plunged; it was getting easier all the time to imagine final defeat. The potential for a restoration seemed greater every day, and, amazing as it may have seemed in the West, the organization that had the best chance to accomplish that restoration was none other than the Communist Party of the Russian Federation.

The imagery of triumph and even comedy that attended the events of August 1991 in Russia had comforted, and ultimately deceived, the world. The men of the Communist Party, the army, and the KGB who had tried to seize power in the name of Leninist principles and imperial preservation betrayed their weakness before the cameras: their hands trembled, they drank themselves senseless, they could not bear to pull the trigger (except in the case of one conspirator, Interior Minister Boris Pugo, who, when all was lost, shot his wife, then himself). The images of

RESTORATION TRAGEDY? | 293

Soviet collapse that August were as vivid as anything in Sergei Eisenstein's unforgettable portrait of the Russian Revolution in his film *October*. The morning after the coup failed, aides loyal to Yeltsin roamed the halls of the Central Committee, giddy and wild, opening safes, rummaging through files and desks—the detritus of the old regime. When Gorbachev returned to Moscow from his house arrest in the Crimea, he tried, if only for a day, to speak up for the Party, but after one of his closest aides, Aleksandr Yakovlev, made it clear to him that trying to rescue the Party was tantamount to "serving tea to a corpse," Gorbachev resigned as general secretary, dissolved the Central Committee, and, it seemed, put an end to the claque of bolshevism once and for all. "The Party Is Over" was the headline dreamed up on a hundred different copy desks around the world.

The imagery of historical closure and beginning was everywhere and irresistible. Four months after the August melodrama, on the night of Christ's birth, Gorbachev resigned, handing over his nuclear baggage to the leader of a new state with a new flag and new symbols. The red banner of the Bolsheviks was lowered from the Kremlin staffs for the last time. The old imperial double-headed eagle became the Russian phoenix. Lenin's face disappeared from the ruble and appeared instead on T-shirts advertising the latest McDonald's franchise.

The truly sly men of the Communist Party, of course, had not waited around for the cataclysm. They used their web of connections to cash in, to position themselves for what would obviously be the biggest privatization and landgrab program in history. There were many ways to get rich in the new Russia; nearly all of them depended on some kind of connection to state power.

Men like Boris Gidaspov, a Leningrad Party chief who had made his name in the late 1980s with his defense of orthodox principles in the face of Gorbachev's perestroika, seemed to disappear for a while and then reemerge in Italian suits. By 1995, I had not heard of or seen Gidaspov for years. One afternoon at Pulkovo Airport in St. Petersburg, I saw him getting off the plane from Moscow. I caught up to him and introduced myself, and we chatted awhile. Then he begged off, saying, "I've got to go. Meetings downtown. You know how it is." As he walked away, Gidaspov clicked open a cellular phone and then ducked into a waiting limousine, a rather sleeker version of his old Party model. I wondered who was paying the bill this time. Gidaspov, it turned out, was president and chairman of a local corporation called TechnoChem.

Gidaspov was a representative man. In the years following the collapse of the Party, interests, rather than ideas, dominated the political scene. The old nomenklatura did not so much give up power as scurry around trying to find their place and privileges on the new map of influence. With the collapse of the central planning system and the loosening of the Party's grip on regional activity, a Party chieftain in a distant place like Vladivostok could, with the right amount of guile and cooperation with local mafias, transform himself into a baron. Former Party men quickly got into the oil business, the natural gas business, the gold and diamonds business; they started banks, commodities exchanges, and dozens of other businesses—all of which operated in an atmosphere of virtual lawlessness.

While all this was happening, a small corps of devout communists, energized by what they saw as Gorbachev's betrayal and the collapse of a glorious empire, refused to swim with the rest. In 1992, less than a year after the coup, they went to the Constitutional Court to fight the Yeltsin government's edict that the Communist Party of the Soviet Union (the CPSU) was illegal. Yeltsin banned the Party entirely under the pretext that the CPSU was never a party the way the rest of the world understood the word but rather a political organization "of a special type," as Lenin put it, which had unchallenged and absolute control over every aspect of the public lives of its subjects. One functionary after another went to court to speak up for the Party's history, and, what was more, they vowed that if they were outlawed, they would return all the same. One Party representative, Dmitri Stepanov, said that more people had been killed in traffic accidents than by Stalin's executioners. The Party, he said, would use "the same methods" to get back into power as the leaders of the August coup. His message was clear: the Party would call in tanks and troops to the center of Moscow. No one took him very seriously. Yeltsin controlled the tanks now. (In Moscow and later in Chechnya he would prove himself prepared to use them.) The trial ended with just a few people in the courtroom and no one paying much attention. The Party, the court ruled, would have to hand over its vast properties—its buildings, its newspaper plants—but, as one party among many, it could operate on a local basis. Even the Yeltsin forces did not mind: their greatest concern was with the opposition in the parliament.

One of the men in the courtroom who had testified for the Party, an officer in the Central Committee's old ideological department, was Gennady Ivanovich Zyuganov. On the day of the court's decision, he left the building promising that he and his comrades would return to power, and when they did, a red flag would fly once more over the Kremlin towers. His prediction seemed preposterous, even pathetic, at the time. But by December 1995, Zyuganov and the Communist Party of the Russian Federation had won an astonishing victory in the Duma. Even the heartiest optimist in the Kremlin could now see that Zyuganov had to be counted the favorite to defeat Yeltsin for the presidency in June 1996. The first democratic transfer of power in a thousand years of Russian history could well result in the elevation of the leader of the Communist Party of the Russian Federation.

———

At the beginning of 1996, the race was Zyuganov's to lose. Not only was Yeltsin unpopular, he was also sick. Even though Yeltsin wisely kept out of view—often for months at a time—he could not entirely hide the fact that he had deteriorated badly in office. By now he had suffered two heart attacks. His health problems were known to anyone who bothered to pick up a newspaper. Unlike his communist predecessors, moribund men like Brezhnev, Andropov, and Chernenko, Yeltsin did not enjoy the forced discretion of the press. At the start of the Chechen war, Yeltsin declared that he had to be hospitalized indefinitely with difficulties having to do with his nose. True or not, the claim instantly became the source of jokes, most of them playing on Gogol's great story "The Nose." Yeltsin was not only reviled, he was also suffering a fate perhaps as serious to a politician: he had become a punch line.

But with all of Yeltsin's failings and weakness, it was still hard to imagine how he had come to trail someone like Zyuganov. In Moscow and in the Western press, the conventional notion of Zyuganov was that he was a colorless, none too intelligent apparatchik whose sole talent was to make himself appear to be the sort of unthreatening communist that the audience in question was willing to accept. When he traveled to the West, talking at the World Economic Forum in Davos, Switzerland, or on *Larry King Live,* he tried to portray himself as a social democrat, a kind of Russian Olaf Palme, who would not dare to renationalize properties and industries for fear of upsetting the civil peace. He sounded in the West like one who put the social security of his constituents above the interests of the bond market, rather like a Moscow-based representative of the American Association of Retired People. At a meeting with a newspaper editorial board in the United States, one editor asked him why, if he was such a social democrat, he called himself and his party "communist." Zyuganov said that for reasons of tradition in Russia, " 'communist' has always been a good brand name." Like Coca-Cola, or Nike.

Zyuganov found his supporters mainly among urban pensioners and badly paid workers in the smaller, less successful cities and, above all, in the poor, conservative provinces of the Russian *glubinka,* the deep countryside. He played on their deepest suspicions, encouraging them to believe that Stalin was, in fact, a heroic patriot, Gorbachev and Yeltsin guilty of treason, and the United States the culprit for all that was wrong in their lives. To the tremendous cheers of the crowd (a sound Yeltsin had not heard in a very long time), he promised the eventual restoration of the Soviet Union and the demise of an arrogant and corrupted West.

Zyuganov's support came generally among voters who had fared the worst since the economic and social earthquake of 1991. He was understandably popular among those who had been unable to adjust to the collapse of the old patriarchal state and its social welfare system, who were enraged by the new disparity between rich and poor and bewildered by the sudden loss of traditional Soviet power. Even among some liberal intellectuals, hatred of Yeltsin had grown so intense that Zyuganov seemed relatively appealing. Andrei Sinyavsky, who had been jailed in the mid-sixties and now lived mainly in Paris, accepted the idea of Zyuganov as the lesser of evils. "I don't think Zyuganov will begin to reanimate communism," Sinyavsky told an interviewer for the newspaper *Argumenti i Fakti.* "In the first place, the West will not give one kopeck. . . . Second, the people have gotten smarter. Probably this will be something of the social democratic orientation. It seems to me that we can expect something better from Zyuganov."

Zyuganov was born in 1944 in the tiny village of Mimrino in provincial Russia. "I was born in the seventh month, like Churchill," he said. "That's under the sign of Cancer. But if I had been carried to term, to nine months, I would have been a Leo. Therefore I am a Cancer with pretenses toward Leo." The closest city to Zyuganov's village was Oryol, Turgenev's city and the scene of heavy fighting in World War II. Over a quarter million people died during the war in the Oryol region. Zyuganov's parents survived the war years—his father lost a leg in the fighting—and they both earned their living as schoolteachers. The school had once been a church until it was closed by the local Communist Party. His mother, a notably strict teacher in the local rural school, had Gennady as a pupil, and, one magazine informs us, the boy dared call her "Mama" just once. The family lived in a small two-bedroom house with a wood-burning stove and no indoor plumbing.

Zyuganov was a student of modest achievement. His talents and ambitions were directed more at Komsomol activity. At the urging of his teachers, he set out to become a teacher of science and mathematics. In the army in the mid-1960s, Zyuganov served in Germany and the Urals and worked in the intelligence forces concerned with chemical warfare. Like many of his army mates, he joined the Communist Party while in the service. After moving back to Oryol, Zyuganov was asked to go into Party work, and he began, like thousands of officials before him, as a Komsomol officer. He worked his way up the Komsomol ranks and then the ranks of the regional Party organization, but compared to stars of his generation, like Gorbachev, Zyuganov's advancements were not especially fast, nor was he particularly distinguished. He was finally called to Moscow in 1983 to work as an instructor in the department of propaganda, a relatively junior post. In 1989, he became vice chairman of the ideology department; he became, in other words, a lord of an orthodoxy that was two years away from death.

Zyuganov first came to the attention of Russians in the late 1980s when it became possible for Central Committee officials to get up at meetings and give speeches accusing Gorbachev and his circle of betraying "the great Leninist ideas." Zyuganov joined those voices who began calling on Gorbachev to step down as general secretary, and he stood out especially as a public enemy of Gorbachev's top liberal aide, Yakovlev. In what would become a staple of Party papers for years to come, Zyuganov wrote an article in *Sovetskaya Rossiya* called "Architect of the Rubble" implying that Yakovlev, who had studied for a year at Columbia as a young man, was an American "agent of influence," turned by American agents to rise high in the Soviet bureaucracy and undermine the state. "What we can see today can be called a national calamity, comparable with the civil war or the invasion of Hitler's fascism," he wrote. "Glasnost has grown into a hysteria and has become a weapon of ideological war against the people."

Like many orthodox communists who were disenchanted (or worse) with Gorbachev, Zyuganov helped form a separate communist party based in Russia, distinct from the CPSU. The "Russian party" became an especially reactionary power base for opponents of Gorbachev, Yeltsin, and radical reform.

In the summer of 1991, with Gorbachev working with Yeltsin and other republican presidents to reshape and decentralize the Soviet Union, Zyuganov and a group of other leading conservatives in the military, the nationalist intelligentsia, and the Party decided to publish a manifesto of resistance, a call to arms of "all patriots." On July 23, *Sovetskaya Rossiya* published "Slovo k Narodu" ("A Word to the People"): "Our Motherland, this country, this great state which history, Nature, and our predecessors willed us to save, is dying, breaking apart and plunging into darkness and nothingness. . . . What has become of us, brothers? . . . Our home is already burning to the ground . . . the bones of the people are being ground up and the backbone of Russia snapped in two." The Communist Party had given over its power to "frivolous and clumsy parliamentarians who have set us against each other and brought into force thousands of stillborn laws, of which only those function that enslave the people and divide the tormented body of the country into factions. . . . How is it that we have let people come to power who have no love for their country, who kowtow to foreign patrons and seek advice and blessings abroad?" The document directly appealed to the military, above all, to close ranks around all patriots who could not tolerate what Gorbachev and Yeltsin were preparing to do to their country. In Moscow, journalists and politicians considered the document to be a warning of an imminent coup. Three weeks later, the tanks rolled into the center of Moscow.

"You can't say that 'A Word to the People' was directly tied to the coup, but there was a direct *metaphysical* relationship between the document and the event," said Valentin Chikin, the editor of *Sovetskaya Rossiya*.

Two of the signers of "A Word to the People" were directly involved in the coup. Zyuganov, however, was not among them. The coup plotters were at a much higher level. On the morning of August 19, a friend called Zyuganov at home and said there had been a coup.

"Where?" Zyuganov said. "In Bolivia?"

———

After the defeat of the coup and Gorbachev's dissolution of the Central Committee, Yeltsin firmly believed that he had defeated the Communist Party once and for all. In an address before the U.S. Senate, he announced the end of communism. His sense of victory and closure was no less serene than that of the Republican Party. There was triumphalism all around.

In the meantime, the Yeltsin government decided it was unnecessary to try to put forward an ideology, a *national* ideology, to replace the old one. The largely unspoken understanding in the first years of the Yeltsin era was that the new Russia would be more or less democratic, more or less market-oriented—that is, more or less like the United States, Western Europe, Japan.

Russia, in other words, had not only abandoned the Marxism-Leninism of the twentieth century, but also the Slavophile notion that declared for Russia a "special role" in the world, a particularity that set it off from all other nations. Russia, a Eurasian state, would lean westward. Yeltsin's foreign minister, Andrei Kozyrev, announced himself an unabashed Westernizer, and he struck up as good a relationship with his American and European coequals as any Russian emissary in history. In *Transformation,* a book published in 1994, while he was still in office, Kozyrev quoted one Westernizer after another, practically begging his countrymen "to end the traditional isolation" of Russia from the rest of the world and warning of "partisans of an imperial policy" who would, once more, come to power under a banner of furious xenophobia.

But Kozyrev's view was merely his own. As recently as 1995, I asked one of Yeltsin's main political advisers, Giorgi Satarov, why Yeltsin himself had not done more to promote, even loosely, the sort of ideas Kozyrev was advertising. (Almost no one read—or could find—Kozyrev's book.) "When totalitarianism was being destroyed, the idea of ideology was being destroyed, too," Satarov said. "The idea was formed that a national idea is a bad thing. But the baby was thrown out with the bathwater. Our Kremlin polls show that people miss this. In 1989, 1990, and 1991 there was a real sense of mission to destroy communism. After that seemed to be resolved, there was a vacuum that followed." That vacuum, Satarov said, allowed the communists to develop their own ideology and make it a successful political platform in the 1995 elections.

If Yeltsin ever believed in democratic principles, he had lost an opportunity. "The essential national drama is the search for identity, and in this we, the liberal intellectuals, have failed," a prominent literary historian, Andrei Zorin, told me. "There is no sense of what this new country, Russia, really is. This was a pressing intellectual obligation. It should be an exciting intellectual adventure to start a country. Look at France after the revolution—you had everyone going at it from the ultraconservative de Maistre to Madame de Staël. Or in eighteenth-century Britain, after the Glorious Revolution, there was Locke. And this was done over time in the United States as well. These last four or five years in Russia have produced little else than pure hysteria. The Gaidar government, in this regard, was too technocratic. They were anti-Marxist but still held the Marxist idea that the economy decides everything. The one symbol we might have had—the White House in 1991—was promptly lost in 1993."

———

The Constitutional Court's ruling in 1992 that communists were free to begin parties on a local and regional level was precisely the organizational opening that the remaining true believers needed. To the horror of the Kremlin, Zyuganov and cohorts from the old regime like Valentin Kuptsov began forming organizations, parties, and alliances in the open. In February 1993, Zyuganov was elected chairman of the Communist Party of the Russian Federation, which was the biggest of many communist parties. Zyuganov was able to bring into the fold countless provincial pols who yearned for the old structures, and with his flexible rhetoric, he was able to make the CPRF into the dominant left-wing party. By the time of its triumph in the December 1995 parliamentary elections, Zyuganov's party had about 560,000 members—tiny compared to the twenty million of the old CPSU, but gigantic compared to any other party planning to make a run at the presidency in 1996. Yeltsin, for one, still had no political party at all—one of his greatest oversights.

At the same time as he was rebuilding the party on an organizational level, Zyuganov also had to create a new ideology. He realized that the old notion of a communist party—an unchallenged vanguard party that was lord of a centralized state—would be a loser at the polls. Shopworn phrases like "the dictatorship of the proletariat," a foreign policy of menace, an economy of absolute central control: none of it had any attraction to voters. Zyuganov also had to take into account the theme of Russian nationalism—a traditional *enemy* of the Communist Party. To beat Yeltsin, he would have to find a way to graft nationalism onto the still-useful qualities of the communist idea; he would have to make use of a lingering nostalgia for the old regime without blatantly painting himself a neo-Stalinist. This was not merely intellectually challenging, it was also a political necessity.

"Now a new sort of party is being born," Zyuganov told his comrades in the first days of the new party. "Much is being taken from the past: solidarity, social justice, and great spirituality. The Party should also take in Russian patriotism, love of one's motherland, and an interest in Russian power."

In 1992 and 1993, Zyuganov explored the possibility of joining forces with far-right nationalists, setting off talk of a "Red-Brown coalition." Acting as the chief Red, Zyuganov became chairman of the coordinating council of the People's Patriotic Front of Russia, and a leader of the National Salvation Front, a group that included Bolsheviks, fascists, and a general of the KGB. The most important aspect of his increasing association with the nationalists was the way the experience rubbed off on his ideas. He began to develop an eclectic ideology, drawing on whatever was still appealing from Soviet history and ideology but also borrowing from whatever sources from the pre-Soviet era seemed appropriate and potentially popular.

The best-known of Zyuganov's ideological mentors in this project was Aleksandr Prokhanov, a newspaper editor and novelist whose work was so celebratory of the military in Afghanistan that he became known as "the nightingale of the general staff." Even though Prokhanov was Zyuganov's main intellectual mentor, very few people outside the world of Moscow politics and journalism knew much about him.

In Moscow, I met frequently with Prokhanov, sometimes at his apartment downtown or at the offices of his newspapers. Prokhanov, in his fifties, and usually in a well-worn suit, was possessed of a strange charm. He fairly paraded his extremism, and yet he was utterly open, thoroughly enjoying the sport of granting interviews and meeting with people he knew could not bear his politics.

Prokhanov's background was peculiar. One of his grandfathers was an evangelical Baptist and a self-described futurologist. Even earlier in the family lineage there were Molokanes from the Tambov region, a sect that emphasized a return to the most ancient prayers and traditions in Orthodoxy. Prokhanov was born in Tbilisi and grew up in Moscow. He was a child of the postwar era, a time, Prokhanov told me, "of the glorious sound of the sonic boom, a Soviet civilization at its height in military affairs and in outer space." Twice a year, on May 1 and on Revolution Day, November 7, new models of planes screamed across the sky in Moscow, Prokhanov said, "and this created a fantastic impression on me." Inspired by the "thrilling propaganda of the state and the romance of the technosphere," he studied to become an aviation engineer.

"But I was a skeptic, not a conformist," he went on. "I did not like what had happened in Budapest in 1956. I met people who returned home from the camps. I saw many victims of Soviet power. At the same time, there was another mood growing in me: a romance with the Russian tradition of folklore and folk language, an awareness of Khrushchev's assault on the countryside. The villages had survived collectivization somehow, but Khrushchev absolutely liquidated the peasantry with his various rural programs. People started flooding into the city, to Moscow, and I got to know these people. Because I was a hunter, I also started going out into the countryside, and I began to understand and value these rural things: the folklore, the poems, the language."

In 1960, Prokhanov finished his studies at the Institute of Aviation and moved to a village in northern Karelia. "I became a kind of monk," he said. "There was something mystical about it, the connection with the earth and the Russian peasantry. So there was this peculiar mix of the military-technological strength with the mystical metaphysics of the Russian folklore. This is what formed me. It's the avant-garde, the myth of the future, married to an ideal of Russia, a myth of the past."

Prokhanov began writing fiction in the late sixties, and over the years his books reflected his political obsessions. He wrote of futurology in *Eternal City,* about the Russian countryside in various short stories, about the glories of the Soviet army's war in Afghanistan in *The Tree in the Center of Kabul.* With the sponsorship of a grateful Soviet military command, Prokhanov was allowed to make countless reporting trips: to Afghanistan, Angola, Nicaragua, Ethiopia, Kampuchea, and Mozambique. During perestroika—an "anti-imperial, antistate" era that "destroyed everything"—Prokhanov made his name as a journalist crusading for the preservation of an imperial Russia.

The newspapers he published—first there was *Dyen* ("The Day") and then *Zavtra* ("Tomorrow")—were printed monthly on cheap paper and featured apocalyptic cartoons (usually of a Yeltsin figure, made grotesque and murderous), tabloid headlines reminiscent of the *New York Post* or the *London Sun,* and endless screeds in tiny, bleeding type. Prokhanov called his papers the voice of "the spiritual opposition," and membership in that opposition did not require a particular orthodoxy so much as it did a hatred of all that had come after 1985. "I invited in all forces opposed to Gorbachev, all forces opposed to the Westernizers under Yeltsin," Prokhanov said. "I accumulated them all and tried to synthesize them and create a real opposition." In *Zavtra,* Prokhanov printed interviews with and articles by the seemingly irreconcilable: "maximalist" communists like Viktor Anpilov; crackpot military men like Colonel Viktor Alksnis, General Valentin Varennikov, and General Albert Makashov; the profoundly anti-Semitic nationalist and world-class mathematician Igor Shafarevich; rural writers like Rasputin and Vasily Belov. Gennady Zyuganov, the head of the growing Communist Party of the Russian Federation, appeared so often that in interviews with Prokhanov he called him "Sasha."

What energized Prokhanov and united every voice in his paper had little to do with nostalgia for Marx or Lenin, but rather an intense longing for an empire and a hatred for the West. Above all, these voices were *gosudarsvenniki,* statists; their mourning for a lost empire and their determination to rebuild it was their common cause. There was enough slander, bile, and anti-Semitism in *Zavtra* to fill an issue of *Der Sturmer.* Prokhanov's deputy editor, Vladimir Bondarenko, once told me after he had made a trip to the United States that while David Duke's views might be a bit extreme, he did feel in ideological sync with Pat Buchanan.

Like so many of the new extremists, Prokhanov was perfectly willing to perform his role as the ogre for foreign consumption. He was not shy about inviting over visiting Westerners and describing for them precisely why they represented Satan. One day some *Washington Post* reporters took Ben Bradlee, the former executive editor, and Katharine Graham, the chairman of the board, to see Prokhanov as part of their political tour of Moscow; after Prokhanov delivered his usual fire and brimstone, complete with a few choice cracks about Zionist influences, he left the room to take care of some newspaper business. Bradlee, in his boredom, reached over to a dish of candy. "Don't touch it, Ben," said Katharine Graham. "It's probably poisoned."

After Yeltsin began coloring his own rhetoric and politics with the accents of nationalism, Prokhanov could smell victory. "The president's men have read our newspaper well and have borrowed our slogans and doctrines," Prokhanov told me. "This is a great victory for the opposition." Prokhanov could see that the "Westernizing capitalists"—men like Gaidar, Kozyrev, Chubais—were in trouble, while "national capitalists"—like the bodyguard Korzhakov—appeared to be in control. But Yeltsin could never shift enough to satisfy Prokhanov. What Yeltsin had done in breaking up the union was unforgivable. "To get rid of Gorbachev, Yeltsin had to get rid of the USSR," he said. "It was like the Russian folktale in which a peasant with a fly on his forehead gets a bear to help him swat the fly. But, meanwhile, the bear kills the peasant, too."

Prokhanov was not himself an orthodox communist, but his greatest accomplishment, he believed, was helping communists drop their "old and useless dogma" (dictatorship of the proletariat, etc.) and replace it with elements of nationalism that would help them build a broader political base. In other words, he tried to bring together the opposing sides of the civil war of the twenties. His reasoning was purely pragmatic. The nationalists, on their own, could not win a presidential election.

"The communists have the best political organization," he said. "Their popularity also comes from a widespread urge among people to live the way we did ten years ago. Send your kids to camp in the Crimea. Work well at your factory. No crime, minimal poverty, social guarantees, even if modest. The guarantees of being a citizen of a great power. If you are an aerospace engineer, you want to know that your shuttles are flying in space and not being converted into gambling casinos or sold to the French.

"The communists, like the nationalists, understand that Russians have a specific mission in history, and the first priority is to organize this huge territory, a great political machine on the Eurasian continent. This is a territorial, cosmic imperative. We are a land of many peoples and nations, and so there is an imperial component to this. There is a kind of voluntary submission to the empire, open to each other, not dominating. Then there is the mystical component, a people who have in this world the defined task of finding utopia. Utopias, after all, happen. Then there is the primacy of justice. Freedom is about the victory of the strong over the weak. In Russia the idea of freedom is secondary to justice. The point is how to organize society, to organize its power, to conduct a social experiment. All this is essential to a Russian soul, and the Yeltsin people have never understood this. So now the Yeltsin experiment is dead. The liberal idea proved ruinous for Russia, and, mark my words, it will be replaced. One way or another."

———

With Prokhanov's help, Zyuganov had developed an ideology of national bolshevism. But he was not entirely equipped for the modern world. For one thing, he was pretty bad on television. He was portly and bald and spoke in the drone of old Soviet newscasts.

In most things, Zyuganov affected a Leninist modesty and sobriety. When an interviewer complimented him on the cut and cloth of his suit, he protested that it was not foreign-made, but rather the product of a Russian shop inside GUM, the huge shopping center on Red Square. When he was asked how he celebrated winning his doctoral degree in 1995, he said, well, of course there was a party, "but no caviar." Nor did he drink too much, he was quick to remind the voters grown weary of Yeltsin's well-publicized benders. "I'm not against a good glass of wine or a little shot of vodka," he said. "But I drink quite modestly. I can't handle more than three vodkas. Someone has to be sober among today's politicians."

Zyuganov's singular vanity was the pride he betrayed in the range of his intellect. Although he started out in the sciences, he won his advanced degree in 1995 in matters closer to the affairs of state. "My specialty is a rare one: political philosophy," he said. "I got my doctorate with a thesis on the fate of Russia in the world in the coming decades." At Moscow State University, he defended his dissertation on Russia and the modern world in front of a panel of like-minded professors, many of whom continued to declare Marxism-Leninism as their academic specialty. In speeches and interviews, Zyuganov bragged of having read "all the philosophers." When I heard him lecture, it was clear that he did know the names of many of them.

In the three books Zyuganov published in the two or three years leading up to the campaign, he unleashed a torrent of these names, and the names one might have expected (Marx, Lenin, Engels, etc.) do not enjoy pride of place. Zyuganov, after all, was out to remake, not restate, the ideology of his party.

As the leader of the new communist movement, his first obligation was to advance a version of the Party's history that was believable enough to a majority of the Russian electorate. Ever since Gorbachev reopened the debate on Soviet history in 1987, conservatives in the Party had railed against the "blackening" of the Party and its past leaders. By the time the criticism reached the sacred hem of Lenin it was clear that the attempt to reform the old regime had been overtaken by a movement to destroy it entirely. In a speech called "Twelve Lessons of History" delivered in 1995 on the anniversary of the Bolshevik Revolution, Zyuganov claimed that Gorbachev had set off an orgy of "libel" against history and that the Yeltsin regime had so thoroughly distorted a glorious Russian and Soviet past that it was no longer possible to read about Tolstoy, much less 1917, in new textbooks.

This was rubbish, of course, but adherence to fact is not what Zyuganovism is about. On a campaign trip to Siberia, Zyuganov gave a speech on the various evils of Western invaders and compared them to the Nazis, who, he said, had been ordered to replace Orthodox churches with Protestant churches. When a reporter from *The New York Times* questioned that piece of history, Zyuganov's spokesman allowed that the candidate had permitted himself some "poetic license." It was his custom to flash that license often.

Zyuganov, as the leader of the Party restoration, rejected any notion that Leninism represented a break either with Russian history or with an international lineage of humanistic thought. "On the entire planet, all educated people well understand that Lenin is one of the great political figures and thinkers of modern times. In his nearly fifty-four years he wrote fifty volumes, more or less, and is a presence in every library in the world. His work is studied everywhere. He had one of the great minds of the epoch, and what he wrote remains relevant today. Take, for example, his work on the theory of imperialism: today we see how this pertains to what is happening with transnational corporations. . . ." Needless to say, Lenin's brutality—his assault on the peasantry, his war on the church and the intelligentsia, his establishment of the first labor camps on Solovetsky Island—was not part of the portrait. Rather, for Zyuganov, Leninism drew on "the greatest idea in the history of humanism: brotherhood, justice. . . . These were not the idea of seventy-five years but of thousands of years. . . . Buddha, Jesus Christ, Muhammad, Mahatma Gandhi, Lenin: they are all of the highest moral order, champions of the fellowship among men, and therefore the vast majority of people go for them."

Zyuganov, through some willful act of forgetting, seemed sincere in his view of the Soviet past. Although he told me and many other journalists that he could not recall any victims of Stalin's repressions in his hometown, his claim is on the edge of absurdity. According to *Requiem,* a directory of victims of Stalin's repression in the city, more than seventeen thousand people in Oryol were arrested in 1936–37, one of the worst periods of terror. Zyuganov's in-laws lived in the nearby village of Glotovo, and they, too, were visited by Stalinist horror. Alessandra Stanley of *The New York Times* visited Vasily and Olga Omelichev, who still lived in the same small house where Zyuganov's wife grew up. Vasily said his father had been declared a kulak and lost his land and possessions during collectivization: members of the family starved to death as a result of the confiscation. Although the Omelichevs told Stanley they were still close to their daughter and son-in-law and even brought them potatoes from their garden when they traveled to Moscow, they also said that Zyuganov was willfully ignorant of the family's encounter with Stalinist horror. "He still doesn't know," Vasily said. "He's not interested in my past."

In his analysis of history, Zyuganov determined that there were actually two Communist Parties: the party of heroic men like Stakhanov, the legendary worker, and Kurchatov, the legendary scientist, and Marshal Zhukov and Yuri Gagarin; and then there was the party of "betrayers": Yezhov and Beria, Gorbachev and Yeltsin. As leaders of the secret police, Yezhov and Beria were guilty of tremendous cruelty; Gorbachev and Yeltsin "sold out" the Party and the empire, all under the influence of a rapacious West and the West's "agents of influence."

Zyuganov also defended one of the traditional whipping posts of anti-Soviet dissent: the enormous and privileged nomenklatura that ran the country. "The qualified apparat served the Soviet state well for three quarters of a century," he wrote. "There were mistakes . . . but this nomenklatura all the same created and supported a great and powerful state." The apparatchiks, then, were in the party of the good. Here, of course, Zyuganov was not only defending his own species; he also knew that there were millions of old apparatchiks still alive, and they all had families, and they all could vote.

But where was Stalin in Zyuganov's "two-party" system? In speech after speech, Zyuganov rejected any notion that tens of millions of Soviet citizens had been destroyed under Stalin. He claimed special access to the archives, and there were, he said, only about half a million people killed under Stalin, "and most of them were Party members." Zyuganov's numbers, of course, contradicted by many millions every major scholar in the field, Russian and Western.

Stalin, despite all the contrary evidence, was also credited as a great military leader in the war, and thus the savior of humanity against Nazism. Zyuganov could not reach the poll numbers he enjoyed at the beginning of 1996—about 20 to 25 percent to Yeltsin's 6 or 7—with the support solely of the older Russians who still believed in the goodness of the Generalissimo or the even smaller percentage who carried his portrait at Communist Party rallies. Zyuganov did not risk his chance at broader support by openly speaking out in favor of Stalin. But he did have the occasional nice thing to say. In fact, Zyuganov saw in Stalin a wise ideologist, one who tried to combine imperial pride with communist ideology. Stalin, Zyuganov said, "understood the urgent necessity of harmonizing new realities with a centuries-long Russian tradition." Stalin was a true "patriot" who "understood the special destiny of the country, while Khrushchev was oriented toward crude consumerism." If Stalin, who ruled from 1927 to 1953, had only lived "a few more years," he would have "restored Russia and saved it from the cosmopolitans." Zyuganov, of course, was referring to the Jews. In fact, if Stalin had lived, the Doctors' Plot prosecution would have continued apace, as would the expected massive attempt to purge Russian Jews and, at the very least, deport them to the "homeland" established in the Far Eastern hamlet of Birobidzhan.

Zyuganov also claimed that Stalin, who had obliterated the peasantry in Ukraine and southern Russia through forced collectivization and artificial famine, was bound to have made life fine again for the farmers on the kolkhoz. "You know, I am acquainted with the documents," Zyuganov told one interviewer, "and I was shocked when Stalin, not long before his death, said we are obliged to return our debt to the peasantry."

This cynicism about Soviet history was not peculiar to the top leader of the new Communist Party, as I discovered when I met with Igor Bratishchev, one of Zyuganov's closest allies in the Duma. Bratishchev, who helped draft Zyuganov's economic plan, was slated for a top job in a communist government. His willful and convenient forgetfulness, his ability to rearrange history, was typical of his Party. When I asked him about Stalin, he wanted it all ways. Stalin was a "great general" who "saved the world," Bratishchev said.

Five minutes later, he was saying, "And as for Stalin and those who did terrible things, they were not communists. They carried Party membership cards. This is true. But anyone can enter a church holding a candle. That doesn't make him a believer, does it? We see Yeltsin in churches, but do you really think he's a believer? If there were repressions, they were organized by people, not communists, and they were directed, first and foremost, against communists. The only real privilege of being communist was to lead your brigade into battle and then to work in an atmosphere of self-denial. For example, you are writing this to make money, and I am giving this interview for free."

Zyuganov's telling of Communist Party history featured a turn from celebration to repugnance quite early in the Party chronology. Khrushchev represented a period of "unnecessary" reforms and vulgar consumerism. Brezhnev's era was sclerotic and overlooked the urgent need to modernize the economy. Gorbachev, of course, sold out the country and the Party entirely, "simply to hear his name chanted in the capitals of Western Europe and the United States."

The only post-Stalin leader lionized by Zyuganov and the new communists was Yuri Andropov. Zyuganov had a difficult time forgiving Andropov for playing mentor to Gorbachev, but he complimented his intelligence, his relative modesty, and, above all, his discipline and commitment to the Soviet Union as a great power. Andropov's reign in office lasted little more than a year, and there are many communists in Russia even today who are convinced that the only thing that separated the empire from oblivion was Andropov's failed kidneys.

As chief of the KGB, Andropov helped lead the Soviet assault on Prague in 1968 and a general war on dissidents at home. Zyuganov, especially when he was in the West, promised he would never clamp down on dissenting opinion, but it was clear that he had no argument with the old methods. He greatly admired the Chinese model of reform and wished "we had taken the advice" of the Chinese Communist Party leaders when they· warned Gorbachev about taking glasnost too far. And as far as the events at Tiananmen Square were concerned, the Chinese powers did what was necessary, though it was a "difficult" situation. "I can't imagine what would happen if such a situation took place," Zyuganov said. The West, in its sanctimony and self-interest, made too much of its notion of human rights. "In our time, we had three hundred or so dissidents, and there was endless noise about them everywhere," he writes. "But today there are six million refugees in Russia. Our countrymen in the Baltic are treated as second-class citizens. Every other workingman in Russia is not paid on time. Who of these patented democrats is speaking out in their interest?"

Zyuganov's ideological sleight of hand had been to graft onto a left-wing party an enormous degree of old-fashioned Russian nationalism. This was a maneuver with important roots in Party history. In the Brezhnev years, most foreign diplomats, politicians, and scholars understood the Communist Party as a monolith, unshakable in its power and resolve, and utterly united and disciplined in its adherence to orthodox principles. Brezhnev's ideologist, the "gray cardinal," Mikhail Suslov, was thought to be in absolute charge of his province; there could be no dissent, especially in the top Party ranks or on the pages of the official newspapers, magazines, and "thick journals."

In fact, there was great division within the Party, though it required tremendous attention to find it. It now seems self-evident that there was a significant cadre of aides and officials in the sixties who were sympathetic to a Dubček-style reform, "socialism with a human face." Gorbachev himself had been extremely close in university days to Zdenek Mlynar, one of the top officials in the Dubček government. When Gorbachev assumed power he surrounded himself with *shestidyesatniki,* men and women of the sixties generation who had been deeply affected by the Prague Spring but had continued working within official structures.

What is less well known is that there were also officials within the Party who were interested in Russian nationalism. The orthodox myth was one of internationalism, "the friendship of peoples," but this strain in the Party made little secret of its belief that Sovietism was, at its root, a Russian project, an imperial matter with a red gloss. In April 1968, the journal *Molodaya Gvardia* published articles attacking Western-leaning intellectuals inside and outside the Party; such thinking was anathema to the "Russian national spirit." Those articles were answered first by *Novy Mir* and then, more dramatically, in October 1972, by a Central Committee propagandist named Aleksandr Yakovlev. In a long article titled "Against Anti-Historicism," Yakovlev used the ritual wooden language of Party Newspeak to condemn the nationalists and their romanticized vision of prerevolutionary, imperial Russia and for creating a "cult of the patriarchal peasantry." Yakovlev must have been sanctioned to write his piece, but he must also have offended someone in the Politburo. He was made a virtual exile; he was "sentenced" to serving as ambassador to Canada for more than ten years. It took Gorbachev to bring him back to Moscow.

In the seventies, communist-nationalists had to conceal themselves behind the veil of approved Party language. Zyuganov's language and emotions, his sense of persecution, were uninhibited and, at times, chilling. His writing and speeches were often as rife with ugly conspiracy fantasies as anything found in the works of Pat Robertson, as filled with bogus mists-in-the-forest Wagnerian mythology as early Nazi primers. This kind of stuff had been floating around for years in Moscow—the various political extremists were always holding open public meetings and you could always buy an armful of bizarre papers and magazines from various eccentrics outside the Lenin Museum on fair-weather afternoons—but now, with Zyuganov still leading in the polls, it all felt extremely dangerous. Yegor Gaidar wrote in the weekly magazine *Novoye Vremya* ("New Times") that if one simply changed the word "Slavic" to "Germanic" in Zyuganov's work, "everything will be clear."

"I am convinced," Gaidar wrote, "that today's Communist Party of the Russian Federation is not communist but rather national socialist. The seriousness of the possible threat of their coming power does not consist simply in massive renationalization, but rather in populist and military adventures and the practically inescapable move to destroying the already fragile market instruments in Russia." The threat of a remilitarized economy and a Soviet-era KGB was "not propaganda, but rather part of their worldview."

Zyuganov's book was repetitious and fairly easy to summarize. An empire, led by a "special" civilization, has been betrayed. It is the duty of a united front of patriotic forces to rebuild it. The West has undercut us at every turn, expanding its imperial hegemony over the rest of humanity. Only Russia has the might and the resources and the will to challenge the West and provide balance in the world. The choice we face (in this election) is among three variants: a "worldwide" version of Chechen-Yugoslavian unrest; a Colombian-style criminal dictatorship; or a powerful and stable state with structures amenable not to the West but to Russian traditions. A Yeltsin victory will provide the first two options, Zyuganov the third.

"The struggle between the anti-people forces and the patriotic forces is reaching its decisive phase," he wrote. "The outcome of the struggle will decide the future of the country, its unity and values, its independence and authority, its life and the fate of millions of citizens."

When Zyuganov shifted into his nationalist mode, we no longer heard much about Lenin. Rather he quoted Toynbee and Spengler, and nineteenth-century Russian reactionaries like Nikolai Danielevsky on the rot and decline of the West. He praised Danielevsky's major work, *Russia and Europe* (1869), in which Russians are the declared "chosen people" and the challenger to the rotting West. Zyuganov was especially fond of Danielevsky, who was convinced that Russia must reject Western models—parliaments, presidents, etc.—and develop only those traditions that were inherently Russian. In the end, Danielevsky wrote, Russia would prevail in an apocalyptic battle with the West. Zyuganov, too, talked of the "millennium-long" struggle between the Orthodox and Catholic worlds that began with the great schism of 1054.

For Zyuganov, like nearly all nationalists, Russia was a special case, a "special world," a "special type of civilization" based on "collectivism, unity, statehood, and the aspiration to attain the highest ideals of good and justice." Russia, he wrote, was hostile in its soul to the West, which was infected with "extreme individualism, militant soullessness, religious indifference, adherence to mass culture, antitraditionalism, and the principle of the primacy of quantity over quality."

Zyuganov blamed Yeltsin and his circle of "radical Westernizers" for destroying the Soviet Union and trying to graft onto the new Russian state the sort of alien features embodied by the stock exchanges, strip joints, and burger palaces that so infuriate all nationalists. But soon, he wrote, "it became evident that a significant number of Russians did not accept this path of development that the radical democrats were trying to take. The dissatisfied people grew in number into a real mass opposed to the general and deepening chaos that was the unavoidable result of the political and economic course of the Russian leadership. This dissatisfaction reached a critical mass."

There was probably no phrase that infuriated Zyuganov and the nationalists more than "the New World Order." The American-led alliance in the Gulf War in 1991 marked for Zyuganov a humiliation and a warning: the United States now clearly treated its once-great rival and super-power, the Soviet Union, as a "junior partner." George Bush's notion of a New World Order meant unchallenged American power. The New World Order, Zyuganov said, was the fulfillment of a "messianic, escha-tological, religious project, thought out and based on plans long known in 'the history of planetary utopias, like the Roman imperialism in the time of Tiberius and Diocletian . . . and the movement of Protestant fundamentalists in Europe or the Trotskyist notion of World Revolution." The New World Order, he went on, was part of a "post-Christian" reli-gion. "Its ideology (we recall 'the end of history' by F. Fukiyama) comes in the form of the messianic dream, held by the West for many centuries, of a liberal-democratic 'heaven on earth.' This same ideology of mondial-ism is convinced of an imminent arrival on earth of Messiah, which would confirm on Earth the laws of 'the true religion' and provide the basis for a 'golden age' of humanity." The planet would be ruled over by "a united world government" supported by representatives of the Bilder-burg club, the Trilateral Commission, the American Council on Foreign Relations, and, of course, "other intellectual centers of mondialism." Harvard University was the suspect "brain trust of world liberalism" where Western intellectuals and policymakers worked out the New World Order prior to the final collapse of the Soviet Union and the "bipolar geopolitical construct." There was also much conspiratorial dis-cussion about the United Nations, the World Bank, the International Monetary Fund, Jacques Attali and the European Bank for Reconstruc-tion and Development and the ways they go out of their way to undercut the power of Russia. The IMF's $10 billion loan to Russia in early in 1996 was simply another way to make Russia beholden to the West.

Zyuganov, of course, skipped over these fantastical notions of the West when he visited Davos, Washington, or New York. He never mentioned them when he was invited to a group meeting with President Clinton at the American embassy in Moscow in 1995. Nor was he foolish enough to give voice to a kind of ritual anti-Semitism that ran through so much of the nationalist movement. Like his varied compatriots on the pages of Prokhanov's newspaper, Zyuganov wrote in *I Believe in Russia* that there was much to fear in the Jews: "The ideology, culture, and world outlook of the Western world are becoming more and more influenced by the

Jews scattered around the world. Jewish influence grows not by the day, but by the hour. The Jewish Diaspora traditionally controlled the financial life of the [European] continent and is becoming more and more the owner of the controlling interest in all the stocks of Western civilization and its socioeconomic system."

Like Stalin in wartime, Zyuganov decided that the Russian Orthodox Church was an essential aspect of Russianness and patriotism. He supported not only maximum freedom for the church, but also a kind of spiritual singularity. The God of the Jews and of Western Christianity was alien to the Russian people, and for them he promised nothing. It was on the question of his own spiritual life that Zyuganov revealed just one of the oddities of trying to reconcile his fealty to bolshevism and Slavophilic nationalism. He told one interviewer that, for him, Christ was "the first communist," since both Jesus and the Party came "from the same principle of social justice on earth." He didn't go to church, exactly, but he was spiritual, "rather like Marshal Zhukov," who did not go to church either but kept an icon hanging in his house.

Zyuganov made it clear that Russia could expect Russia, under his leadership, to assert itself strongly and, possibly, erratically, largely out of a sense of vengeance. His insistence that the West had brought Russia low and was now out to suck it dry of all strength and resources was a strain present in all of his essays, speeches, and interviews. "It is extremely important," he wrote, "that Russia avoid deepening its integration in the 'world economic system' and the 'international labor force.' That could bring on a dangerous dependence of the country on external factors. There is a need for maximal autonomy."

Zyuganov said that Russia must go through a period of healing and "internal evolution" after the trauma of 1991, but he also had in mind a reexertion of some unspecified degree of influence over the countries of the old empire. He wrote with great admiration about Alexander III, who reigned while Russia's "southern border went one thousand kilometers toward Afghanistan." These were not pleasant notes to hear if one was living in, say, Estonia, Ukraine, or possibly even Eastern Europe.

The idea that Russia, as a great power, should be able to develop its own sense of identity and presence in the world free of Western pressure was now widespread and quite natural. There were no politicians of consequence in Moscow—not Yeltsin, not even the liberal opposition leader, Grigory Yavlinsky—who said otherwise. There was no inherent harm in this, and for Americans to treat Russia with anything less than respect was not only arrogant, it was politically counterproductive. It was also natural that in its search for itself and bearing in the world, Russia should sort through what Zyuganov called the "thousand-year experience of Russian statehood." But Zyuganov's vision of Russians as a people apart—a people with a superior sense of spirituality, with an innate belief in the collective over the individual, with a mission in the world to battle the West—was an ideology bound to have consequences were it to come to power. Zyuganov came from a stream of the Communist Party and of the nationalist world that bore a hatred for the West that was hard to imagine. He may not have revealed it in Davos, but in his words to the Russian people it was unconcealed. He was prepared to take legal actions against his predecessors for ending the Soviet Union, and he was ready to reinstitute a swagger that the world had not seen from Moscow in a decade.

"I always want to make it clear to the [West]," Zyuganov wrote, "that you cannot destabilize a great country. You cannot force upon another your values and force on us your vulgar films, this consumer psychology, these endless advertisements, which cause division in every family. You are instilling in us an anti-Americanism. Even during the Cold War, there was not the anti-Americanism there is now."

At the beginning of 1996, there were plenty of analysts in both Russia and in the West who claimed that restoration of any kind was impossible in Russia. But considering how fragile were Russia's new political and economic institutions, considering Russia's historical penchant for xenophobia and tragedy, one wondered at the origin of such complacency. After Zhirinovsky's party had scored so well in the parliamentary elections of 1993, reporters asked one liberal democrat, Anatoly Shabad, what the West could do in the face of such depressing results. Shabad answered, "Wait and tremble." With Zyuganov on the brink of power, and with Yeltsin showing no signs of life or democratic impulse, the time to tremble had surely come.

CHAPTER 11

THE WAR
FOR THE KREMLIN

In the spring of 1996, in the midst of the Russian presidential campaign, a message arrived in terms both exacting and absurd: at exactly nine in the morning, I was to stand in the doorway of a McDonald's on the Old Arbat and look for one Igor Prelin, a middle-aged man "with a short white beard and dark hair." Prelin would then lead me to the apartment of Vladimir Kryuchkov, the last chief of the Soviet Union's Committee for State Security—the KGB—and the man who had led the botched coup d'état of August 1991.

It was no exaggeration to say that the outcome of the election would greatly influence the course of Russian history, and for half a year every day of the campaign was so crowded with Kremlin intrigue and tension that few had time to notice that Kryuchkov, the embodiment of the old regime and its vast secret police, had published a two-volume memoir called, fetchingly enough, *Lichnoye Delo,* "A Personal File." I snapped up a set one day at the bookstand at the Duma and devoured them over the next couple of nights. Kryuchkov had much to answer for: as a young spy in Budapest, he helped crush the Hungarian uprising of 1956, thus launching a career that ended when he was arrested in 1991 and charged as a "betrayer of the motherland." He was released from prison in 1993 after the

Yeltsin government seemed to sense that with the nationalist and communist opposition on the rise, there would be no political sense in pursuing
the prosecution. While some of the plotters returned to politics—some
won seats in the Duma, in fact—Kryuchkov retired, a defeated man.

On the appointed morning, it poured, and to stay out of the rain
I stood inside the restaurant next to a life-size, hard-plastic Ronald
McDonald. I had come with my friend Masha Lipman, the deputy editor
of *Itogi*, a new weekly magazine in Moscow funded by (who else?)
Vladimir Gusinsky. Masha and I had worked together at the Moscow bureau of *The Washington Post* in the days when an interview with the head of
the KGB was unimaginable. One would sooner apply for an interview
with Augustine of Hippo.

"Are you sure this is really happening?" Masha said. Since her teens,
Masha had been friends with various refuseniks, dissidents, and others
whom Kryuchkov would surely have deemed "anti-Soviet elements."

While Masha and I cooked up some questions, McDonald's was doing
a brisk breakfast trade, mostly to mobsters finishing up a long night on
the streets and the casinos and a few tourists hoping the rain would stop
so they could cruise the pedestrian mall outside. All around was the good
American smell of coffee and grease.

At nine exactly, Masha and I walked out the front door of McDonald's,
and there, standing outside, was our man. Trimmed white beard, dark
hair, expectant eyes.

"Igor Nikolayevich?"

"It's you?" the man said. "You came early."

"A few minutes, yes."

"Then let's go."

Prelin snapped open an umbrella and walked quickly along the Arbat
and then turned right onto a side street. These are among the oldest and
most legendary streets of Moscow, the stuff of popular song. We entered
a ten-story apartment building that was much cleaner than most. Having
ordered his president under house arrest during the 1991 coup seemed
to have done Kryuchkov no harm in the real estate department. He was
obviously well fixed. Prelin explained that Kryuchkov spent most of his
time at a dacha outside of Moscow.

We got out of the elevator and came to Kryuchkov's door. Someone had slashed it up with a razor or a knife, leaving a zigzag gash.

"The 'democrats' were here," Prelin explained as he pressed the buzzer. "They did this."

It was quiet for a while behind the door. We waited, not quite sure that anyone would come. Then a faint scratching sound, then a frail and distant voice.

"Who is it?"

"It's me," Prelin said.

The bolt clicked open. Vladimir Kryuchkov, dressed in a dark suit, stood in the doorframe.

"You are welcome," the spymaster said. "Please come in." His stooped and silent wife stood at his side. Then she padded down the hall and out of sight.

———

The apartment had an empty look. There were no more than a few dozen books on the shelves, and only one volume, Yeltsin's memoirs, bristled with bookmarks—each one, I had no doubt, stashed there by Kryuchkov to note another outrage. Yeltsin had defeated the coup and now, to make the agony more intense for Kryuchkov, he was hoping to win reelection against the Communist Party candidate, Gennady Zyuganov.

Kryuchkov led us into the living room. The paintings on the wall were the sort of generic seascapes and dawns ordered up by the gross by Holiday Inn. There was no sign anywhere of a human hand, of decoration, of taste or nontaste or of life of any kind. The apartment may, in fact, have been Kryuchkov's, but it seemed more like a safe house than a home. Kryuchkov, for his part, looked more lived-in, more worn-out, than I had remembered. He was distinctly less vigorous, moving with a sad deliberation, as if guarding against a fall. His small cherubic face was pale, his small eyes narrow and lifeless behind rimless glasses. He seemed always to squint against the light of the world.

"We don't have much time," he said soon after we sat down. "I'm in a rush."

Where Kryuchkov was rushing to, what urgent business awaited him, he did not say. It seemed to me an old gambit, in case he wanted to cut out early; but, as it happened, he was in no rush. We had plenty of time to talk.

I began with a few dutiful Cold War questions. I asked about Lee Harvey Oswald's prolonged stay in Minsk, and the Kennedy assassination, about spies and suspected spies, about Alger Hiss. I was rebuffed with dutiful answers.

"The Soviet Union had nothing to do with the assassination," Kryuchkov said. "I know that for sure, because I was at the head of Soviet intelligence and it goes without saying that I took an interest in the assassination. Any insinuation otherwise is ill-founded.

"I do, however, think a time will come when you will know," Kryuchkov went on cryptically. "The forces responsible are still not allowing you to find the truth or make it public. Some time will have to pass—five or ten years maybe—but I hope this will be as short as possible. Anyway, I think the Oswald case is one of the most disgraceful phenomena in the States, because one person after another was killed who was involved in it."

When I asked about Hiss, Kryuchkov looked utterly bewildered.

"Alger who?"

"Hiss. Alger Hiss."

"Who is that?"

Prelin, it turned out, was Kryuchkov's longtime aide, and he jumped in to help his boss, explaining that Hiss had been a State Department official in the Roosevelt administration and had been suspected of spying for Soviet intelligence.

"Ah," Kryuchkov said. "Well. If there had been something, I wouldn't know."

Finally, I asked about a contemporary case, the mole Aldrich Ames, a CIA agent who spied for the Soviet Union for nine years before American intelligence began to wonder how one of their own could possibly afford to pay for a Jaguar and a half-million-dollar house on a government salary.

The subject brought a look of infinite satisfaction to Kryuchkov's face, a contented look, as if he had just finished a good meal and were halfway through a Cohiba.

"I think Ames behaves well," Kryuchkov said. "He is a man of principle. High politics meant a lot to him and urged him on to action."

"Really?" I said. "Wasn't it a matter of money?"

"I'm sure money played a certain role, but not the determining role," Kryuchkov said. "If you look at our special services, money was not the top priority. We had many ideological allies in the U.S. who looked at us favorably in the political sense. I am sure that at least a part of American society cannot be seen as antagonistic to Ames. I don't say the majority, but a sizable part."

I said that Americans were still debating what had been decisive in the union's collapse. Reaganites were sure that it was the pressure of Star Wars. Others had more complicated explanations. How did he see it?

"Despite the fact that the external pressures were strong, the decisive factors were domestic," he said. "I don't think there was any objective necessity to destroy the Soviet Union. The entire world is moving toward integration and we are collapsing! The main role was played by subjective factors connected to very specific people: Gorbachev, Yakovlev, and Shevardnadze, and their supporters."

"You were the head of a powerful KGB," I said. "How could you have let them dupe you? Why did you wait so long to act?"

"We were hostages of our own illusions," Kryuchkov said sadly. "You know how it is with a president: you come to him with some material, he agrees with you and tells you you're right, things are bad, he'll carry out the struggle, but then it turned out to be all lies."

It was an odd tack. Kryuchkov, who had tapped Gorbachev's phones and stuffed his memos to the general secretary with reams of disinformation, was now feigning gullibility.

"How could you have been so easily deluded?" I asked.

"It all happened because by that time we had turned into law-abiding people," Kryuchkov said. "We obeyed the law and the president, and Gorbachev had one quality: his hypocrisy was so great that it was not easy to tell the difference between truth and lies."

Kryuchkov was quick to defend some of the most notorious of all KGB operations, including the invasion of Hungary in 1956. Speaking of the same period, I asked how he now felt about the KGB's assault on dissent, the attacks on Sakharov, Solzhenitsyn, and the rest.

Kryuchkov smiled thinly. "I wouldn't want to deny anything, but in fact I had nothing to do with the struggle against dissent," said the former chairman of the KGB.

Kryuchkov seemed perfectly capable of lying with a serene sense of self-possession and righteousness. When I asked about the August 1991 coup—an assault he led with a grotesque lineup of leaders who were either incompetent or drunk or both—he simply smiled.

"There were no others to work with," he said. "I myself am a sober person. Of course, you can't resort to many 'ifs' in high politics. If you could rewind your life's tape, probably I would change some frames. . . . We didn't really want to perform a putsch. If we were real putschists I could have assumed all the power, but we had different goals. The integrity of the union was more important than anything else. We didn't carry it out to the end because there would have been blood."

At one point, I said, "Mr. Kryuchkov"—"Mr." has now become a part of the postcommunist lexicon, replacing "Comrade," and it was a treat to use it now—"Mr. Kryuchkov, isn't it a wonderful thing to live in a country where a former KGB man can publish his memoirs without any censorship?"

Kryuchkov screwed on a frown and thought awhile. He took off his glasses and rubbed his eyes.

"As for this country being free, I think we had more freedom in 1991 and before," he said. "You think America is a free country, but you can't do everything there. Some things are banned, and there are punishments. Before 1991, we didn't have any restrictive laws. The law allowed anyone to act against the state. That is banned in the States! We paid a high cost for that."

"Mr. Kryuchkov," I said, "people talk a great deal about repentance these days. I wonder if you, as a former chief of the KGB, feel compelled to repent for anything?"

This did not please him at all. "If there has to be repentance," he said, "then let everyone repent. You should repent for what you've done to the Indians. I haven't heard that from you. If you repent, we will, too. My attitude toward Stalin is clear: I condemn the repressions. I condemn the totalitarian forms of rule that Stalin developed. But Churchill was right when he talked about Stalin's historic role. He became the head of the Soviet state when there was only a plow, and he left it when the state had an atomic bomb. Stalin is far from being a simple figure. Believe me, in twenty or thirty years, no matter what we think, Stalin will be referred to as a kind of genius."

Finally, Kryuchkov had had enough. Yes, he said, he would be voting for Zyuganov. He even thought that Zyuganov would win. But when I had shut off my tape recorder, Kryuchkov and Prelin asked me to switch it back on. Be sure to tell your audience, they said, how fine Kryuchkov's memoir was, how there was a deal "in the works" with someone in Maryland to bring out an English-language edition. "I even want to write another book," Kryuchkov explained. "I wrote the memoir in prison. Now I'll work here. I think I have real potential!"

———

In 1991, Russians would sooner have believed that a spymaster would be hustling an American visitor for publicity than they would believe that in 1996 they might be facing the possibility of a return to power of the Communist Party. And yet, by December 1995, the Communist Party of the Russian Federation had won a decisive victory in elections to the State Duma. Under the leadership of Gennady Zyuganov, the communists had seized on Yeltsin's plummeting popularity and had made themselves the odds-on favorite to win the presidency. That Zyuganov was a dull and edgy personality was hardly the point. The communists were the only political party with a degree of organization and an identifiable set of myths to connect with the amorphous opposition to Yeltsin.

In the weeks leading up to the first round of elections on June 16, I visited the offices of numerous Party politicians, workers, and ideologues and found them all to be confident of victory. I began by visiting the Party's designated rabble-rouser, Viktor Anpilov, who led the radical group Workers of Russia. His rank-and-file members were old ladies who carried portraits of Stalin and nasty unemployed kids who could be counted on to hurl rocks at the police. Anpilov, who had helped stir up antigovernment violence on the streets of Moscow in 1993, worked out of an abandoned house in a muddy courtyard near the Paveletsky train station. Anpilov used to work as Party propagandist for Radio Moscow, and he was loath to abandon the old truths. Even though Zyuganov was usually "too hesitant," too soft, to be a true revolutionary, he said, the Party's "inevitable victory" would lead to a "democracy of a new type."

"If we win," he said, "it will be a great breakthrough, like October 1917. We will get rid of private property. We will end the exploitation of man against man. Look at what this so-called democracy has accomplished! Nothing! Socialism, on the other hand, gave us progress. It gave us literacy. It gave us electric power stations, an end to unemployment. It gave us buildings to live in, no one slept on the streets."

I noticed that among Anpilov's home decorations were portraits of old general secretaries and, incongruously, a map of Israel. This latter was quite odd. Anpilov, unlike other, more clever Party leaders, did not bother to hide his anti-Semitism, and his followers often carried charming signs like "Save Russia, Destroy the Yids!" What's with the map? I asked.

"Oh, it's not a Jewish map," he said, taking it down from the wall. All the place-names were written, I now noticed, in Arabic. "This is the true Palestine."

With an American visitor, however, Anpilov felt he had to go through the motions of ceremony and tolerance. "We are not anti-Semites, we are internationalists. And yet when we turn on the television we see nothing but Jewish faces on every station. This insults us, because after all we live in an international country."

And what about the Stalin portraits his followers carried?

"The people were happy under Stalin," Anpilov said. "There was bread, food to eat. The prices were low. He was one of the greatest figures in the history of the country. He gave this country its true independence. After all, Stalin refused your General Marshall when he offered us help after the war. It was us, the Soviet Union, that rebuilt the country after the war."

Zyuganov and his circle of advisers relied on Anpilov to get people on the streets for demonstrations but distanced themselves from him when it came time to talk to more mainstream voters. But Anpilov was far from alone in his views. General Valentin Varennikov had helped lead the 1991 coup but had a soft landing, winning a seat in the Duma. At a closed session of army generals in the spring of 1996, he told a collegium of officers that they should set aside any fears that Zyuganov was a mere social democrat, a pink. In fact, he told them, the Party had put out an economic recovery plan called Program Minimum for public consumption, but also planned to implement a secret Program Maximum once in power. Program Maximum, he reassured them, would certainly make any Bolshevik proud.

"I told the officers we cannot reverse history, we cannot undo what has been done by betrayers of our motherland," Varennikov told me. "We must be realists. . . . If we talk about our Program Maximum too soon, it would be too strange and utopian. But that is our aspiration, our striving for human justice. Remember, the program of the Communist Party of the Russian Federation and the Bible do not much diverge."

There were some in the Party who tried desperately to modify its image and history. The businessman Vladimir Semago ("Hi, I'm just back from my factory in Cyprus!") greeted me in his Duma office wearing an Armani tie. Semago was the Party's designated millionaire and he was friendly with the oligarchs supporting the other side, the government. He talked about having a mixed economy and a free press and various other trappings of modernity. He said the government should work like "a giant management company," more or less "just like they do it in China."

Since Semago ran the Moscow Commercial Club, the popular haven for the business elite modeled on an English gentleman's club, he was familiar with the jargon of modern times. But when it came to the Stalin question, he, too, could go only so far.

"If we leave to the side the tragedies of the Stalin period and the position of Stalin in communist ideology, we must remember that Stalin, if he had lived another five, six, seven years, would have created an even stronger Soviet Union. The portraits of Stalin you see in demonstrations really represent a form of protest. When you hear 'Beat the Jews,' that's a weakness of the national patriotic movement. These are manifestations of the temper of the times. We absorb these people into the body of the movement, but we also want to change their outlook and their tactics."

The hardest thing to capture about the Communist Party was its sullen darkness, the strangeness of some of its leaders. One afternoon during the campaign, I went to visit Aleksei Podberiozkin, a shadowy figure who used to be an instructor of young diplomats and KGB officers and now ran something called the Spiritual Heritage Society. He published a magazine that pushed the very sort of nationalist-communist mélange that Zyuganov himself had adopted. And like so many others in modern Russia, he also ran a little bank on the side.

Podberiozkin proudly (and not incorrectly) pointed out that since 1991, Yeltsin himself had gradually jettisoned a purely Western democratic outlook and taken on nationalist trappings. Certainly Yeltsin was talking (when he deigned to talk at all) more about the need for a strong state, about the glories of Russian history and power. "In fact," he said, "Mr. Yeltsin himself accepts more and more of our positions, and it becomes harder and harder for us to argue with him."

But as the conversation went on, Podberiozkin unveiled his crackpot self. By way of discussing the demographics of the electorate he knotted his brow, leaned forward across the desk, and said, "Usually, about three percent of the Russian population is crazy. But now in our troubled times, I would say it's higher—maybe seven percent are crazy."

It turned out that at the root of Zyuganov's ideology was something called the "Theory of the Noosphere," the invention in 1919 of a scientist-philosopher named Vernadsky. I am not expert enough to recount the theory either as Podberiozkin explained it to me or as Vernadsky wrote about it; suffice it to say that there is much concern about "the interrelated world."

"Vernadsky proved that we live in a nature larger than the dead one, and so on," Podberiozkin said. Or whatever.

"If all this is the case, then why," I asked gamely, "does Mr. Zyuganov tend to talk more about communism than the noosphere?"

"Of course we did not explain the noosphere to the people," he said. "We tried to use terms the people were familiar with. So we use older terms."

The neocommunists tried hard to have it both ways. They forgave themselves the persecution of religion, the better to win over a population that now saw the Russian Orthodox Church as a powerful element of the new state. They forgave themselves the purges, saying it was the Party that had suffered most of all. They forgave themselves the suppression of dissent, saying that the Party would have been even stronger had it learned the art of political debate.

One afternoon I paid a visit to Svetlana Goryacheva, the deputy speaker of the Duma and one of Zyuganov's closest allies. Before coming to Moscow, Goryacheva had been a prosecutor in the Far East. She had a high hairdo and a stern gaze. A small crucifix nestled in her bosom, and so I asked her if she was a believer.

Goryacheva fixed me with a nasty look. "I was baptized on October 4, 1993, in the White House," she said, recalling the days of the armed battle between the parliament and the Yeltsin forces. "When I saw the tanks firing and at the same time I saw priests inside with us, with their icons and crosses, I decided that this force of Russian Orthodoxy must be far greater than the forces outside. I met a priest who had turned an office in the White House into a monk's cell. I told him, 'If I am doomed to die, then I would like to die with the faith of my fathers.' I realize that the repression of the church was a terrible mistake of the Communist Party."

We talked awhile about her youth and her years in the Party. She seemed to relax, even warm to the subject.

"As for Stalin, you must know that both my grandparents on my father's side were repressed in Ukraine," she said. "They were sent to the camps—to Solovki—and they died there. They were arrested because they belonged to the sect of Old Believers. My father was an orphan by the time he was five years old. I read Solzhenitsyn in the late 1980s and my soul was filled with outrage. I won't justify these repressions. But I also remember how my father, who was born in 1918, told me when I was a girl, 'Soviet power took away a great deal from me. It took my parents from me. But I also got an education. I built a house. I started a family.' So I can't judge Stalin too strictly. These were difficult times, and it was tough to distinguish between friends and enemies."

The Party murdered her father's parents but gave him an education—and therefore, on balance, he was an ardent communist. To tell the truth, I didn't know what to say after that.

It hardly mattered what I, or any other Westerner, thought: the Communist Party was still the best-organized party in Russia, and at the beginning of the year, Zyuganov's chances looked excellent. His popularity rating was in the twenties, while Yeltsin's was at 5 or 6 percent. Meanwhile, Yeltsin's fragile health had become the visible embodiment of conditions in so much of the country.

At least as troubling was the fact that the war in Chechnya persisted and had made Yeltsin an even more insular leader than before. Moreover, his loyalty to his bodyguard, the former auto mechanic Aleksandr Korzhakov, had only intensified. Over time, Korzhakov had stayed with Yeltsin through all his trials: his firing from the Politburo in 1987, his stand against the coup in 1991, his war with the parliament in 1993. There was no vassal more loyal. Yeltsin, in turn, rewarded him, allowing this lightly educated bodyguard to give advice in high politics and to control access to the president. They were together all the time. They played tennis, took saunas, stayed up through the night talking, drinking.

"Of course, Korzhakov is not very well educated and has some odd ideas about human rights, but he was extremely loyal to Yeltsin," said one former Kremlin adviser, Galina Starovoitova. Korzhakov's address reflected his status: he lived at 4 Osennii Street in southwest Moscow, the same building that housed Yeltsin, Prime Minister Viktor Chernomyrdin, mayor of Moscow Yuri Luzhkov, and other top officials. Korzhakov was also given one of Stalin's old dachas just outside of town. The only other people who could claim a greater intimacy with Yeltsin were his wife, Naina, and his daughter, Tatyana, who played the role of personal gatekeeper. No one else could even feign to know his moods, the source of his abrupt decisions.

"Yeltsin is a black box," said Igor Malashenko, the head of Yeltsin's media campaign and the chairman of the NTV television network. "There is not a single person in this country who can pretend to know what goes on inside that head. It's like the black box in cybernetics: you can look at the inputs and the outputs, but never inside the box. Yeltsin never really shares his concerns. He is an extraordinarily closed person."

Inside the Kremlin, Korzhakov led the hard-line team that included secret police chief Mikhail Barsukov and First Deputy Prime Minister Oleg Soskovets. Together, they had prodded Yeltsin to embark on the disastrous invasion of Chechnya. Now, as 1996 began, the party of war began to encourage Yeltsin to call off the presidential elections. In fact, the only factor that seemed to prevent a summary cancellation of the elections right at the start was the president's own befogged notion of his standing in the country. When his presidential council got together at the end of February to discuss a campaign strategy, the polls were hopeless. And yet, at the meeting, he got up and said that surely his rating was the highest of any politician's.

"It was crazy," said Emil Pain, one of Yeltsin's more moderate advisers. "We all sat there in silence. We were shocked, wondering, where did he get this idea? A few tried to suggest, very gently, that maybe the numbers were not so high—but only gently."

At the beginning of the year, Yeltsin had appointed Oleg Soskovets to run the campaign. He and Korzhakov, in turn, invited a number of their friends in the media and the emerging business world for meetings. They even invited a team of American consultants who had worked for Pete Wilson when the California governor made his dismal run for the presidency. Boris Berezovsky, the head of a vast conglomerate of car dealerships, media outlets, banking concerns, and other companies, was one of the richest men in the country and had met Korzhakov and other members of the presidential entourage when he was invited to join one of Yeltsin's pet projects, the presidential tennis club. Berezovsky, who operated out of a mansion that once belonged to the Smirnoff vodka family, told me that he had joined the campaign team thinking that he would be contributing to a real election.

"But after two or three meetings in January, I could see that these meetings were not at all constructive," he told me. "These were very primitive people, ministers of metallurgy and the like, absolutely *Homo sovieticus*. They just did not understand the media or elections. I said this to Soskovets, but he said, 'Don't worry, be quiet, everything will be fine.' But after some time, I realized that there were two games going on at once. One was to guide the elections. The other was to cancel them and hold on to power through force. Okay, I said to myself. This is not my game. We need to use only legal means, otherwise we will have a president who is nothing more than a marionette."

In January, a wide range of Russians went to the World Economic Forum held every year at a ski resort in Davos, Switzerland. Zyuganov tried to win over Western businesspeople by sounding less like a Soviet communist and more like a social democrat. Some people even believed him. Elsewhere in Davos, Berezovsky met privately with several Russian businessmen, including Vladimir Gusinsky, who had returned from his exile in England to run MOST Bank and the independent television station NTV from Moscow again, and Anatoly Chubais, the former head of Yeltsin's privatization program. Berezovsky and Gusinsky had despised each other; they had bid on the same properties, pursued the same capital. There were even rumors printed in the press that Berezovsky had considered having Gusinsky murdered. But now their interests coincided. Without Yeltsin in office, they would no doubt lose everything, not least their media properties; the communists would set up their own banks, their own elites.

"We talked and decided to work together," Gusinsky told me. "There was no choice."

The group decided to form a new campaign team, and when they got back to Moscow they asked for a private meeting with Yeltsin at the Kremlin. Yeltsin was certainly not prepared to jettison Soskovets and Korzhakov, but he agreed, in effect, to establish a parallel campaign team, which would work just one floor below Korzhakov's crew in the President Hotel. The new team, led by Chubais, promised millions in capital, control of television, and media sophistication. Yeltsin was already growing displeased with Soskovets, who had almost botched the campaign to gather one million signatures to get Yeltsin on the ballot—a legal requirement.

From the start, the two teams fought and conspired against each other. Korzhakov, for example, would approach various politicians and try to prove to them that people within the campaign—on the other team—were out to betray Boris Nikolayevich. "When I met with Korzhakov he tried to show me how his opponents were trying to undermine or sabotage Yeltsin," said Galina Starovoitova. "Here is one tiny detail. Yeltsin was going to visit a military plant called Akhtuba. In his speech there, Yeltsin was supposed to have said something to the effect that the conversion of military factories to nonmilitary production is not like collectivization in the twenties, it's a long and serious process. As written, the speech said, according to Korzhakov, 'Before you were producing missiles, now you are making useful consumer products, like *phallo-imitators*' "—

commonly known in the West as dildos. "Korzhakov showed me the paper. And we were both shocked! In his view, this was proof that he had to control the rest of the campaign. Yeltsin, of course, never read this passage, because, Korzhakov claimed, it was cut just in time.

"Korzhakov also told me, 'I worry about Clinton's influence on Boris Nikolayevich. He's convinced him that we should have elections.' Korzhakov felt that elections were too risky, that elections are just a Western idea and that 'democracy could be preserved without them.' It's not as if Korzhakov is a devil. He is out to save himself and his boss and he thinks, 'Why risk everything just to have some people put pieces of paper into something called a ballot box?' "

The Korzhakov team tried to get Yeltsin to see that he was going to lose, that he could even lose to the communists in the first round of voting on June 16. Cancellation of the election would bring disapproval from the West and from liberal circles in Moscow, they said, but it would be a greater sin to give up power to the communists. In the meantime, Korzhakov, Soskovets, and other figures in the secret services wrote up possible scenarios for cancellation, various pretexts and decrees. They thought about using the war in Chechnya as an excuse, or possibly terrorism in Moscow or a reunification with tiny Belarus.

In early March, Yeltsin himself started to lean in the direction of canceling the election. He instructed Korzhakov to look more deeply into how it could be done. Korzhakov gladly complied.

On Friday, March 15, Korzhakov and his team identified what they thought might be the perfect excuse. The communists and nationalists in the Duma pushed through a resolution denouncing the agreement in December 1991 among Yeltsin and the leaders of Ukraine and Belarus to dissolve the Soviet Union. Korzhakov and Soskovets tried to convince Yeltsin that the resolution could well be a step toward even greater confrontation—even, in the case of a loss at the polls, arrest and prosecution.

"They were pressuring him every single day," said Berezovsky. "And so on March 16, Yeltsin decided he would take a final decision."

Yeltsin came to Moscow in the early morning of the 16th from his dacha. He was leaning toward the Korzhakov option. One of Yeltsin's aides had already drafted a series of *ukazi,* or decrees, on the dissolution of parliament, the banning of the Communist Party, and the cancellation of the June 16 elections. The paperwork, at least, for what was called inside the Kremlin the *silovoi variant*—the force variation—was in place. Democracy would end with the stroke of Yeltsin's pen.

Korzhakov's men also did not want to repeat the tactical mistake of 1993, when members of the legislature found out in advance that the parliament was about to be dissolved and holed up inside the building—a move that led to a violent showdown. According to sources in various opposition parties and inside Yeltsin's own campaign, troops used the pretense of a bomb threat to seal off the Duma building on Saturday, March 16, and searched the office of Valentin Kuptsov, one of the leaders of the Communist Party in the Duma. Two armored personnel carriers parked outside the building.

As these preparatory maneuvers began, Yeltsin held a series of one-on-one meetings to discuss the force variation. He immediately met with resistance. Prime Minister Chernomyrdin told Yeltsin he was against the plan, a senior diplomat told me, "but in a shrugging sort of way." Chubais made the same point, though more vigorously. The truly decisive meeting, however, was with the minister of internal affairs, Anatoly Kulikov. A career police chief, Kulikov had been brought in to clean up the ministry after it had badly botched the hostage rescue attempt in 1995 near the Chechen border in the town of Budyonnovsk. Yeltsin respected Kulikov as an honest broker and a hard-liner with ties to the security services, and so when Kulikov told the president that he could not guarantee the loyalty of his troops in such an action, that it could lead to terrible bloodshed in the streets of Moscow, Yeltsin was taken aback, to say the least.

Yeltsin balked more out of a sense of politics than ethics. For his entire life, he had been steeped in the methods and tactics and habits of the Communist Party; only in 1989 did he join ranks with liberal intellectuals in the democratic opposition. His allegiance to democratic method, as former deputy prime minister Gennady Burbulis reminded me, was "purely situational."

Over the past few years, Yeltsin had abandoned Western-leaning men like his former foreign minister, Andrei Kozyrev, and his former economic adviser, Yegor Gaidar. Even the American administration had been of little help. Top-level advisers told me, with great frustration, that Bill Clinton seemed ready at all times to forgive Yeltsin anything, including showing up to a summit meeting with an obvious hangover. The Russian president, they said, had lost respect for Clinton and felt he could do anything and say anything and never lose support from Washington.

"But if there is one factor that is still capable of pushing Yeltsin in the right direction," Andrei Kozyrev told me, "it's history itself. He desperately wants to be thought of as a force for good in history."

And so, for reasons of both fear and history, Yeltsin made his decision. He told Korzhakov that he would go forward with the presidential elections. The team led by Chubais would take the lead role in the campaign. The APCs and troops retreated from the Duma. Deputies arrived for work on Monday the 17th as usual.

Until the crisis was over, the banker Vladimir Gusinsky said, "no one slept." In fact, the crisis was not over at all.

Having decided to run, Yeltsin now had to find a way to win. Zyuganov, the communist, was still leading in the polls. A potential "third force," led by the liberal economist Grigory Yavlinsky and the popular army general Aleksandr Lebed, threatened to drain off voters who were in favor of reform but had grown disgusted with the ills of the post-Soviet era.

To get his campaign moving, Yeltsin established an election council of fourteen members drawn from both the warring teams. Like a traditional Politburo, the council met privately in Yeltsin's new Kremlin office, but it soon became apparent that the council was unworkable. Korzhakov's people were not going to work easily with Chubais's people, and vice versa.

"In reality, for two months, there was not a single meeting," said Igor Malashenko, the former Party bureaucrat who had become Yeltsin's chief image-maker. "When we did have these meetings, there was always criticism of the mass media, that the media were doing a lot of terrible things to the image of Boris Yeltsin, talking about the Chechen war, blah, blah, blah. It was always Barsukov or Korzhakov or Soskovets. So then there was a decision that I should present a report on how I see the mass media and how we can get the media to cover Yeltsin in a more positive way and bring him toward a victory. Korzhakov and Barsukov were appointed as my official opponents in the discussion. I made a brief presentation, saying we had to make news every day so that these things would be covered by the press. That way, if we made the right sort of news we'd get the right sort of coverage and the right perception of Yeltsin. Very primitive. I talked about advertising strategy, images, slogans. Then Korzhakov made a presentation. He was reading from a paper, of course. On his own, he can talk only in brief sentences. He criticized television, especially NTV, and said it was undermining the president. He said that we, the media, were enemies of Boris Yeltsin and trying to get him defeated. Well, at that point, I relaxed. I knew it wouldn't be a discussion. It was just a matter of black and white, and if Yeltsin was ready to agree that this piece of white paper is black, well, then what could I say? But actually Yeltsin got mad at Korzhakov and attacked him, saying that all he was saying was a bunch of nonsense and he doesn't understand the media, that Korzhakov wanted to make another Brezhnev out of him."

Yeltsin had already made one important concession to the campaign. He had stopped drinking. Now the trick was to get him to appear in public, to create at least the image of vigor. The team of American advisers working secretly for Yeltsin was naive in many ways, but they may have earned their pay when they wrote memos that were forwarded to Yeltsin urging him to get out of the Kremlin and run a campaign in which he showed contrition for his mistakes and reminded voters of the ills of communist rule. Malashenko and others on his team agreed and tried to convince Yeltsin that he would have to travel widely in the provinces, create a "story of the day" strategy straight out of the Michael Deaver–Ronald Reagan handbook. So far, his travels had produced only the wrong sort of imagery.

"We discussed a trip that Yeltsin had taken to Krasnodar, which had been a real disaster," Malashenko said. "The trip had been managed by the others and it was just like an old-fashioned tour of the provinces by a general secretary of the Communist Party—no one too close, frozen, artificial smiles on all the faces of the local big shots. The pictures were absolutely terrible. So afterward, Chubais and I came to Yeltsin and showed him pictures of the trip. Then we showed him pictures of himself in 1991, surrounded by the crowds, practically swimming in them, a man of the people. Yeltsin looked at these pictures and immediately grasped the problem. After that the campaign started to roll."

The Yeltsin campaign gave new meaning to the phrase "the advantages of incumbency." Those of delicate sensibility might even say that his team, with the help of friendly media, was determined to win at any cost. While Zyuganov traveled on commercial flights with a small team of aides, Yeltsin flew in the presidential jet, cosseted from the rigors of Aeroflot. While Zyuganov depended mainly on door-to-door campaigning and a series of clumsy old-fashioned television ads, Yeltsin was guaranteed constant and flattering attention on the networks (which were owned by the men supporting him) and in the newspapers (which quite reasonably feared being shut down or censored under a new and vengeful communist regime). The vast majority of journalists did not need any extra incentive to report favorably on Yeltsin. But some operatives working at arm's length from the campaign distributed money to the few journalists who were not already on board for love. The bribes ranged from thousands of dollars for a favorable report on television to a pittance for complimentary notice in a regional newspaper.

Taking thirty-three trips in four months, Yeltsin went from town to town acting like a czarist-era governor, dispensing every sort of favor, from a cultural center to Muslims in Yaroslavl to a telephone for an old woman who had been on a waiting list for eight years; from tax breaks for ailing industries to billions of rubles in back pay to miners and workers. To capture the youth vote, rock stars and entertainers were sent cross-country putting on pro-Yeltsin concerts, a tour that culminated in a concert that drew over a hundred thousand people to Red Square. Most important of all, Yeltsin's financial backers, including Inkombank, began pouring money into the Lebed campaign, because they thought that Lebed, with his image of blunt honesty and strength, could draw off voters from both Zyuganov and the nationalist fanatic Vladimir Zhirinovsky; Lebed, they guessed, might then deliver those votes in a second round of voting in July. And if that was not enough, some Yeltsin aides, especially in Korzhakov's orbit, even spoke rather openly of falsifying the results if necessary.

In the end, economists estimated that Yeltsin's various campaign-related expenses and promises would cost the state billions of dollars, making a farce of his commitment to containing budget deficits and keeping within the guidelines set by the International Monetary Fund.

Zyuganov and his advisers were, not surprisingly, enraged. Anatoly Lukyanov, who had made his way back into the parliament despite his involvement in the 1991 coup attempt, told me, "Whitewater made a big splash in your country, but I must tell you that the corruption in these elections, call it Yeltsin-gate, dwarfs anything you have imagined. Imagine if your president were to banish Bob Dole from the airwaves and take funds from the state budget for his campaign, and all the rest. What would be the response?"

The response among the Yeltsin backers was unabashed pride. Plutocrats like Berezovsky and Gusinsky and journalists for television and newspapers all insisted that the election was unlike anything in the West. Russia was faced with a stark choice between two social systems: a transitional system of state capitalism and "half democracy" that held out promise for the future and a system of communism that, for all of Zyuganov's promises, meant a return to a familiar and even brutal past. That Igor Malashenko ran both NTV and the Yeltsin ad campaign, for example, shocked most Westerners. Dan Quayle, on a visit to Moscow, said it was the equivalent of having Dan Rather run an American presidential campaign. Yeltsin's supporters dismissed such rhetoric as self-righteous cant.

"Look, there were two ways to influence the electorate," said Leonid Radzikhovsky, a journalist who wrote speeches for Lebed and tried to "liberalize" the general's image. "There was the way of force and there was the way Malashenko did it. In essence, Malashenko's way saved hundreds of lives that might have been lost to the tanks and guns that would have been used in the cancellation of elections and the rise of presidential rule. Yeltsin had alternatives before him. It's true, in a truly fair election, he might have lost. He violated various rules in the end. So call it the softer variant of what might have been. But Yeltsin plays cards only when he knows he can win. He always wants a fifth ace up his sleeve. Otherwise he'll take out the Smith & Wesson and start firing. In the election, Malashenko played the role of the fifth ace. Let's at least praise Malashenko for that."

While the more visible part of the campaign reaped its rewards—Yeltsin's ratings were pulling even with Zyuganov everywhere but in the southern farming and industrial cities known as the Red Belt—Korzhakov's troops had not shut down their operations. Korzhakov started to shift his attention to gaining credit and power after the battle was over. He was determined to make sure that Yeltsin would not forget his old allies in the security forces, that he would not surround himself once more with outsiders and liberals like Chubais and Malashenko. "There was still an atmosphere of hate among the president's assistants," said one Kremlin aide.

It is usually an advantage in a political campaign when you can accuse your opponent's party of, among other things, the murder of innocents. And so, in the last days before June 16, Yeltsin flooded the airwaves with the ultimate in "negative" campaign propaganda. Television showed a series of films meant to fuel an anticommunist fever: there were documentaries about collectivization and the purges and films like Nikita Mikhailkov's anti-Stalinist allegory *Burnt by the Sun,* which won an Oscar in 1995. Nor could Yeltsin's ads be accused of being "off-message." One showed black-and-white footage of Stalin voting at a Communist Party ballot in the forties; in case anyone missed the point, the narrator asked whether Russians wanted to return to this sort of "democracy" in the near future.

In the meantime, Korzhakov's people seemed to keep up their dark game. In early May, Korzhakov had told a British newspaper that the elections should be called off—a suggestion that was quickly slapped down in public by Yeltsin himself. There were also rumors that Korzhakov was in contact with the Communist Party hierarchy; he was trying to attract support from the "moderates" with the promise that both sides would jettison their radicals—democratic liberals and orthodox communists alike. More ominously, in early June, a bomb exploded in a subway station in southern Moscow, killing four people. A candidate for deputy mayor of Moscow was nearly killed in an assassination attempt. There was no official blame assigned, no damning evidence, but many suspected Korzhakov.

To win in this first round, one of the ten candidates would have to score a majority. None of the polls suggested that anyone would do that well, but Yeltsin said on television that he expected to win reelection on the first try. His advisers discovered, to their astonishment, that he really meant it. What was more troubling was that Yeltsin showed no inclination toward an orderly transfer of power should he lose. "I will not allow the communists into power," he said.

On election day, I went to Yeltsin's campaign headquarters and met there with Sergei Karaganov, a foreign policy expert on Yeltsin's presidential council. There were computers and wire machines all around, and the very early information coming in from the Far East, from places like Vladivostok and Khabarovsk, was not encouraging.

Karaganov frowned as he scanned a computer screen. Yeltsin, he said with a long sigh, was far from being an ideal candidate for reelection. "He carries with him the baggage of his mistakes," he said. "He's not a candidate for whom people would just love to vote. They vote for him more with the mind than with the heart, if they vote for him at all. His main negative is the suffering the whole society has had to endure under transformation. If he wins, it will be one of the rare moments in history when someone who leads a revolution is not swept away by it."

"And if he loses?" I asked. "Would he pack his bags and greet the moving vans at the Kremlin gates?"

"If Yeltsin loses, he will not give power to the communists," Karaganov said. "He has said that more than once."

"I'm sorry. You said . . ."

"I would say that he could give up power, but not to communists."

This was getting more cryptic and chilling by the moment. Russian power still depended mightily on the politics of its "force structures"— the army, the KGB, the police—and would go on doing so until it went through a peaceful and uneventful experience of transition.

———

At about nine that night, I went with Masha Lipman and her husband, the historian Sergei Ivanov, to the apartment of their close friends Maria Volkenshtein and Igor Primakov. Maria ran a polling and market research company called Validata, and in recent months she had been doing some polling about the political situation. More than anyone else I knew, she had traveled all over the country, through the depressed cities of the Red Belt in the south and to the more prosperous cities in Siberia and the Urals. As well as anyone she knew just how disenchanted Russians had grown with Yeltsin. But she also discovered that in the eyes of most Russians Zyuganov was no savior, that the memory of the communist past, the empty shelves of the eighties as much as the purges of the thirties, was still vivid.

"If it's a matter of slogans, Yeltsin will win because of 'Forward, Not Backward' and the communists will win because of 'Let's Be Great Again,' " she said. The exit polls showed Yeltsin slightly ahead of the ten-man field, but Maria had no confidence at all that he would win.

As we watched the various election-night specials on television and waited for the first returns to be announced at eleven, we all ate greedily. All except Maria. "I'm too nervous," she said.

We tuned in to NTV. The anchor, Yevgeny Kiselyov, an unabashed Yeltsin supporter, did not look at all well. His expression hinted at defeat. The people at NTV undoubtedly knew some of the voting trends already.

But at eleven exactly, the polls closed and Kiselyov could announce the first returns. He seemed relieved, though he spared us the indignity of a smile. Yeltsin was running four points or so ahead of Zyuganov. General Aleksandr Lebed was making an extraordinary showing at about 15 percent. Grigory Yavlinsky had won enough liberal votes to place fourth, and Zhirinovsky was fifth. The rest of the field were marginalia. Among the marginalia was the most important historical figure of the postwar era, Mikhail Gorbachev. By the time the night was through, he would have a grand total of one-half of 1 percent, only a pinch more than a former Olympic weightlifter, Yuri Vlasov, and an oddball businessman, Vladimir Brintsalov. As much as Gorbachev was hated, one wondered why Gorbachev could not surge past the likes of Brintsalov on name recognition alone. Brintsalov was known mainly because of his young and pretty wife. (On television, Mrs. Brintsalov volunteered that her husband gave her $26,000 every time they had sex; on another show, she turned her back to the camera and pulled down her pants, revealing a spandexed bottom. Gorbachev may have ended the Cold War and ended decades of repression, but he never did that.)

At about two-thirty in the morning, Maria finally got out of her chair and piled some food on a plate. She could eat now with confidence. There would be a runoff between Yeltsin and Zyuganov in July, and there were already signs that both Lebed and Yavlinksy would, in one way or another, back Yeltsin.

A little while later, NTV switched from its election coverage to an episode of its hilarious political puppet show, *Kukly*. The episode featured all the presidential candidates aboard a luxurious boat floating down the Moscow River. Yeltsin, of course, was a bear, Zhirinovsky a nut, Yavlinsky a boyish prig, Zyuganov an unsophisticated bore. But it was Gorbachev who got the most bruising treatment; he was portrayed as a pathetic *boltun,* a chatterbox who talks on and on. At one point, Gorbachev despairs of finding someone to talk to and he takes out a cellular phone and calls a local 900 number, a sex line.

"No one will listen to me," he said sadly into the phone. There is obviously a sex worker at the other end of the line.

After a long soliloquy, he says, "I still have great potential."

But even the sex worker, it seems, is barely listening.

"Stop moaning," Gorbachev says.

The next day, the real Gorbachev gave a press conference. About one hundred reporters were there at the start. Gorbachev declared that he was "not discouraged" by his vote count. "I felt that in all these dramatic events I have the chance to continue in my efforts, and I will do this," he went on. In fact, he went on for two hours. By the end of the session only a handful of reporters remained.

The real morning-after story was not Gorbachev or Zyuganov or even Yeltsin—it was General Lebed. Until 1996, Russian liberals despaired of Lebed's popularity and worried that he would try to become a Russian Pinochet. But now many of those same liberals spoke highly of Lebed because he seemed honest and was willing, at least occasionally, to mouth positive slogans about the market economy.

After a series of meetings at the Kremlin, Yeltsin made a dual announcement: he was appointing Lebed head of his Security Council—the *über* council responsible for the military, police, and secret services—

and, even more shocking, he was firing his longtime defense minister, Pavel Grachev. Grachev was almost comically unpopular in the country. His entourage was famously corrupt—so much so that he was known in the press as "Pasha Mercedes." Although Grachev had promised to end the Chechen conflict in "two hours," the army's inept prosecution of the war had led to thousands of deaths. Grachev had carried out Yeltsin's orders during the October 1993 crisis, but only after hours of hesitation and double-dealing. He had ingratiated himself with the president, but now Yeltsin could keep him no longer. What was more, Lebed despised Grachev. The price of his participation in the Yeltsin government was his rival's head.

Just hours after Lebed was appointed, he went on television and declared that he had uncovered and quashed a potential putsch among the generals loyal to Grachev. Lebed said that on June 18, between 9:00 and 10:00 A.M., in a lounge in the Defense Ministry, five generals and some other officials had talked about putting pressure on Yeltsin to not fire Grachev. Lebed said he went to the general staff officers and told them not to take any orders from the former minister, and then sent a telegram to the Moscow military garrisons instructing them to refuse any orders from Grachev. He also visited a garrison of paratroopers near the capital and told them, "You have only one commander in chief."

Accurate or not, Lebed's voice was a like a distinct horn in the political fog. Yeltsin would have to get used to the sound of it. "Lebed's voice is worth two or three battalions," said Leonid Radzikhovsky, his speechwriter during the campaign. "All he has to do is roar and people will obey." In fact, Lebed's swagger was reminiscent of his new partner. Even in civilian clothes he walked as if to battle, and to complete the picture he smoked cigarettes from a holder worthy of a Victorian duke. "To me he looks not like Augusto Pinochet but like a nice hooligan from the old neighborhood, like Yeltsin in 1988 or 1989 in fact, before Yeltsin was spoiled by civilization," Radzikhovsky said. "This was the beloved Yeltsin who was always showing his fist. Alas, Yeltsin developed a love for vodka and the bourgeois game of tennis. He became a czar and a sybarite."

The best expression of Lebed's character was his autobiography, *I Pity Our Great Power,* a lament for his country's lost honor and his own hard times. Lebed provided tales of a modest, even brutal, childhood, of military derring-do, of injuries and wounds, of humiliation and sweet revenge. In excruciating detail he described how he broke his clavicle in boyhood and then had to have it rebroken after a botched operation; how he had his face smashed with an iron bar by a vengeful soccer opponent; how he broke his tailbone in a parachuting accident; how he had to have a painful sinus operation, the mere memory of which evokes the smell "of burning meat." Lebed also loved to talk about honor and its protection: once he discovered that some soldiers were brutally hazing recruits, and so he called together the offending dozen and, one by one, slugged them, breaking twelve jaws in all. Or so he said.

Lebed's military biography was a veritable history of Soviet adventure and disaster. A paratroop commander in Afghanistan, he took part in the Soviet crackdown on nationalist dissent in Azerbaijan in 1990. During the August coup, he led troops into Moscow only to end up defending Yeltsin; Lebed admitted later, however, that he barely knew what was going on during those three tense days and had to verify his orders from a phone booth. He became a kind of nationalist hero beginning in 1992 when he led the Fourteenth Army in the Russian province of Trans-Dniestria inside Moldova. Lebed had orders to keep a neutral presence, but he decided on his own to use military force to defend the local Russians against Moldovan troops. Central command in Moscow kept imploring him to withdraw to Russian territory. He refused. Lebed humiliated the defense minister, Pavel Grachev, by sending cables to Moscow telling him, in effect, to stay out of the business of the Fourteenth Army. When the American UN representative Madeleine Albright said that Washington was concerned about the Moldovan operation, Lebed responded by saying that no "third party" had a right to "butt into" his business. "It's time all those uninvited advisers got a boot in the behind," he said.

Time and again, Lebed used his gift for rhetoric to attract political attention. A stream of journalists, Russian and foreign, came to his office in Tiraspol to hear him dispense his foghorn quips. From behind his desk, and with a sour expression reminiscent of Lurch the Butler in *The Addams Family*, Lebed spoke up for the humiliated Russian military, cracked wise about corruption among the top brass in Moscow, and expressed his admiration for Pinochet. Lebed said that Pinochet had been able to revive the Chilean economy while killing "no more than three thousand people." In Russia, he added helpfully, "sometimes more people get killed and no one is held responsible. Pinochet found a way to transfer power legitimately to a civilian government and now the country is stable and flourishing." Later, under the refining pressures of the campaign, Lebed said he actually preferred de Gaulle as a role model.

In 1995, Lebed ended his war with the Kremlin and retired from active duty. He ran for parliament in December 1995 as the cochairman of a small party called the Congress of Russian Communities, or KRO. Lebed himself won a single-mandate seat in the Duma, but the party won only 4 percent of the vote and failed to secure a party slate in the legislature.

The results indicated that Lebed's chances for the presidency were almost nil. But he ran anyway. Although he was fond of lobbing verbal grenades at the Kremlin, he hired a pro-government member of parliament, Aleksei Golovkov, to help run his campaign. Golovkov, in turn, helped refashion Lebed. He jettisoned some Soviet-style economic advisers and installed one Vitaly Naishul, an economist of the Chicago School. The imagery of the campaign also changed. Suddenly, Lebed had a new suit, a new haircut, new scripted one-liners, and a political future. When the history of the Russian transition is written, it will describe how Vladimir Zhirinovsky, playing the clown in the early nineties, introduced nationalist sentiment to politics and how Lebed, a far more serious figure, went on from there.

"Lebed stole my act and he stole my votes," Zhirinovsky complained to me. "I should take him to court."

The Yeltsin forces saw that development ahead of time and cut a deal with Lebed. Sources in both the Yeltsin and Lebed campaigns said that money from the Yeltsin side began streaming to Lebed as early as March—all with the clear understanding that the general would eventually get a high-level job in exchange for a few kind and supportive words. "The idea was to put Lebed on track, and it was understood that this would be at the expense of Zhirinovsky," Radzikhovsky said. "If Lebed took these votes, they would not turn back so easily to Zyuganov. Lebed, after all, was talking, in his own style, about democracy and the market. Maybe, we thought, the people could somehow get used to these words in the second round and not return to Zyuganov. So Lebed had his game and we had our game. Our interests coincided."

After Lebed was installed as security adviser on June 17, however, he lost control of his rhetoric. With Yeltsin now exhausted from his travels, obviously ill, and mainly out of sight, everyone focused on Lebed and could not help but see how he felt compelled to vent on everything from the presence of foreign missionaries in Russia ("mold and scum") to the influence of Western pop culture on Russian television ("sexual trash"). He managed to insult Mormons, though no one I have ever met in Russia has ever met a Mormon. His standard-issue anti-Semitism was also plain enough. At one meeting, a Cossack got up from his seat rather shyly and started to ask a question. Lebed interrupted, saying, "You call yourself a Cossack, but you talk like a Jew." Eventually, Lebed apologized for all his remarks, though it was becoming clearer that a loose cannon had been rolled onto the political stage.

"Lebed is atrociously educated. He is unimaginably stupid," said Sergei Kovalyov, Yeltsin's former aide on human rights. "The whole idea of a Yeltsin-Lebed team makes me extremely nervous."

Finally, Lebed said he would not be doing any campaigning for Yeltsin. After all, he had already said he didn't really care for the president, and what was more, he said, "Do I even remotely resemble an entertainer to you?"

The election rules called for a two-week interregnum between the first and second rounds of voting, and so with the balloting set for July 3, I went off for a couple of days to St. Petersburg to see friends and go to the annual Stars of the White Nights music festival. The conductor of the Kirov Opera, Valery Gergiyev, is probably the most significant figure in Russian music who has not left the country, and he was premiering a new production of Shostakovich's opera *Lady Macbeth of the Mtsensk District*.

Even the flight up to St. Petersburg was instructive. Aeroflot, an airline once known for such touches as straphangers in the aisle and green chicken for lunch, now has business class on some flights. Up front, the clientele was roughly that of a Moscow casino. The fellow next to me looked like an agent of obscure commerce, and while we waited on the tarmac in Moscow he spent the entire time barking into a cellular telephone. Something about "units." While we were up in the air, he drank a half-dozen vodkas and napped fitfully. When we touched down at Pulkovo Airport, he stirred to life, snapped open his phone again, and began screaming above the engine whine: "Misha! You amazing fuck! I'm already here! Yes, in Peter! Send the limo!"

Compared to Moscow, which is far and away Russia's richest city, St. Petersburg seemed to be in a funk. The shelves in the stores were all full, of course, but the mayor, Anatoly Sobchak, did not seem capable of paving the roads or cleaning the city in quite the startling way his Moscow counterpart, Yuri Luzhkov, had. Sobchak, for his part, was licking his wounds in Europe; just a few days before, he had been voted out of office. The news elsewhere in town was not at all unusual. A local mobster, Vladislav "the Brick" Kirpichev, had been shot to death while drinking a glass of wine in the Joy Restaurant on the Griboyedov Canal. Kirpichev probably thought he was sitting pretty; not long before, he had been on trial with other members of the Malyshev gang for fifty-two crimes, but they were all released after all sixty-three witnesses amazingly decided to retract their testimony to the police. "The Brick" was fifty-nine and was survived by his twenty-five-year-old wife. Elsewhere in town, a huge cast and crew were shooting a remake of *Anna Karenina*. And at a meeting with the Union of Scientists, Aleksandr Solzhenitsyn made his first appearance in St. Petersburg since his return from exile. He told the scholars assembled there that he was, as usual, fed up. In the election he would mark the box designated "none of the above."

With the elections coming, the timing of Gergiyev's production of *Lady Macbeth of the Mtsensk District* was astonishing. "I am terrified of a communist return," the music critic Lev Ginzburg told me, "and the fate of this opera tells you a little bit about why." Stalin first saw *Lady Macbeth* in January 1936 and left the theater disgusted; the libretto is filled with sexual intrigue, and the music confused the dictator. A few days later, at Stalin's order, of course, *Pravda* denounced Shostakovich in an article headlined "Chaos Instead of Music": "From the first moment, the listener is shocked by a deliberately dissonant, confused stream of sound. Fragments of melody and embryonic phrases appear, only to disappear again in the din, the grinding, and the screaming. . . ."

I took my seat in the orchestra of the Mariinsky Theater. Gergiyev was almost always late in starting his performances, and I had a chance to talk with a doctor who was sitting next to me. She had been going to the Mariinsky for so long she remembered seeing Mikhail Baryshnikov dance here—"Oh, God knows how many years ago." She told me that the previous head of the theater had been bounced for taking bribes, but that Gergiyev was keeping the place alive with a stream of new productions of operas from Tchaikovsky, Rimsky-Korsakov, and Shostakovich. She turned in her seat and pointed out that one of the restorations in the Mariinsky was the placing of a czarist-era crown over the royal box. "But only as decoration!" she was quick to say. "We aren't monarchists here. We're just interested in our own past."

The curtain went up. The opera began.

On the night of June 19, in Moscow, two senior aides in the Yeltsin campaign walked down a path from the White House. They headed toward a gate, where the cars and drivers awaited them. The two aides, Sergei Lisovsky and Arkady Yevstafiev, were members of the campaign team close to Anatoly Chubais.

Both men knew well that Korzhakov was not finished with his intrigues. Just the day before, Boris Fyodorov, the former head of the National Sports Fund, had been parked outside Moscow State University with a female companion at around midnight. A man leaned through the window, drew a 9mm Luger, and shot Fyodorov in the stomach. When the pistol jammed, the gunman brought out a knife and stabbed Fyodorov four times in the chest. In May, Fyodorov had been arrested on drug possession charges and replaced at the fund by a KGB colonel, a crony of Korzhakov's. The sports fund was an immense boondoggle; thanks to a decree issued by Yeltsin, it was allowed to import cigarettes and liquor tariff-free, an arrangement that cost the state over $200 million per month in lost tax revenue. Of course, no one knew for sure who had attacked Fyodorov or if Korzhakov had anything to do with it, but the atmosphere of the election had darkened once more.

In any event, before the two aides, Lisovsky and Yevstafiev, could get through the gate, they were arrested by members of Korzhakov's presidential security service. According to Lisovsky, the guards "produced" a box filled with American currency, and the two men were charged with trying to sneak half a million dollars out of a government building without proper documents. They were brought back into the White House and subjected to an eleven-hour interrogation. Lisovsky, a wealthy advertising magnate, had an extremely dicey reputation. Even some of his closest colleagues did not trust him. And few doubted that there was a lot of money in the White House offices. "People would believe anything about him," Malashenko said. "That's why he was an excellent target for a frame-up."

Meanwhile, at a business club owned by Boris Berezovsky, key members of the Yeltsin campaign team and some leading business magnates were talking strategy. At about nine, Chubais got a call on his mobile phone, and as he listened he paced around a long table, a stricken look on his face. The others, including Igor Malashenko, Berezovsky, and Vladimir Gusinsky, watched him intently. Then the others began to get calls on their cell phones. The message everywhere was the same: Lisovsky and Yevstafiev—the Rosencrantz and Guildenstern of the drama—had been arrested.

"It was clear that a showdown of some kind had begun," Malashenko told me later. "Within twenty-four hours, someone would be gone, either Chubais or Barsukov and Korzhakov. It was a clear-cut situation."

Malashenko traded information with his colleagues in television; as a result, bulletins began popping up on the air. The group failed to get through to Yeltsin himself, but they did get through to someone almost as crucial: Yeltsin's daughter, Tatyana. Tatyana had played a crucial role in the campaign; it was Tatyana who handled the data churned out by the American consultants, and it was Tatyana who mediated between the two Russian factions and had constant access to her father. She came to the club and promised to arrange a meeting first thing in the morning between the president and Chubais.

"We realized on the night of the 19th that even if Yeltsin were to win we wouldn't be able to build a normal country if Korzhakov, Barsukov, and Soskovets kept their posts," Berezovsky said. "If they were to stay, we'd have to leave the country."

Gusinsky was even more nervous and at least as self-dramatic. "We waited to be arrested or thought, 'Maybe they'll just kill us,' " he said.

"We had no illusions. I called my wife at our house in Spain and said, 'Don't have any illusions.' She was furious. I can hardly repeat what she said. She said she'd come to Moscow and kill everyone."

Sometime just after midnight, Chubais called General Trofimov, a deputy to Barsukov and the head of the Moscow secret services, to get more information. In fact, the only hard information was coming from television. By about two-thirty, Chubais reached Barsukov himself. Barsukov claimed he was "not very aware" of what was going on but asked that Chubais come to his office early the next morning. Chubais was incensed.

"Look, I am not your subordinate and I want to warn you," he said. "If something happens to Yevstafiev, you are going to pay for it."

At the White House, meanwhile, the interrogators had been demanding that the two detainees cough up compromising "evidence" aimed against Chubais and/or the prime minister, Chernomyrdin. (Korzhakov despised Chernomyrdin and hoped to have him replaced after the election with his own ally, Soskovets.)

"Boris Yeltsin is going to win anyway," one interrogator barked at Yevstafiev, "but this victory is going to be brought to him by real patriots, not guys like you."

But with the airwaves now flooded with nervous news bulletins, the interrogators backed off. They started trying to convince their two detainees that they would soon be released and when they were, please, don't make too much out of it. According to Malashenko, "They were saying, 'Oh, everything is fine, we think you're also not interested in too much media attention. Let's forget the whole thing.' They were suddenly obsessed with one thing: media coverage. And they realized it could blow up in their faces."

Lisovsky and Yevstafiev were released at dawn.

After the opera, I went back to my room at the Astoria Hotel and watched television through the night. But like anyone else—including the campaign aides and the businessmen at Berezovsky's club on Novokuznetskaya Street—I would not find out how the story ended until Yeltsin, now barely able to speak a coherent sentence or walk across a room, moved to write its finish.

It was far from guaranteed that Yeltsin would side with Chubais over Korzhakov, Barsukov, and Soskovets. Even if he understood that the "party of war" was provoking the other team, trying to smear it with the appearance of scandal, Yeltsin was like a blood brother to Korzhakov. They played tennis together, they went hunting together, they drank and went to the sauna together. Korzhakov also claimed to know Yeltsin's "secrets," and one could only guess at their nature. The early-morning hours were like a "dead zone" to the Chubais team as they awaited their turn to meet with Yeltsin at the Kremlin. "I was extremely tense," Malashenko told me. "I was afraid that Yeltsin would not do anything and pretend that this frame-up was a minor incident and sweep it under the rug. I had already made a clear decision for myself. I had decided that it could not be business as usual. If it had just gone on as always, I would have resigned immediately from the election campaign. Probably Chubais would have done the same."

While the Chubais team waited, they also made sure to get in contact with the newest and most unpredictable force in Kremlin politics, Aleksandr Lebed. Lebed drove quickly to his office on Old Square. He, too, would have his chance to see Yeltsin.

Chubais finally reached Yeltsin on the phone and told him what he knew. He told the president that he had a press conference scheduled for 10:00 A.M. Yeltsin told him to cancel the press conference until later in the day when he would have had a chance to sort out the intrigue.

Yeltsin met first with Korzhakov and Barsukov, who gave their side of the story. Then he met with his Security Council, which quickly approved the nomination of Lebed as its chairman. After that session, Yeltsin met privately with Lebed, then with Chernomyrdin, and finally with Chubais. All three advised Yeltsin, in one way or another, to move quickly against "the party of war." And, amazingly, he did. Within minutes of his meeting with Chubais, Yeltsin walked blockily in front of the television cameras and declared it was time "for fresh faces" in the leadership. Korzhakov, Barsukov, and Soskovets were out. "They were taking too much and giving too little," Yeltsin said.

The Chubais team was jubilant. In a country that had always relied on force and the threat of force as the pivot of all public life, Yeltsin had jettisoned his most forceful ally. Gusinsky, a former theater director, said the whole affair reminded him of *Antigone,* which he saw as a play about a ruler who destroys his family in order to preserve the state order. "You have to credit Yeltsin for this," he told me. "For him, this was no simple matter. Yeltsin killed his son, he allowed his son to be taken away from him."

Yeltsin's wife, Naina, told a television interviewer that the decision to fire Korzhakov was one of the most painful of her husband's career. "It was very difficult. Even the word 'difficult' does not do it justice," she said. "It's like losing a member of your family."

At noon, Chubais called a press conference and said in a tense and rambling monologue that with the firings Yeltsin had "driven the last nail" into the coffin of a military regime. Korzhakov, for his part, was less dramatic. "I have backed the president and will continue to do so," he said in one of his rare statements to the press. "I am not quitting the president's team and will do my best for the president's victory."

In fact, within a day or two it became known that Korzhakov had not left the Kremlin. Everyone was sure that after the election he would be back, if not as the head of the presidential guard, then at least somewhere not terribly distant from Yeltsin. Chubais had won the battle, but he betrayed no great confidence. One of his allies compared Korzhakov and his men to Papa Doc Duvalier's vengeful army of Tonton Macoutes. Sometime after his ostensibly victorious press conference, Chubais began riding around town with a full complement of armed guards in a bulletproof Mercedes-Benz.

———

A few days later, I traveled to the small city of Tula, a region famous for its rifles and samovars. Now it was also famous for being the home of Aleksandr Lebed. In the parliament, Lebed was the delegate from Tula, and the city had also turned out in droves for the general in the presidential election. The question was whether the Lebed voters could now bring themselves to Yeltsin. Or would they spurn their man's recommendation and turn to the communist, Zyuganov? The answer would be the greatest clue to who would win the election.

My friend Maria Volkenshtein set up a series of focus groups in Tula and I went along. After a three-hour drive south from Moscow, we arrived in town. With a little time to kill, I took a walk downtown and saw a woman in her fifties watering the flowers outside Tula's own self-described "White House," the main government building. Her name was Tasya Kuprina. She had been born in Ukraine and had come to Russia with her husband. She was not a fanatic, not crazy, not even especially interested in communism. But she had voted for Zyuganov and she would vote for him again on July 3.

"Isn't it obvious why?" she said. "We live terribly now. Two, three months go by sometimes before I get paid, and when I do get paid it's sixty dollars a month. In the winter I'm working outside in terrible cold. The collapse of the Soviet Union has been a disaster in my own life. Try to imagine what it's like living in a huge country and then it splits apart. My daughter lives in Ukraine and I have seen her once in three years."

But while there were many people in town who would vote communist, Maria's focus groups provided the more overwhelming trend. By a clear margin, the Lebed voters—as well as the Yavlinsky voters—would go for Yeltsin.

Back in Moscow, the mood was less nervous. "Yeltsin will win, but it's a question whether or not he can survive the victory party," said Leonid Radzikhovsky, the journalist who worked for Lebed. "That will be really dangerous. But of course, for the next three or four years, Yeltsin can look forward to a sea of vodka and endless tennis tournaments and the great warm hug of Bill Clinton. Isn't that reason to live?"

As it happened, the days leading up to the final ballot were nerve-racking. Yeltsin canceled one appearance after another. It became plain that he was at best completely worn out, and at worst quite ill. Only later would we learn that Yeltsin had probably suffered yet another heart attack sometime between the two rounds of voting. His aides lied in the old style. They said that Yeltsin had merely caught a cold, that his voice had given out. The truth was that they were terrified that Yeltsin would die before the runoff, and so they let their man rest in isolation while they betrayed what was left of a democratic process. Reporters at television stations and news bureaus all over Moscow nervously watched the wires. Finally, Yeltsin appeared on July 1, giving a two-minute-long speech. He seemed waxy, unfocused, thick-tongued, a (barely) living evocation of the last days of Brezhnev and Andropov. "The man is a living corpse," the ever-solicitous Vladimir Zhirinovsky told me at his office in the Duma. "We're just waiting for him to drop dead."

A few days before the final balloting, I managed to attend the happiest event I had seen in Moscow for a long time. The Russian State Institute for the Humanities, a new university run by the perestroika-era leader Yuri Afanasyev, was graduating its first crop of graduate students in Jewish studies. Since the institute began in 1991—it had once been the Higher Party School, an institute for aspiring communist leaders— Afanasyev had been bringing in support and top-level scholars from two of the main Jewish centers of learning in New York: the Jewish Theological Seminary and the YIVO Institute for Yiddish Studies.

I arrived just in time to see YIVO's research director, Allan Nadler, get up in his cap and gown and speak to the graduates and their families. Cameras clicked and babies cried—just as at a graduation anywhere. "There is a verse in the Psalms," Nadler said, "that says that when God returned the exiles to Zion, it was as if we were living in a dream. And although Russia is for most Jews not Zion, there was the feeling that this country would harbor great hopes and be a source of knowledge. That dream was shattered over the years of totalitarian rule. But now we live in a different dream—the return of freedom and Jewish knowledge."

While Nadler spoke, I remembered that I had spent a lot of time in this auditorium: in 1989, I had heard a debate here about the future of the Communist Party; in 1991, I had watched a crowd of visiting communists from Vietnam watch a dubbed version of Michael Douglas playing the greedy investment banker in *Wall Street*.

"We are witnessing a mystifying inversion of the trends of recent history," Nadler went on. "The surreal moment for me, the dreamlike state, was when a professor, a Russian professor from the institute, recommended to one student that she ought to take more time to look at the KGB documents on the repression of Jewish dissidents."

Then one of the top students, a young woman named Irina Astashkevich, took the podium and delivered her speech, first in Russian and then in gorgeous English. "In August and September 1991, it was impossible to imagine what, if anything, would come out of the putsch," she said. "It turns out this was a coup not only in our politics, but in our culture and our history. . . . I now look at a diploma that says I am a specialist in Jewish studies. I feel like a pioneer in a new land. . . . It is a great feeling to be not only a witness to a historical event, but also to participate in it. I feel as if I am standing in the center of the world."

———

The Yeltsin strategy in the last days was simple: get out the vote, hide the president, and scare the hell out of the population. The ad campaign on television dropped all pretense of subtlety and ran haunting footage of Bolshevik atrocities and disasters. "No one in 1917 thought that whole families would be executed and entire peoples destroyed," a grave narrator said as footage of an execution, coffins, prison camps, unspooled. "Now the communists have not even bothered to change the name of their party. . . . It's not too late to prevent a civil war. Save and Preserve Russia. Don't Allow the Red Storm." Zyuganov's ads were, in the main, Zyuganov speechlets. He was, in terms of Madison Avenue, out of his depth. With a day or two to go, Zyuganov sensed defeat and tried to appeal for a "coalition government," but it was far too late for that.

Once more, my friends and I gathered at Maria Volkenshtein's place on Leninsky Prospekt, but no one was much in doubt about the result. Yeltsin won by fourteen points. Zyuganov's voters in the Red Belt seemed resigned at the end, and many did not bother going to the polls.

Yeltsin, for his part, made no appearances on the night of his victory. No victory speech, not even a statement for the press. His new security chief, however, had already taken to throwing his weight around. One well-informed Russian journalist told me that at one point on the 3rd, Lebed asked Yeltsin's chief of staff, Viktor Ilyushin, for an appointment with the president. Lebed was told that such a meeting was not possible. Lebed was furious. He informed the presidential staff that if he was blocked from seeing Yeltsin, he would drive straight to the Kempinski Hotel, where CNN was broadcasting round-the-clock from the roof, "and tell the world that Boris Nikolayevich is dead!" Lebed got his meeting.

Businessmen and oligarchs like Berezovsky and Gusinsky were immensely relieved and looked forward to their rewards. Berezovsky talked about the triumph of "capital over ideology." Gusinsky was looking forward to expanding his television enterprises; with the help of a huge investment from Gazprom, the natural gas behemoth once run by the prime minister, he was preparing to establish a satellite system covering the entire former Soviet Union. NTV would soon be on round-the-clock, and Gusinsky would start negotiations for new stations modeled on CNN, Home Box Office, and ESPN. "I'm thinking big," he said.

EPILOGUE:
CAN RUSSIA CHANGE?

There was celebration in the State Department when Boris Yeltsin won reelection, but polls show that in Moscow and in other Russian cities and towns there was, at most, only relief, a sense of having dodged a return to the past and the Communist Party. Political celebration, after all, usually welcomes a beginning, and the Yeltsin regime, everyone understood, was no beginning at all. Yeltsin had accomplished a great deal as both an outsider and as a president, but now, in his senescence, he represented the exhaustion of promise.

To prevail, Yeltsin had been willing to do anything, countenance anything, promise anything. Without regard to his collapsed budget, he doled out subsidies and election-year favors worth billions of dollars; he gave power to men he did not trust (Aleksandr Lebed); he was willing to hide from, and lie to, the press in the last weeks of the campaign, the better to obscure his serious illness.

Power in Russia now is at once adrift, unpredictable, and corrupt. Just three months after appointing Lebed head of his Security Council, Yeltsin fired him for repeated insubordination, instantly securing the general's position as martyr, peacemaker, and pretender to the presidency. On the night of his dismissal, Lebed giddily traipsed off to see a production of Aleksei Tolstoy's play *Ivan the Terrible*. "I want to learn how to rule," he said.

In the new Russia, freedom has led to disappointment. If the triumph of 1991 seemed the triumph of liberal democrats, Yeltsin's victory in 1996 was distinguished by the rise to power of a new class of oligarchs. After the election, the bankers, media barons, and industrialists who had financed and, in large measure, run the campaign got the rewards they wanted: positions in the Kremlin, broadcasting and commercial licenses, access to the national resource pile. Anatoly Chubais, who led Yeltsin's privatization campaign and then the presidential campaign, suddenly forgot his vow never to rejoin the government and became chief of staff, a position made all the mightier by Yeltsin's bad health. Perhaps as a way to personify the shamelessness of the Kremlin, Chubais led the push to appoint one of the leading oligarchs, Boris Berezovsky, as deputy minister of security. Those few Muscovites with enough patience left to care about Kremlin politics wondered what qualifications Berezovsky, who had made his fortune in the automobile business, brought to his new job.

The new oligarchs do not feign innocence of the new map of power. They see themselves as undeniably lucky, but worthy as well. They righteously insist that their fortunes will spawn a middle class, property rights, democratic values. No matter that the Kremlin lets them acquire an industrial giant like the Norilsk nickel works for a thieves' price; in the end, they claim, they are helping to build Russia. They rationalize the rest. Mikhail Smolensky, who runs the powerful Stolichnii Bank in Moscow, invited me to his offices, the restored mansion of a nineteenth-century merchant, and told me, "Look, unfortunately, the only lawyer in this country is the Kalashnikov. People mostly solve their problems in this way. In this country there is no respect for the law, no culture of law, no judicial system—it's just being created." In the meantime, in a lawless environment, bribery is the grease of commerce. Government officials, who issue licenses and permissions of all sorts, "practically have a price list hanging on the office wall," Smolensky said.

The enormous power of the new oligarchs is humiliating to Russians, not because they are wealthy, but because so little of their wealth is funneled back through the Russian economy. According to Interpol and the Russian Interior Ministry, rich Russians have sent more than $300 billion to foreign banks, and much of that capital leaves the country illegally, untaxed. Yeltsin's "Kremlin capitalism" has so far failed to create "a nation of shopkeepers"—the British middle-class model—but it has spawned hundreds of thousands of *chelnoki,* or shuttle traders, young people who travel back and forth to countries like China, Turkey, and the United Arab Emirates carrying all manner of goods for sale. While this sort of trade is probably only a transitional form of crude capitalism, it is also uncontrolled, untaxed, and mafia-ridden.

Under Yeltsin, Kremlin power has become almost as remote from the people it presumably serves as it was under the last general secretaries. In its arrogance, in the way it so rarely deigns to answer the questions of the press, Yeltsin's Kremlin usually seems to believe that its duty to democratic practice ended with the 1996 elections. The Russian people, understandably, believe the government has much to answer for. The poverty rate soars; life expectancy for men plunges. The murder rate is twice as high as it is in the United States and many times higher than in the capitals of Europe. According to Russian government statistics, by late 1995, eight thousand criminal gangs were at work in Russia—proportionately as many as in Italy. The fastest-growing service industry in Russia is "personal security." Hundreds of thousands of men and women now work as armed security guards for businesses. The police are too few, and usually too corrupt, to do the job.

The press is far freer than it was in Soviet times, but it is still a mixed bag. State television, which is owned largely by the new oligarchs, is extremely cautious, even sycophantic when it comes to Yeltsin. After acting as cheerleaders during the election campaign, some newspapers and magazines have once again become more aggressive, more critical, even going so far as to probe impolitely into the state of Yeltsin's health. (*Itogi* magazine's investigations forced Yeltsin to go public with his heart ailments, which, in turn, led him to agree to his quintuple bypass surgery in November.) But there is still no institution—not the press, not parliament, certainly not the weak judiciary—with the authority to keep the Kremlin honest.

One of the most troubling deficiencies in modern Russia is the absence of moral authority. The country lacks the ethical compass provided by Andrei Sakharov, who died in December 1989. Human rights groups like Memorial, which were in the forefront of the democratic reform movement under Gorbachev, are now marginal. If Sakharov had a leading protégé it was Sergei Kovalyov, a biologist who spent many years in prison under Brezhnev and then helped lead the human rights movement. One of Yeltsin's most promising gestures was his appointment of Kovalyov as commissioner of human rights, and one of the most depressing events of his reign was Kovalyov's recognition that he could not persuade the government to end the war in Chechnya and his subsequent resignation. These days, Kovalyov is hardly a presence in public life—he appears more often and more prominently in *The New York Review of Books* than he does in *Izvestia*—and no one seems to have replaced him. Even most liberal journalists seem uninterested in Kovalyov; after years of talking about ideas and ideals, they are cynical, intent only on discussing economic interests; the worst sin is to seem naive or woolly or bookish—or hopeful.

"The quality of democracy depends heavily on the quality of the democrats," Kovalyov told me after the elections. "We have to wait for a critical mass to accumulate of people with democratic principles. It's like a nuclear explosion: the critical mass has to accrue. Without this, everything will be like it is now, always in fits and starts. Our era of romantic democracy is long over. We have finally fallen to earth."

———

When and how will that critical mass accumulate? Russia cannot be mistaken for a democratic state; rather, it is a nascent state with some *features* of democracy (and, alas, many features of oligarchy and authoritarianism). When and how will a more complete transformation happen? Is Russia capable of building a stable and democratic state or is it forever doomed to follow its historical pattern in which long stretches of absolutism are interrupted by fleeting periods of reform? In other words, is it reasonable to expect or even hope for a radical change in Russia's political culture?

First, it pays to review the legacy—the damage report—of history. Russian history seems at times to have been *organized* to maximize the isolation of the people and, in modern times, to prevent the possibility of democratic capitalism. The Russian Orthodox Church, for example, was the dominant institution in Russian life for centuries and by nature was deeply suspicious of, even hostile to, the outside world. After the fall of Constantinople in the fifteenth century, the church distanced itself from transnational creeds like Protestantism, Catholicism, Judaism, and Buddhism; xenophobia became a leading characteristic of both church and state. The xenophobia only intensified during the Soviet epoch. Under the banner of internationalism, the Bolsheviks successfully kept the world at bay until the glasnost policy of the late 1980s.

Russian history has also proved unique in the endurance and degree of its absolutism. In many regards, the authority of the czars exceeded that of nearly all other monarchs. Richard Pipes points out that "throughout Europe, even in countries living under absolutist regimes, it was considered a truism that kings ruled but did not own: a popular formula taken from the Roman philosopher Seneca that 'unto kings belongs the power of all things and unto individual men, property.' Violations of this principle were perceived as a hallmark of tyranny. This whole complex of ideas was foreign to Russia. The Muscovite crown treated the entire realm as its property and all secular landowners as the czars' tenants-in-chief, who held their estate at his mercy on the condition of faithful service." Czarist absolutism was far more severe than English absolutism because of its far greater control of property. With the rise of the Bolshevik regime, property became, in the theoretical jargon of the epoch, the property of all, but in practice remained the property of the sovereign—the Communist Party and its general secretary. The communists were even less inclined to develop a culture of legality—of property rights, human rights, and independent courts—than the last of the Romanovs had been.

Also, under both the czars and the general secretaries, the legitimacy of the government was, in Mikhail Gorbachev's rueful phrase, "the legitimacy of the bayonet." Violence and the threat of violence characterized nearly all of Russian history. The two great breakthroughs—the fall of Nicholas II in February 1917, and the fall of Gorbachev as Communist Party leader in August 1991—came only after it was clear that both figures would refuse, or were incapable of, the slaughter necessary to prolong their regimes. Many Russian intellectuals today, including camp survivors like the writer Lev Razgon, believe that the capacity to create a democratic critical mass was diminished *genetically* by the communist regime's policy of forced exile, imprisonment, and execution. "When one begins to tally up the millions of men and women, the best and the brightest of their day, who were killed or forced out of the country, then one begins to calculate how much moral and intellectual capacity we lost," Razgon told me. "Think of how many voices of understanding we lost, think of how many independent-minded people we lost, and how those voices were kept from the ears of Soviet citizens. Yes, I am furious beyond words at Yeltsin for the war in Chechnya and for other mistakes. But we have to look at our capacities, the injuries this people has absorbed over time."

Finally, Russia will have to learn to alter its intellectual approach to political life. Even though Gennady Zyuganov failed to win the 1996 elections with his national bolshevik ideology, he did prove that maximalist ideas still resonate among a certain proportion of the population. In 1957, writing for *Foreign Affairs,* Isaiah Berlin described accurately a traditional Russian yearning for all-embracing ideologies rooted in the anti-intellectual and eschatological style of the Russian Orthodox Church. As Berlin points out, the Russian revolutionaries of the nineteenth and twentieth centuries were not obsessed with liberal ideas, much less the liberal idea of political and intellectual pluralism, but instead were given to a systemic cast of mind. In the most extreme ways, they absorbed German historicism in its Hegelian form (history as a genuine science tending in a certain direction) and then the utopian prophecies of Saint-Simon and Fourier.

Unlike the West, where such systems often languished and declined amid cynical indifference, in the Russian Empire they became fighting faiths, thriving on the opposition to them of contrary ideologies— mystical monarchism, Slavophil nostalgia, clericalism, and the like; and under absolutism, where ideas and daydreams are liable to become substitutes for action, ballooned out into fantastic shapes, dominating the lives of their devotees to a degree scarcely known elsewhere. To turn history or logic or one of the natural sciences—biology or sociology— into a theodicy; to seek, and affect to find, within them solutions to agonizing moral or religious doubts and perplexities; to transform them into secular theologies—all that is nothing new in human history. But the Russians indulged in this process on a heroic and desperate scale, and in the course of it brought forth what today is called the attitude of total commitment, at least of its modern form.

Russian intellectuals—and not least, Lenin himself—derided the weakness, the unsystematic thought, of Western liberalism. For Lenin, Marxism provided a scientific explanation for human behavior. All he needed was the technological means of altering that behavior.

But while the Russian and Soviet leaderships have been predominantly characterized by xenophobia, absolutism, violence, and extremist political thought, there have always been signs of what the scholar Nicolai Petro calls an "alternative political culture." If Russians today were to attempt to create a modern state purely out of foreign models and experience, if there were nothing at all in Russian history to learn from, rely on, or invest pride in, one could hardly expect much. But that is not the case. Even if Russian history cannot rely, as the Founding Fathers did, on a legacy like English constitutionalism, the soil of Russian history is far from barren.

Even the briefest survey of alternative currents in Russian history must take note of the resistance to absolutism visible under Peter I and Catherine the Great or, in the nineteenth century, the Decembrist rebellion against Nicholas I. While Nicholas was able to crush the Decembrists, their demands for greater civil and political authority did not fade; in fact, those demands became instead the banner of rebellion that persisted, in various forms and movements, until the February Revolution of 1917. Alexander II's decree to abolish serfdom was followed by the establishment of local governing boards called *zemstvo*s, and out of that form of limited grassroots politics even more pressure was applied to the czar. In May 1905, after a long series of strikes, the Third Zemstvo Congress appealed to the czar for a transition to constitutional government, and the czar soon issued the edict accepting constitutional monarchy. The constitution published in 1906 guaranteed the inviolability of the person, residence, and property, the right of assembly, freedom of religion, and freedom of the press—so long as the press was not criticizing the czar.

Under Soviet rule, the Communist Party was far quicker to suppress signs of an alternative political culture than Nicholas II had been, but there were expressions of resistance and creative thought. Under Khrushchev, in the thaw years, a few artists and journalists began to reveal the alternative intellectual and artistic currents flowing under the thick ice of official culture, and, beginning in the late sixties, one began to see the varied currents of political dissent: Sakharov and the Western-oriented human rights movement; "reform" socialists like Roy Medvedev; religious dissidents like Aleksandr Men' and Gleb Yakunin; traditionalist neo-Slavophil dissidents like Solzhenitsyn and the authors of *From Under the Rubble.*

Yeltsin's government has not been especially successful in articulating the nature of the new Russian state. But however formless, the new Russian state has made a series of symbolic overtures. By adopting the pre-revolutionary tricolor and the double-headed eagle as national emblems, the government has deliberately reached back to revive a sense of possibility from the past. Similarly, the mayor of Moscow, Yuri Luzhkov, has restored and rebuilt dozens of churches and monuments destroyed during the Soviet period, not least the enormous Cathedral of Christ the Savior on the banks of the Moscow River. One also sees a revived interest in Ivan Ilyin, Nikolai Berdyayev, and other émigré philosophers who tried to describe Russian political and spiritual values. Academics are struggling to write new textbooks. Religious leaders are coping with the revival of the Russian Orthodox Church among a people with little religious education and only a sentimental attachment to their faith. These phenomena are not mere kitsch or intellectual fashion, but rather an attempt to reconnect Russians to their own history and the idea of a national development that was shattered with the Bolshevik coup of 1917.

While it is undoubtedly true that daily life in Russia today suffers from a painful economic, political, and social transition, the Russian prospect over the coming years and decades is more promising than ever before in its history. Or as the former deputy prime minister Yegor Gaidar has put it, "Russia today is not a bad subject for long-term prognostication, and a very inappropriate subject for short-term analysis." I see no reason that Russia cannot make a break with its absolutist past much in the way that Germany and Japan did after the war.

Since the late 1980s, Russia has already gone a long way in this direction. The decades of confrontation with the West are over. Russia has withdrawn its talons, and except for the need to vent some nationalist rhetoric once in a great while, it offers little threat to the world. For all the hand-wringing by Henry Kissinger and other Russophobes, there is no imminent threat of a renewed imperialism even within the borders of the old Soviet Union. The threat of conflict between Russia and Ukraine over the Crimea or between Russia and Kazakhstan over northern Kazakhstan has diminished greatly in the last few years. After centuries of isolation, Russia seems ready to live not merely with the world but in it. Russians are free to travel. They are free to consume as much foreign journalism, intellectual history, and pop culture as they desire. Foreign influence and business are encouraged by the authorities: there are more than 200,000 foreigners resident now in Moscow (many times the number before 1990). Communications with the outside world are limited only by Russia's dismal international telephone capacity; happily, scholars and business people have finessed that limitation with the rapid appearance of personal computers and electronic mail.

In the short term, most Russians cannot hope for much, especially not from their politicians. If, after his surgery, Yeltsin's health does not improve dramatically, there will likely be an atmosphere of permanent crisis in Moscow. "I lived through the last days of Brezhnev, Andropov, and Chernenko, and I know how illness in power leads to danger," Mikhail Gorbachev told me shortly after the 1996 elections. "We survived back then only thanks to the inertia of the Soviet system. But Russia needs dynamic people in office, and now, well . . ." Gorbachev, obviously, has never shown much charity toward Yeltsin (nor Yeltsin toward Gorbachev), but he was right.

The most important figures in the government will be Yeltsin's chief of staff, Chubais, the prime minister, Viktor Chernomyrdin, and, not least, his daughter, Tatyana Dyachenko. Such a government is likely to continue a more or less friendly relationship with Washington and the West and will continue to preside over a semicapitalist, semioligarchic economy. But unless the government begins to fight corruption and work toward the creation of a legal order and a strengthened court system, the state will continue to be compared to the Latin America and South Korea of the 1970s.

If Yeltsin dies sooner rather than later, his circle will either follow the letter of the constitution and go forward with presidential elections after three months or it will find an excuse to avoid them. The latter choice would be unforgivable, and would go a long way toward negating the limited progress since 1991. Russia has yet to prove it can undergo a peaceful and orderly transfer of power—one of the most crucial tests in the development of a democracy. If the government does go forward with elections, however, the likely combatants would include Chernomyrdin, Moscow mayor Yuri Luzhkov, General Lebed, and communist leader Gennady Zyuganov.

Lebed's popularity is the highest of the four, but who he is, what sort of president he would be, is unknown. Lebed is considered "flexible" and "educable" by many Western visitors to Moscow, but his is a flexibility born mainly of ignorance. Lebed is a military man, but unlike Colin Powell or Dwight Eisenhower—to say nothing of his hero, de Gaulle—he has hardly any experience beyond the military. Lebed must be given credit for signing a peace treaty with the Chechens during his short tenure as security minister. He is also, by most accounts, a decent and honest man, which sets him apart from most who have set foot in the Kremlin. But he also displayed a willful, even outrageous, disregard for the president he was ostensibly serving. Aleksandr Lebed's first priority, so far, appears to be Aleksandr Lebed. It is discouraging that the most visible political alliance he formed after leaving the Kremlin was with Aleksandr Korzhakov, Yeltsin's crony and bodyguard before being bounced from the government during the campaign. Korzhakov, for his part, has landed easily on his feet after being fired; he has decided to run for parliament from Lebed's home district (Tula), and should any of his old rivals threaten him, he has promised to release "incriminating evidence" against Yeltsin and his aides.

Lebed's potential rivals are probably more fixed in their views and political behavior, but they are not a promising lot. Zyuganov still has supporters, especially among the oldest and poorest sectors of the population, but he has little or no chance to win if he repeats the tactics and rhetoric of 1996. The communists would do well to jettison any memory of the past and adopt, as some are proposing, a new name for the party and younger faces to run it. A party of social democrats is inevitable in Russia, but not under Zyuganov.

Chernomyrdin represents a longed-for predictability abroad, but to Russians he represents the worst of Yeltsin's government: suspicion of corruption, oligarchy, and an almost fantastical disregard for the public. Chernomyrdin is singularly inarticulate, and the only way he could win the presidency would be to exploit the resources of the Kremlin and gain the support of the media to an even greater degree than Yeltsin did in 1996. Luzhkov is extremely popular in Moscow—a kind of Russian Richard Daley—but he would have to cope with a traditional tendency in Russia to be suspicious of political figures from the capital.

In all, the Kremlin depends, at this writing, on the heart tissues of one man, Boris Yeltsin, and the conflicting economic and political interests of his would-be inheritors.

But not all depends on Yeltsin, and not all depends on Moscow. Far from it. Russia is a far less centralized country than the Soviet Union was, for while Moscow political life is rife with intrigue and the whiff of authoritarian arrogance, it is also relatively weak. One decree after another is issued, but local authorities adopt the ones they like and ignore the rest.

The levels of development and progress are wildly different in the country's eighty-nine regions, and much depends on the local political map. Beyond Moscow, the most encouraging region is centered around Nizhny Novgorod, where young and progressive politicians like Boris Nemtsov have made good on their promises to create "capitalism in one country." One of the biggest problems with the Soviet economy was that it was so heavily militarized; Nizhny Novgorod, the third-largest city in the country, has been one of the most militarized of all. And yet not only has the city managed, through privatization, demonopolization, and bond issues, to create thriving service and production economies, it has also managed to convert 90 percent of its collective farms to private hands. Meanwhile, five hundred miles down the Volga River, the conservative communist-run city government of Ulyanovsk (Lenin's hometown) has refused to participate in radical reform. Ulyanovsk's economy is a shambles.

Not all regions, however, can thrive simply by adopting the market reforms of Nizhny Novgorod. The coal-mining regions of western Siberia will continue to suffer for the same reasons so many other mining regions in other countries have suffered: the mines are nearly mined out and no alternative economy has developed. Except for some areas, farming regions have resisted the difficult transformation to private farming, largely because of the inevitable reduction in workforces and the capital needed for modern equipment. Agricultural areas like the Kuban or Gorbachev's home region of Stavropol have only suffered since 1991.

Morality and the level of mafia involvement also play a local role. In Khabarovsk the mobster Vladimir "the Poodle" Podiatev controls the city to such a degree that he has his own political party and television station. Chechnya will continue to gnaw at the attention, if not the conscience, of Moscow. Its capital city is in ruins and the local authorities consider themselves victors; the rule of Islam, of Sharia, prevails in Chechnya, not the rule of Moscow.

In trying to analyze the situation in Russia and the Russian prospect, all analysts, myself included, tend to grope for analogies with other countries and other eras. The rise of oligarchy summons Argentina, the vacuum of power evokes Weimar Germany, the dominance of the mafia hints at postwar Italy, the presidential constitution recalls de Gaulle's constitution of 1958. But while Russia's problems alarm the world on occasion, none of these analogies takes into account the country's possibilities.

Since 1991, Russia has broken so dramatically with its absolutist past that the break cannot be ignored or underestimated. The almost uniformly rosy predictions for China and the almost uniformly gloomy ones for Russia seem wrong to me. Political reform is not the only advantage Russia has in its favor. Unlike China, whose population is still dominated by rural poverty and illiteracy, Russia is an increasingly urban nation with a literacy rate of 99 percent. Nearly 80 percent of the Russian economy is in private hands. Inflation, a feature of all postcommunist countries, has dropped from 2,500 percent in 1992 to 130 percent in 1995. The natural resource base is unparalleled. Richard Layard of the London School of Economics and John Parker, a former Moscow correspondent for *The Economist,* predict that by the year 2020 Russia "may well have outstripped countries like Poland, Hungary, Brazil and Mexico with China far behind." They are more optimistic than I am ready to be, but it is not an unreasonable view.

Not least in Russia's list of advantages is that its citizens show every indication of refusing a return to the maximalism of communism or the xenophobia of hard-line nationalism. The idea of Russia's "separate path" of development is increasingly a losing proposition for communists and nationalists alike. The highly vulgarized versions of a national idea—Zyuganov's national bolshevism or the various anti-Semitic, anti-Western platforms of people like Aleksandr Prokhanov—have repelled most Russian voters, no matter how disappointed they are with Yeltsin. Anti-Semitism, for example, has no political attraction, as many feared it would; even Lebed, who has betrayed moments of nationalist resentment, has felt it necessary to apologize after making various racist comments. He will not win as an extremist. Rather his appeal is to the popular disgust with the corruption, violence, and general lack of integrity associated with the Yeltsin government.

Perhaps it is a legacy of the Cold War that so many American analysts demand so much so soon from Russia. Russia is no longer an enemy or anything resembling one, and yet we demand to know why, for example, there are no developed political parties in Russia; somehow we fail to remember that it took the United States (with all its historical advantages, including its founders) more than sixty years after independence to develop its two-party system, that in France nearly all the parties have been vehicles for the likes of Mitterrand or Chirac. The drama of 1991 so accelerated our notion of Russian history that expectations became outlandish; and now that many of those expectations have been disappointed, deferred, and even betrayed, it seems as if we have gone back to expecting only the worst from Russia.

The most famous of all nineteenth-century visitors to Russia, the Marquis de Custine, ended his trip and his narrative by writing, "One needs to have lived in that solitude without tranquillity, that prison without leisure that is called Russia, to appreciate all the freedom enjoyed in other European countries, no matter what form of government they have chosen. . . . It is always good to know that there exists a society in which no happiness is possible, because, by reason of nature, man cannot be happy unless he is free." But that has changed. An entirely new era has begun. Russia has entered the world, and everything, even freedom, even happiness, is now possible.

AFTERWORD
TO THE VINTAGE EDITION

The Tsar and the Seven Boyars

If we have learned anything from the strange and epic story of Boris Nikolayevich Yeltsin these past ten years, it is that no tsar is hero to his bodyguard. Or not for long, anyway. We know this because, in the new tradition of Russian politics, the bodyguard in question, having been fired at last from the inner circle, responded by writing a marvelously venomous memoir, "From Dawn to Dusk," that seems truthful in spirit, if not in every fact.

Aleksandr Korzhakov writes of Yeltsin as provincial chieftain, a "genuine Communist Party despot." As Yeltsin's powers increased, as he moved, in the course of a decade, from Politburo member to folk hero to imperial wrecker to Russian president, as his health declined and he no longer felt the urgent need to appear very much on television or in the papers, he began to behave very much like a tsar. He became more and more isolated and withdrawn from public life, more dependent on a very few aides. Those same aides came to refer to Yeltsin, alternately, as "The Boss" and "Tsar Boris." Yeltsin was meant to overhear these epithets as tribute.

But even while Yeltsin had been bestowed with the title of a Romanov, he often acted rather more like the captain of the Bensonhurst Democratic Party clubhouse. From Korzhakov's memoirs, one gets the sense that by 1994 or so running the country ran a distant second to the more serious business of recreation: boozy swims in the Black Sea, boozy deer shoots in Zavidovo, and tennis—lots and lots of tennis. It is, as Mel Brooks says, good to be the king.

Yeltsin loves a good time. He is, it appears, a musically minded tsar. He is fond of singing traditional Russian drinking songs, though he is only good for remembering a line or two. He is more of an instrumentalist. "Yeltsin's sense of rhythm was good and he was good player on the spoons," Korzhakov writes. "Even on official trips, he would demand, 'Bring spoons!' Yeltsin was born in the village of Butka, where playing spoons must have been prestigious." Yeltsin's favorite trick was to play knick-knack paddy-whack with his spoons on the head of Yuri Zagainov, the chief of the president's administrative department. "At first the boss would beat on his leg, as is normally done, and then he beat loudly on the head of his subordinate. The latter did not dare to take offense and smiled affectedly. The audience burst out laughing." On one occasion, Yeltsin took aside the president of one of the former Soviet states, Askar Akayev of Kyrgyzstan, and played the spoons on his head. As Korzhakov writes, "He could torture one to death with this musical instrument."

Yeltsin's international prestige drooped in the mid-1990s after the assault on the Russian parliament and the war in Chechnya. He became increasingly depressed. There was less spoon-playing, more drinking. He talked about resigning. He was constantly telling his chief of staff, Viktor Ilyushin, to stop bringing him "all that shit," meaning his paperwork. He came to resent the imprecations of the precious few intellectuals in the street and in the press who were protesting the carnage in Chechnya. He had started out his career as a reformer surrounded by intellectuals—he courted Sakharov intensely, he brought young academics into the Kremlin—but that was all in the past. He referred to one of his more liberal advisers, Sergei Filatov, as "a man who looks as if he has two flies fucking in his mouth." Even losing in tennis would send Yeltsin into a funk, and so his faithful bodyguard, Korzhakov, always made sure that the president was paired with a professional.

For ten years, Korzhakov could not have been more loyal to Yeltsin. When Yeltsin was fired from the Politburo, Korzhakov stayed with him and even drove him around town in his own car, a tuna-can-sized Neva.

He was with Yeltsin on top of the tank when they faced down the coup in August 1991, and he was with him when they faced a dozen crises thereafter. Like mafia blood brothers they sliced open their arms and mixed together their vital bodily fluids—not once, but twice.

It was Korzhakov who came to the rescue when Yeltsin was mysteriously thrown into a river outside Moscow and was dragged to a guardhouse where he sat waiting, and weeping, on the cold floor. Korzhakov stripped the president to his underwear, wrapped him in a blanket, fed him sips of moonshine, and then rubbed the warming booze all over the presidential corpus. "It worked beautifully." It was Korzhakov who organized the construction of a luxury apartment building for Yeltsin and his favorite aides on the southwestern edge of Moscow. Yeltsin had long since jettisoned his populist "campaign against privileges" and fallen deeply in love with the perquisites of power. "He also didn't want to have to run into Gorbachev in the elevator," Korzhakov explains.

When a subordinate came running from the presidential office yelling, "What should I do? Boris Nikolayevich gave me a hundred-dollar bill and told me to go fetch a bottle," it was Korzhakov who calmly cracked open his secret supply of watered-down vodka supplied especially for this purpose by the Department of the Interior. ("To give him no vodka at all was, alas, not an option.") When Yeltsin, bombed on beer, spilled coffee all over himself in the car on the way to see Helmut Kohl, it was Korzhakov who helped him into the extra suit on hand for just such occasions. Poor Korzhakov. "Even after he got strict doctor's orders not to drink," he writes, "Naina [the president's wife] continued to give her husband cognac. Yeltsin always knew how to get around my ban. If he really needed a drink, he would invite in one of his most trusted friends for 'an audience.' "

Korzhakov's memoirs promise intimacy and, on some level, they do deliver. There are no fewer than six color photographs of the President of the Russian Federation wearing a tiny Speedo bathing suit. Yeltsin has the coloring of a mushroom and the belly of a hippo; if Korzhakov meant to discredit Yeltsin as candidate for the Mr. Universe title, then he was quite effective.

But, in fact, Korzhakov tells his readers very little they did not know already. Russians have long understood that their president has a drinking problem and a barrel-like physique. The man could be played in the movies by Wallace Beery or Broderick Crawford. And ever since the full press coverage of his multiple-bypass operation after the election, they have also known of his precarious health. The people are, in short, well-informed on the peccadilloes and weaknesses of their president.

"Strangely enough," writes Aleksandr Pumpyansky, the editor of *Novoye Vremya,* "The people not only understand but forgive their drinking leader, swearing and cursing him nonetheless. Reagan was called a Teflon president because all his mistakes were forgiven. Similarly, Yeltsin's pranks do not cling to him, they go off him like water off a duck's back. One can only guess why. He is far from an ideal ruler. Our people do not tolerate ideal rulers. He is bone of the bone, flesh of the flesh of his nation. And the whole set of the entire nation's weaknesses and inclinations can be read in his face. No doubt he has played enough pranks in his life, but he has also had enough trouble and enough enemies, with whom he did away with so deftly, and the demon rum is far from the most dangerous of them."

The average Russian, Pumpyansky is pointing out, is himself quite familiar with the bottle, does not expect to live as long as they do in the West, and sees himself as long-suffering. And so it is not this collection of Russian traits that threatens Yeltsin in his quest for a decent place in history.

———

For the more profound argument against Yeltsin, we might turn away from the likes of Korzhakov's "From Dawn to Dusk" and to "The Russian Intelligentsia," a series of lectures given at Columbia University by the great novelist and critic Andrei Sinyavsky shortly before his death in 1997.

Sinyavsky's credentials, of course, are on a far higher plane than Korzhakov's. He was born in 1925, served in the Soviet army during the war against Germany, and, by the 1950s, began writing essays critical of the reigning aesthetic of socialist realism, "a phantasmagoric art with hypotheses instead of a purpose." Sinyavsky adopted the pseudonym Abram Tertz, borrowed from Abrashka Tertz, a Jewish outlaw bandit celebrated in the folksongs of Odessa. Like Pasternak before him, Sinyavsky attracted the notice of the Kremlin authorities when he began publishing his fiction and essays abroad. In October 1965, he was arrested along with his friend, the writer Yuli Daniel, who was publishing abroad under the name Nikolai Arzhak. Sinyavsky and Daniel's four-day trial in Moscow in 1966—along with Joseph Brodsky's trial in Leningrad in 1964—marked the re-establishment of Stalinism in both the arts and in society after the all-too-brief period of thaw. But unlike the Stalinist show trials of the thirties, Sinyavsky and Daniel, as well as Brodsky, improvised remarkable defenses, the transcripts of which became samizdat classics. The verdict, of course, was never in doubt. Sinyavsky and Daniel were found guilty of "anti-Soviet agitation" under the notorious article 70 of the penal code and shipped off to Dubrovlag, an island of the gulag archipelago in Mordovia. During his sentence of hard labor, Sinyavsky managed to write two masterworks, *A Voice from the Chorus,* a kind of pastiche memoir fashioned out of his letters home to his wife, and *Strolls with Pushkin,* an irreverent portrait of the great Russian literary demigod which, when it was published in Moscow during the perestroika years, came as a far greater shock to many intellectuals than any work of Solzhenitsyn, Orwell, or Grossman. Sinyavsky emigrated to France in 1973, where he wrote, taught at the Sorbonne, and was active in émigré polemics and literary magazines.

Considering Sinyavsky's literary achievement, as well as his reputation for honesty and courage, it is not easy to challenge his judgments about contemporary Russia. But they are deeply flawed judgments based on surprisingly erratic observation.

The core argument of Sinyavsky's three lectures is that the Russian intelligentsia has abdicated its traditional role of opposition to power and has instead adopted a sickening affection for Yeltsin that resembles nothing less than the intelligentsia's capitulation to Stalin in the thirties. At the same time, Sinyavsky argues, the same intellectuals who roundly mocked Gorbachev for his errors now forgive Yeltsin's far greater errors—especially the draconian market reforms of 1992 devised by the economist Yegor Gaidar, the violent assault on parliament in October 1993, and the war waged in Chechnya in 1995. Sinyavsky draws an acid caricature of contemporary Russian intellectuals as a tribe thoroughly divorced from reality, as artists, writers, and scholars who are so grateful for their new freedoms and opportunities to travel abroad that they disdain "the people" as hopelessly retrograde. Using a phrase from Nekrasov's "Elegy," Sinyavsky asks, "Why in the past did the intelligentsia pity the people, sympathize with them, declare 'I dedicated my lyre to the people,' but now tremble? What happened?"

Sinyavsky spent the last twenty-four years of his life living in France and not speaking much French; like so many older literary émigrés, he concentrated on his books and on learning what he could of home from Russian-language radio broadcasts, newspaper clippings, and other sources. Writing both of his life inside the Soviet Union and then in France, Sinyavsky says, "Before perestroika, I had a wonderful life. The Soviet regime seemed unshakable. It was possible to clash with it and to end up in prison, as had happened to me. It was possible to thumb one's nose at it behind its back, as many intellectuals did. It was possible to adapt to it—and even to love it. In a purely abstract sense, I understood that at some point it would collapse, perhaps in a hundred or two hundred years, but I did not think I would live to see that. There was no hope of that, nor could there have been any such hope. Instead, there was stability." Sinyavsky was being partly ironic, of course—his arrest and imprisonment were hardly "wonderful." And yet I think he was absolutely sincere about his sense of stability; almost no one expected anything like the cataclysm of 1991 and no one at all was fully prepared for the shock, the pleasures, and the tragedies it would bring.

In the summer of 1992, Sinyavsky went to "Gaidar's Moscow" and, to his horror, discovered a new world of beggars and dirt, widows selling off the contents of their closets. "We had the feeling that we had returned to the wartime years of our youth," he writes. "History was repeating itself!" When his fellow intellectuals told him that every country in the West had poverty and crime, Sinyavsky would not accept it. "I am not an economist," he writes. "If you ask me what a monetary system is, I answer that I don't know. The International Monetary Fund? I don't know about that either. But I do know that economics—perhaps more than any other area of human activity—must be based on common sense." And common sense, he adds, does not entail workers being paid in sanitary napkins or vodka or bras or newborn calves—all legal tender, at times and in various places, in modern Russia.

One can easily understand Sinyavsky's despair. The collapse of communism was soon followed by industrial collapse, rising crime, disappearing funding for the arts and sciences, and, perhaps worst of all, the increasing violence and isolation of central power. One can argue about the economic policies of 1992, but not about the Kremlin's ever-increasing indifference to corruption and bloodshed.

And yet Sinyavsky's understanding of the Russian transition is terribly incomplete. There is no sense at all that every country in the East has experienced to one degree or another all the ills—the organized crime, the economic uncertainty—that Russia has. Considering the degree of calcification in the Soviet Union compared to Poland or the Czech republic, considering the degree of economic, social, and political pathology experienced in Russia since 1917, it is only natural that the transition would be so much more painful and long-lasting. There is also little mention in Sinyavsky's lectures of even the partial freedoms that have been won: the freedom of worship and expression, the irreversible dismantling of the command economy, the end of an imperial and hostile foreign policy, the sense of promise among millions of young people. Sinyavsky fails to see the seeds of entrepreneurship in the cities, the openness to useful western influences even in the deepest provinces.

Sinyavsky's is an analysis based on emotion, conspicuous omission, disorientation, and anecdote. He writes of newspapers and political parties being shut down after the October 1993 crisis, but does not care to remind the reader that they were all quickly reopened and reactivated. He writes of street beggars, but fails to remind his American audience that the Soviet Union in its waning years was already a landscape of poverty, a region of terrible infant mortality rates, rural collapse, rampant alcoholism, overburdened and insufficient health-care facilities, and on and on. Sinyavsky seems to give the impression that a purely benevolent Gorbachev, whom he rightly admires, unleashed perestroika *in order* to publish censored books and to screen unseen films. He did not. Glasnost, the policy of openness in the arts and sciences, was a deliberate means of encouraging the intelligentsia to join the world and work for *obnovleniye*—the renewal of the communist system. Yeltsin can be criticized for his inadequate response to corruption, but he must also be given credit for encouraging foreign investment, the rise of normal market mechanisms, the privatization of state enterprises, and a reversal of initially terrible inflation rates.

Sinyavsky's most wounding charge, that the intelligentsia has behaved miserably, is as anecdotal and errant as his economics. "Once again the flower of the Russian intelligentsia went over to the authorities, supporting Gaidar's looting and Yeltsin's firing on the White House, chanting: 'Right on, Boria! Give it to them, Boria, go to it, Boria! Crush our enemies!' " he writes. "No one thinks of what our children and grandchildren will say or whether they will be ashamed of us. Our times are interesting because they are so ironically congruent with our unhappy past." He condemns such intellectuals as Sergei Averintsev, Bulat Okhudzhava, Bella Akhmadulina, and Marietta Chudakova for signing letters in support of Yeltsin during the October crisis. Never once does Sinyavsky mention that the "parliamentarians" who precipitated the October crisis amended the constitution *hundreds* of times as part of a political battle waged against Yeltsin. Nor does he mention repeated rejections at a political settlement or, worst of all, the leader of the insurrection, Aleksandr Rutskoi (Yeltsin's former vice-president), calling on armed crowds to capture key buildings around Moscow. Sinyavsky says that the intellectuals have failed to point out the fall in living standards among ordinary people. "This reminded me of the beginning of the 1930s when the intelligentsia closed its eyes to the horrendous famines and disasters in the villages and maintained its silence."

There are undoubtedly a few intellectuals in contemporary Russia who have made fools of themselves, who sold themselves out simply "to clink glasses" with Yeltsin at a Kremlin reception. And in the October crisis there were some whose fury led them to bloody rhetoric. But to compare Yeltsin to Stalin? To compare monetary reform to Stalin's artificially induced famines, his slaughter of the peasantry? To say that the intelligentsia has kept silent on poverty?

And yet the most astonishing statement in Sinyavsky's lectures was this: "The democrats have let their opportunity slip. I don't like the Communists, but they are better for the people than the democrats. It is not fortuitous that the very word *democrat* has been compromised and that people call democrats 'demo-thieves.' Democracy is associated with poverty, theft, corruption, and other horrors. Against that background the Communists look wonderful." Sinyavsky could not have met the current leadership of the Communist Party and made that statement; they are much like the old leadership, but dumber, less competent. The cream of the Party has long since left to set up businesses. All the real supporters of the Gorbachev reforms, the reforms Sinyavsky so admires, abandoned the Communist Party before its collapse or soon thereafter. What's left are the true believers, the cranks. Sinyavsky rightly points out that Yeltsin has failed to deliver on his promise of erecting a European model of civilization, but what was he thinking when he said that "everything in Russia is being done the way things were done in Uganda under President Idi Amin"?

Both Korzhakov's and Sinyavsky's critiques are insufficient—Korzhakov's because it is limited to personal anecdote and the dorsal vantage point of the bodyguard, Sinyavsky's because it is limited to economic anecdote and a kind of intellectual version of sensationalism. And while it is true that Yeltsin continues to flounder at times, making such bewildering public statements that his own aides have to scramble to retract them, he has also restocked the Kremlin with far more promising men than Korzhakov. An array of young reformers, led by Boris Nemtsov, seems to be steering the country into an at least rough approximation of stability.

And yet even as contemporary Russia fades from the front pages and becomes a gigantic developing nation with nuclear weapons, there is a serious critique to be made. Yeltsin's commitment to democracy remains, as one of his former chiefs of staff, Gennady Burbulis, told me, "purely situational." He is a democrat when it suits him. Happily, democratic means appealed to him between 1988 and 1992: the result was the dissolution of communism and an imperial state. But had Yeltsin believed in 1996 that he had no chance to win the elections, he would surely have postponed it indefinitely. The present Russian constitution allows a president only two terms in office, but I am not at all sure that Yeltsin, despite his health, will retire gracefully. Will he once more come to believe that he, and only he, can save Russia? Will he try to amend the constitution to allow for a third try in the year 2000?

But to concentrate too much on Yeltsin himself is to overlook the structures of power, property, and influence that are taking hold in Russia today. Constitutionally, the Russian presidency is enormously powerful, far more so than the American office, but, in fact, the most powerful men in the country today are seven business barons—"the seven boyars," "the Magnificent Seven"—who own nearly the entire news media and a fantastic proportion of the national wealth. These boyars are not mentioned at all in Sinyavsky's lectures and yet they are at the core of the "crony capitalism" that now dominates Russian public life.

The seven men are Boris Berezovsky of Logovaz (automobiles, television, oil); Mikhail Friedman of the Alfa Group (oil, tea, sugar, cement); Mikhail Khodorkovsky of Ros-Prom (banking, oil); Vladimir Gusinsky of Media-Most Group (television, newspapers, banking, real estate); Vladimir Potanin of Uneximbank (banking, real estate, oil and gas, media, ferrous metals); Mikhail Smolensky of SBS-Agro (banking); Vladimir Vinogradov of Inkombank (banking, metals, oil). Potanin alone has major interests in seven of Russia's twenty largest companies. Other imperial beacheads include Gazprom, the country's immense natural gas conglomerate, and various regional potentates, including the mayor of Moscow, Yuri Luzhkov.

The ascent of this oligarchy began with the collapse of the old system and the legalization of commercial banking in 1988, but it really accelerated in 1995, when Yeltsin instituted a "loans-for-shares" privatization scheme whereby the new breed of Russian bankers, who had made their initial fortunes by speculating on the international currency markets at a time of runaway inflation, could make loans to the cash-starved state. The state could not pay back the loans and instead allowed the bankers to participate in rigged insider auctions for some of the most valuable industrial properties in the country. The bankers were pleased to be picking up these bargains, and Yeltsin was pleased to give them out to friendly bankers rather than to the provincial industrialists who backed the communists. And the bargains! It was like shopping for conglomerates at Filene's Basement. Berezovsky, for example, paid $100 million for Sibneft, the Siberian oil giant; western investors, who were going to join with Berezovsky on the deal backed out because they were nervous that Yeltsin might be voted out of office. After Yeltsin won, Berezovsky claimed he was offered a billion dollars for the property. Khodorkovsky bought three-quarters of Yukos oil for $168 million; annual revenues for Yukos are now around $3 billion.

The various empires resemble one another in that they always have a political patron, a series of media outlets to protect their business and political interests, and a vast "security" apparatus that acts as a kind of private army and KGB, shielding them from physical attack and gathering intelligence on their rivals and other businesses. The new barons have also acquired a certain style gleaned from their trips to the West: posh business clubs, private jets, fleets of armored cars, immense gated dacha-mansions on the edge of Moscow, vacation retreats in Cyprus, London, Switzerland, Vienna. All of them can get a Kremlin minister on the phone in an instant.

With Chubais as their leader and patron, the barons (some of whom had been intense rivals) came together in 1996 to insure that Yeltsin would defeat the Communist Party. They had a lot to offer: money, control of the media, expertise. After the election, Berezovsky and Potanin spent some time in the Russian government before leaving again to pursue their increasing fortunes.

Business Week has declared Potanin "the most powerful man in Russia." And not without reason. His companies are worth around $32 billion and his personal wealth is somewhere between $1.5 billion and $3 billion. His Uneximbank is the biggest private bank in the country and owns major stakes in credit-card and insurance companies; he is co-founder of MFK-Renaissance, the biggest investment bank in Russia; he owns 85 percent of Sidanko, the third biggest oil producer; he owns the Norilsk Nickel works, which he bought for a song; he owns the majority share in *Izvestia, Komsomolskaya Pravda,* and *Russky Telegraf;* he owns the Central Army basketball and hockey teams. Potanin is thirty-six years old and a former leader of the Young Communists. He plays chess and likes jet-skiing very much.

In a series of articles for the *Washington Post,* David Hoffman compared the new Russian conglomerates to the South Korean model; others have mentioned the Japanese *keiretsu.* Hoffman compares the barons themselves to the railroad barons of the late 19th century who, using the Pacific Railroad Act of 1862, won land grants from the government, formed companies to develop and sell the lands, and then used the money to hire their own construction companies to build the rails at inflated prices. The situation in Russia is similar: a small core of businessmen who call themselves capitalists without yielding any of the monopolistic tendencies of their Soviet predecessors dominate the economy.

The Russians, however, still suffer by comparison with South Korea and Japan. The rise of those economies in the seventies and eighties was based on the export of cheap, well-made manufactured goods to highly competitive foreign markets. The Russian model is based mainly on the exploitation of natural resources, where competition is minimal and government connections are at a premium. The seven boyars and the other monopolies dominate the stock markets but they do not, generally, make anything; there is minimal technological innovation. At the same time, tens of thousands of medium-sized businesses are floundering because they attract minimal foreign or domestic investment, suffer from punishing tax codes, continually battle organized crime, and get no favors from political patrons.

The creation of capitalism on the ash-heap of communism has not been a pretty sight. The question is whether the economy will develop over time into something resembling the West's or whether it will calcify into a stagnant oligarchic arrangement. The optimistic view is that the new barons will become increasingly competitive among themselves and that they will also begin investing more heavily in smaller enterprises— a turn of events that will hasten the creation of a middle class not merely in Moscow, where it is already evident, but elsewhere in Russia. There is little doubt, too, that the business culture of Russia is growing more sophisticated. The biggest business story of 1994 was the collapse of a gigantic pyramid scheme called MMM run by a con man named Sergei Mavrodi. The likes of Mavrodi have been replaced on the pages of the newspapers by the latest arrivals from Morgan Stanley, WestDeutsche LandesBank, and dozens of others.

One of the most encouraging signs in the Russian political scene in 1997 was the appearance of the first real fissure in the seven-sided oligarchy. Customarily, one of the seven barons would enter into the privatization auctions as a "walkaway" partner—a designated low bidder present only to give the appearance of fair play. Last year, the government put up 25 percent of an enormous corporation called Svyazinvest for auction. The company is the parent concern of eighty-eight local telephone companies and the main long-distance carrier. Gusinsky, who had not been very active in the snatching up of other industrial properties in the past, was especially interested in this deal and assembled a bidding consortium that included Friedman, the Spanish telephone company Telefonica, and Credit Suisse/First Boston. He thought he had clear sailing. At the time the deal was first mentioned, Potanin was still in the government—he was vice-premier in charge of economic policy and privatization—and could not participate, but unfortunately for Gusinsky, he quit his Kremlin post in time to take part. Potanin had been instrumental in designing the "loans for shares" scheme in the first place that ensured that the oligarchs—and not the communist factory chieftains—would win the most valuable properties. The two first deputy prime ministers, Chubais and Nemtsov, told Gusinsky that this time the bidding would be open and real. The auction was scheduled for July 25, 1997. In the run-up, Potanin's newspapers attacked Gusinsky for corruption and foul deeds, and Gusinsky's media outlets did the same to Potanin. To compete with Gusinsky, Potanin brought in $980 million from George Soros's Quantum Fund and help from Morgan Stanley and Deutsche Morgan Grenfell and came up with a bid of $1.87 billion, topping Gusinsky by $160 million. It was perhaps the most significant deal in the short history of Russian capitalism and by far the largest foreign investment. The final price was 50 percent more than the government had expected. Leonid Rozhetskin, a member of the Renaissance Capital investment bank, predicted that the consortium's investment would triple by the year 2000.

"From a bandit-like amassing of capital, the country is moving to a more or less civilized regime," the first deputy premier, Boris Nemtsov, said. Perhaps.

Granted, this new and dominant story of Russian politics does not have the euphoria and allure of perestroika in the late 1980s or the heroic battles of 1991. Sakharov is gone, Solzhenitsyn is ignored, and heroes, in general, are absent from the scene. It is hard to warm to an auction as a heroic event. And yet if business can advance in a way that begins to benefit more than a few Moscow tycoons, if Yeltsin finally fades away in a peaceful transition of power, then Russia will move farther down the road toward becoming what so many of its people have hoped for for so long: to be part of the world, to be a normal country.

David Remnick
New York City
February 1998

NOTES ON SOURCES

My main source of information was personal interviews. I am indebted to those who took the time to talk with me. (Some people have, for obvious reasons, asked not to be named either in the text or in these chapter notes, but that was rare; that happens less often in Moscow now than in Washington, D.C.) I also benefited greatly from steady reading of *Izvestia, The Moscow Times, Moscow News, Nezavisimaya Gazeta, Sevodnya, Zavtra, Kommersant, Sovetskaya Rossiya, Pravda,* and other papers, as well as the newsweekly *Itogi.* The coverage of Russia in *The New York Times* (notably Michael Specter's remarkable work in Chechnya), in *The Washington Post,* and in the *Financial Times* (especially John Lloyd's dispatches on the new economic scene) was invaluable.

CHAPTER 1: THE LOST EMPIRE

The most important interviews were with former Soviet president Mikhail Gorbachev; Boris Yeltsin (these interviews were in 1988, 1989, and 1990— that is, before he became Russian president); Duma member Galina Starovoitova; Gorbachev's adviser Anatoly Chernyaev; former foreign minister Andrei Kozyrev; Duma member Grigory Yavlinsky; Duma member Vladimir Zhirinovsky; playwright Aleksandr Gelman; former Politburo member Yegor Ligachev; communist leader Gennady Zyuganov; Duma member Anatoly Lukyanov; former Gorbachev adviser Aleksandr Yakovlev; newspaper editor Aleksandr Prokhanov; former Soviet vice president Gennady Yanayev; former KGB chief Vladimir Kryuchkov; former Russian first deputy prime minister Gennady Burbulis; former deputy prime minister Yegor Gaidar; author Allen Weinstein; presidential adviser Giorgi Satarov; former presidential adviser Sergei Stankevich; and residents of Privolnoye, including Dmitri and Maria Kraiko and Aleksandr Yakovenko.

Among the books that were helpful were Yeltsin's memoirs *The Struggle for Russia* and *Against the Grain;* Yeltsin biographies by John Morrison and by Vladimir Solovyov and Elena Klepikov; Gorbachev's two-volume memoir, which has been abridged and translated (rather badly) into English as *Memoirs,* and his *Dekabr' 91: Moya Pozitsiya* ("December '91: My Position") and *Soyuz Mozhno Sokhranit'* ("The Union Can Be Preserved"); and memoirs by three of Gorbachev's aides: Andrei Grachev's *Final Days: The Inside Story of the Soviet Union,* Giorgy Shakhnazarov's *Tsena Svobodi* ("The Price of Freedom"), Anatoly Chernyaev's *Shest' lyet s Gorbachevym* ("Six Years with Gorbachev"). Also helpful were Archie Brown's *The Gorbachev Factor,* David Satter's *Age of Delirium,* and John Kampfner's *Inside Yeltsin's Russia,* as well as articles by Michael Dobbs in *The Washington Post* and Sergei Parkhomenko in *Nezavisimaya Gazeta* and *Sevodnya.*

CHAPTER 2: THE OCTOBER REVOLUTION

Interviews with Andrei Sakharov (in 1989 about Yeltsin as a political and moral figure); Yeltsin aide Lev Sukhanov; Gennady Burbulis; Yegor Gaidar; Andrei Kozyrev; newspaper editor Aleksandr Prokhanov; former Moscow mayor Gavriil Popov; Duma deputy Oleg Rumyantsev; economist Stanislav Shatalin; Deputy Prime Minister Anatoly Chubais; Aleksandr Solzhenitsyn; former legislator Arkady Volsky; Colonel Viktor Alksnis; General Valentin Varennikov; *Sovetskaya Rossiya* editor Valentin Chikin; radical communist leader Viktor Anpilov; journalist Leonid Radzikhovsky; General Dmitri Volkogonov; Giorgi Satarov; presidential adviser Yuri Baturin; and presidential adviser Sergei Filatov.

Anders Aslund's *How Russia Became a Market Economy* is a lucid, and decidedly optimistic, analysis of economic policy under Yeltsin from a former Swedish diplomat who then went to work as an economic adviser to the Yeltsin-Gaidar team. Stephen Handelman's *Comrade Criminal* is the best book on organized crime. Jonathan Steele's *Eternal Russia* and Bruce Clark's *An Empire's New Clothes* both, in their own way, advance a theory of the October events that is more conspiratorial than my reporting bore out, but both journalists provide interesting details. Ruslan Khasbulatov's two-volume memoir, *Velikaya Rossiskaya Tragediya* ("The Great Russian Tragedy"), is the best insider's memoir from the anti-Yeltsin forces. *Moskva Ocyen'-93 Khronika Protivostoyaniya* ("Moscow, Fall '93, Chronicle of a Clash") is a collection of transcripts, decrees, articles, and interviews that, while tilted toward the government point of view, is reliable, if only as a compendium. *Bloody October in Moscow* by Aleksandr Buzgalin and Andrei Kolganov is a pro-Khasbulatov-and-Rutskoi book featuring interviews with partisans inside the White House. Veronika Kutsillo's *Zapiski iz Belovo Doma* ("Notes from the White House") is a relatively impartial, and remarkably brave, account by a young reporter who stayed inside the White House throughout the confrontation. I am also indebted to the reporting of Lee Hockstader, Masha Lipman, Margaret Shapiro, and Fred Hiatt of *The Washington Post,* John Lloyd of the *Financial Times,* Sergei Parkhomenko in *Sevodnya,* Veronika Kutsillo in *Kommersant,* and various reporters in *Izvestia,* as well as to the constant coverage provided by the Moscow bureau of CNN, which was the main source of live information for both Russia and the rest of the world throughout the October events.

CHAPTER 3: THE GREAT DICTATOR

Interviews with Vladimir Zhirinovsky; members of Zhirinovsky's Falcons; Dmitri Nalbandyan; Arkady Murashev; Vladimir Boxer; Gennady Burbulis; Galina Starovoitova; Sergei Stankevich; Aleksandr Prokhanov; Yuri Baturin; Leonid Radzikhovsky; former adviser in charge of corruption Yuri Boldyrev; and historian Sergei Ivanov.

Zhirinovsky has published numerous books and pamphlets, including *Poslednii Brosok na Yug* ("The Last Thrust to the South") and *Poslednii Vagon na Sever* ("The Last Wagon to the North"). *Absolute Zhirinovsky,* edited by Graham Frazer and George Lancelle, is a useful compilation of the great man's statements. *Zhirinovsky: Russian Fascism and the Making of a Dictator,* by Vladimir Solovyov and Elena Klepikova, is the best biography—more reliable than the rather odd *!Zhirinovsky!* by Vladimir Kartsev, Zhirinovsky's former boss at Mir Publishing. Also helpful were Isaiah Berlin's *Russian Thinkers;* Bruce Clark's excellent book *An Empire's New Clothes;* Walter Laqueur's *Black Hundred;* Nikolai Karamzin's *Memoir on Ancient and Modern Russia;* Dostoevsky's *The Diary of a Writer;* Iver B. Neumann's *Russia and the Idea of Europe,* a trove of interesting quotations as well as acute analysis; Nikolai Danilyevsky's *Russia and Europe;* Grigory Fedotov's "Russia, Europe, and We"; Igor Shafarevich's modern Slavophile manifesto, *Russophobia;* and Nikolai Berdyaev's *The Russian Idea.*

CHAPTER 4: THE EXILE

I interviewed Solzhenitsyn in Cavendish, Vermont, and, after his return to Russia, in Moscow. I am grateful to him and to his family for their time. Also helpful were discussions with numerous writers and editors, including Joseph Brodsky, Susan Sontag, Lydia Chukovskaya, Elena Chukovskaya, Lev Razgon,

Alexis Klimoff, Nikita Struve, Sergei Zalygin, Andrei Bitov, Vitaly Korotich, and Vassily Aksyonov. Gorbachev, Aleksandr Yakovlev, and Yegor Ligachev all talked with me about Solzhenitsyn as well. Solzhenitsyn's recent books, including his essays and manifestos, have all been published by Farrar, Straus & Giroux. The best biography remains Michael Scammell's *Solzhenitsyn*. Scammell also edited *The Solzhenitsyn Files*, which contains numerous Politburo documents. Also helpful were Paul Hollander's *Political Pilgrims;* Edward Ericson's *Solzhenitsyn and the Modern World;* and *Solzhenitsyn in Exile*, edited by John Dunlop, Richard Haugh, and Michael Nicholson.

CHAPTER 5: MOSCOW, OPEN CITY

Interviews were mainly with ordinary people—shopkeepers, bankers, the poor—but also helpful were former mayor Gavriil Popov; former deputy mayor Sergei Stankevich; architectural scholar Aleksei Komech; television broadcaster Leonid Parfyonov; U.S. diplomat Thomas Graham; Giorgi Satarov; and sociologist Andrei Bystritsky.

Timothy Colton's history of Moscow is a remarkable work and of great help. Yuri Luzhkov's book *Moscow, We Are Your Children* is dull as history but helpful as a self-portrait of a vain master builder. In *The New York Times*, Alessandra Stanley has written extensively and with wit about the New Russians and the changing mores of Moscow life. Masha Lipman, Sergei Ivanov, Maria Pavlenko, Fred Hiatt, Lee Hockstader, and other friends were very helpful in showing me the new sites around town. There have been many helpful articles in the Russian and American press about the Cathedral of Christ the Savior, but one of the best pieces is a long riff in Ryszard Kapuściński's *Imperium*. There are many articles on the Gazprom conglomerate in the financial and industry press; also helpful were David Hoffman's profile in *The Washington Post* (December 3, 1995) and a piece in *U.S. News & World Report* (December 11, 1995).

CHAPTER 6: THE BANKER, THE PRESIDENT, AND THE PRESIDENT'S GUARD

I had several extensive interviews with Vladimir Gusinsky in Moscow and New York. I also talked with key figures in his media empire, including Igor Malashenko and Yevgeny Kiselyev of NTV, editors at *Sevodnya*, and broadcasters at the radio station Ekho Moskvi. Many others were helpful in explaining the new economic culture of Moscow, including the banker Mikhail Smolensky; industrialist Boris Berezovsky; Grigory Yavlinsky; journalists Mikhail Leontiyev and Mikhail Berger; sociologist Igor Bunin; Aleksandr Yakovlev; Duma member and journalist Yuri Shchekochikin; former Yeltsin adviser Boris Fyodorov; Duma member Irina Khakamada; industrialist Kakha Bendukidze; Dr. Svyatoslav Fyodorov; and Yegor Gaidar.

CHAPTER 7: RESURRECTIONS EVERYWHERE

Interviews with writers and editors Aleksandr Solzhenitsyn, Vitaly Tretyakov, Aleksandr Kushner, Joseph Brodsky, Ludmilla Petrushevskaya, Tatyana Tolstaya, Vladimir Novikov, Natalya Ivanova, Viktor Yerofeyev, Leonid Radzikhovsky, Alla Marchenko, Andrei Zorin, Zufar Gureyev, Aleksandr Terekhov, Yevgeny Popov, Dmitri Prigov, Arkady Rein, Vladimir Voinovich, Irina Prokhorova, and Vladimir Sorokin. The best English-language source for new Russian fiction is the journal *Glas.*

CHAPTER 8: THE BLACK BOX

The best source of information about Russian television was endless viewing of the various stations. In addition, interviews with the following broadcasters and television executives were essential: Vladislav Listyev (1988), Leonid Parfyonov, Igor Malashenko, Aleksandr Yakovlev, Yevgeny Kiselyov, Sergei Zverev, Vsevold Vilchek, Eduard Sagalayev, Aleksandr Lyubimov, Artyom Borovik, and Boris Berezovsky. I am grateful as well to Jonathan Sanders of CBS and Eileen O'Connor of CNN for allowing me to watch numerous tapes of Russian programs and events archived at their respective network bureaus in Moscow. The Russian press was filled with information on the Listyev murder—the incident is also the basis for two popular novels—but a special issue of *Kommersant* magazine (No. 8, 1995) was especially helpful.

CHAPTER 9: YELTSIN'S VIETNAM

I am indebted to Michael Specter of *The New York Times* not only for his reporting from Chechnya but also for setting me up with contacts on my trip to the Caucasus. The interviews done there are self-evident from the text except for the many conversations I had in Grozny and villages outside the regional capital with Chechen rebels, Russian soldiers, and refugees and victims of the fighting. In Moscow, the human rights group Memorial provided reams of documents on various atrocities, including the massacre in the village of Samashky. I am also grateful to Lee Hockstader for his reporting in *The Washington Post,* the late Fred Cuny for his piece in *The New York Review of Books* ("Killing Chechnya," April 6, 1995), the reporters for NTV, *Izvestia,* and *Itogi,* and various works by Marie Bennigsen Broxup on Chechen history.

CHAPTER 10: RESTORATION TRAGEDY?

Interviews with Aleksandr Prokhanov, Gennady Zyuganov, Viktor Anpilov, Valentin Chikin, Andrei Kozyrev, Valentin Varennikov, Mikhail Gorbachev, Aleksandr Yakovlev, and others helped provide the context of the fall and rebirth of the communist movement led by Zyuganov. The most valuable secondary source materials were issues of *Sovetskaya Rossiya, Pravda,* and *Zavtra,* as well as Zyuganov's books (see bibliography). Alessandra Stanley's May 1996 cover story in *The New York Times Magazine* is filled with interesting material on Zyuganov's past.

CHAPTER 11: THE WAR FOR THE KREMLIN

Interviews with Vladimir Kryuchkov; Viktor Anpilov; General Valentin Varennikov; businessman and communist leader Vladimir Semago; ideologist Aleksei Podberiozkin; Anatoly Lukyanov; deputy Duma speaker Svetlana Goryacheva; Galina Starovoitova; Boris Berezovsky; Igor Malashenko; American political consultant Dick Dresner; Yevgeny Kiselyov; Vladimir Gusinsky; Vladimir Zhirinovsky; Grigory Yavlinsky; Leonid Radzikhovsky; Arkady Murashev; Yeltsin's foreign policy adviser Sergei Karaganov; Andrei Kozyrev; pollster Maria Volkenshtein; conductor of the Kirov State Opera, Valery Gergiyev; music critic Lev Ginzburg; and human rights activist and former Yeltsin adviser Sergei Kovalyov. Andrei Karatnycky of Freedom House supplied me with very helpful Zyuganov material.

The best information on Lebed is from his memoir, *Za Derzhavu Obidno* ("I Pity Our Great Power"). Michael Specter's October 13, 1996, profile in *The New York Times Magazine* was also helpful. The *St. Petersburg Times* and *The Moscow Times,* two excellent English-language dailies, provided useful material, as did the usual Russian dailies, NTV, and *Itogi.* The involvement of American consultants in the Yeltsin campaign is laid out in *Time,* July 15, 1996.

EPILOGUE: CAN RUSSIA CHANGE?

Besides the texts used on the subject of Russian identity, I also relied on Isaiah Berlin's essay "The Silence in Russian Culture" (*Foreign Affairs*, October 1957), Richard Pipes's essay "Russia's Past, Russia's Future" (*Commentary*, June 1996), and Stephen Cohen's discussion of the "continuity thesis" in *Rethinking the Soviet Experience: Politics & History Since 1917*. Richard Layard and John Parker's *The Coming Russian Boom* was helpful, especially with economic and polling numbers, as was Nicolai Petro's study of "alternative political culture" in *The Rebirth of Russian Democracy*.

BIBLIOGRAPHY

Albats, Yevgenia. *The State Within a State*. New York: Farrar, Straus & Giroux, 1994.

Aslund, Anders. *How Russia Became a Market Economy*. Washington, D.C.: Brookings Institution, 1995.

Berdyaev, Nikolai. *The Russian Idea*. London: Lindisfarne Press, 1992.

Berlin, Isaiah. *Russian Thinkers*. London: Hogarth, 1978.

Beschloss, Michael R., and Strobe Talbott. *At the Highest Levels: The Inside Story of the End of the Cold War*. Boston: Little, Brown, 1993.

Boldin, Valery. *Ten Years That Shook the World: The Gorbachev Era as Witnessed by His Chief of Staff*. New York: Basic Books, 1994.

Brown, Archie. *The Gorbachev Factor*. New York: Oxford University Press, 1996.

Buzgalin, Aleksandr, and Andrei Kolganov. *Bloody October in Moscow*. New York: Monthly Review Press, 1994.

Chernyaev, Anatoly. *Shest' lyet s Gorbachevym* ("Six Years with Gorbachev"). Moscow: Izdatelskaya Gruppa Progress, Kultura, 1993.

Clark, Bruce. *An Empire's New Clothes*. London: Vintage, 1995.

Cohen, Stephen F. *Rethinking the Soviet Experience: Politics & History Since 1917*. New York: Oxford University Press, 1985.

Colton, Timothy. *Moscow*. Cambridge, Mass.: Harvard University Press, 1996.

Dostoevsky, Feodor. *The Diary of a Writer*. New York: Braziller, 1954.

Dunlop, John. *The Rise and Fall of the Soviet Empire*. Princeton: Princeton University Press, 1993.

Dunlop, John, Richard Haugh, and Michael Nicholson, eds. *Solzhenitsyn in Exile: Critical Essays and Documentary Materials*. Stanford: Stanford University Press, 1985.

Ericson, Edward. *Solzhenitsyn and the Modern World*. Washington, D.C.: Regnery Gateway, 1993.

Fedotov, Grigory. "Russia, Europe, and We." *New Times,* November 27, 1990.

Frazer, Graham, and George Lancelle. *Absolute Zhirinovsky*. New York: Penguin, 1994.

Gaidar, Yegor. *Gosudarstvo i Evolutsiya* ("State and Evolution"). Moscow: Eurasia, 1995.

Goldman, Marshall. *What Went Wrong with Perestroika*. New York: W. W. Norton, 1992.

Gorbachev, Mikhail. *Memoirs*. New York: Doubleday, 1996.

—————. *Dekabr' 91: Moya Pozitsiya* ("December '91: My Position"). Moscow: Novosti, 1992.

—————. *Soyuz Mozhno Sokhranit'* ("The Union Can Be Preserved"). Moscow: April-85, 1995.

Grachev, Andrei. *Final Days: The Inside Story of the Soviet Union*. Boulder: Westview Press, 1995.

Handelman, Stephen. *Comrade Criminal: Russia's New Mafiya*. New Haven: Yale University Press, 1995.

Hollander, Paul. *Political Pilgrims*. New York: Oxford University Press, 1981.

Kampfner, John. *Inside Yeltsin's Russia*. London: Cassell, 1994.

Kapuściński, Ryszard. *Imperium*. New York: Knopf, 1994.

Karamzin, Nikolai. *Karamzin's Memoir on Ancient and Modern Russia: A Translation and Analysis*. Ed. Richard Pipes. New York: Atheneum, 1966.

Khasbulatov, Ruslan. *Velikaya Rossiskaya Tragediya* ("The Great Russian Tragedy"). 2 vols. Moscow: Too Sims, 1994.

Kozyrev, Andrei. *Proobrazheniye* ("Transformation"). Moscow: International Relations, 1994.

Kryuchkov, Vladimir. *Lichnoye Delo* ("Personal File"). 2 vols. Moscow: Olymp, 1996.

Kutsillo, Veronika. *Zapiski iz Belovo Doma* ("Notes from the White House"). Moscow: Kommersant Publishers, 1993.

Laqueur, Walter. *Black Hundred: The Rise of the Extreme Right in Russia*. New York: HarperCollins, 1993.

Layard, Richard, and John Parker. *The Coming Russian Boom*. New York: Free Press, 1996.

Lebed, Aleksandr. *Za Derzhavu Obidno* ("I Pity Our Great Power"). Moscow: Moskovskaya Pravda, 1995.

Lewin, Moshe. *Russia/USSR/Russia*. New York: New Press, 1995.

Ligachev, Yegor. *Tak Zhit' Nevozmozhno* ("We Cannot Live This Way"). Moscow: Korina, 1992.

Malia, Martin. *The Soviet Tragedy: A History of Socialism in Russia, 1917–1991*. New York: Free Press, 1994.

Matlock, Jack F., Jr. *Autopsy on an Empire*. New York: Random House, 1995.

McFaul, Michael. *Post-Communist Politics*. Washington, D.C.: Center for Strategic and International Studies, 1993.

Morrison, John. *Boris Yeltsin: From Bolshevik to Democrat*. New York: Dutton, 1991.

Neumann, Iver B. *Russia and the Idea of Europe*. London: Routledge, 1996.

Petro, Nicolai. *The Rebirth of Russian Democracy*. Cambridge, Mass.: Harvard University Press, 1995.

Pipes, Richard. *The Russian Revolution*. New York: Knopf, 1990.

Remnick, David. *Lenin's Tomb: The Last Days of the Soviet Empire*. New York: Random House, 1993.

Satter, David. *Age of Delirium*. New York: Knopf, 1996.

Scammell, Michael. *Solzhenitsyn*. New York: W. W. Norton, 1984.

———, ed. *The Solzhenitsyn Files*. Chicago: Edition q., 1996.

Sestanovich, Stephen, ed. *Rethinking Russia's National Interests*. Washington, D.C.: Center for Strategic and International Studies, 1994.

Shakhnazarov, Giorgy. *Tsena Svobodi* ("The Price of Freedom"). Moscow: Rossika, 1993.

Sinyavsky, Andrei. *Soviet Civilization*. Boston: Little, Brown, 1990.

Sobchak, Anatoly. *For a New Russia*. New York: Free Press, 1992.

Solovyov, Vladimir, and Elena Klepikova. *Boris Yeltsin: A Political Biography*. New York: Putnam, 1992.

———. *Zhirinovsky: Russian Fascism and the Making of a Dictator*. Reading, Mass.: Addison-Wesley, 1995.

Solzhenitsyn, Aleksandr. *The Russian Question at the End of the Twentieth Century*. New York: Farrar, Straus & Giroux, 1995.

Steele, Jonathan. *Eternal Russia*. London: Faber & Faber, 1994.

Sukhanov, Lev. *Tri goda s Yel'tsynym* ("Three Years with Yeltsin"). Riga: Vaga, 1992.

Tolstoy, Leo. *Resurrection*. London: Penguin, 1969.

Yanov, Alexander. *Weimar Russia*. New York: Slovo, 1995.

Yeltsin, Boris. *Against the Grain: An Autobiography*. New York: Summit Books, 1990.

———. *The Struggle for Russia*. New York: Times Books, 1994.

Yergin, Daniel, and Thane Gustafson. *Russia 2010 and What It Means for the World*. New York: Random House, 1993.

Zhirinovsky, Vladimir. *Poslednii Brosok na Yug* ("The Last Thrust to the South"). Moscow: Rait, 1994.

——. *Poslednii Vagon na Sever* ("The Last Wagon to the North"). Moscow: LDPR, 1995.

Zyuganov, Gennady. *Za Gorizontom* ("Beyond the Horizon"). Oryol: Veshniye Vodi Publishers, 1996.

——. *Veru v Rossiyu* ("I Believe in Russia"). Voronezh: Voronezh Publishers, 1996.

——. *Rossiya i Sovremenii Mir* ("Russia and the Modern World"). Moscow: Obozryevatel' Publishers, 1996.

ACKNOWLEDGMENTS

Each time I have visited Russia since 1991 I have been an unending annoyance to my friends; I am forever asking for yet another favor, for another piece of advice, and somehow the indulgence has been unending. Masha Lipman, who started out as a translator at *The Washington Post* bureau in Moscow, was foremost among these friends. For five years, while working for the *Post,* she worked intermittently on behalf of this book, and she deserves no end of credit for its pluses, whatever they may be, and is wholly exempt from its minuses. Masha and her husband, Sergei Ivanov, both read the manuscript with care. Most of all, I am grateful to Masha and Sergei, as well as Igor Primakov and Masha Volkenshtein, and Sergei and Katya Parkhomenko, for their friendship.

In Moscow, I was also the recipient of numerous kindnesses from Michael Dobbs, Eleanor Randolph, Fred Hiatt, Margaret Shapiro, David Hoffman, and Lee Hockstader of *The Washington Post;* John Bilotta of ABC and Eileen O'Connor of CNN (the nation's innkeepers); and, above all, Alessandra Stanley and Michael Specter of *The New York Times.* Besides providing me office space and about a thousand meals, Michael and Alessandra also extended extremely helpful counsel on everything from the proper flak jacket to take to Grozny to where to find an all-night diner in Moscow. I'd also like to thank the staff of the *Times* for their hospitality.

Tina Brown sponsored a great deal of the reporting in this book and was kind enough to publish versions of several chapters in *The New Yorker.* Her support has been invaluable to me. Jeff Frank, my editor at the magazine, read and edited an early draft of the book. My gratitude to both.

Stephen Kotkin of Princeton and Michael McFaul of Stanford University, two of the best young scholars in Russian studies, traded ideas with me and, to my relief, pointed out errors of fact and judgment. I am also grateful for the friendship and counsel of Harry Evans, Barbara Epstein, Murray Kempton, David Halberstam, Richard Brody, Maurie Perl, Henry Finder, Hendrik

Hertzberg, Dorothy Wickenden, Nancy Franklin, Michael Shapiro and Susan Chira, Jeff Toobin and Amy MacIntosh, Joy de Menil, Ted Johnson, Fareed Zakaria, Eva Gamota, Amelia Dundee, Marc Fisher and Jody Goodman, and my oldest and dearest friends, Eric Lewis and Elise Hoffmann. I also want to thank my loving family—Edward and Barbara Remnick; Richard Remnick, Lisa Fernandez, and Will; the Feins; and Miriam Seigel.

Jason Epstein is the finest book editor in publishing and I am grateful for his readings, his encouragement, and his kindnesses, which are countless. In my agent, Kathy Robbins, I am truly blessed.

My deepest thanks are for my sons, Alex and Noah, who indulged the absences this project required, and for my wife, Esther, to whom this book is dedicated.

INDEX

ALSO BY DAVID REMNICK

"Remnick is a gifted storyteller and
a master of the short profile."
—*Newsweek*

LENIN'S TOMB

The Last Days of the Soviet Empire

In the tradition of John Reed, George Orwell, and Nadezhda Mandelstam, this monumental account of the collapse of the Soviet Union combines the vision of the best historical scholarship with the immediacy of eyewitness journalism. Out of his years as Moscow correspondent for the *Washington Post*, Remnick has created a narrative that arcs from the rise of glasnost to the start of the post-Communist age in 1992.

Winner of the Pulitzer Prize
History/Current Affairs/0-679-75125-4

THE DEVIL PROBLEM

And Other True Stories

In this brilliant collection of profiles, Remnick trains his gaze on figures from Mario Cuomo to Dennis Rodman and from Ralph Ellison to Ben Bradlee to illuminate their characters and the character of our time. Other profiles include those of Marion Barry, whose arrest and reelection as mayor of Washington, D.C., stand as metaphors for the ways in which black and white communities view transgression and redemption, and of the religious historian Elaine Pagels, whose personal tragedies led her to seek out the origins of the devil.

Current Affairs/0-679-77752-0

VINTAGE BOOKS
Available at your local bookstore, or call toll-free to order:
1-800-793-2665 (credit cards only).